Alexander Holloway

BOTTLED WATER

~ a novel ~

Jaunt Publishing

Jaunt Publishing
Atlanta, Georgia

Published in 2006

Copyright © Alexander Holloway, 2006
All rights reserved.

PUBLISHER'S NOTE:
This is a work of fiction. Names, characters, places and incidents either are the product of the author's imagination or are used fictitiously, and any resemblance to actual persons, living or dead, events, or locales is coincidental.

ISBN 0-9787773-3-6
13-digit ISBN 978-0-9787773-3-3

Printed in the United States of America.
Cover design by Timothy Scott DeGroot
Cover photo by Arkadiy Yakubov

Without limiting rights under copyright reserved above, no part of this publication may be reproduc ed, stored in or introduced into a retrieval system, or transmitted, in any form or by any other means (electronic, mechanical, photocopying, recording or otherwise), without the prior written permission of both the copyright owner and the publisher of this book.

www.alexanderholloway.com
www.jaunt publishing.com

ACKNOWLEDGMENTS

To Anna, Herman, and Aaron.
To everyone in Malaga and Barcelona who put up with me
during this marathon of inspiration
and to those oceans away
whom I thought of continuously.

BOTTLED WATER

Prologue

Chapter One: Thailand

Chapter Two: Corporate Life

Chapter Three: Cuba

Chapter Four: Back to Corporate

Chapter Five: Israel

Chapter Six: Turkey

Chapter Seven: Bulgaria

PROLOGUE

I was a full year into the job. Today I would begin working the financial audit of a new client. Waiting in the lobby area was a little nerve-wracking, because although I had talked to the manager over the phone a number of times, I hadn't actually met her. I had heard horrible things about this new client, that their going through bankruptcy required my firm to work abnormal hours, that everyone was stressed out, not only the client but my firm. But the manager's voice over the phone had seemed pleasant enough. She was definitely taking a long time. How large was this building anyway? Maybe she had a long corridor to journey down before finally making it to the elevator. That's if she took the elevator. She could be the ambitious type, trying to fit in a quick workout down the stairwell.

I looked around. The lobby was impressive. It had flat panel televisions, sturdy, dark maple furniture, and leather chairs. The coffee table held all the financial magazines, like *Forbes*, *Financial Times*, and the *Journal*. Further down the stacks of magazines appeared the corners of a bright yellow cover, and I didn't need to read a title to know what it was. Immediately I was taken back.

At three years of age I liked to look at *National Geographic* magazines while sitting in my mother's lap. I couldn't read, but flipping the large shiny pages filled with vibrant colors and blasting contrasts struck me with awe, and silenced me, most likely my mother's only peaceful pauses of the day. Some of the images were so striking that I would point to them and ask questions. She would tell me the names of the places in the world where these pictures were taken and read key sentences from the articles, helping me to conceptualize these new truths. One article was on Angkor Wat in Cambodia. In the pictures, shiny metallic trees sprawled, plush with green leaves, their roots growing uninhibited through old stone structures, while bald-headed monks draped in bright orange robes smiled enormously in stoic poses along weathered stone steps. Within the article there were elephants and monkeys and a long moat surrounding what seemed a fortress with a long bridge guarded at the front by two ferocious lion statues.

I promised her that one day I would travel as far as that magical kingdom. And over the years my mother would remind me of that promise. Finally, I had done it. I had traveled to Cambodia, but it wouldn't be my most memorable trip. So far, Thailand had won that prize.

THAILAND

The Full Moon Party was like nothing we had ever seen. From the mountainous terrain on either side of the bay and between the clubs and sea, thousands of gleeful foreigners and Thais from all over the country covered the bay like a mound of disturbed ants. The party extended continuously from inside the clubs onto the beach. Outside, the glowing light from the moon competed with bon fires and fire dancers twirling batons with oil-soaked cloth flaming at either end. A man with long, dark hair casually draped along both sides of his face and down the front of his shoulders and back wore painted henna tattoos and tribal art, and even more popular were his glow-in-the-dark tattoos. A glowing blackboard full of neon designs stood behind him. I watched as he balanced a cigarette in his mouth and drew a Playboy bunny along the cleavage of some giggly girl, to the laughter of her friends. They all wanted one after seeing how well it came out.

The Full Moon Party was more like a beach circus. Everything was possible and tolerable. No one was out of place or anything out of the ordinary. There was an energy felt through the crowd of arbitrariness, of being exempt from any laws or cultural norms. People were free, dancing like they were in some sort of trance, rolling their heads from side to side, so that their chins touched the tops of their chests, releasing their hands and arms in full circular motions. Some exaggerated their presence even more, with neon yellow and green glow sticks clasped between moving hands, sprouting out of the mouth, or hanging from their neck and ankles. Smiles and laughter were the rules. The night was warm and the air light, the sound of the sea was drowned out by the music resonating from inside the clubs. Nonetheless, the sea was visible. Every light source, from the fires and candles, the bar lights and Christmas lights, the fire dancers and glow sticks, the moon and stars, reflected off the slow moving waves, crumbling lightly as the waves fizzled onto the shore. Thousands of people crowded the beaches and clubs, and still infinite space extended to the celestial bodies and across the sea to India or Africa, eliminating any feeling of claustrophobia.

A day or two before, the three of us, Seb, Leo and I, had flown twenty-three hours from JFK in New York, including a lay-over of about two hours in Tokyo, Japan, then on to Bangkok, Thailand, before boarding a domestic flight to Ko Samui Island, another hour and a half, and then taking a thirty-minute ferry boat ride jam-packed with young backpacking foreigners and a few native Thais. Fishing boats, ferry boats, "tuk tuk" taxi boats, and even jet skis were populating Koh Phan Gan, which was full of visitors, all of them waiting to party the night away under tropical clear skies and a full moon. On the boat ride over, we were sandwiched in between these loud boisterous Norwegians, excited about their previous adventures in Phuket, a very commercial island on the west coast. More thankfully, on the other side, were two very sneaky looking Swedish blondes who furtively guarded a knapsack full of beer. The sun was beaming heavily on the front deck of the boat, and without the refuge of a quick swim or shade, we were like pizza dough baking to a crust. Knowing the conditions and finding it hard to conceal the sparkle of beer bottles perspiring from the sun, they eventually invited us. We toasted our bottles, they chanted "skol," and we immediately became friends. After a brief chat about the formalities of birthplaces and names, and the game of blabbing out what you already know or have in common with the other person's country, which for us was practically nothing, we shifted our conversation to the task at hand: the Full Moon Party. They told us that some friends were awaiting them at one of the family-owned bungalow clusters scattered around the island, and that they heard you should watch out who offers you drinks or drugs; it could be an undercover cop or someone slipping a "micky." Seb thought it hilarious that some girl might slip him any such drugs, but then we reminded him that it was a woman only if he was lucky. And he changed the topic.

As we were disembarking the ferryboat, confusion and chaos erupted from all the anxious travelers hurrying to find their bags before stepping off into paradise. Everyone rushed to find a truck or van that would take them further into the island, and in the middle of all of this we lost track of the girls. We hesitated longer than we should have, thinking maybe they hadn't left, until we almost didn't have a ride at all. We were lucky and managed to catch the last truck leaving. The truck was rusted, beat-up and, from the sound of the engine, struggling to stay alive. With the finesse of hitchhikers, we pushed our heavy extra-duty REI backpacks over the tailgate of the truck and climbed in, trusting that the driver would lead us to wherever we were supposed to go. The truck was clearly over capacity. It took us treacherously up and down the rocky dirt roads of the hilly terrain to the point where I could feel my stomach rising and falling. We rode alongside cliffs overlooking spectacular views of the sea and pieces of land breaking and crumbling like offerings to the great hungry blue. At one point, we had to jump off the truck to help push it up the last little bit of steep hill. I could see a bit of embarrassment on the face of the driver as he signaled us to get off.

The truck's engine roared, and its tires spit up stones and red dirt into clouds of dust. For a while after that, I wasn't sure we would make it to our destination. But I left it to fate, and, after the ride went beyond my own mental odometer, I began to reflect and have that anxious feeling that I got as a child taking long family trips—the four of us, my father and mother riding in the front of a red, two-door Sentra and my brother and me squashed in the back seat between a large red cooler and the millions of gadgets and toys that my brother couldn't bear to live without for just a few days. Our only trip for the year was usually to Jekyll Island on the coast of Georgia. The salty breeze and rhythmic sounds associated with the ocean, the excitement of jumping through the dark mysterious waves or letting them carry me on a cheap styrofoam board all the way to the shore, the strange pleasure of sticking my feet in the dark milky sand and competing with my brother for who could stand the longest in the same spot without giving way to the ocean's force—all of these thoughts created a longing for the beach that would last each time an entire year. I had always wished as a child that I was growing up closer to the sea; at heart I was a surfer, a beach bum, or a lifeguard. In the water, I felt free and sublime; the mystery of what lived and existed beneath me in the dark Atlantic Ocean always intrigued and thrilled me. Some of my best memories as a child were from those trips when I felt a cohesiveness and camaraderie that I was never guaranteed to feel with my family.

The truck suddenly stopped. We were being motioned by the driver, through the long glass window, to get off. He placed us in front of a narrow dirt path leading to the back of a small wooden shack and a cluster of "bungalows" and palm trees. We were lucky to find vacancies.

We showed up at the beachfront the next day, the afternoon before the party. After we'd observed enough through the opening between the restaurants, we decided to go forward onto the beach itself and take our chances. We were entering a scene all the travel agencies try their best to capture in photos: flour-soft white sand, transparent turquoise sea, calm water rippling like short breaths of air, lush green landscape, all backed by a mountain terrain jutting up from the coastline. We saw a small cluster of open-air bars pushed tightly together like green monopoly houses, no more than a back yard's reach from the sea, their patrons indistinguishable from the crowd of sun worshippers.

The famous Full Moon Party on the small island of Koh Phan Gan was coined "essential Thailand for Uni Grads" by Seb's internship boss in Manhattan. He hadn't told Seb we would also be the rare Coca-Cola babies in attendance. Considering what a web our economics and trade had spun over the rest of the world, we were surprised, if not refreshed, by this development. Maybe September 11th had something to do with the absence of Americans, especially young college grads high in debt and still arm's length from Mommy and Daddy's bank account and ultimate influence. It was the summer of 2002, and the world we had escaped was now in the throes of military vengeance and prideful last words. We, on the other hand, were far removed. Our occupation was with the mostly European mix of women sun bathing, paddle balling, drinking and strolling up and down the beach, wearing hardly a care in the world.

"Jesus!" Seb blurted out, not at all religiously. Of course, we all turned to see what he was looking at. "Aren't those the two Swedish girls we met on the ferry yesterday?"

"Good God, you're right!" said Leo, dropping his jaw.

I finally caught on. The sight was enough to reincarnate a dead man. The word "Damn!" came out of me like a trombone staccato.

The two girls caught sight of us standing along the beach ready with our beach towels, flip-flops and beer, and waved us over. They were dressed in that European arrangement of beach attire, and I didn't have to ask Seb or Leo what they were thinking, though I thought I heard Seb blurt out, under his breath, "Thank you!" We walked over, trying not to appear overly excited at our invitation. The taller one, Emma, had beautiful light green eyes and was the more outgoing of the two.

"Hey, how are you! We wondered what happened to you after the ferry!" They seemed happy to see us.

"Yeah, we looked back and you ladies had vanished . . . and along with the beer," I said half-jokingly. I was trying my best to focus on her eyes and not the other impressive duo. "You mind if we sit here?"

"Sure . . . I mean, No, we don't mind . . . please join us."

"This time beer's on us," Leo chimed in.

We laid out our towels and sat our beer down on the sand in front of the girls, took off our shirts and flip-flops and continued talking. After a couple of beers, everyone decided to get in the water and cool off. It was the middle of May and the year-round tropical weather was reaching its peak. The water was crowded with people nearer to the shore, so we walked further until we passed behind a group of Brits who were too wasted to throw a Frisbee with any accuracy. I was a bit annoyed when I heard a whistle of wind passing, the Frisbee just missing my ear. And I pretended to return the Frisbee, which ended up flying towards the cluster of people along the beach.

The water was warm, but still refreshing in comparison to the sun and its thick humid air. We waded in the water, the girls and us, somehow finding ourselves in a conversation about the ubiquity of American television, cinema and music in Sweden. I was amazed that they could watch the soap opera, *Days of Our Lives*, and see episodes of *Friends*. I talked about hip-hop and Atlanta's strong music industry presence, and they said they were fans of Outkast and Ludacris. The Swedish girls seemed to be an extension of our culture as much as we were of theirs. We were hitting it off like we had known each other for years.

Beer was getting low, so I decided to walk to the bar in search for more. The Thai bartender greeted me in English when I walked up. I asked him for five Singhas. At the same time, I noticed a dark-haired guy sitting down at the bar, staring at me with an inquisitive look, through a somewhat disdainful expression.

"American! You must be American!" he shouted in an accent that I couldn't recognize from among the fifty states. I didn't know whether to welcome this conversation or frown upon it. I could sense something in his tone, a sort of challenge to my existence. It wasn't a friendly, "I want to be your friend" approach. It was more a smug challenge for me to prove my self-worth to him. And I hadn't the time or need. But I still engaged his words.

"Yes. I'm Mr. America. Where are you from?" I asked.

"Canadian. I'm from Montreal. Do you know where that is?" he wisecracked, looking around to the bartender and whoever else was sitting the bar, proud of his little insult.

"No. I usually don't venture past the Great Lakes on the map. Cold weather and barren land doesn't interest me much," I cut back.

"Right," he said slowly drawing the word. He was about to make another smart remark, when I made a truce.

"Just kidding," I said, and I laughed. "What brings you to these parts?" I wasn't really interested to know, but I always seemed to regret conflict, and at that moment I just wanted to walk away with a free conscience and five cold beers.

Early in the conversation, I realized that Todd, the Canadian, was a bit tipsy and had a preoccupation with politics and Americans in general. I had never known that any of this mattered that much to Canadians, before meeting him. But he continued to pour it on, and I, being sort of stunned by the topic, continued to receive it. The conversation for a while was going rather civilly, until I made the mistake of saying that Canada and America were a lot alike. I didn't really know that to be exactly true, but the few Canadians I had met in my life all seemed to talk pretty similarly, dress the same, and, considering we were sharing the same continent, I had no reason to ever view them as any different. Todd went into a rage at my hypothesis. That's when he went on to say that Canadians are nothing like Americans.

"We want peace with the rest of the world. Not like you warmongering capitalists. Everyone knows that your country goes into other countries forcing your economics and McDonald's culture on them, and if they don't take the bait or succumb to your exploitation then you just throw bombs on them—go in and kill their leaders, massacre their women and children, until you can set up your McDonalds' and KFCs or steal their oil, until the entire world is one big Capitalist wasteland of conniving Corporate Bosses and overweight consumers. Look at what happened to the Indians!"

I honestly didn't have a rebuttal to the flurry of accusations. They were obviously a bit one-sided, and Todd was talking out of anger. But I'd never really had to defend my country to others or even seen a need because America, the land of the free, had always been my ideal model of human civilization. As far as I was concerned, people from other countries died to enter my country and become a part of the American Dream. Why would anyone ever have a reason to hate us? I paid the bill, and then, fumbling the five bottles of beers in my arms, took off without saying goodbye or continuing the argument. I wasn't going to spoil the day talking politics, not when two lovely Swedes were awaiting my return.

The rest of the day went by under the sun. We laughed and cavorted in the waters. We strolled along the shoreline all the way to the rocks enclosing the cove on either end. We convinced those Brits to lend us their Frisbee for a while so that we could also terrorize the waters and be a little obnoxious, and we finally rested on our towels until the sun evaporated every bit of moisture from our bodies, except for the invisible trace of humidity that always lingered. It wasn't really obvious how fast the day had flown by until the sun's final descent. Then, at that point, in a moment where time seemed to have slowed down, the sun exited, bit by bit, in a sort of ceremonial march, leaving behind it streaks of violet and purple clouds, and, not long after its farewell, revealing an entourage of stars and a bluish-white moon in all its fullness. The beautiful goddess of the night sky in all her grandeur was now out for everyone to marvel at, inaugurating the night's theme and setting in motion the tone of events to follow. It was time for us to get back to our bungalows. We told the girls we would see them later at the party.

Our bungalow cluster was run by a small Thai family who did everything from cleaning our bungalows and setting our bed sheets everyday to serving drinks at the tiny bamboo bar and preparing authentic Thai dishes. Our bungalows were a fifteen-minute walk from the main action, nicely stretched along a calmer side of the island. Each individual bungalow was a simple wooden hut with straw roofing. Ours was equipped with three twin-sized beds, a ceiling fan, a small bathroom, and handmade double doors that scraped along the floors, opening up to saintly white sand and the sight of sea, so enticing you could literally run right into it. That same morning, I had experienced the euphoric feeling of opening those double doors, like a great prince facing the dawn of day. I walked a straight line from the log steps until every inch of my body submerged slowly into the comfort of the water. The sea was at bathwater temperature, just slightly cooler than during the day, and I floated on my back without any distractions or sounds from my friends or anyone in the outside world, only the calm rhythm of waves passing underneath. Our small Southeast Asian hideaway fell somewhere in the definition of exotic paradises, and we were only paying three dollars a night, per person, a little extra for meals and drinks—a spiritual lottery that I could have fallen knees first to the ground and kissed the sand for; I was in heaven.

We were starving by the time we'd dragged our tired, sun-drenched bodies back to the bungalows. I didn't waste time ordering grilled fish whole with a pineapple dressing and hot Thai chili peppers; Seb had fried calamari, and Leo had the fish. On this island it seemed common for bungalows to have an outside deck or awning with low-lying tables and large pillows for lounging around, something to offer shade from the sun. We leaned back on the gigantic pillows with all our dead weight, half awake, waiting for the food. A little girl, smiling from every corner of her face, probably the daughter of the family, came and served us our food. She was the most polite person ever to serve me, I considered for a moment. The seafood was fresh and the special combination of hot and spicy flavorings had my taste buds somersaulting and mounting triple flips. There was more than enough, and bearing in mind the ease of tropical life and the way those pillows seemed to form around my body contours, it wasn't long before I dropped my fork, and I fell unconscious. I woke up about two hours later in the same spot. Seb was gone, and Leo was snoring loudly to the snickers of this Aussie couple sitting a couple tables over. They were also loud. It took me at least four nudges before he woke up, with his mouth gaping wide and a bit of drool forming a corner.

"Leo, Leo, Get up dog, we gotta get ready soon," I said trying not to be too loud. It was embarrassing.

"Damn. I was just getting in a kiss with that Swedish girl on the beach when you woke me up," Leo mumbled, sounding as if a fishbone had lodged near his vocal chords.

"Which one?" I asked. I was curious if he liked Emma. The fact was I still couldn't block those jumpy breasts from my mind. That was probably the same reason I was hit twice in the head with a Frisbee.

"Lovisa . . . don't worry . . . it wasn't Emma."

"It wouldn't matter to me," I remarked, not wanting to make a deal of it.

We ambled back to the bungalow, got showered up and started dressing for the big night. I slid on a baby-blue linen shirt, which I had paid an exorbitant amount for at the Banana Republic back in Lennox Mall in Atlanta, also a pair of white linen pants and trainers. I always regretted my carelessness and impatience in shopping for clothes. If it wowed me in the first seconds, and I could somehow manage it within my meager pittance, I never gave up on having it. I decided against sandals; I would be dancing tonight, and drunk people tend to step on your feet at parties. Leo dressed in A & F cargo shorts, a polo shirt, and braided-leather sandals. He had a short, almost military hairstyle and was of average height and solid build. He would forever be the preppy one out of the group. Maybe that was his reaction against having lived in a tough D.C. neighborhood at one point during his childhood, though he'd moved later to a much more affluent setting. Seb proudly put on his new "fisherman pants," which are of this really soft, light-weight material, perfect for tropical temperatures and with an enormous waistline and draw strings that could tie up to fit an elephant. Of course, Seb is built more like a white panther than an elephant. He was mostly proud that he had purchased the pants on the beach earlier that day, in a negotiating frenzy that ended up with him agreeing to buy three different colors to knock the price down from 200 bahts to 100 bahts or about two dollars a pair.

It was close to 11 p.m. when we were finally leaving our shack. We took a right after the footpath leading from our bungalows and walked down a main dirt road connecting all the other bungalow clusters on our side of the island. This road would lead us back to "Haadrin Beach," the central site of decadence and the Full Moon Party. Along the way, we experienced periods of darkness where the absence of street lamps or any nearby bungalows made us aware of our tropical surroundings. In the thick brush of trees growing wildly into the road, you could hear crickets and other insects screaming in a litany of high-pitched tones; you could hear birds chanting aggressively as if the darkness shielded them from aggressors or critics, and frogs shouting back and forth in drum-like patterns. The mixing of sounds and melodic rhythms reminded me of the chaos produced when an entire orchestra has to warm up and each musician is responsible for hammering notes at his or her own pace, octaves and levels. The nightfall made us realize how dominated this small island was by nature. Long before this patch of red dirt road was plowed and exposed or before the Full Moon Party idea had ever been conceived of, the rawness of wild nature prevailed, and still to this day it held court. I was hopeful this island would remain this way: just a few family-owned bungalows, a few bars, and clubs, enough infrastructure for a beach party every full moon, but not for the development of resorts and shopping malls, those indiscriminate projects, characteristic of many tropical destinations around the world. It would kill the purity and charm of this place.

Our brief breaks in darkness were from other bungalow communities and an occasional mo-ped speeding by, with its lights first blinding us. The further we walked, the more obvious it was we were fast approaching "Haad Rin." Then there were increasingly smaller breaks between darkness and light, bungalow clusters were spaced tighter together, and people were starting to fill up the tiny dirt road. The wild orchestra of anonymity was no more. Now you could hear and feel the energy building from the crowd that gathered and walked the road. It was like a great march to freedom, only where banners or any type of order was prohibited. We could even see flashing lights coming from the beach. We were almost there.

The party atmosphere was free moving and light, and the tropical island exuded an instinctive ease of pressure, a sort of natural high. Still, a significant amount of people expressed their freedom through drugs, which ranged from alcohol to speed. Apparently, according to the rumors floating around the island, harsh penalties could be served to those caught by undercover cops selling or using illegal drugs. Yet, ironically, Thailand was famous for its thriving underground market of any kind of drug or indulgence imaginable. I was sure the same undercover cops, condemning and accusing, were apt for bribes. That's how the country worked. That night, I was offered ecstasy pills, which are supposed to give the person taking them a feeling of immense elation, heightened emotions, and a light, fluid feeling, which would explain the trance-like dancing of many partygoers. I was also offered a couple of drugs I had only heard of recently, while casually walking through the crowd, one named Yaba and the other, "K." Yaba, I had read before leaving the U.S., had recently gained popularity in Bangkok, and users were considered unpredictable and some times dangerous. The drug, if used by someone vulnerable to violent eruptions, could act as a gateway to those aggressions. Someone wrote in an internet blog that they had seen on the streets of Bangkok a middle-aged man dressed in an old shabby white t-shirt and dingy shorts grappling another man on the sidewalk pavement with one hand, and holding a kitchen knife to the guy's neck with the other. The guy was clearly out of his mind screaming at the top of his lungs. The police and neighbors all stood outside helpless in the situation, not able to apprehend the guy for fear that he would act on his threats and kill his captive. They tried continually to reason with the guy, yelling at times and pleading in other moments, but the guy never gave in. The blogger watched the spectacle for at least ten minutes, and, although he didn't know the outcome, he said the guy never acted on his threats. The other drug, "K," I found out, only after asking the hippy who was touting it to me and saying, "you've never felt better in your life," was legally used to tranquilize horses. The drug was typically made into a liquid serum to be injected into these massive animals. But this guy had cooked the liquid into a dry white substance, to be snorted like cocaine. Thailand, for better or for worse, was a playground for life's vices and indulgences, and drug use was not exempt. Seb, Leo and I were content with the drug called alcohol. It was a liquid first and afterwards, a liquid to be palmed in a cup or bottle and drunk at your own pace.

    We made our way through the crowds of people in pursuit of the bar. Everyone was walking around gripping super-sized plastic cups that had at least five straws sprouting out of the top in all directions. We wanted to try this drink that appeared so popular. I asked some random girls hovering around the bar, and as far as they knew it was called a bucket drink and "you can't taste the liquor, but it definitely sneaks up on you." We asked for three bucket drinks. We all watched as the bartender first grabbed a bottle of obscure Vodka, emptied it in the kind of cups you see at the great Cineplexes, then poured a couple cans of Red Bull, and lastly tipped over a no-name bottle of this light brown liquid. The last ingredient was foreign to us, but we never questioned him. "It was not everyday we were in Thailand," and no one around us seemed to be falling over dead. Lastly, the guy threw in a hand-full of straws and handed us the drinks. We realized the magic of this concoction while standing near the middle of the dance floor. It was a conversation piece if nothing else. Girls would walk up, choose a color straw and start drinking, the whole time looking up and staring you in the eyes. I was thinking if somehow I fell broke on the island, down to my last baht, I would just go around bumming sips. Though the drinks were at most one U.S. dollar, it seemed shameful.

    The bucket drink was now kicking in with speed. We were

happy with the hip-hop music, but decided to walk around a bit more while we finished our first drink. As we were stepping back out through the entrance, which spread the length of the club, we happened to bump into the Swedish girls coming in. It was like a small reunion! Everyone hugged and lit up like firecrackers. I lifted Emma off the ground with my hug. We had only been apart for a few hours. Nevertheless, we carried on as if we were old friends meeting after years. The girls were always alive and fresh, possessing the optimism and freedom we all had, being in our early twenties. And, I noticed a change in our mood for the better, some synergy sparked between men and beautiful women. I was shocked at what seemed to be costumes. Anywhere else I would have probably been blushing, but at this party it was obvious anything goes. Emma wore silver thongs with shiny sequins in the front that sort of dangled and trapped light like a disco ball. She also wore a small round patch covering each nipple, with a little tassel that never stopped bouncing around. I was scared if I watched too long there was the possibility of becoming hypnotized. The girls had dressed alike, but in different colors. They obviously had planned out this night. Lovisa wore black instead of silver, a little more classy. The truth was they looked like showgirls from Las Vegas. It was a very bold move, not that these girls really needed the attention. But we weren't complaining.

"Where are you going? Don't you want to dance?" said Emma, especially exuberant this time.

"Are you kidding! You know how we feel about hip-hop and gorgeous ladies!" I responded.

"We didn't realize how crazy the guys would be . . . already, I had to hit this guy for grabbing my ass! You have to protect us tonight!" Lovisa said. It was an ironic statement because I was sure she enjoyed the undisguised attention she was receiving. Even now, out of the corner of my eyes, I could see men drooling. It was nice being on the winning team this time.

We walked to the back of the club where there was more room to dance. Emma had been extremely talkative and was proud of her dance moves. The more she danced, the closer and more daring she became. She loved lowering herself slowly towards the dance floor, while facing away from me. When I followed she would get so low to the floor, I had trouble getting back up. She was a pro at this limbo competition. Lovisa appeared much livelier tonight than she did on the beach. Whether her penchant was for Seb or Leo wasn't very clear in the beginning, but at this point it seemed that Lovisa was gravitating more towards Seb. Now he was on the dance floor clasping her hand in some algorithm, spinning her in a circle away from him and then back closer. I remember back in University how he was always ranting about the Havana Club in Buckhead, and this Argentinean girl he picked up, who later taught him a few salsa moves. He was now exhibiting how one complicates hip-hop with too much order. Leo didn't wait, once he realized he was wasting his time with Lovisa. He found this cute copper-skinned girl from the U.K., who seemed quiet at first; but all that changed when she stepped foot on the dance floor. We danced for at least a few hours, only breaking for bucket drinks and bathroom. It was easy to get carried away into yet another song and continue dancing, like a phone conversation that never ends, each dance another tangent to discuss and maneuver, until someone finally hangs up. I cut it after I heard the deejay scratching in "Hip-Hop-Hooray" by Naughty by Nature over the end of a Jay-Z song. I wasn't staying around so that I could throw my hands side-to-side, the way bleacher fans in basketball arenas pass time between quarters.

    I pulled Emma off the dance floor. We were sweating, in need of water and fresh air. I bought a couple of bottles of water at the bar, first checking the cap. The other more despicable rumor floating around was about some places refilling old bottles with tap water and reselling them. I'm all for recycling, but apparently Thailand water wasn't fresh from the Alps. When we left the dance floor, Seb and Leo were off in their own worlds, so we walked outside unnoticed. Emma spotted a couple of vacant beach chairs next to the sea. We plopped our bodies down, finally realizing the extent of our dance workout.

    The night was still young though, and we just needed to pace ourselves. We sat there for a few minutes, quiet, listening to the sounds of the clubs in the background clashing music the way disc jockeys battle, listening to the hum of the crowds laughing, chanting, the fullness of energy. At that point of the evening everyone was at the height of inebriation. But the waves alleviated some of the noise, and we were able to re-energize.

    "It's lucky we ran into you on the boat," said Emma.

    "I know—right? It's amazing what a few beers and a scorching sun can do. If it wasn't for our eyeballing those beers with so much yearning, we probably wouldn't be here right now together." We both paused for a few seconds.

"A lot of the guys here are just druggies with no idea how to talk to a girl. Their idea of talking is touching. They see us on the beach all day topless and now they're acting like animals."

She had a point. They were wearing less on the beach, but I thought she had to be a bit naïve not to expect at least some male harassment. They were bombshells in thongs. And guys are drunk and horny. Wasn't that part of the risk and fun? Still, she wasn't the most outrageous scene at the party. I spotted a couple of topless girls parading in body paint. And I almost vomited at the sight of this one guy walking around in Speedos. What is up with Europeans?!

"No need to worry. I will protect you tonight," I told Emma. And before I could utter another word, she leaned in to kiss me on the lips. Here I was, just a couple of nights in Thailand, thousands of miles away on the other side of the planet, sitting before a beautiful sea, on a small island that I could barely pronounce let alone spell correctly, and the prototypical Swedish goddess was initiating a kiss, in the midst of a massive all night beach party. I didn't want to wake up if I was dreaming. And little did I know this was only the beginning. It was an insignificant drop in what would be my life as a traveler. However, for a young man fresh out of college, I was on top of the world.

When we returned to the club, Leo was still with the girl he had been dancing with earlier, and there were no traces of either Seb or Lovisa. Leo was grinning when we walked up.

"What's up dog?"

"Chris, Emma . . . I want you to meet Lisa. She's from the U.K.," Leo said, still grinning.

"Have you seen Seb?"

"No, when they slipped out I didn't see them. What do you say? Another round of bucket drinks?"

"No, I think we're going to wait. I've had at least two of those in the last three hours, and it's starting to really sneak up." I turned to Emma. "I think we're going club hopping." She nodded. "Anyways, haven't you two had enough dancing? . . . you should go outside and rest, this is a party, not a gym class, you know."

"Never get bored to hip-hop, my friend, still can't believe I just heard that old Kriss-Kross song."

"What did they play? 'Jump, Jump'?" I started laughing. It was a random song to be heard way out here.

"The daddy-mack will make you . . . jump, jump . . . kriss-kross will make you jump, jump . . ." Leo started singing.

"Now you're really tripping!" I laughed some more, then said, "We'll catch you later. Gonna walk around a little."

Leo was still singing the Kriss-Kross tune as we walked away. "I'm tha migudee-migudee-migudee-migudee-mack-daddy . . . ."

Emma and I walked around a bit. We passed by a few bars, and not for any real reason did we decide against those bars. Then, Emma and I stopped in front of a peculiar place. It had a dark wooden façade that looked as if it was made with scrap materials, large holes dotting each of the planks. The sign was cut in an asymmetrical shape, flaring out from the top of the entrance, making it impossible for someone with my height to enter without bending down. It read: "The Mushroom Shack." For some reason, an odd energy seeped out of this place. Everyone that walked out seemed somewhat spooked, often looking off into the sky or other undeterminable places. Some people were laughing mad. I wondered what was so damn funny. Was this place a comedy bar? And so it went; curiosity is what pulled us in through the front entrance, and further into this dark dungeon of a club. Glowing red lights radiated from somewhere inside, their light clinging to the clouds of smoke, as if sunset was happening all over. It was hard to realize the size and depth of this club from the darkness. Every step forward was like driving through a thick foggy rain, where objects aren't visible until the last second. People in this club seemed to lurk around, some expressionless and zombie-like, others animated the way of cartoon characters. I often wondered what they were thinking when we passed by: were they looking at me or were they looking through me? Did they enjoy the lounge music playing or were they oblivious? They definitely noticed Emma. At moments, when we broke through a cloud and passed by someone seemingly deep in thought, suddenly then they would burst into laughter and then their friends would burst into laughter. It was the contagious kind of laughter, and I would catch myself laughing, until Emma elbowed me in the side. I had decided whoever these people were and whatever this bar was serving, they were happy people and that was all that mattered. We then walked to the inside bar, which was an island in the middle of a dark-red sea of people. The bartender asked us if we were having the usual. I didn't understand what "the usual" meant, so I asked for my usual, a bucket drink. We enjoyed the music but finally decided it was putting us to sleep and left the bar.

    We could hear music pounding from the next club, even before passing in front. I was never a house music fan, but the club had an upbeat energy and we were still in the partying mode, so we ventured in. As soon as we entered, the force of so many people concentrated in one space felt like ocean waves passing and sometimes crashing. It was almost impossible for us to bring our bodies to a halt or keep our feet planted in one place for too long. And even when I tried my hardest to resist one point of pressure, the crowd pushed me from another direction. We maneuvered the crowd by waiting for the next wave that propelled us forward. On the second level, I could see people really letting free and dancing. Emma stayed burrowed under my chest and in the grasp of my arms. Every minute or so she would look back and I would smile. We finally found our way upstairs, where there was enough room to maneuver a dance move. The alcohol had really kicked in by this point, and I was no longer responsible for the wild animal gesticulations I was concocting on the dance floor. We ended up grinding at every chance, our bodies never parting. There were ceiling fans up above revolving the entire time. But we were in tropical weather, amidst a crowd's body heat, and we were in full throttle on the dance floor. We were sweating profusely, to the point our bodies were now slipping and sliding, as opposed to bumping and grinding. I really enjoyed Emma's company. We were parading around this whole night as if we were some item, and maybe for this very moment we were something. I was amazed at the speed and ease of our relationship. We both knew the chances of us seeing each other for much longer or in the future were very slim, though none of that mattered. Right now is what counted. She was here for me, just as I for her. I wanted to protect her and show her as much care and affection as my young, inexperienced mind was able to show. I was living for the moment, along with everyone else on this crazy island. I didn't want to explore too profoundly into her past or background. I didn't care if she had a boyfriend back home or if she ever wanted to see me again. My simple mind didn't think that far, and furthermore, Thailand was too new and fresh. I also didn't realize then, at that moment, that true love with compatibility doesn't appear when it's convenient or when you need or expect it; often logic or sound reasoning need not be involved at all. I knew Emma was a wonderful temporary acquaintance, a brief partner in crime, and I was feverishly attracted to her.

We continued to dance and sweat. So much so, that I took off my shirt, and wrung out a puddle of water on the dance floor. Afterwards, I just wrapped it around my waist. We struggled to one of the inside bars situated in the corner of the club and bought more water. At this point we were in need of the outside. As we stepped outside, the sun was casting up its first light, gradually transforming the dark blue sky to a purplish-red. This had no effect on the party going on around us. People were still in the clubs and outside on the beach, still dancing the same trance. The bars were still serving those magical drinks, and while there were a few causalities of people who had passed out in the sand or were escorted away by friends, the daylight emerging only added more insanity and awareness to the chaos. The backbones of the party, the diehards, had a post-festival to look forward to after the beach lost its gusto. Somewhere around 10 a.m., people found their way to an after party in the mountains on a cliff overlooking the bay. I had heard that there were enough drugs at this party to keep the entire country of Thailand awake for days. I intended to make the party, but Emma would have other plans.

"Let's get a massage!" I saw Emma's face light up at the sound of her own idea.

"But, it's eight in the morning. You think anyone will be up serving massages? Shouldn't their hands be tired from all day massaging?" It was a logical conclusion. Plus, the whole idea sounded shady to me.

"I know a place where the people are always ready to give massages. Come. Walk with me. We can get one together. You right next to me the whole time," she said. And I was sold.

I had always heard of the infamous massage parlors in Thailand, the ones set up as fronts for prostitution, where you walk into a small viewing room and through the glass window on the other side are rows of Thai girls watching a television placed above the window, so it looks like they're watching you, each with a designated number tag for selection. It was the sad side of Thailand, the dark secret reverberating from the poor countryside to every back alley in Bangkok. Many of these girls, from the Northern region of Thailand, the more poverty stricken areas, were said to be sold by their families or they had left voluntarily, ironically seeking a better life in Bangkok or Chang-Mai or any of the other high-traffic cities along the coast. But this island seemed to me void of such darkness. It was at most a few days' backpacker retreat for the Full Moon Party, with not enough of the kind of travelers to support any brothels. Plus, I didn't think Emma was as kinky as she carried herself tonight. We walked through a small neighborhood of knick-knack shops behind the clubs searching for this supposed parlor. Emma was exhausted from being on her feet dancing all night, so I gave her a piggyback ride. We stomped through the criss-crossing dirt alleys of the neighborhood, consisting of mostly huts and shacks, finally managing on this narrow wooden shack with low hanging straw roofing. Emma knocked lightly on the door. We waited. Outside was ghostly. No one was in the streets and the fact we were interrupting this parlor at early dawn seemed odd to me. But Emma was sure someone would come.

The door opened and a small Thai lady dressed in white robes contrasting with her dark sun-baked skin—probably in her late 20's—opened the door and waited silently to the side while we walked in. I caught some sort of formal eye contact between her and Emma. We followed the lady down a long narrow hallway; the ceiling was low, and it felt the whole time like we were moving through a dark portal. The corridor opened up and people were knocked out flat asleep on the floor, between dividers. They must have felt so relaxed after their massage that they couldn't muster the strength to walk back home. White sheets had been kindly draped over them. At the end of the corridor, she directed us to the bathroom to change out of our clothes, and the Thai lady gave us both towels. I stood there admiring Emma for a few seconds as she changed out of her showgirl outfit. Standing there, stark naked, she fiddled with her wristband, turning it from bottom to top. She had a secret pocket with a zipper and from inside it she pulled out a little pill.

"What is that?" I asked

"Valium. It's going to relax me, finally," she said.

"Isn't that what the massage is for?" I asked, a bit confused.

"Yeah, but this will make it even better. Here . . . you should take one with me." And she pulled out another pill.

I knew it was a prescription painkiller, which didn't seem so dramatic. Plus, I was still responding to the Redbull Vodkas running though my system—probably the perfect reason not to take painkillers—and, so I wasn't in my right mind.

"Yeah, sure!" I replied.

She went over to turn the sink on, carefully placed her face under the faucet, lowering her mouth sideways under the flow of water, took a quick gulp and swallowed the pill. I followed the same procedures, not knowing I would pay dearly for my actions later in the trip, and took a mouthful of the good old Thailand tap water and swallowed down the other. We walked back out into the parlor with complete silence surrounding us. The hovering silence and darkness was a strange world for someone in my shape to be in, but somehow I made the effort not to fall over or laugh obnoxiously before making it to my mat. The Thai lady never uttered a single word. She just directed us with one hand, stiff as a log. I wondered was she a mute or had she vowed silence with the monks.

Two mats were laid out nicely in the corner of the parlor where we were given our own parcel of space, between bamboo poles and bristly rope, dividing us from the others. My head was feeling cloudy. I watched Emma dreamily as she gently unwrapped her towel and slowly lowered herself down onto her stomach. The entire parlor was dark; only a thin light shown from a candle that was fast running out of time; most of its wax had hardened along the floor. From the darkness appeared a young Thai lady with a dark colored tank-top exposing heavy strong arms; behind her a young Thai man, shirtless, in the shape of a "muy thai" (kick boxer) fighter. The young girl was more alert than the Thai guy at this time in the morning; she smiled warmly without words. The young guy was sleep walking, going through the normal motions of rubbing his hands warm with the oil, then spreading the first layer across Emma's entire back. Emma and I were close enough to hold hands and it felt natural to caress each other during the massage. The light smell of incense and the masseuse's deliberate motions penetrated my muscles and intoxicated my mind, releasing me from the world. My body lay so tranquil from it all, that eventually I forgot I was holding Emma's hand at all. Soon our grasp fell limp and dormant. Warmth continued to pour from our touch, but we were now in the dream world.

A blinding light entered through a sliding garage door, illuminating the inside of the parlor where we had been lying for most of the morning and afternoon. Not a single crack of light could be seen the morning before. Once my pupils stopped rejecting the new source of light, I could begin focusing vividly on the bright yellow birds chirping right outside, perched on vibrant green bushes and vines that were spilling over from the grass into a tiny pond. Rich blue skies with only faint cloud strokes colored in the background and added depth. A pleasant breeze blew in a thick smell of sweet honeysuckles, and the richness of the air seemed to flush open my throat and chest. The whole scene was a magical awakening where only flourishing tropical life filled my range of senses. I took a moment to lean my body forward—at which point, I could feel all the blood rushing to my head. The night had done its best to wipe me out. I managed to rest on the backs of my elbows while my legs overflowed the tiny mat, built for little Thai people. The alertness and tenacity of nature, and my sluggishness after a long night out, played guilt trips on my mind, now that I had slept so long into the pride of the day. Sunlight exposed the privacy of the parlor, and shined right through the ethereal cotton sheets covering our naked bodies. That's when I promptly gazed over at Emma. She was like a work of fine art beneath the silent veil of covers. I watched as she motioned through that final stage of sleep, where the body responds slowly to the inundation of outside noise. Sporadically she changed positions: her back to me at first, then balling up like a fist, then releasing her legs, then turning over and resting her body against my side. A strange feeling of freedom swept over me, lying there in my bare essentials with Emma, alongside nature. We were like one of those wacky nudist colonies shedding our inhibitions and sharing ourselves with the openness of God's green earth. Emma was now opening her eyes to the suddenness of a mid-summer's day. I could see it around her eyes: she had slept mountains. They puffed out in bags, the distance of her cheeks, and her eyelids never fully opened.

"Good morning!" I whispered. A few seconds went by while she struggled to gain equilibrium.

"Hey," she grumbled hoarsely.

I waited a moment before I made any drastic movements or started any substantial conversations; she was still cuddled up next to me, comfortable, not yet ready to start the day. The Thai lady that invited us in that morning came by our mats with a round wooden platter. On top of it, rustic red clay cups and a matching clay pot steamed slowly in the direction of the incoming breeze, leaving with it a delicate lotus scent. The lady smiled much more enthusiastically than she had earlier that morning but continued her vow of silence and left just as hastily as she had entered. I almost preferred her style of service to the way Americans often overdo hospitality, with the implied tip at the end. I would pay upfront for sincerity any day. It turned out the tea was the burst of inspiration Emma and I both needed. We sat up at our mats, carefully sipping the green tea as not to burn our mouths or lips. I still hadn't fully left that dreamy state, and while marveling at how relaxing and cleansing the sensation of tea was, I somehow went off on a tangent, remembering when I had been forced to enter the coffee-drinking world as a university student.

    I remembered having to focus and concentrate for extreme periods of time during those end-of-senior-year exams. At the end, professors had become much more challenging and irritating, and were demanding much more of my overall time. I had had the sobering feeling of entering boot camp at the end of my college career. Senior year had proven to be a tough time. I could see the light at the end, though I was sick of returning to the same concrete campus, day after day, for the fourth year in a row. Part of my problem was I had goofed off during my second and third years, and so I spent the last year racing to catch up and finally get the whole monotony of college life done and over. To make matters worse, professors at this stage were aware of their power as diploma gatekeepers, and made us pay for our circumstances every painstaking second. At that time, I found myself retreating to Caribou Coffee in East Atlanta at least once a day if not more, where I was on a first name basis with the drug dealers in green aprons and had developed a fondness for coffee with hazelnut syrup. If I was the type to blame my childhood for every bad habit or bad fortune, I would look to my mother who had always prepared large pots of coffee in the morning before rushing off with a huge mug to another day at work. But, every once in awhile a person consciously has an epiphany, and at this very moment, I resolved to abandon the coffee world for tea.

    Emma began to talk again, and we laughed and chatted about the night, about how drunk we had been, how people had stared at Emma, even making all types of whistling noises, about the unimaginable energy and outrageousness of the crowd, about us getting lost on the way to the parlor, and taking a Valium pill before lying down to a massage. That's when Emma admitted she hadn't slept for three days up until this morning. I knew what that probably meant, but she seemed a little embarrassed or ashamed to go into details. So I left the conversation alone. We got dressed and walked to the main entrance where the owner was sitting, chatting, and drinking tea with his wife. He was Thai and she was very English. A pleasant couple, they informed us of their intensive two-week Thai massage lessons, where we would become certified at the end, and also their new Swedish massage lessons. Emma smiled at that and told me if I was lucky, she would show me a real Swedish massage. We politely took the little brochure and walked back towards Emma's bungalow. While walking down the dirt path, with tropical wilderness seeming to swallow us up, I had a strange feeling of being lost and floating around in the world, with no clear purpose. As if I had a five-speed manual clutch in that moment, I was probably coasting in second gear, not in any rush, with nowhere pressing to be. It was a strange concept to digest, after experiencing an entire childhood and college career of goals and deadlines. My vacation didn't really have a clear ending in the near future, either. I would start work in about four months, which left a lot of uncertainties. I didn't have a schedule to follow, no reserved hotels or rental cars, no idea how I would travel from city to town, town to village.

Emma was beginning to open her eyelids, appearing fresh and lively. This was amazing considering she hadn't slept in three nights. Her bungalow was very close to Haad Rin beach, where all the main action had played out the night before. When we approached, I had this feeling of entering in a campsite. Many more trees were concentrated between each of the bungalows than at my place, providing plenty of shade. A pack of dogs, in all shades of grey and black and brown, jumped on each other and rolled around in the sand at the edge of the canopy. I wondered if there was a connection between these bungalows and the dogs, because they were extremely well-fed and joyful. I remembered watching the little children at my bungalows handing out all kinds of tasty leftovers to the dogs the day before. I had already seen enough to know these dogs had a better life than me. They roamed the beach freely, socialized in groups, played and swam, not a care in the world. They didn't have to scavenge or hunt; the Thai families fed them amply everyday. And you could almost see that they were taunting the humans with their wonderful doggy lives. They hung around close but never bothered socializing with the tourists, as if we weren't good enough for them. Before arriving, I had heard that the dogs in Bangkok had a hard knock life. There were rumors floating around the net that the government didn't kill stray dogs roaming the streets, because it was against Buddhist principles. There was an overpopulation of dogs in that city, and humans were warned to stay away for fear of catching rabies. If Bangkok was a dog's purgatory, then the islands were heaven on earth. Here it seemed every dog was happy.

It had been a rough night for all the people lying around the campsite. There was this mental hospital look about everyone who managed to stay awake. People were lying around in hammocks, on the steps of their bungalows, and under the wooden awning near the beach, not moving much, or socializing, just off in their empty thoughts. Emma's paradise pad was four bungalows down from the center, a front row seat to the beach. She stuck her head in the door to the absence of Lovisa and her other mates.

"Want to come in while I go take a shower?" she asked.

I followed her in. The ceiling fan was on blast, and I wondered did it have the power to suck up clothes from the open backpacks, and disperse them haphazardly around the room.

"Please excuse the mess!" She giggled as she spoke and pushed all her clothes and belongings from her bed into a backpack, and she quickly threw back the bed sheets and placed her small pillow back to its normal position for me to sit down. She gathered her towel and toiletries, slipping through to the bathroom. I observed what could have been the aftermath of a small tornado: the open pack of cigarettes lying on the floor, the small clock-radio with empty beer bottle resting on top, sandy flip-flops separated from each other like lost twins, and candy wrappers with Swedish writing on them. I picked up an old Lonely Planet travel guide that lay beneath a black bra and shirt tangled together on the other bed. I still couldn't believe I had done it! I actually booked a plane ticket and flew all the way across the world to a place I had only seen briefly in a travel guide just like the one I held in my hands. It seemed this whole book was my life at the moment, my story. I smiled at the thought of some adventurous soul in that very moment probably sifting through the very same copy at some bookstore or through a travel magazine in the dentist's office, day dreaming, imagining how great this world could be, how exotic and unforgettable, how different and exciting an adventure in Southeast Asia would be compared to the person's everyday routine, and how difficult it would be to find money and time to seek out such an experience. And I had just found and booked a cheap ticket without thinking too much. I was now living the very dream that drifts by the contemplator. I flipped through the pages aimlessly, landing on large picturesque photos with bright red and yellow colors and magnificent temples, exultant Thai children and sun-baked elders with deep smiles that covered their entire face, amazing overhanging cliffs next to white sand beaches and turquoise sea, boat markets along the river, with locals selling all types of fruits and vegetables. It occurred to me how much there was still left to do, so much to look forward to. I flipped through the pages planning silently what should fall under my itinerary. I must go there to see these shiny gold temples atop the mountain, I have to get my scuba diving license and experience the night dive and glow-in-the-dark specimens and take pictures at sunset. Emma shouted in an echo from under the water splattering, "What do you want to do today?"

I shouted back, "It's almost night time."

"Oh . . . you're right," she replied. I could hear the soap drop in the middle of her sentence.

Her loss of time perspective was no surprise. One thing I was beginning to notice about the island lifestyle is that no one wore watches and, accordingly, no one really knew the correct time. Not the foreigners and definitely not the Thais themselves. They didn't even know the correct day. I would later ask someone on the trip, on one of those small islands, what the day was, and he would reply Wednesday. I would ask another person the same question to confirm and she would answer Friday, and all the time I had thought it to be Saturday. To anyone living this island lifestyle, time didn't have any consequences. For instance, if you told someone to meet you later at the bar, it meant some point in the late afternoon or night and if you never showed up, it just meant you would meet another day. People here viewed the world as a series of events all tied into destiny and whatever happens is exactly what was supposed to happen. No arguments, regrets, or condemnations. The basic principle was never to rush or hurry. I was almost certain the Thais here in the south didn't use alarm clocks. They were biological clocks incarnate. They didn't need some battery-operated doohickey to tell them when it was time to fish or plant the next crop. If the sun set, then certain outside activities would have to wait for the following sunrise. It was that simple. The downside for foreigners was the island afterlife. It was dangerously easy to absorb the island rhythm: performing activities only when inspired, adjusting to the tropical climate, indulging in the ability to do absolutely nothing at times, praising the sun for all its heat and worshiping the sunset for all its relief. The bursts of energy and the sudden entrapments of tranquility had the power to push waves of hours in a day to a crashing end, and with it, the loss of time perspective. Any modest yearly savings from a first world country could allow an easy living in this country. So, with the struggle to survive lifted, many other nuisances like watches are relaxed.

I calculated the day, as such. When the sun was still in the sky, people rested in hammocks under the shade of palm trees or sunbathed, cooling off in the water periodically. More ambitious travelers were out kayaking, scuba diving, or snorkeling. After peak time when the sun was less intense, more people were in the water, the volleyball games and soccer games along the sand commenced, and if people weren't already sipping fruity mango drinks during the day, they were at this point. Later, when the soccer ball was missing your entire foot or the volley ball was smacking you in the face from the lack of sunlight, it was now time to eat and get ready for another night of drinking, smoking, and sitting around the local Bob Marley singing songs of freedom and strumming a guitar. It was common for people to lose track of time to the point that they were no longer on vacation and had started a whole other life in Southeast Asia. I was willing to bet that the main airport in Bangkok probably had the highest number of missed plane flights in the world, and later I wouldn't be an exception. Life was great out here. I didn't have the pressure of passing another university semester with a grade high enough to maintain my scholarship or have the pressure of keeping up with the latest fashions or impressing the lot of opportunists back in Atlanta. In fact, material items were meaningless in a place like the south of Thailand. More important here was your attitude towards life. The kinds of things popping up in conversation around here besides food, drugs, and sex were anything having to do with your experiences in your country versus someone else's, the stereotypes and customs, or myths, dispelled. Even more important was what you had in common with the people from other far away countries. Those realizations proved the essence of humanity; those were the everlasting bonds connecting our species. When you actually found someone who reminded you of a good friend or an old relationship back home, it felt as if you were shrinking the world to fit the palms of your hands.

I waited awhile for Emma as she got cleaned up fresh. Of

course, I wasn't going to leave Emma to be prancing around the way she was, so I decided to take a shower. A couple hours later, Seb and Lovisa barged through the door, without thinking to knock first. Emma, suddenly feeling shy and caught off guard, snatched the covers and wrapped them around herself; I had to fend for myself, finding my boxers and using them for cover.

"Oops, did we come at a bad time?" Lovisa said, grinning, the way people do when they aren't at all remorseful.

"No. It's okay," Emma muttered, getting dressed.

"How was your night?" Lovisa asked, as if she wanted to answer that question more than ask it. Before we could answer, she continued talking. "We had a wonderful time. Had the bungalow all to ourselves." She looked into Seb's eyes in the same moment, smiling passionately. "Where did you both run off to? Didn't see you for most of the night!"

"We, well it's a long story. We went to some more clubs. Ended up at that massage parlor, remember the one we went to the other night?"

Lovisa nodded.

"We fell asleep after the massage and didn't wake up until this afternoon," Emma said.

"Have you guys seen Leo? He didn't show up to the bungalow last night," Seb asked, not at all worried. I still hadn't known Leo that long or as well as Seb knew him. They had spent two years of university together in New York before graduating and taking this trip. But Leo struck me as a character, highly unpredictable, though very in control of his own destiny. I was sure he would be the cause of great stories to tell, sooner or later.

"No. I have no idea. Maybe we should go look for him," I said. I had spent enough time with Emma, and I was sure Seb wanted to unload all that happened last night—most likely in the crudest detail.

It was becoming dark outside as Seb and I left to look for Leo. The concentration of palm trees filtered the moonlight even more. The coolness of the air, felt after the intense heat of the day, seemed to clear my mind, and I felt lighter on my feet. At times a soft breeze enveloped my face like a mask of light air as I walked; it invited back life and I could feel my energy coming back to me again. This was how the nights felt in tropical Thailand; it was another chance to live out the same day, equally as important as the bright sun. We decided to walk back towards Haad Rin Beach; the few restaurants and shops were all behind the bars and clubs. Seb started yapping about Lovisa, how she had gone down on him at the end, and how he didn't think to warn her of his finale. I had heard all of these stories before, but he continued telling them with the same intensity and pride, which led to him asking how things had gone between Emma and me, and I couldn't let him down. We were now walking the part of the dirt road that passed in between small family-owned restaurants and led up to the main beach. Seb stopped for a moment, the way he always did when he needed to emphasize a thought in his head. Seb was full of thoughts and mental workings. His brain never stopped moving, and, consequently, neither did his mouth. They were almost one in the same. I was preparing myself for another one of his personal reveries.

  I had always known Seb as the bright-eyed and cheery victor. Regardless of all he had seen and done, he always chose to outwardly view the world with untainted innocence. Even later on, after his tumultuous experience on Wall Street, he would still carry with him this positive filter of appreciation for the world. I had heard that Investment Banking could turn the biggest optimist into a cold-hearted cynic. And although he could be the most abusive critic of human behavior—those humans outside of himself, essentially he had the ability to create wins and gains out of life's situations, never losses or regrets. He had a remarkable talent for promoting only the benefits and greatness from each of his actions. The truth was Seb had a most excellent perception of himself, and neither human nor God could break his self-esteem. Of course, no one really knew all the innermost workings of Seb's brain, and none of us are completely void of darkness or regret. But if words and emotions are the best indicator of a man's true self, then Seb was forever a forward thinker. Negative feelings or rotten memories kept no place in Seb's oratory or outward self-image, and even those could be transformed into highlights with the proper presentation. As proud and conceited as Seb may have appeared to those who didn't truly know him, there, within his lofty talk and optimism, lay the formula for perpetual success.

  Seb was on the verge of laughing. This time he wasn't thinking of himself. He was staring into a small yard. The house at the far end of the yard had a round stone walkway adjoining the restaurant next to it. I suspected it had the same owners as the restaurant.

  "Only in Thailand!" he started.

"What?" I said.

"Where else in the world can you see a chicken, a dog, and a cat living side by side in perfect harmony!" he said. It was a detail that my mind had been prepared to ignore, for me to walk right by without any thought, until he mentioned it. But Seb was right. It was a very odd coexistence, a concept that goes against my whole understanding of animal relations. I always thought the cat eats the chicken, the dog eats the cat or the chicken, or at least harasses it, and the chicken just lays eggs. The food chain was being yanked apart right before our eyes. And that's when Leo popped up.

"There goes Leo!" I was now looking inside the restaurant with no windows. He was his usual self, chatting it up at full speed, his audience this time, the owner and a cute Thai waitress. They were both sitting back in awe, seemingly mesmerized, elbows on the counter, jaws resting in the palms of their hands, as if they were listening to a distinguished president speak.

"I bet he's blabbin' about New York," I told Seb sarcastically as we walked over.

Leo was an extremely talkative guy and had learned to conquer a conversation, talking for hours, with the sole topic being New York City. He had relocated from his mother's apartment in D.C. to an upscale part of New York when he was just finishing middle school, where his father had made fortuitous contacts in the real estate market. Not only did he adapt to his new home, but also a certain pride came with being a New Yorker. He knew the average foreigner's impression of New York was one of intimidation and awe, excitement and mystery, curiosity and dreams. As soon as he mentioned the city, most people automatically reverted to listener and digested his stories with a glow of exhilaration. I had noticed before how he would anticipate the question, "Where are you from?" almost like a lion in the wild stalking his prey or a spider spinning its web, waiting the exact moment to spring forward to launch a surprise attack. He would then conquer his victim in a sort of oratorical dance. Okay, maybe I was a little envious at times. As much pride as I could have had for Georgia, the fact was that the world didn't have as much knowledge or interest about the place. And setting up a proper presentation was draining. First, I had to warm them up with familiarities, like Coca-Cola or the '96 Olympics; then, music such as Otis Redding and James Brown or Usher and Outkast, and so on. The bright side was that I didn't come with so many stereotypes, other than "you American." So, I could be a clean canvas, drawing the picture as I chose to see it, like Picasso or Van Gogh, emphasizing what was important to me.

Aside from his usual spiel about NYC, Leo was really a sharp, witty guy. He could strum up a conversation with almost anyone, in that sense not a whole lot different than Seb. But Leo was pure unfiltered energy. He had a way of exploding onto people with all focus and lack of trepidation. This served him well as a speaker. Seb had told me once that there was no one better in his graduating class at NYU for giving speeches. Leo had a natural propensity for getting up in front of people; in fact, he thrived on it. Oddly enough, considering his background, I always envisioned him as Mr. Corporate, big man about the boardroom, making decisions and giving orders; and not only because he could speak well, but because he was also a very clean-cut, well-mannered gentleman and always acted with an official air. He was arrogant to put it bluntly, but with no malicious intent. He was only being Leo. He, like me, was a product of a multi-racial family, his mother being African-American and his father German-Jewish. My mother is a Northerner of Swedish-Canadian origin, my father an African-American Southerner. Partly for this reason, we seemed to connect almost immediately. He had had some of the same experiences as me growing up, sliding in and out of different social and cultural circles, never making the full commitment to just one group or ever feeling fully accepted, but rather sort of keeping one foot in and the other out. It was the gift of a mulatto to be a human chameleon. We both had the ability to feel confident and comfortable around the broad sects of society and ethnic lineages and to gain people's trust and time effortlessly. It was a complex dance handed to us in the same way Cubans inherited salsa and rhumba.

Leo poured his arm out in our direction welcoming us in the restaurant, as if he already owned the place. He said, "These are my buddies from the states. Fellas, I was just telling them about September 11th and how you could just see the buildings crumbling to the ground right before your eyes."

"This guy giving you all trouble?" Seb said laughing. Leo ended his conversation prematurely with them. He wanted to talk about the last twenty-four hours.

"How was your night?" He stood up, slapping Seb around the shoulders as we found a table in the corner and sat down. A wave of excitement seemed to come over him.

"It was good!" Seb reacted with a smile. "The girl was a total freak! We drank most of the night, and then back to our bungalow, where I smashed it all night!"

"Right! That's good, man! What happened to you Chris? Don't tell me it fell through?! Aaaarrrgh! No?!" Leo said wild with energy.

"No, things went well. I mean it's a long story. It was going well today, right before Seb and his girl came bursting through the door!" I replied.

"Your girl has a bangin' body!" Seb said, laughing.

"Anyways, what happened to you?! We saw you leaving with that one chick. Where did you guys end up?!"

"Guys it was absolutely nuts! First, we went down to the rocks at the corner of the beach, right below where the hills creep up like mountains, and she whipped me out right then and there and went at it! It was unbelievable! Later, we went back to her bungalow where her friend was sleeping in the bed next to us and she wanted to go at it again. Unbelievable, guys! Unbelievable night!" Leo said.

"Who would have thought us three naïve Americans would be conquering this small island in the South of Thailand. God bless America!" Seb remarked. We all laughed. After catching up on the night before, we finally ordered food to eat. I hadn't eaten all day and was starving. We all shared Pad Thai, papaya salad, masumum curry chicken, and mango shakes. The food calmed us down and settled our moods, and we began more profound conversations.

"You realize that just in a few months we will be starting our new careers?" Seb said, not sure if he was happy about that idea or not.

"I know, that's crazy—right?! Life is going to change dramatically. Soon one of us will have kids, and then life will never turn back as we now know it," I said.

"Can you imagine Leo with two little sons running around, teaching them how to mack on girls!" Seb remarked. We all laughed. "Guys, you have to promise we're going to come back here for a ten-year anniversary. I mean, no matter what happens, kids, job, wife. It doesn't matter. We'll escape again." Seb didn't realize at that time, our travel anniversary, although elsewhere, would come sooner than imagined.

"I hear you. I'm down for that," I said. And Leo nodded.

"But, seriously, I'm looking forward to the big pay days. For most of my life, I've had to ask for money or work a part-time job paying nothing. Pretty soon we'll be able to make our own moves. That's if our job doesn't take our lives," Leo said.

"The first couple of years are going to be hard. You have to prove yourself constantly and outshine your colleagues. Then, when people know you could be taking their job one day, they start stabbing you in the back," said Seb.

"I don't think it's that bad," Leo said. "Everyone at my internship seems pretty cool."

"But that's because you are no threat at the moment, and the bosses don't want to scare you away too early in the game," Seb responded.

"That's true," I said. "They try and make the job look all glamorous and agreeable to interns by taking them to fancy dinners, sending them to training near the beach."

But, what did I really know about a career job in one of the toughest financial or accounting firms in the world? I, myself, had only done an internship in tax at this multi-billion dollar corporation in Atlanta. I had learned some useful skills, mingled with the tax professionals, and worked on some of their tax-saving projects. But I didn't receive any serious pressure from my supervisors, because they didn't really need an intern. The position was created to help the image of the company, showing how they reached out to the community and local universities. As far as the head tax guys were concerned, they had a budget set up for one paid tax internship, and I filled that hole. Now I had accepted an offer before leaving the States to work at one of the Big Four accounting firms (at that time it was still the Big Five). My only experience with the Big Five was through a series of interviews, extravagant lunches and dinners, special functions at the Ritz Hotel, where you meet and greet the entire hierarchy from associates to partners of the firm. It was, to say the least, a circus act. Everyone greeted you with a fantastic smile, told you how great the firm was and how you were a special candidate, key to the future development and success of the firm. They wanted to all appear cool and young, knowledgeable about things in life other than financial statements, which meant talks about professional and college football or basketball; the partners would make some lame comment about Britney Spears or a famous young person that they probably overheard their kids talking about. They all tried to make you feel as excited and welcomed as possible. I had to be skeptical, but from my eyes or any candidate's eyes, stepping into the Big Five (in my case) or an Investment Bank (Seb's and Leo's case) was like stepping into a world of freebees. It was very appealing. For graduates fresh out of university, these positions in the business world were considered golden. If you made it in, you were part of the elite and were on the path to affluence. That's if you climbed the ladder properly. We weren't so sure what all climbing the ladder entailed, but we had secured an opportunity to climb. The Thailand trip in that sense was not only a celebration of graduating university, but also graduating right. All of us had worked diligently in college, kissed the right professors' asses and now had jobs lined up. We were having the times of our lives, letting go and living free in Thailand, and all the time subconsciously a part of us was also awaiting our new corporate careers in the U.S. and ready to explore the next chapter in our lives.

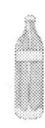

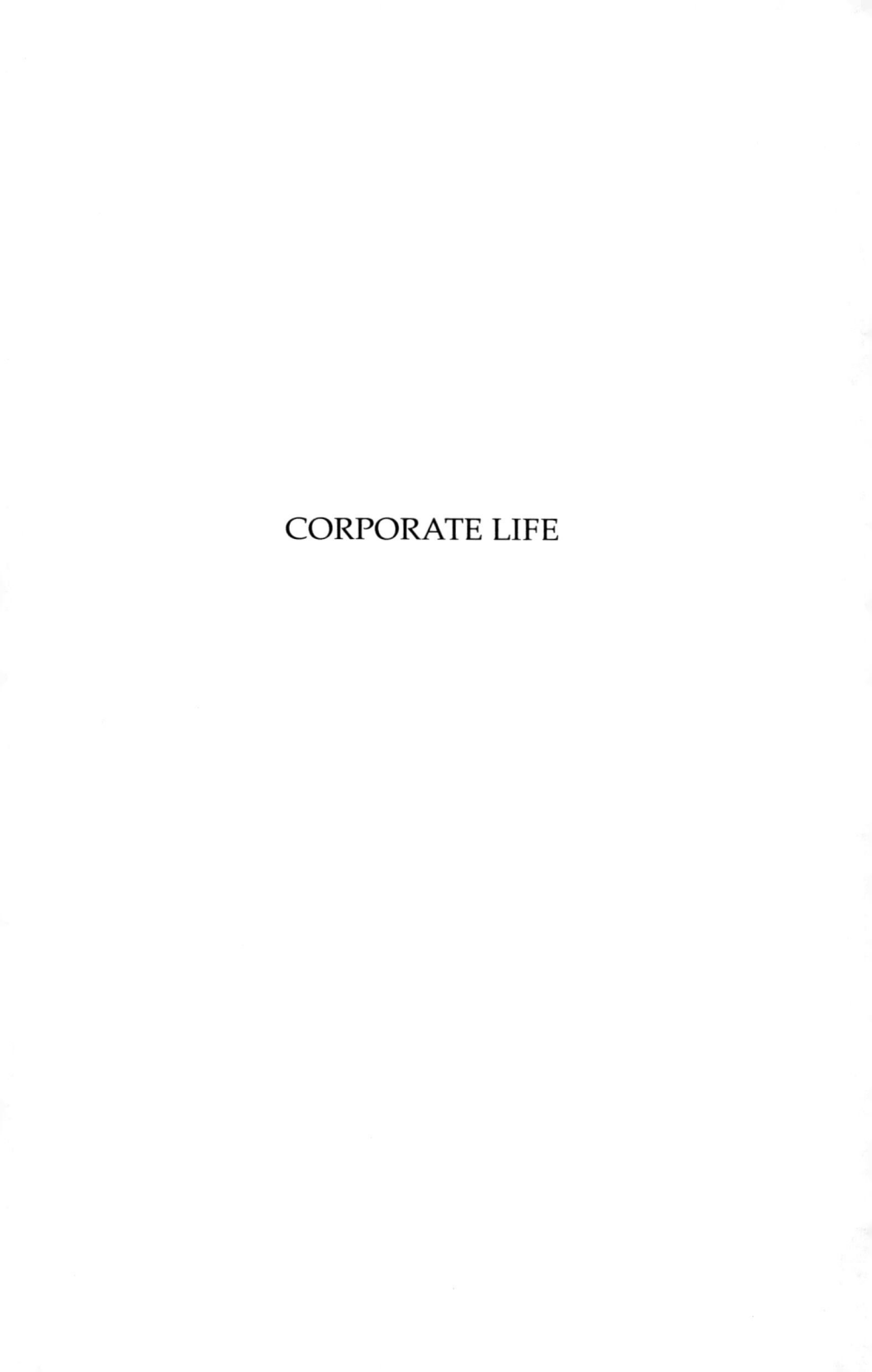

CORPORATE LIFE

It was too late; two years later, and still the indelible images were burnt, engraved in my psyche, like a vision of freedom planted before a revolution. Visions and memories of Mexico, Bahamas, Puerto Rico, Thailand, Cambodia, Hong Kong, and Singapore repeated themselves, over and over, diverting me from my corporate prison, saving me and torturing me in the same moment—recollections miles away in the past, and yet I still felt anxiety and nervous excitement from them, experiencing some of them with almost the same intensity and clarity. My heart would beat blood faster and faster, my eyes open wide in wonder, my head seeming to float, disconnected from the rest of my body, momentarily elated, locking in and focusing steadily, as if I were, in that very moment, atop an elephant traversing the jungles of Northern Thailand, or flying down the Mekong River in a speed boat barely skimming the top of the water, on my way to Phenom Phen, the capital city of Cambodia, just having left Angkor Wat and all the mysterious ruins of Angkor Thom. Then suddenly, those visions would begin to be blurred and infiltrated by the reality of my distance and the confines of my corporate monotony, and my mind would try to fight back and reject the sobering thoughts, in the process dead-locking my brain's neurons and ending the battle without compromise or truce. This fierce yearning for adventure and search for the unknown was much like a drug addiction, and these relapses were part of my withdrawal. But it was even worse, because the body can overcome the typical known drug addictions, like cocaine, heroine, or cigarettes in a matter of days or months. I couldn't escape these moments where my mind would completely shut down.

The small fishing boat cut its engine off in the middle of the Andaman Sea between the western Thai island, Ko Phi Phi and the small deserted island we were en route to, drifting only a few more yards before completely stopping. Ti-Ti, our private boat guide for today and our marijuana connection on the island, bent over, rummaging through the rusted metal chest between the two sitting planks on the small boat, grabbing two snorkels and goggles. It was a surprise, sprung on us at the last minute. Who would have ever thought that a coral reef prospered right below us, in the middle of the sea, ten minutes from the nearest island by boat? Maggie gave that deep gorgeous smile, her little dimples glowing, excited about the boat trip and now all of a sudden our little adventure gift. Before I knew it, Maggie dived overboard, hands first, black shiny hair back, submerging herself, then springing back to the surface a few seconds later. "Jump in! All types of colorful fish and coral! Throw me the goggles!" she gleefully shouted over quick, short breaths. I threw her the goggles, then plunged in feet first with my goggles already strapped on, snorkel popping out the side. The cool slippery feel of the water received me as I entered in; it was a welcome relief and I tried to savor every moment of its new refreshing quality, before my body would fully adjust, becoming immune to its new sensation. Bubbles whizzed by my face violently, like a blast of spritzer, clouding my vision. Then, all of a sudden—Wow! I had entered another world. Not far from the surface was a colorful realm, mute, with smaller bubbles, fish with orange and white stripes, bright red fish, and black eels. A funny looking crab-like crustacean popped his head out from behind a crevice in the coral, seemingly just as curious about me as I was of his world, then he disappeared. Now, my focus shifted to a school of clear, yellowish round fish. I noticed how they kept perfect distance and symmetry, even when something had startled them, shifting their direction in milliseconds. I continued to watch these fish in awe, but I was no longer submerged under water and that cool, free flowing feeling had faded completely away. Now the fish from Thailand were morphing into one-dimensional fish animations, swimming in a space the size of a fishbowl. I was watching the screensaver on my laptop at work.

    It was happening again. "Please not at a time like this," pleaded the person inside me, the dominant voice of reason, health and happiness. The recollections of past travels were a welcomed break at times, calming me down when I was irritated and angry, lifting my spirits when I needed dreams to look towards, reasons to continue pushing forward. But now, I was in a moment of proving myself. I urgently needed to finish this memo and turn it into my senior for review before I left the office tonight. And, I was hungry. Today I had felt the pressure of finishing the memo, like a consistent unrelenting weight of someone's hand, never letting off, and I had worked straight through lunch, without a thought to the mental or health consequences: the environment of the entire office was such that not even the partners stopped our determined work ethic to mention the principal nourishment the body would need to last through to another grueling night of testing, analyzing, understanding mountains of data. "Not at a time like this, when I need every ounce of my capacity for concentration" —and I was being put on the spot this time. I just knew it. The manager over this review was far behind her schedule, having made promises to her partner of a quick turnover, deadline and delivery, ironically, the same type of lofty goals that put our current client into bankruptcy, after committing financial fraud to achieve over-ambitious revenue, stock price projections. Now, my manager was desperate for a scapegoat at this point or a saving grace. She had given me an even heavier responsibility at the last minute, a seemingly impossible goal of decoding the audit trail on an accounts receivable of an obsolete subsidiary; and, with hardly any assistance, I was destined to fail.

But the thought that, because of a delay in the finishing of my project, the entire higher up deadline of reporting the 2000 year could be jeopardized sent adrenaline pumping through my veins, and I refused to be the weakest link after such an arduous struggle to survive the last eight months of a systemic chaos within this particular client and our firm. "I can't give up now. Maybe a quick break is what I need to refresh my energy, and I can come back and pick right back up where I left off. I need to stand up, stretch, and walk around a little." When I tried moving my legs, I realized they had fallen asleep; I stood up on numb logs, waiting for the ants to begin a flood of bites, as my legs regained balance in blood. At the same time, I could feel the temporary dizziness as blood rushed to my head. It seemed blood was rushing back to all parts of my body, like a bursting of river water through an open dam, regaining all its old levels and streams.

I stuck my head around to Chip's cubicle and whispered, "I'm taking a break for a few minutes in the stairwell; cover for me if the boss comes around. Tell her I went down to the first floor to make photo copies of the original client books." He nodded okay, not missing a beat, as he continued hammering away at the keys. It seemed stupid to need to make up stories for a few minute's break down the hallway, but in the business I was in, image was a large percentage of everything you did, and consequently the way you were perceived by your bosses and in return, the type of bonuses you received. I often felt like delivery took precedence over content. Bosses typically didn't like the idea of a break, even if it made logical sense, because this created images of a slacker, someone not suited to the auditor's world: always fast at work, asking clients difficult, decisive questions with the professional hard stare, one hand on the special edition HP 10-key calculator, body bent forward connected to the laptop by an invisible cord, downloading and uploading information continuously, like a corporate cyborg. Even at times when there clearly was nothing to do at the office, the bosses wanted everyone to appear busy, and with the client paying extortionate hourly fees, bosses had their reasons.

    I passed through the hallway of cubicles in swift, confident strides, keeping an appearance of focus and destination, hoping not to run into any of the managers, who would vent their negative energy my direction, and especially not the partners on this engagement, who flicked the awkward obligated smile of insincerity and distance. I hated that smile that seemed practiced and sharpened, polished and sedated after years and years in this business; to their credit they were accountants, not very good actors. This time I would be lucky; I made it to my usual hideout and refuge, the stairway to the fire escape, without anyone noticing. I continued to stand, with my right foot on a higher step and resting my body on the railings, while looking out towards downtown Atlanta and the marble island of skyscrapers. The cubicles, where I had been sitting for the last eight months, unfortunately didn't have access to windows. Only the offices housing the managers, partners and client executives had windows, and these offices lined the outer core of the building, like a moat surrounding a castle. A lot was on my mind, and escaping to my spot allowed a quick moment to refresh and purge all the distracting thoughts—like the love of my life, Maggie, thousands of miles away on the other side of the world, or the misery of wasting away my soul and happiness at this job. I was afraid I had forgotten how to be happy after almost two years of it. I didn't remember how to socialize in a functional, normal setting, with people that wouldn't stab you in the back at work the next day, or how to talk to my family and friends, the ones I owed my life to in ways. I felt I was losing touch with not only the people that meant the most to me, but also with myself. With no one to talk to for the moment, I began talking to myself, almost the way my father did down in the basement of our home when he was fast at work on one of his new projects or inventions. I missed those simple days, and, at times, wished my only pressure was making it home in time for dinner.

    After almost two years, it was still difficult to accept: devoting almost every waking hour of my life to pleasing some good old boy with corporate blood running through his veins; having to walk to the only functioning printer on the other side of the building in order to pick up his too many happy-hour drinking beer belly and McDonald's drive-through ordering ass a photo copy or listening to another unnecessary, condescendingly delivered speech about how they would approach the most mundane task, which really meant in manager talk, how I needed to perform the task if I were to continue in their world. I constantly needed to maintain a breath of conversation among colleagues forced upon me for at least sixty, sixty-five hours during the week, ten, fifteen hours on weekends, when the only thing we have in common is a university degree and a diehard desire to reach a new income level in order to step ahead of our peers, and hopefully retire rich and early. Or maybe, one day, even say to the girl we had a crush on during high school, but who ignored us for four long adolescent years, that "I told you so, should have stuck with me, a winner." Ironically, as un-athletic and out of shape as many of my colleagues were, sports were the main thing they knew to talk about, almost as if nothing else existed. I didn't have the slightest interest in watching and talking about college football or any other sport for that matter, unless I was actually playing the sport myself, and more than fifty percent of socializing amongst the firm employees involved fantasy football games or memory competitions on the most inconsequential trivia about athlete statistics and anything remotely related to the lives of these athletes. Hardly anyone had very much appreciation for art, music, or traveling, unless travel consisted of flying to Hawaii for a honeymoon, and these were the essential passions that kept me alive and breathing. There were exceptions to the rule, but the main topics of interest revolved around sports or domestic politics. And, when we weren't working our lives away, glued to our cubicle chairs, the bosses wanted to celebrate our hard work ethic and loyalty by throwing happy hours and feasts at snazzy restaurants and bars all around the city. This was a chance for all the opportunists, the entire lower hierarchy of our firm, to get in closer with the managers and partners and secure spots with the best clients and sell ourselves for better bonuses at the end of the year. In any business environment, this was probably only a logical system, but it meant the couple hours of free time I had at night would be spent with the same group of people that were boring me to death during the other waking hours of the day.

    Still, I couldn't forget why I was here, why I continued to work myself through the system, climb the corporate mountain. For the first time in my life, I was earning enough money to support myself, invest in a 401k, stocks, mutual funds, and real estate, pay back loans, eat and drink sumptuously, and purchase many items without too much thought. Although I was learning over and over again, like a stubborn child, that I didn't enjoy accounting, my bank account was much fatter than in my childhood or college years. And, my understanding of accounting, deemed the business language, had advanced on an applicable level, and, therefore, I was more prepared to start a business of my own, one of the long-term goals I entered the profession with. Furthermore, I was acquiring tools for success, such as time-management, mental endurance, analytical thinking, oratory, etc., useful to any business or profession. Other employers and headhunters were aware of the military minds that firms like mine were molding and conditioning; so, it was normal to receive voice mails and emails from people wanting to set up job interviews, intent on stealing us from our present warden. More than any skill I could have obtained or any amount of money received, nothing could have matched the feeling from my parents, when they knew that their somewhat rebellious son, growing up, had finished high school and university unscathed (still in one piece without a police record) and landed a respectable career job.

Still, I was miserable and I had been miserable for a long time, almost two years. Something was not right in my life. I wasn't healthy. I ate enormously through the job, but I was becoming frail and skinny. I didn't see sun. I was about as pale as a mulatto kid could become, almost a phantasm, and my hair was dry and falling thin. For the first time in my life I wasn't working out or athletic: I was a member at LA Fitness, a gym franchise all over the Atlanta area, but I didn't have the time necessary to go. The irony was that I felt weaker and lower in energy, at a time when I needed all the energy I could muster, and to counter this, I was back binging on coffee to keep awake, like I had in my last year at university. Mentally, I felt depressive. If laughter was a sign of happiness, and I mean real laughs, not the ones created to stroke the managers, I couldn't be happy. I honestly couldn't remember my last true laugh or smile, for that matter. What was I becoming? What was happening to me?!

When I realized these thoughts, running through my head like a panicking crowd, were now being mumbled into the cold stairwell, I silenced immediately. I looked around in both directions, embarrassed, as if someone could see me; but no one was with me in the stairway. If someone had been watching, they probably would think I had lost my mind, the long hours finally taking their toll. Look at Chris! Look at him, I told you he wasn't cut out for this line of work; he's not one of us, he never should have attempted the accounting field. I was not denying these thoughts myself. Maybe they would be right. Was I losing my mind? I sat down near the top of the flight of stairs, left elbow on my knee, palm holding the weight of all my thoughts at the chin, wishing in ways that I could transport myself, just run away, find a new situation; but I couldn't quit, not this far along. I had to force myself to get up and walk back to my cubicle, and finish the memo.

It had been another exhausting night. Finally, at 3 a.m. in the morning, I had finished the memo, and after a meager two hours of sleep, I was now back driving in famous Atlanta rush hour traffic, below the Midtown bridges taking 85 North at the split, on my way towards Alpharetta, back to the client location and back to work. With ambulance sirens blaring in the background and rotating lights edging closer and closer from behind, I knew it was only a matter of minutes before all traffic would come to a complete halt, making me late for work again. The Kanye West and Twister song was blasting from my speakers, but like I was to my alarm clock on the tiny nightstand in my bedroom, I was immune to the noise, and it was hardly helping me to stay awake. Traffic was now coming to a stop, and the look of other drivers reflected this reality; the guy in the BMW to the right of me threw his hands up in a rage, spitting out venomous words at the traffic ahead of him, and a sullen lady, probably in her mid-fifties, leaned her face on the steering wheel of a new Volkswagen Bug in exhaustion and somber acceptance. I too, soaked up the frustration, not having the energy to vent and release. I wondered how, when the time arrived, I would ever get out so much built up frustration I had acquired over the last couple of years. I, like most men, had learned to suppress all of the emotions inside of me, stacking each of the negative thoughts in a closet somewhere in the back of my mind. And I kept seeing images of one day opening that closet, drowning in the mass of clutter that would flow out of it.

After an hour stuck in traffic, I pushed myself out of my little car with laptop briefcase in hand and walked the ritualistic path from parking lot to front entrance, waved my badge across the sensor, waited for the green light and belated beep, tilted my head upwards in salute to the receptionist as I was walking in. I enjoyed basking in what his life must be like, coming home from work right after five p.m. everyday, probably to a loving wife and kids. Not perpetrating a fancy life, driving an expensive Mercedes Sedan, flaunting a luxurious home or trips out the country, but enjoying afternoons with his kids, throwing the football in the local park, and barbecuing chicken and corn on the cob on Saturday afternoons. He was always smiling and seemed at peace with himself and his job, even when he wasn't aware that I was watching. I continued through the flashy lobby, past the enormous flat screen monitors marketing the company, up the elevators to the fourth floor. I dreaded seeing the manager's face, her disdainful look of discontent, but it was too late to change things, and I did have a memo with spreadsheets and graphs supporting my conclusions to show for this morning. I saw Libby walk cautiously out of the break room, so as not to spill the freshly made machine coffee out of her giant blue mug with company logo she won in a raffle at training this year. She had flowing blonde hair, an elegant, professional style, and a pleasant smile that appeared genuine, still not fully corrupted, after only one year at the firm. She was the only bit of eye candy we had swimming in the company pool, although she wasn't interested in dating accountants, and even she looked five years older than she did the first day we met, about a year ago at a company recruiting dinner. She smiled with a slight smirk, knowing that I was walking in late. I lifted my eyebrows slightly, acknowledging her in return, and stealthy whizzed through my row of cubicles, quietly connecting my laptop, anxiously waiting for the computer to boot up, so that I could log on and appear to have been at my cubicle working all along before my manager walked up. The horizontal meter at the bottom of the screen indicating the booting progress slowly nudged further and further to the right, like watching a marathon race, almost reaching the end. It was too late. Already, peering from the top of the cubicle wall, downwards at my computer, the angry eyes of my manager, Kumiko, spoke violently, before she asked out loud, "Are you just getting here?"

    I swallowed air first, my heart started beating fast, and my breathing pattern was suddenly interrupted, making it hard for me to answer right away.

    "Do you know what time we need you here in the morning? Kumiko continued. "Eight a.m., just like everyone else. I don't think I need to mention this again!"

    I caught the rhythm of my breath again, "Yes. It won't happen again."

    "It better well not! Do you have the memo and test work I

asked you to complete? You know last night was the deadline?" she clamored before I could answer.

    She caught me off guard. I was delayed in my responses, appearing guilty—when I was not in agreement, not happy with the way she was accusing, leaving me to retreat and defend myself. "Yes, I just need to print it out. Everything is right here," I said. I couldn't believe my response; I was in someway condoning this treatment, almost apologizing for my actions, when I had stayed here slaving until three in the morning. She, on the other hand, had left briskly at 10 p.m., not at all concerned that she had hammered me with a last minute project or when I would leave the office. And now I was getting stepped on for coming to work thirty minutes late.

    I was amazed at the abuse I was able to absorb without lashing back. I was not the same Chris from college, and especially not from high school, when I was always fighting for the slightest disrespect received. My senior year in high school I had even been in three separate fights in one day. One of them started right after lunch before the change in class. One of the kids, jokingly called me White Boy, a comment that I felt was an attempt to alienate me, draw unneeded attention to the fact my parents were of different races, try and make me out as a soft kid, an outcast to society and the other kids at school. Without much thought, I swung on him, right hook, then a left hook, making him pay for his comment, proving that I could hold my own, that I wasn't a pansy. It all happened so fast. We were now rolling on the floor in the lunchroom lobby, and I managed to force my weight on him, pinning him down, so that I could throw more blows. The other kids were running over frantically from all directions, from the lunchroom, from the hallways leading to the classrooms, and a couple of kids were shouting, "Fight! Fight!" like bookies at one of those underground boxing matches, like they were going to make money off gambling the odds. A crowd had gathered around the spectacle, like we were gladiators in a Roman Amphitheater, all of which fueled my adrenaline even more. Then, out of nowhere, I can remember being hoisted up in the air from under my armpits, powerful arms gripping my chest, throwing me to my feet. It was Randy, one of the assistant football coaches. He had heard the chants and laughter, the commotion projecting from the lobby, the crowd of kids hovering over an opening in the middle. And he knew that it couldn't have been just another break dancing competition. I realized after the fight that one of my enemies had kicked me when I was on the ground fighting. I was infuriated and that day waited for him, with my little gang of friends, to get off the bus from school, near my neighborhood, to fight him one-on-one; and then finally fight his brother who was infuriated seeing his younger brother losing a well deserved fight. I was an animal back then, and I didn't take well to disrespect or injustice.

But now, I was sitting here in my cubicle, hunched over, weak, listening to a stream of ungrateful, fiery comments from my boss, and even apologizing to her. Before leaving, Kumiko plopped a heavy binder on my desk. "Look over this and understand it, while I go review your work." She marched off. At least I was awake now.

How did I get here? At what point in my life did I say to myself, "Accounting, now that's a fulfilling life!" I was a musician at one point: disk jockeyed throughout high school, played jazz with my trombone, and performed hip-hop with my friends. I was an athlete, even: I ran track, played soccer, even basketball at times, and frequented the new state of the art gym at GSU. I functioned in more exciting realms of life, spoke the lingo, hung with the cool kids at school and attracted my share of ladies. But now, now I was an accountant, immobile and dying, and women now seemed to tune me out as soon as I uttered a word of my occupation. How did I get here was a question that I often reverted back to, and the answer made logical perfect sense. My passion was music, so I entered university as a music industry major, took music theory classes, industry introductions and blew my long brassy instrument as much as possible. Only, the more I had to haul my awkward instrument around town, and the more I learned that my school was first and foremost a business portal, the more I realized that music was not guaranteeing much money and that I had a world of companies at my feet if I graduated with a business degree. My school was located in the heart of downtown Atlanta, among multi-billion dollar corporate headquarters, such as Coca-Cola, Georgia-Pacific and Home Depot, and many of the school's alumni were powerful executives, managers, and owners around town. So, I naturally converted to the business school. Only, majoring exclusively in business was not an option; you had to further focus your interest within the business degree. The counselors allowed me to start with the generally required courses, in hopes that I would soon make up my mind. I took a management introduction course and wasn't impressed, a computer information systems course and was lost, a finance course and hated the professor, a marketing class and heard how weak the starting pay would be after college, and finally an accounting class, which wasn't exactly exciting, but I did well in the class, while all the other students were struggling, some even dropping the course.

Furthermore, Mr. Benton, our professor, invigorated the class right from the beginning, brought dollar signs and visions of success to our eyes. He spoke of his experience working at practically all of the Big Five accounting firms and how it had changed his life and propelled him to a place among the business elite. He said that his experience had prepared him as an investor, and that if it wasn't for business knowledge gained in accounting, he wouldn't have invested $5,000 in Microsoft the month after its Initial Public Offering, at that time worth close to $5,000,000. I remember that first day in class like it was yesterday. "Listen, I'm set for life. I'm not here standing before you today because I need to teach. I want to teach. I want to help you learn and be able to compete in today's highly competitive business climate," he preached. And I devoured every word of his speech. I wanted to be just as successful; maybe that was the reason I could focus so well and excel in his class. Seb happened to be in that class, too, just as enamored by the speech, and during that time, while the Nasdaq was hitting its all-time peak, no one could go wrong if they invested in technology stocks. Seb and I gave each other stock tips we had picked up from other people, excited at the thought of making it rich; this is when we became friends. Mr. Benton would tell us, "If you know accounting, you know the language of business. It is the most fundamental aspect of business. You will be able to run your own business, sail through the corporate hierarchy, or whatever business-related passion you endeavor." I was sold.

Now, the next step was finding a job. My most lucrative option with an accounting background was to work at one of the Big 5 firms, so I interviewed and secured a job, to begin after graduation, four months after the start of my Thailand trip. Life had been a chain of events for me, each decision leading to another logical decision. In an ironic way, I had chosen the accounting road contrary to millions of other different paths of which my background up until university screamed out loud, "This is you! This is who you are!" Part of my determination to pursue accounting stemmed from a rebellious nature. I wanted to prove something to myself and to a society of Americans, who I felt underestimated my ability to succeed within what was historically a good old boy network of professionals. For me, it was the ultimate challenge and expression of individuality to pursue a profession that most people, including myself, didn't expect me to enter. Throughout my time in university and even now, I've surprised people and baffled them with my occupation, all the feelings and stereotypes associated with it, because I don't fit the typical profile of an accountant.

    So, here I was, working my logical outcome, trying to find my piece of the American Pie or at least understand what that statement meant. Heaps of accounting analysis and transaction-filled binders flooded my cubicle area, cluttering the top shelf above my desk, jamming my cabinet drawers, covering the floor space in boxes surrounding my legs; I had the cramped feeling of flying coach on United Airlines from Atlanta to Hong Kong, my knees pressed against the magazine storage of the passenger's seat in front of me, the snug armrests of my seat pushing my thighs inward. Normally, work paper documents and client copies no longer useful to an engagement would be discarded, or even shredded if deemed confidential, but because our client had been accused of shredding documents vital to the court's investigation of fraud, the bankruptcy court had ordered the client to save any and all documents. After an entire year of saving and storing every single piece of paper and binder produced, the offices and cubicles on each and every floor of the building appeared as if a giant snow blizzard had hit; the client's core business, its sole reason for existing, to any random passerby would probably seem to be to recycle or process paper. It was a crazy mess, and the first and second years had the esteemed job of organizing and cleaning up the chaos after the client exited from its bankruptcy, that's if they were ever to exit. I wondered if the client was going to be happy paying between 100 and 150 dollars per hour, per accountant, for us to stuff boxes full of paper and ship them away as evidence.

    Of course, the client also wouldn't be happy if it knew that the partners of my firm were skillful in finding ways to convince us that we needed to work excessive hours. Unlike most client contracts, that stated a reasonable amount of hours to be worked for a reasonable amount of time on an engagement, our contract, because our client couldn't afford to negotiate while we held their fate in our hands, stated that for every hour we worked my firm would be guaranteed a certain price for that accountant's level of seniority or expertise (each employee's rank or level at my firm was determined the same way as in the army, you either moved up each year or you moved out). Therefore, our partners were losing out on revenue for every hour that we were away from the office, not working and clocking in hours. I was shocked that my firm, perpetrating as a model of ethics and morality, could be exploiting its employees in order to cheat a client out of millions of dollars. Add that to the fact we were supposed to provide assurance to investors, the SEC, bankruptcy court, and all forms of stakeholders, that our client, who was accused of cheating the system, stated its financials correctly. I was working deep in the belly of the beast, and although I wasn't giving direct orders or asking to work these hours, in some way I was contributing to the corporate corruption. I was learning quickly that even multi-national companies, whose executives had much higher stakes and much more to lose from fraudulent actions, such as overstating revenues or inflating employee hours, were still willing to sell their souls in order to make the highest profits possible . . . by any means possible.

Hours flew by and I continued to sit and flip through the binder I had been given. The client was made up of many different subsidiary companies, which in turn had many different offices around the world with different ways of recording and processing financial transactions (recording sales, expenses, etc.). Fraud was not the only cause of their bankruptcy and misstatement of the financial reports; also the rapid acquisition of many related companies without the integration of their financial reporting systems into the company's central reporting system caused many errors in reporting the final year numbers (revenue, assets, liabilities, etc.). I noticed myself dozing off or daydreaming while trying to understand loads of charts and explanations of various accounting systems. At times, it was like reading another language without anyone or any dictionary to help translate. Most of the accounting department, who worked and compiled all of the data I was now reading, had been fired right after the announcement of fraud more than a year ago. So I couldn't call anyone or set up any appointments. I was basically on my own, in a strange new world that I didn't have any passion of discovering. I pushed and forced myself to concentrate, to continue reading. It wasn't filtering through to my brain.

Then, almost like an alarm clock to wake me up, to remind me that it was only mid-day, and I had many more hours before I would get back home to the comfort of my sofa and bed, the stupid sounding "tropical island" ring began softly and with every millisecond picked up speed and volume, vibrating through my thin wool slacks, by my outer thigh. I had received a text message. I immediately thought to myself, "It could only be one person." Only one person communicated through text messages. (At this time, my American friends were still all faithful phone callers.) My heart pounded a fierce rhythm, an introduction like that of a theme song, a song that I've heard many times over, never preparing for its initial impact, never falling comfortable or ready for its piercing trumpet, its hypnotic melody and deep sorrowful chords. The rhythm reverberated from depths of my being I still wasn't comfortable with, a spot in the core of my soul that I couldn't pinpoint, so that I couldn't be able to start understanding its complex structure. What I knew was that the rhythm was attached to something, another spirit, a beautiful person alive and flourishing, someone who incited within me the strongest passions and emotions, an outlet for all my stubborn, prideful thoughts, the ones I had kept suppressed for so long. I don't know if I believed in soul mates or fate, but the other side of this text message, the person who I knew just finished un-flipping a Nokia phone, pressing the buttons with her elegant tiny touch, pushing "send" just moments ago, entered part of me that I wasn't aware of before. She reflected many of my attitudes towards life, shared my approach, even lived out my dreams, like I was there, a part of every action, enlivening my senses vicariously. The fact that these emotions could be felt far away, from distant continents, thousands of miles away, was in itself remarkable.

That other part of me, that soul mate, like an identical twin, was probably just finishing off the last of a miso soup, gently palming with both hands the bowl to her mouth, and probably right after skillfully extracting beans of edimame with chop sticks. It was our favorite food together. We both preferred sashimi over sushi rolls; she always ordered uni (sea urchin), first asking the cooks at the counter, like a broken record, if it was fresh that day. I loved it all, except the eel. Hong Kong was about twelve hours ahead, and she had been busy shooting photos all day for the new Nokia ad, while I had been working into the wee hours of the morning and fighting for a few hours of sleep. I wondered whom she was with, and if they were also drinking saki together. Probably, it was someone from the photo shoot, another model, the director, or even the cameraman, wining and dining her in attempts to woo her, telling her how long distance never works, and that she's young and has her whole life to be in a serious relationship.

They were probably also stating for the millionth time, like some sort of an agreement with her past pursuers, "Love, you're too young to know what love is."

    This was the main complicating factor of my life: love. And at such an awkward time, a transitional time between my life as a student and my life making a living, making my first mark as professional, and honing applicable skills, un-teachable in school, saving for the future, and building a new life. But my heart was on the other side of the world, and I was here doing the right thing, the responsible thing. Love wasn't enough to describe the complication in my life, because now, with every interaction with Maggie, I was again reminded of life and different ways to approach life, a completely different mentality, that I couldn't have been exposed to the last few years of my life, studying, taking the secure job, and safely preparing for a predictable life with kids, a suburban home, and nice wife. She constantly reminded me, just by effortlessly living her life, of the risks people take, the chances made in search for dreams. I had increasingly forgotten about passionate dreams, those goals in life that send tickles running through your veins, and heartbeats reverberating through your body. In ways, I had been slowly programmed throughout university in the need to follow the safe path in life and forget about those dreams that could one day leave me without a job, ostracized, or worse, hungry and homeless. But Maggie was living her life without these barriers. She went after her passions and never thought in terms of safe and failure. She was making money and enjoying life all in the same breath. True, not everyone is beautiful enough to model for *Elle* magazine or Nivea skincare products, but plenty of other equally, if not better, ways of making money and living passionately were out there, and, through her love, I couldn't forget my dreams or ever want to settle.

    Maggie and I had met a year and a half before, on a small, quasi-commercial island, called Ko Samui, off the Southeastern coast of Thailand, one of the two islands filmed in the Leonardo DiCaprio movie, *The Beach*. It was a week after the Full Moon Party, and Seb, Leo and I had only arrived to the island that day, by ferry, from Ko Phan Ghan. That day, I could finally feel my stomach back to normal, after a long, traumatizing week of diarrhea, where the attacks happened out of nowhere, repeatedly, over and over. I remember being on my knees in prayer formation, caught in a cloud of incense circulating inside this mystical Buddhist temple, while a monk was sprinkling cool water on me from slender bamboo sticks with each flick of his wrist, humming the words of a prayer, then tying a spiritual white rope bracelet around my wrist, when bam! An attack was hitting, and I had to leave the small spiritual ceremony in a hurry, offending the monk and the others waiting their blessing, to find the nearest bathroom, which in Thailand usually means a porcelain hole in the ground and a few squares of the thinnest, cheapest tissue. I remember having to negotiate with the ladies at the bathroom entrances, paying them inflated prices for more of these tiny tissue squares, because they only give you three at a time. All of this, then to squat vulnerably above a dark hole, with fumes I couldn't see, but a smell and quantity of flies landing on my face that helped remind me the place was not a florist shop. Well, all of these outbreaks had slowly come to an end, and I was even shunning alcohol for water at this point, out of fear of another upsurge. Yesterday had been my birthday, but if I were to take time zones into consideration it would still have been my birthday back in the United States. The last day in Koh Phan Ghan had been relatively slow and I hadn't celebrated, so my friends decided to treat me on this island. We were new to the island, so after finding a place to crash owned by this Indian guy who persisted in trying to sell us tailor made suits, we went out exploring the main strip. There were art shops, Italian restaurants, ice cream shops, etc., on the left of the strip and mainly guest inns and small hotels to the right. In the art shop I talked to a painter who was selling his oil paintings at amazingly low prices, considering the quality, and I negotiated for awhile, finally deciding to walk around a bit and, maybe, discuss prices again later with him. The artwork was really impressive. Then we walked past a busy patch of mo-peds and people, and, a little further on, three girls were sitting on the curb in front of a Burger King.

  One of the girls was more focused on me, and I remember her eyes locking with mine as I passed. She was dressed in the normal island attire, white sleeveless shirt, light pants or shorts, I can't remember. What caught my attention was the intensity of her gaze combined with a sort of playfulness that sprang out of her face, a fresh, natural beauty. The abruptness of her appearance and presence was a bit stunning and caught me off guard during the first passing with my friends. My mind chose to hide the initial reaction and feelings, and I reverted to a default cool, shrugging off the fact that a beautiful girl had just been staring directly into my eyes without faltering, and that I would be stupid not to approach her. I kept walking forward with my friends in search of something; we didn't know exactly what. After at least two more minutes walking forward, we noticed everything—shops, people, mo-pads—all started to disappear, and our walk was becoming slower and quieter, just the noise of our flip-flops clomping the pavement. This was our cue to turn back to what must have been the main action.

On the walk back again, the three girls were still sitting, and the girl who was staring at me before presented the same unwavering gaze, only this time she stood up before me, speechless, waiting. I had nowhere to run at this point; this time I had to confront the situation. So, out of all the thoughts, questions, and feelings swirling through my mind at the time, like a lotto machine dropping winning numbers, only a few words, one by one, forced their way through to my mouth, and I asked, "Do you know where the clubs are located?" It was short, abrupt, simple, and not really what my heart had intended to convey. She smiled a flirtatious smile, and pointed in the direction of the bars, the same direction we were back walking, one block on the right where another street full of pedestrians led to the bars and clubs. I made up only marginally with my next comment; at this point my heart was beating closer to normal and breaths were deeper and smoother. I still was feeling a bit stunned, but I followed up, "I hope to see you there tonight." After this encounter, Seb and Leo took me to a strip club to celebrate my birthday. We laughed our heads off most of the time; some of the girls were attractive, and at the mention that it was my birthday, we were from the U.S. and Leo's whole spiel on New York, we ended up attracting most of the attention, but for a short period of time until they realized our lonely pockets. We had entered to warm smiles and soft hospitable words, words we knew from the guidebook, like Saw Wa Dee Kap and Kap Kum Kap and were now exiting with frowns and fast, harsh words that we couldn't understand.

The sun was already down when we left out, and the other guys were tired, had decided to go back and call it an early night. But I couldn't go to sleep just yet. The entire time, from the point I laid eyes on that girl sitting in front of the Burger King and even during the strip show, she hadn't faded from my mind. I had had this girl on my mind, not sure what to think of her, not really sure if it was worth going out, hoping to run into her, and I could have easily followed the guys back, slept early and have wakened up fresh and ready for another day. But I couldn't pass up this opportunity; I had to live out my destiny this time, not make any excuses. So, I decided to go it alone to the clubs this night, no alcohol in my system, just bottles of water and a need to seek out the truth. I proceeded to the small plaza in front of the two main clubs that were facing each other, both completely open and visible from the outside, so much that you could walk directly in without first having to answer to bouncers. It had occurred to me that these establishments were facing each other like two battling disc jockeys, one blasting hip-hop and the other house music. I was still getting used to the idea that I could listen to Biggie Smalls or Snoop Dogg on the other side of the world. I walked closer to the hip-hop club and caught a glance of a sparkling star.

There she was, dancing like the center show among her small cluster of friends. She had a visor on, mostly white with little blue letters reading, NY Yankees. She was light on her feet as if dancing a cloud, and the same two girls I saw earlier followed her every move. But the spotlight was clearly on her. I went up and started dancing next to them, catching her eye and smile again, and then moving closer, so that it seemed everyone else was cheering us on as we danced in their circle. We exchanged moves, back and forth, in a playful manner, each of us on show for the other, as if performing a special mating ritual. Something special came over our display, something liberating and exciting, a whiff of freedom, a magnet meeting its match. I danced until the water had caught up with me, and then excused myself to the bathroom. When I returned, she was gone. I looked around and—nowhere, not even her friends. I wondered what had happened, one second smiling, flirting, gazing in my eyes, and the next second gone. "Was this some sort of cruel joke?" I thought to myself. I went over to the other club, hopeful, partly confused, and still wondering what had just happened. I waited a moment in there, not with any intentions of dancing house or meeting new people, I was just not ready to give up what seemed so real for a moment. Eventually, I walked back to the first club, and there, she was back, this time chilling at the bar. She gazed in my eyes. And I walked over, this time starting a conversation. I remembered telling her that she looked like a model I had seen on TV, in a commercial or magazine, and she smiled and laughed a little. It wasn't a come on line, it was really what I felt to say at that moment. We were talking and dancing, talking and dancing, and became bored with the club scene, the loud, drowning music, the public scene. We decided to take a stroll to the beach. We headed down the small street leading to the club district, across the main strip, past a few small guesthouses, and onto the white sand beach.

The outside air was a tropical warm, and we could faintly hear and see a few people out swimming, playing in the sea. We talked about the idea of taking a dip later that night, but first we walked towards a typical tropical wooden shack along the beach. Closer to the water were nice lounge seats sprawled out and long candles reaching out from the sand, only feet away from the tiny waves. Under the small light on the outer wall of the shack, a sign read "Puc's Place." We walked over to the shack and Maggie introduced me to the owner, Puc, an enthusiastic Thai man, very warm and humble like most of the Thais. Maggie had been here a few days more than me and had already made connections. We walked back out to the beach chairs, and sat down next to each other, finally finding peace and seclusion. Music was coming from the small shack, chill lounge, tranquil alternative, and I remember hearing The Pharcyde song, "She Keeps on Passing Me By," and explaining to Maggie how I hadn't heard that song in such a long time, but how this song was mixed with a lounge beat, slightly different from the original. We talked about London, about Atlanta, about music, about traveling. Time was traveling fast, and we weren't at all aware. Puc came by with a couple of Thai beers and a small joint already half smoked. I had vowed against drinking, but my stomach had been feeling solid all night, so I gave in. We took a few pulls from the joint mixed of marijuana and tobacco. I remember one of us had a camera and was taking photos of our first encounter, even got Puc to snap a photo of us sitting, leaning against each other on the double chair. Who would have thought years later it would be one of the most sentimental pictures of our life? After more laughing and talking, we found ourselves both walking to the edge of the water, touching its warmth and feeling the tickling feeling of the foam barely washing over our toes. We were so close to each other, laughing, completely comfortable as if we had been a couple for years already, somehow married in a previous life. And, it just happened. We began kissing. Right there and then, the mysterious line between strangers and partners was broken. I closed my eyes and I felt something I had never felt before—it was easy, and natural, and never got old, each kiss, each time I caressed her upper lip or bottom lip, or when our tongues met, my body tingled, a real sort of dream world, where my all my senses opened and every part of me was content. It never occurred to me when it would get old, or when to stop, because neither of us wanted to let go, neither of us wanted to part; we were fusing our bodies into one, one spirit, with an energy that flowed continuously in and out of our touch, like one wave of motion.

Eventually, we both opened our eyes, studying each other's gaze, serious for a moment, knowing that something was happening, both a little scared, unsure of the power we were both uncovering. We were locksmiths with a ring of keys, finally matching the right key to the lock after hundreds of tries, now feeling for the first time the key hit all the right grooves, sliding in naturally all the way through to the last click, waiting for a moment, trying not to make assumptions, not to get our hopes too high, and then with a flick of the wrist, Voila! Perfect fit! We were that perfect fit. Opening our eyes briefly had been to make sure this wasn't a dream, that we wouldn't wake up at any moment, sweating and disappointed. The pause was brief and quiet, but powerful. Words didn't stand a chance to something that was out of our reach. It confirmed between us the intensity, the understanding of something we had no understanding of. The next time we would open our eyes, the sun was rising beyond the waters, and the clouds were changing colors, more boisterous and audible than under the moon's dim light. We were now in a way rejoicing, smiling and laughing, amazed at how long we must have been kissing, observing the puffy clouds, making out animals and people faces from the fuzzy puffs of white. We had the power to create whatever we wanted. I picked out what looked like a lion, and she noticed two heads and bodies joined together like twins. We then left to view the rest of the sunset from the rooftop of her guest inn. We walked back cheerfully in a similar direction to the one we came by, her body beneath my shoulder, my arm around her waist.

After that first night, we never left each other's sight more than few minutes at a time for the next four months. We traveled throughout Thailand, meeting Seb and Leo on other islands, then Chang Mai, then Bangkok, after Thailand going to Hong Kong to stay at her house, with her mom, then coming back to Atlanta for her to stay with me for a while before I started work. We were inseparable for a time. Then I had to start work in Atlanta, and she was booked for a few modeling jobs in Asia. Then, long distance set in.

Now, sitting in my cubicle, a message from her, "Baby, wish you were here. You would love it. I'm at this jazz lounge. The band is asking any requests, what should I tell them to play? M."

My heart went weak. That comment, "wish you were here" always killed me and ripped at my insides. I had heard it too many times before, and every time I contemplated leaving my laptop, with all my work still sitting at my cubicle desk, booking the next flight to Hong Kong, just to be with her, to live the excitement with her, to share our love. But, I couldn't do that. I didn't have the guts to do that. Even though I was miserable, I couldn't throw away my career out of impulse and go, following my heart. And these thoughts and considerations were only torture to the heart, because I would be stuck working until Christmas holidays. Then, I would finally get a two-week vacation, after nine solid months of working literally everyday, Monday through Sunday. That was in less than a month now, and I was so looking forward to being away from this insanity, putting my mind to rest, and finally seeing the love of my life. But I had to stay focused here at work. I wrote back to Maggie, "A-Train." I thought, the musician had to know that song. It's a classic.

I walked over to the cubicle of Tlou. He was located in high-traffic, at the corner between the manager's offices and the break room, and for good reason. If my accounting firm was a basketball team, Tlou was the first-round draft pick, an underpaid, highly sought after point-guard for this client, and the bosses wanted to be able to reach him as soon as humanly possible, whenever they needed him. Tlou was a very small guy of sub-Saharan complexion with a lion-sized heart. His name is correctly pronounced "klow," using a strange clicking noise in the beginning, a sound from his African dialect. (It was a lot easier to learn than rolling r's in Spanish.) He had had the bad fortune of landing this job on his two-year rotation from South Africa to the United States. Our firm was based all over the world, and many workers after a few years at the firm were given the option of stationing in another country for a short time, which usually meant in hopes of dodging the mass of work sitting in their home offices. Tlou was not so lucky. He landed arguably the toughest, most intense client my firm has ever worked in its long history. Still, day in and day out, he persisted to keep a smile on his face and never shunned the arduous workload. He was like an angel to some, a lifesaver to most, but to the partners at my firm he was the efficiency of three managers wrapped into one, and at a lower cost for labor. Although he should have been considered a Manager with his experience level, the bosses didn't have the power to promote him here in the U.S. Only his home office in Pretoria, South Africa, had this power; and for some reason they had decided to wait until he returned home to anoint him—probably to guarantee that he would, indeed, return home. He was being exploited from both sides and was too nice to object or fight back. I always felt he deserved better than this old job.

The guy was a genius. He could dissect any accounting system in minutes, even if he wasn't given all the information. He would sit you down and speak to you in a high-pitched voice, matching his size, with a proper British accent he learned while away at boarding school as a child. I remembered him telling me how he earned his spot, the only black boy, at an all-white, private school, by winning an essay competition among thousands of poor children in the villages of South Africa. I would never forget his story, how terrified he had been, not knowing one word of English when he was first dropped off at the school, hundreds of miles away from his home, being thrown in among other children he had nothing in common with and barely knew how to communicate with. He told me about all the racism he had to endure as a child, at a time when the Apartheid was still very much evident in South Africa, a time of oppression and utter segregation. He talked about the time when his school took a field trip to a popular South African beach, and his school was told to leave because the beach didn't allow black people. He was crushed by this experience, holding the guilt, knowing that he was the reason stopping his classmates from celebrating the end of their school year. I could empathize with his experiences and envisioned how it had been for my father, my grandfather, and further generations back into the times of slavery in the South. Tlou had the spirit and heart of a Nelson Mandela. He saved me from time to time when I was in a bind, when I was stuck on a project, not having a clue how to continue, or when I would show up to work, brain dead, because Maggie was in town and I was juggling both the job everyday and her at night. In turn, I was his only true friend at the job, the only person he could confide in and voice his misery to from time to time, the only person that could relate to him having been different all his life, the only other person sick of the monotonous sports conversations. We liked to talk about life, about real things going on in the world, and how we would one day blow this joint, say the hell to XYZ firm and travel.

Tlou smiled when I approached his cubicle with the large

binder my manager had given me; he could see the heavy look in my eyes, that look of "help, I'm lost and the boss is going to kill me if I don't get this current project done." He could also sense more than work was on my mind, that I needed to unload some frustration or hurt. But, I couldn't go off on a tangent this time, talking about all my problems; I needed to wipe Maggie from my mind, and get to the bottom of this analysis. When I first approached I didn't even speak. I was tired and couldn't find the words to begin. I pulled up a chair and balanced the big binder on my lap.

"Is Maggie back in town?" he asked teasingly.

"No. I was here until five in the morning last night finishing this stupid project for Kumiko. I can't get her off my back. One of these days, I'm going to strangle her. Do you believe she had enough nerve to yell at me for being thirty minutes late this morning!"

"Don't let it bother you. She probably just needs to be laid, and she knows you won't help her with that."

I released the heavy, almost cemented, frown I'd been holding since the night before and burst into a hysterical laugh. I laughed with all my energy and breath, even crying, to the point that my face was bright red, eyes bulging with water. Between my lack of sleep and his crude tasteless comment, I couldn't help the outburst, and we both continued to laugh with all our might, like we had been saving up for this moment, finally getting it all out. After laughing like for this for a couple of minutes, I was out of breath and realized how exhausted I really was. I could hear Lambert, in the other cubicle, groan, not happy that someone else could be having a couple of minutes of fun, while he was slaving away.

"We better stop before we get in trouble," Tlou commented. "What do we have here?" He began opening the big white binder, quickly flipping to the most pertinent information, walking me through, step by step, a few systems analyses and explaining that page 1-48 of the binder was useless nonsense written by the client's previous accounting department, that I should not bother reading it. Also, that if I make a photocopy of memo 4, it was descriptive enough, and would save me the time from rewriting the overview in my own words. Before leaving his cubicle, I dapped Tlou up with the handshake I greeted and left all my closest friends with: an abbreviated full-clasp of hands slipping into a half-hand shake, the withdrawal of both hands sliding away at the palms, ending in a finger snap of the other person's finger. I had taught him this handshake, months ago, during a company conference call, when the chief executive of our firm in the company headquarters in New York, sensing the low morale in our group, was giving us a pep talk on how great our career would be after work on this client was finally done. He promised us the sky was the limit, and I remember at the end of the call, when we were allowed to ask questions or give feedback, Rick, a first year at our office asked how big the bonuses would be at the end of the year. With mute pressed down on every phone except Rick's, you could still hear a thunder of laughter reverberating through his phone from the fourth floor. The partners were furious.

It was now about 10 p.m., and the mass exit of my colleagues from their cubicles and offices had already started. I decided to follow as soon as I was certain my manager had left. I shut down my computer, threw on my jacket, slid the laptop into its briefcase, nice and snug between the foam protection layers. I waved at a few people on my way out and vanished into the night. The only positive aspect to leaving so late everyday was the calm flow of cars, the left lane wide open for an uninhibited drive down I-85 south towards downtown, where I had recently invested in a bachelor pad. It was long after 5 p.m. rush hour traffic, where the clutter of cars, noise of horns, and the flicker of finger-birds being shot out of the windows from decent, hardworking people was normally staged. Driving in this manner was therapeutic: the quiet night, the relief of stress, the absence of someone constantly looking over my shoulders at work, the semi-fulfillment of having survived another day. After only forty minutes, I veered off on the carpool lane exit, after North Avenue, confident that it was too late at night for the police to be waiting, handing out fines at the other end of the small off-ramp. I landed nicely onto William Street, stopping at the light, at the intersection crossing Alexander Street. I passed the one-way street lining my condominium, turned right at the next street and right again immediately into a small parking lot, traversing the parking lot, and crossing West Peachtree Street to the automatic opening of the gates and into the garage of my building. I was home. I hesitated for a brief moment, feeling the weight of concentrating mentally and exerting myself all day through the whole of my body. I sat, too exhausted to climb out of my little coupe, knowing that it would be only hours until I would be climbing back in to this old car again, to start another day of work. I eventually hoisted myself up, along with my briefcase, walked through the lobby of the building, saying high to Suzy, the bell lady, and riding the elevator to the fourth floor. Home sweet home.

    I loved the smell of new paint and new hardwood floors that greeted me when I opened the door. The loft-style, high ceilings and open floor plan, shiny chrome appliances, and gigantic window looking out towards the Midtown high rises. I fell in love with this place the moment the real estate agent invited me here at night. At that time, it was bare, just large rooms, not even hardwood over the cement floors. This was to be my investment, a start to claiming my piece of the "American pie," whatever that statement meant. I decorated it myself, chose the blue paint, and, with help from my good friend Russell, sponged a faux paint over the kitchen walls, preserved the cement pillars to keep the rustic loft feeling, and ornamented the halls and lounge area with paintings from my travels. There were two paintings I had bought in Thailand, one with tropical scenery from a village by a river and the other painting of four spiraling naked bodies, fading into each other, in dark blue and black with dark red accents. It was mysterious and usually the favorite of my guests, because the picture could be interpreted in so many ways. Also, there were two paintings from Mexico of heads, abstractly drawn with fiery reds and yellows, a traditional Mexican feature. Along the windowsill, the armoire holding the TV, DVD, and stereo, and along the tops of the kitchen cabinets, I displayed my prized collection of pottery that I had molded with bare hands while at University. For once in my life, I had created works of art. I could never draw or paint, and my handwriting even to this day is like that of a child first learning cursive. This was my introduction into the artist's world. I loved how the pottery complimented the rustic loft ambience.

    I dropped my briefcase in the kitchen, plopped my weak, worn out body on the couch and pulled the phone from between the cushions. I had one message. It was Seb. I wondered what he wanted. He usually hit me at the office. This was strange. I pushed the green button and waited for the robot voice to wail, "You have one new message, ten saved messages. Chris, this is Seb, listen, I couldn't leave this message over your work phone. What are you doing for Christmas and New Years? We're planning to hit Cuba. You missed our debacle in Miami, and dog, the company paid for everything, we gotta bring you up to speed the next time we talk. So don't even think about missing this one. Tell your bosses to fuck off! They aren't paying you enough money. Anyways, dude, gotta run. I'll send you more details by email.

Oh yeah . . . and don't mention Cuba to anybody and especially not your co-workers, it's illegal."

I thought to myself, "Cuba! Wow! Okay, I like it! I like the idea!" To me it was a beautiful tropical paradise, a warm get away from a cold Atlanta winter, traveling to a forbidden country—a country full of culture, salsa, rumba, Santeria, Cohibas, colonial Spanish architecture and Fidel Castro. I had always wanted to travel to the country before he died, as selfish as that sounded, because everyone knew that the place would change dramatically after that point. At the moment, going to Cuba was supposed to be like traveling in time, back to the 50's, old Chevy cars, store fronts unchanged, neighborhoods kept the same, the people unchanged, old revolutionary relics. But to travel during the holidays, and the Christmas holidays at that. How could I? My mom would be disappointed if I wasn't there with the family, putting up the Christmas tree, ornamenting it, and eating boiled shrimp with homemade cocktail sauce for New Year's Eve. Plus, I hadn't seen them in almost a year; I hadn't seen a lot of people in almost a year for that matter, even two years for some people: the members of my church, my grandparents, cousins and uncles, my hometown friends, my mother's cat Shadow. This job sacrificed all of these ties, and the little time I had off over the last two years, I'd enjoyed with Maggie. I had flown to Singapore, Hong Kong, and even London to meet with her before I was thrown on this demanding client. Now, this sudden temptation. I thought about this new idea, debating it, and pondering over it, until my body slumped over sideways onto the length of the sofa, feet hanging carelessly, too worn out to walk to my bed, and eventually fell asleep.

Who was I fooling? Instincts and temptations influence my reality; curiosity fuels my existence, propelling this Classic Cadillac with GPS navigational system to the next mile. I always think, if I know my path, then what incentive do I have to drive towards my destination? I wonder at times how well I know myself, and those things I know, the people I meet, the information I digest, are all bridges to the unknown. I cherish what security could never give me, what many of my acquaintances will never understand, and in some ways, I follow this addiction in the form of destiny to the sacrifice of many I love, many things I loved. I want to slow down my discontent, my mischief, but my curiosity is running its own race, and at the end of each lap, it wants to run the race even better, faster, with more grace.

Plans were already in motion through a lapse of time that increasingly exhibited less importance, a small transition in a larger transition. Before I knew it, systematic procedures were planned and carried out, and only a week from Seb's voicemail, I was already securing a special credit card that would be used while traveling through Cuba. The internet was like Guatanamo Bay, my strategic location for stock piling needed resources that would help me complete a Cuba mission: I received and sent correspondence to the troops, Seb and Leo; set up plane tickets to Mexico and then Havana; reserved a hotel for the first night; got the special credit card from a Canadian bank, and familiarized myself with the target location. I became obsessed with this curiosity about Cuba, as soon as I got the mentality of never looking back or compromising the objective, and I had talked it over with Maggie, receiving her agreement to meet us in Havana.

Only I was still ashamed to explain my intentions over the Christmas Holidays to my mom, who would then dispatch the message to my dad and brother. I knew somewhere in my heart the idea of skipping another gathering with the people who had raised me was wrong, and especially with my mom, who cherished these special days, the sentimental moments that weighed heavy on her heart, carrying far past the actual day. These few days out of the year were earmarked, more resoundingly than all the other calendar days. First was Christmas Eve service at the church, my mother in a long colorful flowery dress, fancy for her standards, also making sure we were presentable in suits and, for a long time, clip-on ties, at her side chanting traditional church hymns and blending our voices with the congregational voices during Christmas carols, songs that always had a special uplifting value, a weapon against all disappointments and hardships during the year. A special banquet followed the ceremony, a chance for all the alcoholics of my church to put down their guilt for a short moment and indulge in eggnog, under the holy roof of God, with his silent permission. Everyone was so joyous and friendly, and the same emptiness I carried walking into house parties, concerts, or even simply a park without the presence of Maggie by my side, was the same void my mother or my brother would surely feel walking through the tall wooden doors with me away. The next day was special: a Christmas Day roast beef dinner and grilled rib-eye steak, and also the days leading up to New Year's were shared and cherished. Long-time friends called and showed up; we talked about all the memorable events of high school, referred to each other by aliases and brought up old girlfriends and nights out. Leaving the country at a time like this didn't feel right, when I consciously soaked in and marinated these tradeoffs. Furthermore, I knew Mom would disapprove of Cuba, for the simple fact I wasn't permitted by the US government to enter. I could rationalize going, because I didn't believe in the trade embargo or ban on travel. But I would feel the pressure to reconsider, like I was back at home, still receiving meals and support, because according to the USA it was illegal, regardless how harmless in nature. But this guilt didn't stop me from pushing forward, finalizing little details of the trip: it was too late, the slender pin locking the grenade had been pulled clean, and it was only a matter of time until an explosion of three travelers would set off into forbidden territory.

Planning for this trip was a little more involved, thanks to the travel ban and the restrictive environment of communism. Precautions had to be taken, many details set up before our arrival. Our mentality going into this trip was still the same, only it was tailored to meet a new set of regulations. The Thailand trip had exemplified our general attitudes toward traveling to new countries: we simply booked a flight to the first island we wanted to explore, and that was ninety percent of our preparation. It was better to leave all options open when traveling, and for good reasons. First, the money factor: middlemen on the internet, travel agencies, and hotel franchises are always scaring clients into thinking that if they don't book accommodations before leaving to their far away destinations, there could be a good chance that everything will be fully booked or prices could be extortionately high when they arrive. So, they entice the customer into a long contract, leaving the option to change, once they have arrived, very difficult and costly. We were not rich, so cutting out the middleman, comparing, negotiating, and paying directly to a local guest inn or bungalow guaranteed lower prices; and the ability to see exactly what we were paying for before pushing over money always proved wiser. Secondly, the exhilaration of arriving to an unfamiliar destination and getting a feel for the new environment was part of the traveling appeal for us, an element of excitement and freedom built into the whole experience. Striking up a conversation with a total stranger at a local bar, talking to the taxi driver on the way from the airport, anyone with current information on the area helped. Unlike the travel agent or internet website, these people could explain to you where they had been recently, could tell you stories of their adventures and experiences, what other cities and locations to travel to, or whether one day or five days was enough in a particular place. There were even special locations for the passing and recycling of such experiences and stories when traveling to a country. Kau San Road in Bangkok, Thailand, was the brief home for many travelers passing in and around Southeast Asia on their way to the coast or other countries, like Cambodia or Vietnam: one street with mountains of cheap accommodations, bars and clubs for *falangs* (foreigners), not far from the heart of the city. Here you could find people who had been through the trenches, witnessed the conditions, could tell you if the family-owned guest inn recommended in the Lonely Planet guidebook for Phenom Phen, Cambodia, was overrun with tourists, the new waiter at the Papaya restaurant in Chang Mai had an attitude problem, or the small village of Chang Rai was so incredibly Thai, that you couldn't pass it up. Instincts also played a large part in where to go and how long to stay in each location. The fewer limitations and barriers there were during a trip the better. We never relied solely on a third party for our information. However, this relaxed, whatever happens . . . happens! attitude had to be altered a little for the Cuba trip.

  American Dollars run the small Caribbean paradise. For years now, Fidel had started allowing regular Cubans to receive dollars from family members abroad, realizing that these dollars could be absorbed by government-owned businesses at inflated prices, finally filtering to pesos for Cubans—of course, after the government takes its share. Therefore, we would be okay bringing dollars, but it wasn't safe carrying three weeks worth of dollars into the country and having to carry it around. Since the U.S. had a trade embargo against Cuba, and one of the restrictions included accessing American banks, we had to find other options for covering costs while on the island. So, we found a Canadian bank, specializing in Cuban travel, and after we sent in applications, identification, and money, they shipped us the "Amigo Card," a bank card useable in most banks around the island. Next, knowing that a travel ban prevented us from flying directly to Cuba from the United States, we were forced to find alternate routes, airports that we had read weren't teaming with customs agents, newly charged and ready to trip up any plans of entering the Communist island and condoning its system by spending tourist dollars. The climate was the worst it had been in years, following a recently televised speech by President Bush reiterating his condemnation of Fidel and his crooked regime and tightening the already restrictive travel ban. Rumors were flying around the internet of immigration officers covertly monitoring travelers with American passports embarking and disembarking Cubana Airlines in Canada, detaining them and charging hefty fines. We played it safe by diverting our itinerary to Cancun, Mexico. And, communism didn't make our travel plans that much easier than the free, democratic borders of the U.S. did. Fidel wants to know where you're living when you enter his island, especially if you represent any symbol of freedom, a possible Cuban exile commando, spy or carrier of a different ideology, one more successful and appealing to his people, contrary to socialism and the cold war. So, not to risk immediate deportation upon entering the country by Cuban custom agents, we reserved hotel rooms for the first couple days of our stay in Havana with our new "Amigo card."

Excited about the new trip and being careful not to overlook anything, the three of us usually set up, in addition to email correspondence, a quick conference call on Fridays, in the midst of our daily grind. This Friday we were only two weeks away from the scheduled departure. I received an email on Microsoft Outlook from Seb as usual, asking us if we were all ready. I had been busy with another deadline—but had a few minutes to spare. The call rang in.

"Chris speaking," I answered.

"We know that asshole," Seb quipped almost as fast as I finished, Leo immediately laughing. These calls were a nice break from the lifeless, civilized atmosphere that I was exposed to day after day in the office.

"A'ight fuckas, what do you want this time?" I sprang back.

"What? You're not happy to hear from us? Don't tell me you're beginning to enjoy your job over there. We can always plan a Cuba trip next life time," Leo chimed in.

"A'ight guys," Seb said, "Before we start today, I want to introduce you to Roman. He's a buddy of mine here in New York . . . works over at Toit & Douche. He wants to get in on the Cuba action. What do you say guys?"

My eyes slanted on the other end of the conversation. I couldn't believe it! What is he doing? I was silently furious and felt somewhat betrayed and sidestepped. How could he invite another person? And at the last minute, without asking us first, when I had already booked my ticket, already committed myself fully to this mission. It was a stupid admission on his part, not to ask us first, and now I was being put on the spot to answer. I couldn't explain how I truly felt in front of whoever it was on the other phone, the new person I know nothing about, had no experience traveling with, that I would have objected immediately to if I had been asked at all first. Seb was now risking the mission, in my mind.

Leo answered first, "Welcome to the team, Roman." I thought to myself, "You guys . . . have to be trippin!" I couldn't object now, not after Leo put his vote in too. I swallowed my anger.

"Yeah . . . welcome Roman." It was too late to turn back now, and when I thought it couldn't get any worse, Leo continued.

"Guys . . . I have a friend at my firm that's dying to go with us. What do you think?" I thought to myself, "You both lost your minds! Listen to what you're saying! Think of what you're doing! You idiots!"

"It's cool with me," Seb answered.

I just didn't say a word. I would give them a piece of my mind later. I wasn't happy with Seb's and Leo's decision to both invite a friend. I knew Seb and Leo, I knew their idiosyncrasies, their rhythm and pace during traveling, and we had grown comfortable traveling together as a team in Thailand, mainly because of our similar interests and objectives. Most importantly we had proven to each other that we were qualified to stand alone, mix and mingle with the locals, communicate without offending or isolating ourselves, abilities not innate in every person; not everyone has the wherewithal, the flexible, diplomatic nature to travel. Furthermore, I knew how it had been living with three other people back at university, splitting a four-bedroom apartment, having to put up with noise when you didn't want to hear it, sharing food when you didn't want to share it or when you were not even around to defend yourself, and having to compromise too many times on too many things. I thought, two travel buddies were sufficient; we were flexible and agile in a group of three, and if one person met a girl, there were still two men left standing. But four and possibly five, that was incomprehensible. We needed to be inconspicuous as possible this trip, and drawing attention to the gullible tourist factor, even worse, our illegal adventure, would be compounded by the larger group. I was distracted by the new turn of events and didn't want to carry on the conversation any further.

"I gotta go fellas, gotta get back to work," I said.

"A few more minutes, Chris, we need to talk about . . ."

"No. I'm out, gotta go. Talk to you guys later," and I hung up the phone. I wanted to kill them. But, it also seemed entirely too late. Maybe this new guy Roman was all right, and Leo's addition to the team, whoever he was. I calmed myself with thoughts that I was going to have fun on this trip at all costs, going to make it work, regardless of the new obstacles. Still, in my eyes, things had suddenly turned from a James Bond mission to a traveling circus, us as the juggling clowns.

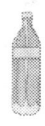

CUBA

> *There are in our existence spots of time,*
> *That with distinct pre-eminence retain*
> *A renovating virtue...*
> *That penetrates, enables us to mount,*
> *When high, more high, and lifts us up*
> *when fallen.*
>
> -William Wordsworth

We had performed all the needed preparations and were one by one flying into Cancun to meet up at the Hilton Hotel for one night. It so happened that the new guy, Roman, was a gold mine of Hilton points; he set up accommodations for our first night, contributing to the team immediately up front. I would be the last to arrive, as the cheapest flight I could find departed from Hartsfield Airport at around 8 p.m. I was not surprised when I landed and was immediately met by a long winding line full of commercial tourists, loud impatient children, and strange people wanting to strike up a conversation and complain about the long wait, anxious about their trip, scared of a little silence in a large concentrated mass of people. The customs line for foreigners, where everyone gets his or her passport stamped and hands in the non-citizen form, was jam-packed with Americans escaping the winter for a taste of the warm Caribbean climate. I put my headphones on, preparing to wait. It was frustrating standing in a theme-park-sized line, when the closest ride to a rollercoaster was the taxicab waiting outside. But I knew every step of the airport process should be calculated with a delay.

Finally I made it out of the airport with its mass of chaos and was now flying down the long strip of land built like an isthmus. It was the site of all the resort hotels, one after another, crammed together like a neighborhood of subdivision houses. The taxi driver rested his elbow outside the window and stared forward into the night as if he wasn't really looking at anything, probably having driven this straight monotonous path from Airport to Hotel, Hotel to Airport too many times. He was blasting "Ranchero," Mexican folk music, which conjured up thoughts of live Mariachi bars and Tequila-tipsy Mexicans reciting word for word the macho cowboy lyrics. The memory carried me back briefly to my school semester abroad in Guadalajara, Mexico, where I had spent many nights out with my new California buddies, and this thought placed a smile on top of the building anxiety I was feeling from not having seen Seb and Leo in two years. So much had changed in the last two years. I wanted to tell them how I had never been the same after leaving Asia, the misery of working so many hours for a job that wasn't fulfilling, the longing for passion and excitement. They were probably the only people in my life that could fully understand my pain and emptiness.

The cab driver looked through me as I paid the fare; I grabbed my backpack, the one I had hauled throughout Southeast Asia, and walked through the sliding glass doors to the receptionist in the lobby. "Roman Shapiro . . . the last name Shapiro," I stated.

"Sixth floor sir, the elevators are around the corner to the right." The hotel felt like the typical, a grand lobby, cold fast air, strangers, sofas around every corner, white signs directing your every turn: toilets, right arrow; pool and sauna, left arrow; bar/lounge, right arrow. I took the elevators up to the sixth floor and followed the signs to the room all the way at the end of the hall. It was a grand suite, and as I fumbled with the key card, the door swung wide open. Leo was almost on his way out. "Hey! What's up dude! Everyone— it's Chris! How have you been man!" Leo yelled.

I heard Seb's voice from around the corner, "It's Chris?!" Leo and I immediately slapped palms together and pulled in for a hug, hands slapping with force on each other's backs.

"What's up man! It's been a long time!" I said.

"I know dude! Looks like you lost weight!" Leo said.

Seb walked up, "What's up dog! How are you man?"

At the same time Leo was still talking, "Dude, you lost a lot of weight, how is Atlanta treating you?!" He turned to Seb at the same time, "You guys are getting murdered at work!" Seb had thinned down, as well. He was never very big. Leo looked like he had been taking steroids; he was solid, like he was prepared to take over the Cuban army by himself.

"What the fuck have you been doing man!" I said to Leo, at the same time punching one of his biceps, "You look like a monster!"

"I've been in the gym, dude. I'm training in Krav Maga, Israeli military combat!" he finished with pride.

"What?!" I looked towards Seb who was already laughing. "I think the job is getting to you too, dog!" I said, smiling largely. By this time, Roman and Leo's friend, Josh, had appeared, slightly further back in the spacious suite, smiling patiently, acknowledging my presence, but careful not to interrupt the reunion taking place.

"Come inside and check out the suite. Roman came through for us, dog!" Seb said. I walked in with my bag, throwing it to the side, arms stretched out in both directions, taking in the space and the different rooms of the suite. We had two bedrooms, a spacious marble bathroom, a small study room for handling business matters, and glass sliding doors leading to a terrace outside.

"Damn! This is the life!" I muttered.

"Meet Roman and Josh," Leo said. I slapped Josh's palm, finishing with a snapping sound and shook Roman's hand. Josh seemed familiar, like any of my buddies back in Atlanta. Roman stood a bit peculiar. He had ghostly pale white skin, which was a clear symptom of workaholism, and greasy dark-brown hair. He wore these perfectly round spectacles that shrank his eyes by at least half. According to Seb, he was working in a similar firm to mine, only in the tax department. I had a lot of respect for tax specialists but knew they hardly saw the light of day. My experience was no different.

"What's up fellas! I like the place, this is nice!" I said.

"That's not all! There is a Jacuzzi outside on the terrace; it has a great view of the beach and the water," Seb said.

I followed Seb outside, "Wow! We need to have a party here tonight!"

"Dude, we are going to celebrate tonight! We haven't been like this, all together, since Thailand," Seb said.

"It's been two years dude . . . two long years," I said introspectively. We both paused for a moment. That thought, ringing in our souls, trapped like an echo in an empty recital hall, meaning different things to both of us, different struggles and obstacles to overcome, reflecting different images and emotions, tugged at each of us somewhere deep.

"Well, it's time to enjoy life now. We have three weeks to let go and say fuck the world!" Seb spoke out, impassioned, emboldened by whatever the words two long years had meant to him. I yelled out to the vast, free air surrounding us, over the rooftops of the surrounding hotels, to the oceans and into the space engulfing Cancun, with my trademark call, a silly loud jungle sound, a cross between a vulture and a monkey, one I had created when traversing the jungle of Northern Thailand, more than two years ago. Seb had created his own unique wild animal call, which he named the "angry ostrich," and which always incited smiles and laughter from our guides and the others during our trek. We yelled our jungle calls, like a secret code among members of a secret society, a sort of brotherhood, and when we finally had enough venting like barbarians, and expelling all the toxins away from our body, we tilted our heads back into laughter. "Let's go back inside," I said.

    The next day began with hope and promise. I woke up with the feeling a child has before opening presents on Christmas day. Beams of sharp light, like light through an opening in a thick forest, shone through the sliding doors between the cracks of the blinds. I walked towards the light. The thought running through my head was that there is a beautiful day, full of life and hope, awaiting us outside. I opened the sliding doors deliberately, knowing I would be helping everyone else awake to this splendor. The view from the balcony terrace as I stepped out and into the spotlight of the sun was like a large flash of continuous bright light, where every crack and speck of earth and building was perfectly illuminated, leaving no shadows. Cancun was truly like all the commercials and leaflets. The water was a magical aqua blue, its movements accented and animated by the sun's reflection, sparkling like bits of white glitter. Only a few clouds stubbornly hovered in the sky. I could count them with one hand and wondered how they still managed to exist amidst the sun's reigning dominance. Everything and everyone else seemed to succumb—the detergent white sand beaches, reflective white-painted stucco encrusting the hotels, white beach furniture, umbrellas, and the white sail boats all seemed to be ruled by an omnipresent sun god. The brilliance of the day spurred me, and I was instantly tired of waiting around. I wanted to get out and move, blend in with the speed of life around me. Today was crucial to the success of the trip; we had an important premier awaiting us in Habana, Cuba, and we needed to leave enough time for any contingencies that could occur. This time, upon reentering, I creaked back the sliding doors wide and pulled on the curtain chords, filling the room with light, and launched pillows.

    "Wakeup! Wakeup! You Bastards!" It was time to depart the luxury suite of the commercial resort and get ready for a more humble experience awaiting us less than a hundred miles away.

    We arrived to the Cancun airport by shuttle bus an hour before the time we were to meet our special travel agent who was supposed to collect our dollars and hand us a voucher, permitting us to receive a boarding ticket at the counter of Cubana Airlines. An hour passed while we waited at the designated meeting place, near the information counter and car rental booths, and no one. Another hour passed. Then two hours. We were worried at this point. We only had forty-five minutes before the scheduled time of our flight departure and not a blink of information. I had heard about the notorious tardiness of the Cuban people and wondered if we would get our vouchers in time. Seb walked to the official counters to see if there was anything we could do, maybe we could pay directly to the airline before boarding this flight. When he returned he told us that the plane for Havana hadn't even arrived yet, and that we still had plenty of time. The time now in Cancun was about 3 p.m., and I wondered if the airlines and travel agents were out for "siesta." Finally, after we had been waiting a total of three hours and a half, a tiny man with a shiny head, like Mr. Clean without muscles, approached us while talking on a cell phone. He wore a plaid button-down shirt, with blue cotton slacks fastened tight above his bellybutton. In the hand not already occupied by his important phone call, he held a black briefcase, hopefully with our flight vouchers. He waved for us to follow him, certain that we were the right ones and not wanting to skip a beat during his phone call. He was speaking Spanish rapidly and intensely. Even though I had studied Spanish in college and in Mexico, I couldn't make out a single word of his breathless conversation; it sounded like every word and phrase he uttered was one extremely long word. We followed him right outside, just past the automatic doors, to the steps of the entrance. He put down the briefcase flat at the top of the handrails and opened it up, all the while continuing to talk. The nerve of this guy, his tardiness and arrogance, was the thought running through our silent expressions. He was trying hard to ignore our stares, avoiding eye contact for fear he would have to acknowledge his rudeness and cut short whoever was capturing his attention. Finally, he flipped down his cell phone and began speaking to us in the same rapid local Spanish he had been using for the last five minutes or more. It seemed that he might have been apologizing for making us wait so long, but none of us could make it out. We stood stunned, mouths slightly ajar, waiting for a clue of comprehension. He started over again, this time in a feeble, sluggish English, skipping verbs, but careful to say key words. "Your money, passport . . . sign here," handing us a pen at the same time. We handed him the cash, and he tore off vouchers one-by-one, said "thank you," picked up his phone as to start dialing and walked off. At this point, we could hear over the intercom the last call for Cubana Airlines. We slung the bags over our shoulders and almost ran with them to the check-in counter. There was never an airport free of drama and stress; almost like a universal law, passengers and airlines are forever rushing, losing bags, yelling and pleading with one another. Today was no exception.

As we were boarding the plane from the ground and walking up the shaky metal steps, the thought kept running through my head, "Cuba . . . I'm actually doing this!" This was a dream I had had since a child, reading *National Geographic* magazines. And I never actually believed it would come to fruition. And now, now I was here, no turning back, boarding an old Soviet jet with a Cuban flag painted at the nose of its white outer shell. I had my reservations about trusting old Russian engineering, knowing that the plane had to be at least fifteen years old, built before the fall of the Soviet Union. But the flight was not abnormally turbulent, and we landed safely in Havana no more than an hour after take off. Before landing, I could view from the small bubble of a window the plush tropical landscape of vibrant green and, for a moment, expansive fields of dark, rich green tobacco leaves. I could imagine how warm, humid the climate had to be, even before setting foot from the plane. The farther the plane descended, the more vivid objects on the ground appeared, and the swarm of ants racing above the ant mound suddenly transformed into small children playing baseball in a reddish-brown dirt field; the small patch of dark green developed into a considerable forest; and the small grey squares turned into large one-door warehouses, bearing only numbers on the outside. We had landed.

We climbed down the ladder and were shuttled quickly to the Arrivals area. Now we were nervously waiting a line to pass customs. And the whole time I was thinking: "What if they see that we're Americans and send us back to the States?" This would mean we were sure to be fined or worse upon returning, and all of our planning and preparing for this trip would have been a waste. The other concern was, "What if they stamp our passports?" We had read everywhere, all over the internet and even the Amigo Card representative lectured, "Whatever happens, don't let them stamp your passport with the Cuban seal; that is the number one piece of evidence that you entered the country illegally and the U.S. Customs will be all over you." The dark green military uniforms and cold facial expressions coming from the agents created even more anxiety as we approached the booth. We were eventually split into different lines, and I ended up first in the line of the third booth from the right with Leo located directly behind me. When I approached the booth, the lady behind the glass barely even looked at me. I handed over my flight ticket and passport and asked quietly in my limited Spanish, as if it was a question that could get both of us in trouble, "Perdon . . . por favor . . . no patea mi passaporte!" She looked at me, expressionless, like she was deaf, waiting for a hand signal. I wasn't sure if she understood me or if she just didn't care. My passport was on her table, a level below the counter, and I couldn't see it anymore, could only hear the small pages being thumbed through quickly. Then, I watched her hand, rising from below the booth, clenching firmly a stamp machine, and before I could say another word, it came crashing down solidly with force. My heart stopped. I couldn't believe it. The last thing I needed was this complication, a special welcoming as I returned back to Atlanta. My friends Justin and Borith laughing their heads off, when I told them why they needed to pick me up so soon, and Justin's favorite phrase, "You dumb ass." The lady handed me back my passport, smiling vindictively as if she had intentionally stamped my passport, knowing the consequences. I walked away from the booth, quickly flipping through my passport to see the fatal Cuban mark. I landed on a page where a green card had been inserted inside. But no fresh ink, nothing new had been stamped. It was the card. She stamped my tourist card. I was in! She had only tried to scare me, and, admittedly, succeeded. I looked back to Leo who was now approaching the booth, and I gave him a thumb down and a sullen expression, at the same time pointing at my passport. I wasn't going to deprive the Cuban lady of a little entertainment.

    Now that I'd passed the customs booth, many anxieties were lifted and the urge to find a bathroom ensued without any prior warning. Adrenaline had its priorities. Without waiting for the others, I walked to the men's toilets, located to the left of the baggage claim. A Cuban lady was waiting inside the bathroom, standing gracefully with hands clasped together. She greeted me with a gorgeous smile and nod upon entering. Normally, the mere fact that I felt obliged to tip someone, handing me a paper towel and forcing a smile or some acknowledgement from me, when the last thing I wanted to do was interact in the privacy of toilets, annoyed the shit out of me. But, the surrealism of a beautiful Cuban lady dressed in uniform as a men's bathroom attendant, confused me, and I quickly dropped her the smallest change in my pocket, a dollar, and said "gracias." When I walked to the baggage claim, the guys were waiting. "Dude, I slipped her a twenty so she wouldn't stamp my passport," Leo said.

"You serious?" I started snickering, "I was only kidding when I gave you thumbs down . . . you didn't have to do that."

"Damn it!" Leo said sulking over his impulsiveness. We gathered our baggage from the old rusty conveyor belt.

"All right! We're all here!" shouted Seb excitedly, looking around to everyone. He had been the first one to come up with the idea for this trip. "Everyone ready!?" he said.

"Let's do it! Yeah!" we shouted in unison, our shoulders slouching slightly from the weight of our bags. And, with all irony, we walked forward, heading for the last doors of Western Communism.

Outside was a frantic rush of men posing as official taxi drivers, who may have been honest but weren't worth the risk at this point. We walked further to the taxi stand, and the entire time the heat greeted us and humidity hugged us. It was the most refreshing feeling! From the time I left cold Atlanta, I had been undergoing a metamorphosis. Blood in my body circulated through my veins with more intensity and fluidity, and my pores were opening wider, perspiring and diluting toxins. A surplus of energy filled my every movement. The sharp contrast in climates, winter nor summer being far from my memory, affirmed me a summer, warm weather soul. I suddenly renounced the cold and all its inadequacies. I wanted to put on a white ribbed tank top and straw hat, like the photos of everyday Cubans, and breathe freely.

"That's the Russian woman and black Cuban guy I was talking about, they're married. He speaks perfect Russian, too," Seb pointed out, right before we reached the small line for taxis. The couple had already begun smiling in Seb's direction and a conversation in Russian ensued. "They're going in the same direction as us. We can split a taxi van with them. It's cheaper," Seb turned back to tell us. The man was probably in his late fifties. He was a massive, burly man with a neck like a heavyweight boxer and kinky graying hair. His wife was almost as burly and had a rough, aggressive voice. She would cut into the conversation at times, eyes sort of droopy and lifeless, never exerting energy towards a smile. The man, on the other hand, was talkative and jovial. But still I sensed he had his other sides. He looked like he would crush anyone who crossed his path. During the drive, Seb was our interpreter. Roman knew how to speak Russian, but so far hadn't opened up and wasn't really talking much, other than to Seb every once in awhile. He would smile at times and observe or look off into the distance of Cuba, as if he was taken away by the whole experience. Josh and I were in the back of the van, and Leo sat in the middle of the conversation with Seb, like he understood the language, even smiling and nodding at times.

The Cuban guy was full of advice. He told us never to walk around the neighborhood at nighttime, to be careful near our hotel, that the district was known to be a hotspot for pimps and prostitutes, and "never purchase drugs," it's the easiest way to find yourself in a Cuban prison. When we approached their neighborhood, houses changed, becoming spacious, antique, and full of grandeur. He said that the area was swarming with high ups in the military and that he and his wife would be watched when they exited the van—"everyone keeps tabs on the other around here, and one has to be careful not to do suspicious things." The way he conveyed his message, searching for fear in our eyes, I wondered if a deeper meaning lay beneath. Was it directed towards us? What did he and his wife do for a living—Cuban-Russian couple in their late fifties, free to travel, a house in an affluent neighborhood, amongst military families? Something was mysterious. The couple had a tough history. You could sense it through their mannerisms and existence. They were around during the Revolution, the great military coup, and when these same houses were confiscated from the Batistas and bourgeoisie were fleeing to Miami and other places abroad. Regular Cubans weren't offered these houses. The taxicab stopped in front of a large Gothic looking house, a long pathway leading up to it. We said our goodbyes, and the couple handed Seb a phone number and said if we had any problems to give them a call.

"What was that all about?" I asked Seb.

"It was strange . . . when I asked the guy what he does, he said he was retired and grinned. He completely avoided my question," Seb answered.

Dusk had set in by the time we dropped off the couple, and soon darkness pervaded. The further we drove, and the closer we reached to the city, the more Havana defined itself. As fast as our taxi driver was moving, it was difficult to digest the small half-rusted Russian car, the size of a Yugo, jetting down a back alley, or the guy in his thirties, wearing beaten sandals and a soiled t-shirt like a second skin, hurrying home with a white plastic bag, too shallow for the long loaf of bread ending up around his wrist. On the other side of the street, two teenagers walked in the opposite direction, a soccer ball at their feet, moving to the rhythm of their steps. I suspected nightfall had forced an ending to a neighborhood game. The night held an unsettling feeling. In every direction, the outer layers of Havana looked troubled and bleak. Not much activity permeated the streets; people were either home or hurrying home, and cars were few. Friday night in Cuba didn't seem to incite the same fervor and activity that my mind stubbornly equated it with. But I was jumping the gun; we still hadn't reached the core of Havana. Maybe the outer layers of the city were sucked inward during the weekend like a flushing toilet.

Our path from the airport to our hotel was unusual. If for some vital reason we needed to back track our steps, or even point in a general direction, it would have been impossible. Every mile or less was riddled with quick turns, as if we were escaping rush hour traffic or something more mysterious. Ever since we'd dropped off the Russian-Cuban couple, I had become suspicious and began creating conspiracy theories in my head: was the taxi driver a domestic spy taking his American captives directly to one of Fidel's famous hideouts, one of his houses said to be secretly located all over the city, all of them preparing and serving three course meals at exactly the same time, just in case he would show up? Or, maybe the driver was just a petty crook now taking us to a secluded neighborhood to rob us of our identity and few items. Maybe he would justify his actions in the name of the Revolution and Socialism. All types of random thoughts were running through my head at this moment. But none of them would prove true.

We were now approaching a new area, and the few working street lamps gave a more inviting atmosphere. A couple of nightclubs spread apart by a small field showed the presence of life, and suddenly, without warning, we turned onto a street full of people. Women were dressed in tight mini-skirts, drawing attention to their African roots, and there were small groups of men, animated, walking with a pronounced swagger, breaking their necks at the passing of shapely girls. Small cafes and bars lined the main street, and lawn chairs and tables were set outside under the awnings that extended from the tops of the first floors. Around the corner was Hotel Vedado, where we would be sleeping for the next two nights. When we exited the van in front of our hotel, hawkers and promoters were already touting in broken English, selling cigars, their bar or restaurant. The doorman to our hotel studied us silently, while we walked up the steps. He opened the door with one hand, and, with the other, pointed towards the front desk. We checked in quickly, and carried our bags up to our rooms. There was no time to rest. We were anxious to get back out into Havana. There was so much to absorb, so many myths to dispel and confirm. Plus, I was feening my first Mojito, and the guys were hungry. Downstairs, we asked the doorman for restaurant recommendations, and without breaking from his oath as a dry, brainless bouncer, he turned methodically to us, back straight, chest sticking out, and pointed to a kid, standing a few feet away from the entrance.

"Damn, the doorman could loosen up a bit," Josh remarked. "You notice that look he gives me?"

"You're just paranoid . . . he gives everyone that same look," Leo replied. When we walked up behind the kid on the street corner, he was in the middle of persuading two older Italian tourists, too polite to release themselves from the sales pitch. I listened in as the couple responded melodically in drawn out accents. The kid aggressively poured out opened-ended questions. Then, seeing the size of our group, he immediately gave up on them and began his pitch on us,

"Do you like comida Cubana? Mmmm, deliciosa . . . I know the best restaurant . . . like nowhere else." He stopped in mid sentence, when he locked eyes with the doorman, probably recognition of a commission. "Follow me!" he said, relieved to finally have won business, and with so little effort. The kid had an instinctive charm and spoke to us in English without much problem. We were led only one block to the corner of a rather run-down apartment building, with no signs in front or visible lights. I had read about these family-run restaurants, called "paladares." If this was one, we were about to experience one of the few legal marks of entrepreneurialism on the island. Only a few lucky individuals had licenses to run these restaurants, and according to law—a strange concoction of communist and capitalist principles—no more than ten or twelve customers could be served at one time. I suspected this one was illegal. The kid put excessive effort towards security and secrecy; first he took a quick look in all directions of the street, then he rang the buzzer twice, and, after only seconds, at least three heavy locks popped in a series of clicks before the door could open.

Already, people were sitting and eating. The room was cozy with four round dining tables. Old black and white photos of what appeared to be Havana decades ago decorated its walls; in the photos, kids were diving into the sea from a city embankment and there were street festivals, where different shades of people wore large innocent smiles while posing for the camera. It must have been a treat to have your picture taken back in those times. As we entered the house, the people sort of paused, the way relatives or close friends would when another guest was welcomed inside, and naturally we felt compelled to greet everyone. I had forgotten I was in a restaurant. The aroma smelled a lot like my grandma's cooking when I used to walk into her small kitchen-dining room where it was always a thick warm. I quickly skimmed through the menu: Arroz y frioles negros con pollo, platanos, cerdo. Aaaha! – I spotted mojito at the bottom. We all ordered the same drink, and when the meal was finished, Seb ordered "ron y miel chupitos" for everyone:

"A'ight guys, here's to our first night out in Cuba! Salud!"

Back on the streets and feeling full and light headed, we ventured back towards our hotel and the bars. At the corner street of our hotel, we ran into Juan, a scrawny slick-dressing Cuban with an accent and mannerisms like Al Pacino in the movie *Scarface*. He wasn't as hard natured as "Tony Montana," so we listened to his spiel hoping to find useful information on the night scene. "Sure . . . there are great clubs just a few minutes walk from here across town. A lot of Cuban chicas tambien," he said. It was a Friday night, and we were interested in going to clubs frequented by locals, not foreigners. We walked down a block filled with bars and groups of people hanging in the streets, enjoying the cooler weather of the night. Many more people were out at this point than when we dropped off our bags. Now, we were walking away from the mainly lit area and heading through neighborhood blocks in a desolate area. It was a bit shady, but our tolerance for risk seemed to be increasing by each experience, and there were five of us. Juan continued to assure us that it would be well worth it once we arrived. "The most beautiful Cuban Chicas!" he continued to say, proud. We turned down another dark street, and at this point, we were at least fifteen minutes away from our hotel.

I turned to Juan, somewhat losing patience, and asked, "How

much further?"

"Right here," he replied. And in between a row of one-story apartments and blank storefronts was a small building, like a town house, with dark tinted glass windows, and a dark blue neon light outlining the top of the door. A bouncer stood at the front, and I was beginning to conclude that no matter where in the world you go they all keep a universal stance, chin up, not looking at you, though aware of your presence. The doors opened to more darkness, and out came two cheerful looking guys with blonde hair, and two scantily dressed Halle Berry look-a-likes, arm in arm.

"Juan . . . you didn't tell us this was a whore house!" Leo said, somewhat concerned now.

"Not all the girls are for sale," he said with a hustler's face.

"What do you think, guys?" I said.

"Why don't we just go in and check it out? We walked all this way," Seb rationalized. I think we were all curious, even though we had no intentions of picking up prostitutes. We waited outside for a moment, still unsure, not able to make any solid decisions, no one wanting to be that guy, the first one walking in a whore house.

Finally after a long hesitation, Juan infiltrated the silence, "Come on. Let's go in, and you can leave if you don't like it." So we followed him up the short flight of stairs; the bouncer clapped hands with Juan and opened the door, and we were in. If we weren't sure of the place being a brothel before we entered, we were damn sure now. Women lined the walls everywhere. They were awkwardly sitting in their tight skirts and dresses at the high tables with bar stools and some were already cajoling clients at the sofa lounge. When we barged through the doors, their immediate attention fled to us as if we were long lost relatives. Each one of them, with every inch of power and ability the eye could muster, tried locking with our eyes and holding on for dear life, as if holding onto the seat of a rollercoaster ride at Six Flags. Their eyes screamed, "Me! Me! Choose me! I'm the one you've been waiting for! I'm the queen of Havana!" No sooner than we walked five paces into the dim light, girls were already clenching our arms and escorting us further into the debauchery. It all happened so fast. Not one of us was prepared for the swarm of attention we were now deeply engulfed in. Our brains were now on autopilot. We continued to walk forward, not missing a step, continued to follow Juan, the stealthy pimp, up a few more stairs and to a large empty table near the bar in the back.

I don't even remember commanding my legs to walk that far, it was as if they were controlling themselves.

The women, I had noticed right from the start, were absolutely breathtaking. They had beautifully tanned skin, bodies only proficient dancers could maintain, and when I focused close enough, which was a dangerous mesmerizing action, some of them had the most exotic light green eyes. They had been rather aggressive at first; but now that we were seated, they only continued to smile and wait, maybe thinking we would make some sort of first move. I imagined they assumed we were expecting this treatment. But we hadn't come here for this. In fact, we really didn't know exactly what to think of it all, now that we were here, other than the most beautiful women in the world were smiling at us, brushing against our legs, and speaking in seductive Spanish. Then, as if a secret signal had been given, they all started to move again. "Vas a comprarme una bebida?" asked the girl sitting to the left of me, the one leaning forward with cleavage in my face.

"Si," I replied. I figured the least I could do was buy two drinks, one for her and one for me, and then when the drinks were done, get up and leave. I leaned over to Seb, "I'm going to buy her a drink. I mean, what the hell. One drink."

"A'ight dude," he replied, extremely suspicious of everything. Next, Seb leaned over to me, "Dude, these women are absolutely gorgeous!"

"Just don't get any crazy ideas," I said. It seemed like every minute that went by other ideas were formulating, and the group was losing track of reality. I looked across the table to Leo, and one of the girls was now sitting in his lap. I flashed him a look, like "do you know what you're getting yourself into?" Seb started to laugh. Leo was sitting there somewhat embarrassed and stiff. I could tell he wanted to enjoy it and look cool, not knowing if he should be letting her sit there at all. Roman was as quiet as ever, and, it seemed, trying with all his might not to touch, talk, or even allow them a look through his glasses. Josh, on the other hand, had the biggest smile I had seen him with since we had met in Cancun. He actually looked rather comfortable over on the far end of the table, and though the table obstructed my view, it seemed his suitor was grabbing at something below the table. After I finished my first drink, a remarkable thing happened—I realized my Spanish had improved. I began remembering words and phrases from my trip in Mexico years ago and was feeling how great it was when someone actually understood me. My Spanish was going so well that I decided to buy another drink, which meant I had to buy one for the girl too. I thought, "Why not? She's teaching me Spanish." Plus, the guys seemed happy and showed no signs of leaving. But, I promised myself, after this second drink, no more games, it was time to leave. I didn't want to lead the women to thinking things would go any further.

During the second drink, the girl who had latched onto me with her enigmatic eyes from the moment I had sat down was now trying to explain that it was fifty dollars for something. I understood that to mean sex, even though I couldn't understand her exact slang. At that point, I knew it was going too far and that we needed to finally leave.

"La cuenta," I yelled over the music to Juan.

"You ready to leave?!" Leo asked, sort of surprised.

"Yes . . . you know what these girls really want! We're just wasting their time, dog," I said, feeling a bit ironic in my words. I don't think Josh noticed a word we were saying. His mind was clearly guttered. Juan returned with the bill, this time not as friendly as before. I thought he was probably annoyed that we didn't go any further with the girls. Then, I looked at the bill: $300! I wanted to say, "Are you crazy! You've really lost your mind to think I would pay this much for a few drinks!"

I said, "Seb come check out the bill!"

"What!?" Seb blasted out, stopping himself in mid-sentence. He called Leo and the rest over and began mumbling under his breath, like a quarterback in a football huddle.

"Should we argue the bill?" I inputted.

"No. It won't do any good. They aren't going to budge. Why didn't you ask the prices of the drinks before you started ordering like some big wig executive?" Leo said loud under his breath."

"You ordered drinks too!" I said.

"Yeah after you!" Leo came back.

"Listen, guys . . . no use arguing now!" Seb said.

"All right . . . I say we drop Juan twenty dollars and make a run for the door!" I said.

"Are you crazy!?" Leo interjected, "Did you see that doorman? The guy is an ogre!"

"Yeah, but he is standing on the other side of the door at the moment, and he won't know what hit him, until it's too late and we're hauling ass down the street!" I said.

"You're right. We don't have three hundred dollars to give anyways, so we don't have any other choice," Seb finished.

"A'ight guys, the second I give Juan the money balled up, start running!" I said. I gathered a few dollars from everyone to make it look like we were sharing the bill, walked over to Juan who was staring at us from the bar, started handing him the money, his palm out, my hand still not revealing what I was handing him, and at the same time I released my hand, I quickly said, "Gracias Adios." And we bolted out of the place, flying over the short flight of inside stairs, Leo, in the process, knocking over a whole platter of drinks one of the girls was carrying, and we bulldozed through the glass door barely hitting the doorman.

The reflex of the doorman was such that he stuck his hand out to grab Seb, though when I came out right behind Seb, I rammed right through the big guy's arm, knocking it out of the way. We were now off down the street like a shooting star. I could hear the doorman and Juan shouting in the background, but I never looked back. By the time we stopped running, we were all out of breath and laughing; we were standing like long distance marathon runners after the big race, our upper bodies bowing back and forth, hands around our waists, and mouths wide-open, inhaling large bursts of air. I hadn't run with so much adrenaline and exertion in at least two or three years. It brought back memories of being a kid running from the neighborhood dogs.

"You . . . guys . . . are . . . crazy!" Leo said between breaths.

"Juan underestimated us! He thought because we were Americans, we were going to pay for that shit! Three hundred dollars! That's almost a year's salary here in Cuba! That fool is nuts!" Seb had become suddenly cocky.

"Damn! Leo! You knocked drinks all over the floor, I almost slipped coming behind you," Josh was laughing and breathing.

Roman had been dragging behind the whole time we ran and breathing hoarsely like the beginnings of an asthma attack. Luckily, he calmed down quickly. Seb and Roman only spoke in Russian to each other. And Roman was now divulging what must have been pure sarcasm and slight condemnation for even going there in the first place. I was learning through his mannerisms and Seb's conversational cues that Roman's humor was dark and cynical. And that he whined a lot. He let out a long muffled "Aaaaa" from the depths of his nasal passages whenever he spoke, and unconsciously rotated his head to the left, as if to remark, "Aaaaaa . . . I can't believe this . . . this time, Seb, you've gone entirely too far." It was a delight to watch.

"Come on, let's keep moving in case they try and catch up," I said, still feeling a bit paranoid, not sure we were in the clear yet. I didn't want to take any more chances.

We backtracked our way towards the hotel. Luckily, our sense of direction put together as a whole aided our return. Seb remembered to turn right by the small dilapidated corner of a two-story building, Josh remembered to continue straight for a few streets, and not to turn at the first narrow alley, there was a similar street further up. Before long we were back near the hotel. Something we hadn't noticed while paying attention to Juan a couple hours ago was a large dark field, a block from our hotel. At the other side of this field in the middle of the city was an awning with a trailer connected to it. A crowd of people under the small shelter and spilling out into the open field were grouped together like they were listening to music, definitely socializing. Facing the open shelter was another small lot; this one had a chain-linked fence and through the holes in the fence people were dancing, maybe to salsa.

"Let's go investigate," Leo said.

"This time let's steer away from fast talkers and Pacino look-alikes!" I said.

Clusters of people walked the street in that direction. Whatever it was, the place was gathering popularity by the second. The closer we approached, the higher the volume increased, and soon I was able to make out the heavy base beat, the steady high hat, and mellow soulful melodies. It was Biggie Smalls, "Juicy." "It's hip-hop!" I confirmed out loud, with a sentimental joy. All this time we had been so close to a gold mine. Not exactly the unique Cuban experience I had been seeking, but everyone was Cuban and I was happy to have something so concretely in common with the Cuban people. I was here in the middle of Communism, and a famous American song with lyrics indirectly espousing capitalism was being blasted across an open field for all of Havana to hear:

> *you never thought that hip-hop would take it this far,*
> *now I'm in the lime light, cause I rhyme tight,*
> *time to get paid, blow up like the world trade . . .*

It was clear that an American-led embargo or a resistant Fidel didn't have the power to shut out musical influences; actually I had read Fidel didn't even represent the typical Cuban that lived for music and dance. He reportedly couldn't dance. The party was completely open without barriers such that we just walked directly into the mass of people, the outer layer of people posing and chatting, the inner layer moving like a tribal dance to the music. The disc jockey was outside in the open breeze, a step slightly above the crowd in a wood-crafted booth, but, like everyone, exposed to the stars and moon. He suddenly switched to "Reggaetone," a popular mix between reggae and Spanish hip-hop. Without warning, an excitement erupted within the crowd, and everyone jolted into a dancing spell, as if a wizard with a voodoo doll was watching over, controlling their every movement. It was like the soul of the people had been captured and invigorated by something not of this earth, something outside of anyone's understanding. At first, the only thing all five of us could do was stand there, in envy and desire, wanting with all our hearts to partake in that which seemed so instinctive and spiritual. I could see African tribal influences, the way the girls dominated every rhythm and beat of the music with powerful twists of the hips and butt in circular thrusts. Dancing was as physical as it was spiritual, sweat beaded up and soared through the late night breeze, muscles were flexed by the men in tank tops, and women maneuvered around the men effortlessly and adroitly. A great joy spread through the crowd, a momentary release from the day's hardships, and I viewed the passion and intensity as invisible bursting flames of toxic energy escaping into the night's atmosphere. Leo and I ventured under the tarp roof, where can beer was being sold and Cuba Libres, mixed with off-brand cola. I purchased a can beer and continued to observe the crowd. Most of the people were Afro-Cuban. I saw a guy sporting a NY Yankees baseball cap, and another wearing a fishnet shirt, reminding me of Jamaican photos I had seen. The girls were dressed in bright colored tops and skirts, all types of oranges and fluorescent greens, some in jeans. By the time I finished my beer, another hip-hop song came on, the recent Fat Joe track, "Lean Back," and it reminded me of home. I couldn't help but bob my head back and forth, and when the chorus hit, I was already melted into the core of the crowd and was now leaning back the way Fat Joe and his cronies do in the music video, noticing I must be the only one with MTV. Seb and Leo joined me out there on the bare ground during the song, and

I was sure the Cuban girls had to be impressed with Seb, dancing with so much soul. We were free and alive out there in the open air, a good start to our first night.

The next day we woke up just in time to catch breakfast. It was not our idea of a good start to the day, but the eggs were edible and the bitter orange juice was tolerable. Seb had taken charge of the Lonely Planet guide, and had already mapped out objectives for our first full day. We decided to play the tourist role and hit all the major landmarks in the city. Most of the action was in the center, in Old Havana a couple of miles away, and we could explore the coastline on the way there. Everything was in walking distance, so I packed up the big Nikon camera in a backpack, I slipped a mini-digital cam in my pocket, and we headed for the coast.

The weather was paradise ideal—barely a cloud worth attention, and a slight breeze could be felt coming from the coast, enough to diminish the sun's sting. The new day washed away the cover of darkness, cleansed and lifted the shadows skillfully employed by people during the night. A more transparent Cuba was revealed, deceivingly free to roam. Many images and theories conceived the night before were discounted, not erased but countered with a devil's advocate view. Now, we were just a few blocks from our hotel, and already the land was declining towards the sea. Our first landmark, secluded in some trees, was undetectable from the end of the street. We approached from the sidewalk, up cement steps, and through an elegant stone passage way, to the foot of a long narrow grass lawn. Two high reaching palm trees shot up from the well-manicured grass, symmetrically placed, one on each side of the driveway bordering the lawn. They were used as sign posts to support a large white banner, drooping in the middle, perpetuating the rhetoric, "Viva La Revolucion," in dark green letters. More palm trees lined the edges of the lawn, until the driveway completed its spectacular oval, leading to a grand front entrance, elegant with white curving stairs, the perfect setting for Cinderella's Ball. Walking up the dramatic approach, I imagined the glory of all those who had been invited here as special guests, arriving by horse and carriage to a special colonial event or more recently by limo to a revolutionary gathering. We had made it to the famous Hotel Nacional.

We moved up the marble steps into a grand lobby adorned by an elaborate crystal chandelier and crossing corridors of ornate

Spanish tile, leading left and right. Not far down the right corridor, a statue stood in the center of a circular room, and forty-year-old photos promoting the revolution were hung along the walls, including pictures of Che Guevera and Fidel Castro in guerilla uniforms riding side by side, recently victorious, Colt revolvers still clenched in their hands. The grand lobby let out into an exotic garden courtyard with ponds and fountains, and the hotel wrapped around the ponds before curving off in opposite directions. It seemed to me the outside area with its angelic white walls and garden display befitted ideally a wedding or sentimental celebration. We watched as an adorable girl posed for photos wearing a fancy white gown and delicate silver tiara. She happened to be celebrating her fifteenth birthday, marking an official arrival into womanhood.

The view from the backyard of the hotel was breathtaking; it turned out to be a plateau, set high above the street and coastline. In between the street and water, a long winding promenade wrapped around the Havana coastline. Called the Malecon, this famous walk was as full of life as the city itself. We found a path down the hill from the Hotel to join this main artery of Havana, which would lead us directly to the historic heart of the old city. Strolling the endless sidewalk, guarded from the sea by broad cement railings, was like time traveling through generations. Images of how it had always been flashed by, one after another, as if projected by an old slide projector: the passing of an old fisherman with freshly dead octopuses draping from his hand; a small family of three holding hands side-by-side in order from tallest to shortest; a young couple settled on the wide cement railings unconcerned with passersby, kissing like not enough time was left, not enough love could fill their yearning. I watched as an older lady was taking her precious time sauntering along, slowly absorbing a moment with her grandson. The wall, which wasn't as greatly built as the wall in China, as controversial as the Berlin Wall in Germany, or as holy as the Wailing Wall in Israel, still held an endearing power and, if nothing else, was an unusual source of entertainment and community. Kids or the occasional "kid at heart" could be seen waiting for the next ocean wave to strike and come crashing over its reaches, an exciting contrast to the afternoon sun. If you were from here, you would even know the best spots along the railings to safely dive, careful to stay away from the shallow depths and painful rocks. You would know that at other points, the wall served as a handy bench for local fishermen or lecturing fathers instructing their kids how to anchor a fishing pole, spring their lines of bait into the ocean, and reel in a fish. The steady wall of the "Malecon" had lasted turbulent decades, not budging from the ocean's force, or the bloodthirsty hurricanes. It was a symbol of longevity for the everyday Cuban who never left or even considered leaving his or her nation, the Cuban not involved in the nation's politics or concerned with the politicians' gluttonous need for power.

I was walking down the famous promenade, proud to be a part of its long history, and at the same time marveling in its potential. The American Pie (they say you are what you eat!) inside of me was imagining a scene similar to that in London, where Big Ben, the millennium wheel, and swanky river wharf flats dazzle and strike awe along the River Thames — or the spectacular neon light show that graces the high rises of Hong Kong next to the Causeway Bay — or even the scene of New Orleans at the mouth of the Mississippi River where the romantic blues and jazz joints make couples fall in love all over again. Apparently, the Malecon did have a glamorous period back in the eighties, before the fall of the Soviet Union, and with it all its enriching subsidies. Back then, all kinds of trendy restaurants and bars faced the coast. Now, I looked across the street to the reality of a country not keeping up, not fulfilling its dreams, wasting away at the hands of systemic neglect. Gigantic blocks of high-rise apartment buildings were badly in need of repair: the cracked windows, chipped paint and crumbling exterior foreshadowed the hazards waiting inside. One corner of a building lay abandoned and crumbled to the ground in a pile of bricks, reminding me of pictures I had seen of war torn cities, like Bosnia or Nablus. Only war hadn't occurred here for quite some time. This was neglect. It's fair to say all cities have their rundown areas, pockets of hidden shame, but not usually on the site of such prime real estate.

It was not long until our path led us to the outskirts of the historic district of Havana. And once we passed Monumento Maximo Gomez, the Malecon changed dramatically. Now the appearance was that of old colonial power, and the small castle of San Salvador de la Punta protected a corner of curving coastline. We took a right onto Paseo de Marti, a lively street cutting into the center of Havana. It was named after the founder and martyr of the revolution whose act of defiance planted the seed of a long war for Cuban Independence from the Spaniards and, economically, the USA. Here vendors were everywhere, selling ice cream and small bite-sized pastries. Old Chevy cars from the fifties, some of them with brand new coats of paint seemingly fresh off the car lot, rolled through to pick up passengers, and at least a couple of times antique convertibles drove by, horn honking, bride and groom sitting above the shiny leather seats, smiling emphatically, waving to the pedestrians as if atop a float in a parade. We crossed by a street barricaded at the end, filled with a crowd of people the size of a small demonstration. We went to investigate. Scattered between the people were more vendor stands where one could buy homemade beer out of rusty barrels; and barbequed pork was a popular item at one stand with an indeterminable queue of people waiting, licking their chops. But if I had been hungry before, the roasted head and snout of a large pig mingling with the already chopped pile of meat would have dissuaded my appetite. I then announced that I was a tourist when I snapped photos of the cheerful vendor and his stand.

    Photo-taking can be like an addiction once past the initial click, so I continued with a shot of an old man with a smile full of wrinkles, dancing with one wooden cane and a shabby straw hat, probably with a cup of homemade beer somewhere nearby. He wasn't alone in the street. Dancing, for Cubans, was like drinking or talking, and there was no shortage of either in the middle of this festive Saturday. Cubanito 20-02, a popular musical group of Reggaetone, salsa, R&B, and hip-hop was dominating the streets of Havana, and kids and adults alike knew every musical lyric, even down to subtle whispers beneath the composition. We waded through the crowd and found a street leading us to the Parque Central, the site of many prominent landmarks, like the Gran Teatro de la Habana and the Museo Nacional de Bellas Artes. Havana was absolutely alive on this Saturday. People could be seen walking a maze of directions. According to our guide map, it was as easy as spinning a bottle on the ground and following whatever path the top pointed to, because the chances were a person would quickly strike something worth investigating.

    I noticed next to the Gran Teatro a small boutique gallery of art and went to explore its shade with Roman and Josh trailing behind, while Seb and Leo searched for anywhere selling water under the afternoon sun. Art was a continuous adventure for me, and ever more important in my life when I began traveling. I was never successful at painting or drawing; somehow those skills skipped over me in my family. Picking up any utensil to write or draw always turned into a disaster once my hand met paper. Not that I wasn't able to visualize beauty, the problem was translating those same thoughts onto paper or canvass. And my penmanship would be a lifelong reminder of this handicap. It hadn't changed since elementary school when even then, sitting in the desk next to Nadia, the librarian's daughter, I had been scolded by the teacher over and over for its unruliness, this further proving to me that there are some talents in life beyond control. So now I admire and marvel at the talents of artists put on this earth to capture "spots of time" and the human experience. They allow passersby a new angle at which to see the world, a kaleidoscope world, created in many patterns, shapes and lights.

In the boutique, a variety of paintings and montages were placed side by side, with no transitions, in no particular order. I wanted to clean my eyes after each work, the same way one inhales coffee beans to renew the sense of smell when comparing fragrances or fine wines, because some of the images were left lingering in my eyes like flashes of light in the dark. Loud and passionate colors affected my spirits. Absurd textures reached out at me, abstract and undecipherable. Naked and disturbed images of human beings were suspended in despair, lonely before my eyes, captured and fossilized. My first reaction, never having focused on Cuban art before, was that these artists were spurred by something intense, something real and burdensome. They were exploding onto the canvas, like suicide bombers, desperate for a reaction or moment of empathy, desperate to release what had been built up inside them and now was almost to the point of boiling. I talked with the lady of the shop about a couple of smaller paintings of odd, colorful faces that looked to be part of a series. I was not ready to pay for paintings so early, but figured this was the best time to negotiate prices—when I wasn't desperate or hurrying through a last day before leaving the island. I was surprised when the owner picked up the phone, called directly to the artist and handed me the old phone with round dial.

The exchange of Spanish between Orozco, the artist, and me was torturous and long and repetitive. We finally agreed to meet another day to talk about the paintings. He said more important than the money was that I understood his artwork and the person behind the brush. I agreed and scribbled down his number. I said "Thanks!" to the owner and realized that I had forgotten all about Roman and Josh. I walked outside to see if they were still around, at the same time wondering what was taking Seb and Leo so long.

When I walked out, Roman and Josh were sitting on the curb, just people-watching. I sat down to join them, and while I was doing so, my body realized how long it had been on its feet since early morning. The sun was now higher in the sky, directly above us. I placed my forehead down on my bent knees, straddling my arms around my legs, hands on my shoes, and tried for a quick power nap before the others would show up. I didn't have my watch on, or the energy to raise my head up, so I asked Roman for the time. It had been over forty minutes since Seb and Leo went looking for water. I pondered lazily over their whereabouts. Then, our answer, in the form of two dark-haired beauties, walked over with them. It woke me up a little bit. I should have known. Send the guys for water, and they bring back even more reason to cool off with cold water. Seb introduced the girls with a deep grin on his face. They did not have any water.

My close friends were all undoubtedly ladies' men. They couldn't help themselves. At any time if they were in the close proximity of an attractive woman, there was a ninety-percent chance they would approach and try their luck. They didn't possess nerves when confronting the opposite sex. They could walk up and immediately spark a conversation, without any hesitation, as if performing an involuntary action, that of tying shoelaces. I, on the other hand, had my rare moments when the timing was just right, a breeze of confidence blew in the air, and I had received eye contact, enough that I would have to kill myself if I didn't give it a try or at least say a few words. The pain and agony on a missed opportunity from a signal-flaring bombshell was worse than an awkward, fruitless conversation. And, sleeping at night was easier when all of the "what ifs" were squashed and dispensed with.

The philosophy that Seb and Leo lived by, though, was that if you talk to ten pretty girls, at least one will find interest and respond to you. I was not one of these guys, and would rather not waste my time on nine girls. Still, I had to give them credit; their record surpassed their philosophy, it was more like eight out of ten. They knew the right things to say and when to say them in most situations. The only characteristic separating Seb and Leo was their taste in women. Leo always sought after a new challenge, a woman far different than any of his previous conquests. He was on a mission to experience every type of female, from Muslim to Jew, short to tall, married with children to divorced with a pet dog. Seb liked to experiment, but, unlike Leo, he had fallen for a certain type of woman that he could not free from his system. Whether, he liked to admit it or not, he was after the women who possessed the same traits as his once golden relationship.

This trip wasn't about meeting women, falling in love or having an exotic fling, but without fail our travels integrated an element of romance. And today seemed to be the introduction of that element. But regardless of how it had been, meeting and chasing new women, all that was in the past for me. I was in a relationship with the love of my life. And as many problems as it had, my heart wouldn't be able to cheat, not on this girl. As far as I was concerned, meeting another girl, other than as a friend, would be a waste of time. There was no excitement or worth in meeting someone who wasn't the one. My heart yearned for only one girl, and I had convinced myself that she would soon be in my arms, celebrating the New Year the way only lovers do.

Seb and Leo were occupied. Roman and Josh were tired of walking, and I was tired of wasting time. We all talked briefly in Parque Central, during which time, Roman expressed a loud "Aaaarh" to Seb, undoubtedly for taking so long without bringing back any signs of water. I decided that I would go off on my own and check out the National Cuban Arts Museum. Roman and Josh decided they would find a street café and shelter from the sun. I had thought another shelter from the sun should be Roman's last requisite. You can't take the Russia out of some people. Still, art wasn't his passion, nothing of the aesthetic order was really his passion, and Josh had heard from someone back in the States that Cubans serve a fresh, strong blend of caffeinated tar. Roman had been in New York long enough to know good coffee deserved company. Finally, the ladies' men, Seb and Leo, took a stroll with their new delights back through the street festival. I flashed a smile at everyone as we ventured off in different directions.

Havana has two separate buildings under the name Museo Nacional Bellas de Artes. I saw that one was located on a short side street adjacent to the Parque Central. It housed a collection of modern and classic art from all over the world, but mainly consisting of work by Hispanic artists such as Mexico's Diego Rivera or Spain's Valezquez and Goya. I had realized years ago during my semester in Mexico that one of the best ways to grasp the culture and history of a society was to understand its great works of art. In Mexico, the frescoes and paintings of Diego Rivera, like "Sueno de una tarde dominical en la Alameda Central" depicted fierce class struggles and dynamics between indigenous

Aztecs, colonial Spaniards, Africans and resulting mestizoes. Diego had a way of explaining, through oil brush strokes, an entire history of Mexico from the native Aztecs to modern day mestizoes. The only pitfall in translating this philosophy to a country like Cuba was that any honest or critical depiction of history and society over the last fifty years would most certainly cease to exist within the confines of a national museum, let alone any private galleries. After all, "Guernica," the large mural painting that depicts the struggle and harsh reality of the Spanish Civil War, wasn't exhibited by Pablo Picasso in Spain until after the death of Franco and fall of Fascism. So I had to consider that a large block of artwork would not exist in the National Museum for as long as Fidel was still around. Nevertheless, past centuries would be enough to satisfy my curiosity. I wondered what, then, would be considered exceptional? What remained? Would there be messages cleverly hidden within the artwork? I headed over to the sister museum, "Edificio Arte Cubano," housing Cuba's native artists, two blocks away.

Upon entering the lobby, I encountered the deadening of sound and emotions that always seems to take place in the hollow immeasurable space of a grand museum lobby. The shiny dark marble, reaching to the ceiling, called back to me in echoes with every step. Faint shadows followed me along the newly burnished black tiles. The receptionist with her elegantly erect body stood formal in a black suit behind the counter like a welcoming bishop, as if she had been expecting me. No one else was around. I admired her long pronounced features: she seemed to fit her noble surroundings. The walk from the heavy metal doors to the counter was long and built up my anxiety. Time was waiting for our conversation, the one we had to exchange before she could fulfill her duty and I could begin my discovery.

"Bienvenido!" she pronounced, warmly and professionally. She then explained at least three times in Spanish, until I was able to understand, that no more guides with the English speaking tour were available today. I would need to wait until tomorrow. I hadn't counted on an English tour guide or even a tour guide before coming to the museum, but the new information created a new decision. I pondered whether to come back another day, putting both days both on hold. That's when a short man with dark spectacles and thinning hair, probably in his late forties, walked up, curious to why I hadn't yet purchased a ticket, why was I so inanimate and his snazzy receptionist idle. He whispered in her ear, anything more would repeat itself in echos, and she whispered

back. He turned to me with a smile.
"Where are you from?" It was obvious I wasn't from here.
"Estados Unido," I answered. His face grew friendlier.
"Que parte?"
"Uhhh . . . Georgia. Sudeste parte."
"Claro! Conozco Georgia! Me llamo Ortero." He stuck his hand out.
"Me llamo Cristof," I answered.
"Mucho gusto Cristof."

He further announced himself as assistant director of the museum. The conversation was shaky, but what I could comprehend was that he would give me a tour of the museum, if I were able to follow his explanations in Spanish. It had been four years since my trip to Mexico, and my Spanish was between rusty and non-existent, but a chance for a personal tour of a national museum by an assistant director didn't come by often, so I agreed without hesitation. I walked with him past the main lobby, through a tiny sculpture garden and up a winding ramp to the third floor. We skipped the second floor full of contemporary works and began with the oldest collection dating back to the sixteenth century. Here I would receive an initiation into the progression of Cuban art.

The layout of the museum was basic: long rectangular rooms, each leading to another, until it reached back to a flight of stairs or elevators completing a circle or square. Rooms were brightly illuminated with framed artwork placed on both walls and the occasional piece of pottery or small statue glassed away. Ortero was animated, using facial expressions and gestures in his explanations. He had to be, in order to overcome the gap in language. The first works were paintings of early colonial landscape, architecture, and people. I was amazed at how much I could understand when Ortero communicated with his hands and arms. All types of things could be explained in this way. He saluted me so that I knew he was speaking of the Spanish military and further talked about their control over the island. He put his hands together as if he was being led handcuffed and shackled at the feet to make note of the large importation of African slaves to the country in order to cultivate tobacco and sugar fields. When he pronounced words deliberately and precisely, with his entire mouth, I had more time to translate. I noticed now more than ever that many Spanish words were almost the same in English. It seemed to me that the small talk and everyday use of both languages was where they strayed from the Latin roots the most.

One painting from the colonial period stuck out in my mind. It was a curious painting, one that left mystery and unanswered questions. I wanted to go back in time, witness the account for myself, see if the painting had been true to reality. "Dia de Reyes en La Habana," painted on oil canvass by Victor Patricio Landaluze, depicted a street parade of Africans dancing, singing, celebrating through the narrow streets of Havana, not far from the actual museum. In the painting, women wore bright, long flowing dresses practically scraping the stone street below. Men dressed ritualistically, in tribal outfits, bare chests with straw dresses and warrior headdresses launched upwards. They filled the streets with exaggerated movements, the men beating tall congo drums clenched between the knees, theatric dancing played out for the onlookers. It was as much a celebration as it was a performance to earn donations. A colonial African dressed in proper bourgeoisie attire, tail tux, even a large ribbon of honor wrapped horizontally around his torso from right to left, accepted money into a top hat. Ortero explained it as a street procession for Africans during colonial times and the only day of the year when slaves were allowed to pass through the historic Havana streets in celebration. I wondered why the artist put so much emphasis on a Catholic cathedral towering in the background. What message was it sending? A message of assimilation? Or was he contrasting the two cultures, who originated from different religious spheres, in order to make some sort of statement for Catholicism? Ortero explained how the religion and traditional worship brought over by Africans had been amalgamated with Catholicism over the years, creating a new religion and identity for many Cubans called Santeria. I think this painting, without knowing it, predicted a future for Cuba, one of integration and common identity.

We passed by more landscape works, old paintings of ships flooding the Havana port at sunset, old portraits of nobility, governors, those with enough money and clout to garner such a luxury as an oil painting. In the last two rooms, already we had entered the modern era of art in Cuba, and I noticed influences from other great painters, such as Monet, the way he used short impressionist brush strokes to paint an image and from Picasso, his way of geometrically breaking down an image to emphasize the essential components; even Frida Kahlo, her bold use of surrealism to portray tragedy and self-conflict.

Cuban artists seemed clever at incorporating these styles in order to communicate their own reality. The third floor had been a history lesson about art and all that encompasses Cuba. We zipped through the second floor devoted to contemporary art. Ortero spoke through most of the pieces without losing wind. One enormous oil painting caught my eye, because from afar it could be seen with the clarity and trueness of a photo. Anna Flavio had painted this masterful work of a beautiful Mulatto lady lying on her side in the grass. It was breathtakingly accurate.

When I left the museum, I was drained mentally. I had been in there for hours, translating, digesting and analyzing information, and my brain needed a rest. The tour was an experience I would never forget, and I would always feel gratitude towards Ortero. But now all I wanted to do was relax, not to think, to act like I was on vacation for once. I stopped at a street vendor, on my way back to the Vedado District, for a vanilla ice cream cone and passed by a corner shop selling dollar pizzas, ordering what tasted more like a thinly coated cheese toast with a dry trace of tomato sauce.

When I reached the hotel, I decided against my immediate urge right away for a siesta, to instead check my email. The main portal to the outside world from Cuba was through the tourist hotels, where one can find CNN (thanks to Ted Turner's diplomacy) and internet access. I waited patiently while the dialup network slowly reached out to Hotmail, and thought how ironic it was to be using the fruits of capitalism under communism. Pop-up windows were slow to appear but slightly faster than the Hotmail page. I had been spoiled by the high-speed access at my job and didn't know what to do with this idle time. Maggie, I wondered if she emailed. We hadn't communicated for a few days. I needed to send my mom an email to let her know everything was safe, if not she would worry; and one email would go to Tlou. The web page appeared, and small blank boxes finally enlarged into a log-on form. I pushed my information through, and I had five new emails, two of them junk mail, one email from my mom, and surprisingly another from Nic, my college buddy—he was finally back using the web, and one from Maggie. I read Nic's email first. "Wud up my nigga! How the chicas lookin! One of these days I'm taking one of these trips wit ya. It's time to take my shit over seas! Make sure to take photos and be safe out there dog. Strap up! Holla at me when you get back." I replied to my mom's email; she wanted to know what city I was in and where I planned to go afterwards. I described my experience at the museum; it was still fresh on my mind. And I sent Tlou an email to liven up his day. I knew he would be at the office working. I had put off reading Maggie's email to the end, as some silly psychological test, a small battle, to see if I could fight the impulse to divert all my attention to her, neglecting everything else.

Before I clicked the closed envelope icon with Maggie's full name outstretched to the right, my heart started beating; in some paradoxical way I was used to feeling this rush of anxiety, whenever I heard from her. Then finally, biting into the main entrée after the salad, or the desert after the entrée, I began reading her out loud in my head, "Hey babieee!" Already, I could picture her talking to me, her pouty lips pronouncing each syllable, coming together like a warm kiss in the air. Though it didn't start out so warm. "Ahh . . . my mum is driving me crazy! I need to get out of Hong Kong, this house is not big enough for the both of us, and the maid is useless, she doesn't do anything. It's too much, really! I have a few castings over the next week here in Hong Kong and then, either come to see you for New Year's or I have to fly out to Seoul for a Samsung commercial. Babieeee . . . I might not be able to see you for New Years! I'm waiting on the client to confirm the dates. They said they may need to shoot at the end of this month. I will let you know when I find out. Wish you were here with me, holding me. I need your love. x." My heart dropped in my chest. I was disappointed. The thought of not seeing her for the New Year's was depressing. But I was too tired to dwell deeply on it. Plus, with Maggie, I had to know to expect anything, and changes to her plans, changes to our plans, were not the exception, they had become the rule. Still, somewhere beneath the thick layer of pessimism, there was hope she would come around. I took the elevator up and crashed out.

When I woke up, I heard the echoes of beating. It occurred to me that someone was knocking. They knocked again. It was Seb and Leo. "Chris, open up! What are you doing in there?"

"Hold on," I tried to say, but my voice was still asleep. I lifted my body up to a sitting position first, the blood heavy in my head from a hard desperate sleep. I stood up and opened the door without looking, walking back to the bed. Then a stream of alert questions exploded from behind me.

"How long were you asleep dude? Where did you go after

we last saw you? You're not going to believe what happened to us? You ready for this?"

"Ready? Ready for what?" I had tuned out the first half. Leo answered.

"First we walked with the girls to the street festival and then to the capitol building, which looks just like Capitol Hill in Washington D.C. After that we walked to the oldest cigar factory in Cuba."

"Go ahead—" I wanted him to get to the point.

"Well anyways . . . how did the girls appear to you?" Leo asked.

"What do you mean?" I asked, knowing the question was rhetorical.

"I mean, how did they appear?" Leo again asked.

"They appeared to be normal, somewhat classy, they were pretty hot. . . .Why? What's your point?" I was tired of the game.

"Well, at first the shorter girl was going on how she studies medicine at the University. Seb's girl said she works as an elementary school teacher. They wanted to go back to their place, so we followed them back, and when we got back to their place," Leo continued.

"Go on," I said.

"My girl told me that she needed to see the money first."

"You mean they were hookers!" I was a bit shocked.

"Yeah!"

"Damn! That's crazy"

"I know. . . . I laughed at first, but she wasn't kidding!" Leo said.

"Well after that we jetted out! They were mad, shooting us fingers, shouting obscenities. I had no clue though. Did you have a clue?" he turned to Seb.

"No, I had no clue," Seb answered while shrugging his shoulders.

It was all a bit shocking for me. But I tried to put myself in the place of the girls. Let's see. I began to do the analysis in my head. I had read that the typical monthly salary for Cubans was between eight and thirteen U.S. dollars' worth of pesos, a currency only dispensable at government shops, barely enough to get by on government-rationed food, clothes and rent, and that was assuming that everything actually existed in stock. Government stores were notorious for selling out of essentials or having the wrong sizes in products such as shoes and clothing. The other options were the black market, special food markets, or government-run shops, all of which accepted only U.S. currency. The only way to live a decent life was to have access to these dollars. And the only ways to access dollars were to have someone sending them from overseas, or to earn them from tourists. "All right," my mind continued walking through the girls' psyches, "if I wasn't one of the fortunate ones who had family in Miami living the American dream, and if I didn't work in a hotel, drive a taxi, attend a bathroom in the airport, operate my home as a guesthouse or private restaurant, then how would I earn these worshipped dollars? Okay, I would probably hustle tourists." Then, I thought, "If I was a female, what was the most lucrative way to hustle?" The reality was disheartening. "I would be a prostitute." I started doing the calculations in my head. A prostitute earns in one day, in dollars, what an average Cuban would have to work an entire year to earn in pesos. It was an astounding realization. Prostitutes were the breadwinners, not doctors, not lawyers, inventors, or savvy businessmen. Working for the government was the other option, but if you weren't critical to the Revolution, or friends or family to the higher ups, then you weren't counted in that pie. Prostitution was a sacrifice to a better life. The pressure must be daunting for Cuban women.

But why? Why was the dollar allowed in Cuba? That question rang to all parts of my brain, in search for a solution. I continued pondering: The goal of socialism, the utopian society that Fidel Castro and Che Guevara had envisioned and fought so hard for, was to create equality, banish the "haves and have-nots" system that capitalism was accused of promoting. But the fact that the dollar was legalized in 1993, creating a double economy where people with dollars had more access to goods, while people with the weak-to-worthless pesos could barely make ends meet, had created the very classist structure that socialism denounced, a society of inequality, haves and have-nots. Something was not right. Questions were still left unanswered.

"Have you seen Roman and Josh?" I asked.

"No," Leo mumbled, sounding unconcerned.

"Let's plan tomorrow. I think we should get out of the city. Let's jump on a bus and just go somewhere," Seb said.

"That's cool with me, as long as we get back soon; there is a lot I still haven't seen here," I replied.

"Where is your Lonely Planet guide?" I asked Leo. Leo threw me the book.

"Let's go up the north coast to the east and look; it says for the nicest beaches near Havana go to Varadero," I said. "What do you guys think?"

"I'm cool with that, let's get on the road," Leo said.

"All right . . . tomorrow off to Varadero," Seb said.

The next morning, feeling refreshed from a full night's rest, I was happy to see the sun yet another day, shining in all its brilliance, a symbol of life. It was a part of nature found anywhere in the world, except for maybe continuous days near the North and South poles. I had missed it. Waking up before sunset for another grueling day as an accountant and finishing up no sooner than 8 p.m., my normal procedures, made it so I had missed the most abundant, life-giving resource on earth. At around the time I was still a senior in high school, I remembered thinking how crazy my brother had been for joining the Navy as a submariner. How could anyone go weeks cooped up in a submarine without seeing sun, talking to the same coworkers everyday, and having no life outside of work? I would constantly tell myself I never could have joined the Navy, let alone volunteer to submerge myself in what seemed an underwater prison.

But, now seven years later, how was I different? How had my precious path changed things? I wasn't underwater for weeks or months on end, but I was locked away in a prison of cubicles, with no windows, only artificial light. I was practically married to my coworkers, who received my first and last words everyday, "Good morning darling and Go fuck yourself good night!" I didn't have a life outside of work, and even worse, my submarine didn't dock every few weeks. I had been working nine straight months on this current client. I had become exactly what I said I could never be, exactly what I thought was completely inhumane, against all morals and principles. And all the time working, I hadn't realized I was no different than someone locked behind bars. The job had been good at sucking me in, relentlessly, never allowing me a second to think or breathe. At first I told myself only a month or two of this insane routine, then they would have to assign me to another client, share the workload with others who consistently go home at six or seven. A month or two went by. Then after two months, I told myself only two more months. Nothing changed. Then half a year, then before I knew it almost a year had flown by, while I sat, day in and day out, in a tiny cubicle, worshipping Saint

Microsoft. My previous year hadn't been fun or particularly interesting, but at least it wasn't modern day slavery. Without knowing that it was happening, I eventually settled, accepted my fate, gave up my dreams, knelt down to the great beast. One thing was for sure though, now I had time to think.

We checked out of the hotel, and now we were walking with all our bags down the street to the bus station, the one our friendly doorman said was in walking distance. Seb led the way; he had gotten the directions. Leo and I were next, and Josh and Roman followed behind, as quiet as the first day in Cancun. I wondered what Roman was thinking the whole time with his thick glasses, never looking you in the eye. The entire morning, I had noticed that everyone seemed a bit irritated. I heard at least three "Aaaarhs" coming from Roman, and this time Seb didn't find a word of his nasal Russian amusing. It started with Josh; he wasn't around last night when we discussed today's plans, and he was upset that we didn't consult him first. He thought we should travel directly to Santiago and then come back to Havana. The only thing was that Santiago was so far away from Havana, all the way on the Eastern tip of this lanky island and we were basically near the northwestern point, which meant we would be on the road for at least a day there and a day back. We only had one-and-a-half weeks left, and we didn't want to spend it on a bus. Right before leaving the hotel, Leo and Seb argued over whether we should take a taxi or walk to the bus station. Seb wanted to save money, and Leo thought it was crazy wasting time and energy, when taxis were so cheap. Seb proved more stubborn than Leo.

We walked fifteen minutes, and nothing, no bus station.

"Dude, let's catch a taxi," Leo hadn't given up. "If you were back in NY, you would be paying ten times as much."

"If you want to take a taxi, go ahead. No one's stopping you," Seb repeated. I could feel the cloud of tension. I wanted to calm things down. When the next taxi passed I waved it down.

"Come on, the taxi ride is on me this time," I said. Seb was not thrilled by my actions, although I had sensed he wanted out of walking.

"Seb . . . I'm going to throw you in this taxi," I said, laughing in the same moment, trying to lighten the mood. Then I snatched the bags off of Seb's back and threw them into the trunk. He got in, shrugging reluctantly.

The bus station was a circus act of people, some rushing, some standing next to the walls not wandering far from their luggage, and others standing around without luggage, like they didn't belong, maybe looking for trouble. We stood out, the five of us, to the stares of everyone not in a particular rush. We checked the bus schedule. We would need to wait for at least four more hours. "The last bus left five minutes ago," the clerk at the ticket booth explained, waving those juicy words, just out of our reach. This was only more ammunition to Leo's lingering war and he wasted no time rubbing it in further. That's when a man walked up to us, his hair shiny and slick like the Fonz from the "Happy Days," while we stood clustered a few feet away from the booth. He had sensed a frustration and disappointment emanating out of our circle from the moment the clerk, just doing her job, opened her mouth.

"Where you go?" he asked with the smile of a salesman, not wasting time. "I have beautiful car outside. I take you." It was almost as if the booth clerk and tout were in cahoots, knowing we didn't want to waste four hours in a dark, smelly station.

"How much to Varadero?" I asked.

"Let's see . . . I have to drive back here and gas . . . 40 dollars," he said.

"40 dollars!" Seb said, sounding like his engine had just kick started again, "Twenty!"

"30 dollars . . . last price!" the driver said.

"Okay," Seb chimed back in. We followed him through a small wing of the bus station, past a couple of dimly lit eateries, of the kind that could ruin an appetite, and out to a side parking lot, where a car show of old Chevys sat idle. The parking lot was like a local hangout for these drivers, jokes were being told, gossip exchanged between old friends. But friendly chatter and business were two different matters; it seemed a jealous, competitive eye flashed over our driver as he opened the heavy metal trunk to put in our bags. He was willing to hawk inside the bus station for customers. He was a threat to them. They knew he was hungrier than them, more determined; maybe they too had been more aggressive sellers in their younger days.

We were finally off, and moving in the right direction, in a car that had had plastic surgery to make it appear younger. It was a bold, beautiful red with big shiny silver hubcaps and a spacious, white interior. However, it smelled thinly of oil, and its engine chugged along in short weak splats, as if Fred Flintstone was panting out of breath beneath the hood. I thought a car like this one, a man's pride and joy, had to have a name, and since the owner couldn't think of anything suitable, we named it Cher (Bono was under the hood). Now, the narrow streets of the city and all its exhaustive energy opened into a vast countryside, filled with long flowing grass, ferns and the occasional isolated tree. A couple of billboards guided us out of the city. One sign espoused old revolutionary rhetoric, "Socialism or Death," and one sign had five faces of men taken like mug shots, referred to like martyrs; they were allegedly imprisoned in the USA unjustly for espionage. One thing was obvious, no signs or billboards marketed products or restaurants, there were no signs reading, "just 5 miles, exit 7, shopping malls and rest stop," nothing advertising Coca-Cola or McDonalds'. This country was commercial-free like PBS. I thought about all the annoying, manipulating, brainwashing commercials played over and over in the U.S., all the billboards cluttering beautiful countryside or defacing magnificent high rises, and could admire a country free from all these headaches. Then, I imagined a whole world full of televisions, every one of them broadcasting PBS—I fell asleep in the middle of that thought.

When I woke up, we were slowly rolling along the rugged country highway. An old, faithful horse was hauling a tattered wagon made of mix-matched wood and wobbly wheels in front of us. Feeling the brunt of every stone or bump inside the stiff carriage were shirtless field hands or farmers shielding themselves from a persistent sun with frayed straw hats. They stared steadily at us through our car windshield, a hard, tired, bitter glare, which was uncomfortable to receive and equally hard to refuse. They continued to stare in our direction the way a cat can force a blink, almost unconsciously. I wondered if they were on the way to work or a death camp.

The mood in the car wasn't any more positive. No one was speaking to the other, and I didn't have the energy or will to break the cold ice. The fact was we were in the midst of taking a trip, a voluntary expedition, spending the rare time we had in our career lives to explore a calling that lurked inside of us. Cuba was a chance of a lifetime, possibly our only real chance before any number of life's haphazard events were to unfold, and we wanted to know that the decision was all ours, every step of the decision. At the end of the day, we wanted our instincts and desires to guide us through this fate, to live as free men without keepers or barriers, not to be tampered with and detoured by someone else's decision making. We were men pushed too suddenly to a realization in our lives; working our jobs had raised, in a round about way, the question of mortality. We had been giving up every day for the last almost two years of our lives to other human beings, coming to work when they ordered, eating lunch when they allowed us, spending every waking hour on call: nothing about our lives on a micro level had anything to do with our own decisions. And it was painfully obvious that this could go on for a large percentage of our lives. Ironically, we had spent four years of our university careers learning how to become leaders and the last two years learning how to be followers. So, as small as the compromise of taking a taxi versus walking, or traveling to Varadero versus Santiago, may appear, these were camel's back breaking straws, and the tiny decisions were small babies of our own creation which for better or worse were ours; nobody could take that away from us. Traveling in a group was not easy, and it was becoming impossible. It meant that at times, each of us had to deny our instincts and better judgment. A rebellion was forming, a culmination of the last two years. Up until now, there had been no outlets to our boiling frustration. The pot was screaming hot, and it was just a matter of time until that pot finally boiled over.

On the way to Varadero, without first asking us, the driver decided to stop in Playas del Este, a popular travel destination for local Cubans escaping the grittiness of Habana. I had imagined Varadero to be much bigger and livelier, but the small beach town had a special charm, so we asked the driver to stop and ask anyone if they knew of private rooms for rent. We were unsuccessful on the first two attempts. Both of them professed knowing about rooms but were certain they had been rented out already. The driver was becoming impatient and colder with each stop, eventually wanting to just drop us off on a main street, though we had no idea where to go. Becoming desperate to find any more information on guesthouses, we flagged down a car that came cruising the neighborhood for a second time. It had passed us earlier when we entered the town. We waved out through the windows, and, after first passing us, it stopped and reversed until we were side to side in the street.

"Perdon . . . pued . . . des . . . decir . . . donde..." Leo was stumbling badly over his words. The smile on the driver's face formed the beginnings of a laugh. He was enjoying every second of the struggle; the entire time Leo's face was becoming redder and redder. Then, the driver asked in the most perfect American accent, "Where are you guys from?"

Leo's face loosened back up. "New York," he said like a reflex, and to my dismay grouping everyone in the car. It was a waste of my breath to correct him.

"Wow! I live in Miami. I'm just over here visiting my parents for the holidays. It's nice to see people my age around here. I grew up in this town as a kid, but a lot has changed and I came back realizing I don't know that many people anymore, many people left, are too busy with kids, etc. Actually, I have kids, but they're back in Miami. I'm taking a break from them and the wife." He said that last part with a sneaky smile. Our driver was very impatient and annoyed hearing our English.

"Que haceis?" our driver asked.

"Listen," I said, ignoring the driver, "we're looking for a guest house, somewhere to stay for the night."

"Sure thing. I have family that owns guesthouses or at least they would know someone who does. Follow me to my house and I'll make a few calls, get you boys settled in," he said.

"Thanks. What is your name, by the way?" I asked.

"Sergio."

We followed him to his house and paid the rest of our fare. But first we took a quick photo of the driver standing beside the Old Chevy for memory's sake. Sergio led us into the small screen porch of a charming beach house. It was painted all white and had a red clay roof, the same color as those of the surrounding houses, a different feel from the mid-rise apartment blocks in Old Havana.

"Wait here on the patio with your bags," Sergio said, and he walked into the house. I felt a little awkward sitting in the patio. An old man, probably an uncle of Sergio, was already sitting down when we tracked our bags and noise in. A dog sat in between his legs, old and quiet like his owner. The old man smiled but didn't say a word. A lady appeared from inside the house wearing a plaid white and blue apron. She had that warm, motherly approach and asked us if we wanted anything, "Café o agua. Pero, no tengo Coca-Cola." She then laughed at her own sarcastic joke. The embargo made acquiring such American novelties difficult. Of course, for the right price it could be smuggled in from Mexico. I asked to use the bathroom.

The inside of the house reminded me of my grandmother's house, the way she had managed to keep every single item and souvenir she had collected over her lifetime and somehow miraculously found a way to display them in her cozy two bedroom house. Sergio's mom had all types of knick knacks jumbling the walls: small porcelain plates, wooden figurines of dogs and horses, antique collector's dolls, and a collage of family photos enough to recreate a family's entire existence. The clutter spanned a few generations, maybe even a couple of dictatorships or military coup d'états. When I came back outside, Sergio was in the middle of telling the guys there was one guest room available, but too small to fit the five of us.

"Listen, my American friends!" he started jovially. Sergio had an energetic and cheerful way of talking about everything. He was full of life. "There is a small hotel that has a ton of vacancies. I'm sure you can find a cheap room there. No worries! It's a few blocks away. We can get some fresh air on the way! Get you settled in and ready for tonight!" he said. So, we lifted our bags onto our shoulders and followed him. The hotel was a cheap rendition of motels anywhere in rural America, though without the flashing bulbs reading "vacancies" or "occupied." The entire second story was a long looping balcony and had a beautiful view of the surrounding neighborhood. Farther out, past a cluster of willow trees where the water met the sky, was the direction of the beach. It was around two in the afternoon after we were all checked in. Sergio said he would meet us later to take us out to the only club open this time of year, a local Cuban hangout sitting on a hill above the city. I was anxious to finally see a beach and tired of waiting on everyone, so I decided to walk ahead and meet the guys on the beach. The walk to the beach was quiet. I was waiting for the large tumbleweed to roll through at any moment. It was obvious, looking around, that winter was upon us, and not because of the weather. The skies were clear and temperature warm, only summer vacation for Cubans would be far off.

When I emerged from behind the thick wall of trees blocking the town's view of the beach, I did find a sparse number of sunbathers. I edged closer to the water, while strolling slowly and aimlessly. I noticed how the white sand appeared a pepper gray from the speckles of debris washed in from the ocean; wet logs were abandoned along the shoreline. A few lonely palm trees sprouted from the sand further back from the tide's reach. The dull coastline seemed to shoot outwards for miles. Something melancholy overtook me in these surroundings. It could have been the lack of joyful, carefree sunbathers and palm trees that I associated with tropical paradises or the monotonous never-ending stretch of coastline. I couldn't figure it out. Maybe it wasn't the beach. Maybe, this emptiness inside of me was a reflection of my already heavy spirits, and the beach was only an innocent bystander, a projection screen capturing my underlying mood. Then it occurred to me, I hadn't really felt the same since I read Maggie's email. I really missed her.

I wondered what she could be doing at that very moment. Probably at a glamorous party, soaking wet from the flood of attention she always commanded, especially on that side of the world, where mixed-race Asians were like rare pearls within the entertainment industry. I didn't even realize that she was half-Asian when we first met. But if I had looked closer at the almond shape of her eyes, the milky pure skin, her delicate shape and jet black hair, I would have seen it. The truth is it never really mattered to me. She was beautiful and full of magnetic energy that was pure enough to breathe. I had no idea, when we met, that she was a model. In a place as un-materialistic and un-superficial as Thailand, those details were inconsequential. Chemistry, liveliness, the spark between people, the ability to embrace and blend were what counted, what people accepted as virtuous. All the other man-made concepts like material success, or names, were not considered in the young backpackers' world.

This beach didn't really deserve my criticism. It was a clean canvass, spray-painted and defaced by my selfish mood, a glass seen for the moment half-empty. Suddenly, distracting me from my self-pity, and a somewhat shocking sight to see marching through the middle of the sunny beach, were two soldiers or maybe they were policemen, both fully dressed from head to toe, in grayish-blue uniforms. They wore heavy black boots tied all the way up their ankles, and both had black pistols visible in holsters. The peculiarity of seeing black boots clumping through soft beach sand, as if patrolling the neighborhoods of Havana, or an open battlefield, was creepy, if not disturbing. It was like time-traveling back forty years to the same revolution. For more than one reason, it seemed pointless and out of place. How many policemen were there in the country? Hardly anyone was on the beach. Were they afraid that rafters could be heading for the shores of Florida? What was the government so paranoid about? For someone who lived most of his life in the U.S., it was a confounding image to see only ninety miles away. Maybe Maggie wasn't the only concern on my mind. Here I was in a relaxed region of Cuba, supposed to be on vacation, and my head was clouded with the limitations experienced by Cubans, the freedoms they had to do without every waking day of their life, freedoms that I took mainly for granted. There had to be something someone could do. But, who to point a finger at? Who could change the repressive system?

Cuba was the center of two warring enemies, the Cuban exiles in Miami and the Fidelistas, similar to a family feud, that in efforts to fight against each other for the ultimate welfare of the country both were actually working together to strangle life out of the country. The entire Revolution under Fidel, which ousted the former dictator Batista, was for the liberation of the Cuban people—or more specifically, the liberation of everyday Cubans, the factory workers and farmers of sugar cane, from exploitation by U.S. companies and other foreign investors. The majority of Cubans, meaning working-class Cubans, not the higher echelons of society, bourgeoisie and government leaders, were fed up with the labor abuses and lack of rights; they were fed up with being controlled like puppet dolls from afar, by investors who had no other interests in Cuba than profits. The U.S. was the big bad opportunist neighbor. While Cuba fought once again for its independence, this time Fidel at the forefront against the giant next door (earlier it had been Spain that exploited and controlled the country from afar), it was slowly cannibalizing itself. This new fight for independence had created a protectionist, scared dictator that used Socialism as a means to lock out his most ardent opponents in the U.S. Fidel tried to eliminate any opportunity for them to gain control over the country's resources for fear that it would lead to another upheaval. This paranoia and over-control by the government eventually led to the oppression of its own people. In order to keep control through Socialism, the government had to shut off its borders, restrict travel and new ideas, and kill off democracy, capitalism and entre-preneurialism. The great revolution that was here to free everyday Cubans eventually ended up doing the exact opposite. And contributing to Fidel's stubborn forty-year rule was the U.S.'s retaliatory trade embargo and travel ban, once credible tools in the fight to rid the Western World of Communism, and now just another barrier to Cuban freedom. The elimination of trade to the island limited the flow of new products, services, and ideas, and the travel ban lessened the influence that a large flock of democratically minded Americans could have had on a relatively closed society. In my opinion, it was a careless mandate that limited the flow of new and different ideas.

With all that said, I had to be careful to put everything in perspective. To Fidel's credit, by luck at many times (the former Soviet Union's subsidies to the country for over a decade), and by lapses into hypocrisy (collection of contributions by Cuban exiles in the U.S. and expatriates living abroad), the country was much better off than many South American countries, in terms of police brutality, corruption, human rights violations, domestic crime, and economic welfare. But still, being so close to these people geographically as an American, having so much in common culturally, and being here and immersing myself in the country all intensified the thoughts of what it would be like if my own friends and family had been forced and restricted to live out someone else's ideology, locked in their own country like socialist lab rats. I was not content basking in the sun and ignoring the issues going on around me. More and more, I realized this trip was not just about Mojitos and warm weather. I needed to ask real questions to real people. I wanted to get back to Havana soon, where the heart of the fire was burning, and I only had about one week left before New Year's, when I would hopefully meet Maggie, party the night away, and end the trip with a bang.

Sergio dropped by our hotel later that night. He was all excited about hitting a club he hadn't been to in years.

"I heard the club hasn't changed a bit, still the spot to be at. That's Cuba for you!" Sergio said. I could still feel tension within the group; something was rotten in the air. We weren't in a partying mood, but no one wanted to sit around the hotel all night staring at the blank white walls. Before we left the hotel, Sergio asked, "But, why Cuba? What are you guys doing down here? Are you looking for women?" No one said anything. "I know. Maybe, you guys are spies for the Pentagon?" he laughed. No one really was in the mood to give the long complicated answer.

"We wanted to do something different this time," I said.

"No worries. You have more time to answer that question. Well, anyway, you guys be careful tonight. The girls, they don't see Americans that often. They don't see many foreign tourists at all for that matter ... sometimes Italians. They're going to jump all over you." The drive from the hotel to the club was dark and dead. The roads were without street lamps, and, aside from Sergio, a silence was still emitted by our group. I wondered what thoughts were traveling through Seb's and Leo's heads as we wound through the darkness of the countryside. Something was weighing heavy in their heads.

We pulled into the gravel parking lot and walked inside the club. Immediately all eyes were on us. At first I thought Sergio could have been another "Juan the pimp," but the women weren't as dazzling and provocatively dressed. We were movie stars walking the red carpet, and it was obvious we weren't from around here. Hard, suspicious stares came from the guys, and the girls in their little groups were competing to catch our attention, often giggling back to their friends when they caught one of our eyes. A range of ages filled the discothèque. Sergio bought a round of mojitos for everyone. We toasted, then walked around the circular bar, out through the back of the club to an open patio, sheltered by a couple of large oak trees. Only then did I realize how high up we were; I walked further out, past the oak trees, and to the edge of the hill. An entire valley of lights sparkled and flickered like stars along the coast. The club had a gorgeous view of the small beach town and its immediate neighbors.

I noticed Roman was opening up with every round of mojitos. He had been dancing all night with a group of girls huddled around him. Watching his awkward moves, I thought to myself, it's amazing what tricks one pulls out of the hat when girls suddenly enter the picture. He seemed enthralled by his newfound mo-jo and the attention from the girls. I wondered if he hadn't had a revelation out there on the dance floor. He was discovering himself in ways he probably never considered before, dancing to hip-hop and reggae music. Ironically, the fact that he couldn't dance made him even more the "Gringo" and helped him stand out even more. Seb and I were getting pure entertainment out of his efforts.

"Check out Romano . . . he's pullin' out some new moves on us," I said.

"I've never seen him act like this. He never dances back in New York," Seb remarked, to which I added,

"It's obvious he never dances anywhere."

"It's amazing what a few mojitos and Cuban girls have the power to do! Did you know that Roman has never even been laid before! He's still a virgin!"

"No! You gotta be kiddin me!" I said. Not that it was unbelievable.

"I'm serious, dude. Never tasted pussy, not one day in his life." Then Seb paused for a moment. I could tell by the squinting of his eyes and self-gratification in his smile that he was up to something.

"I got a plan for tonight." Seb's voice quieted down.

"What?" I was already laughing inside, I knew where he was going with this.

"We gotta get Roman laid. The poor guy has never seen pussy in his life," Seb continued.

"How are you gonna pull that off?" I asked. Roman clashed within our group. He had thick round glasses and pale white cold Russian skin, was chubby and round, walked hunched over, had a million nervous mannerisms, and never looked anyone in the eyes. Now all of these characteristics that no one here had were playing in his favor. Roman, probably for the first time in his life, was a chick magnet.

Later that night, Seb walked up to me. "Those two girls standing over there want Roman and me to go home with them."

"Those two girls?" I asked. Out of all the girls they danced with, these were the least attractive girls. "Which one are you hooking up with?" I asked Seb.

"Are you crazy! I'm just going to keep the other one busy, while Roman handles his business," he said. "Listen . . . Sergio agreed to take us to the girl's house first and come back to pick you guys up. So hang around for a little while longer," Seb finished.

"All right. Good luck," I said. The rest of us danced around more, waiting for Sergio to return. He took us back to our motel.

The next morning, Seb knocked on the door. He came in with his famous, I have a story to tell look.

"Last night, Roman's name changed from Roman to Romeo," Seb said as he burst in.

"Are you serious! Roman got laid?" I asked.

"Yes he did. And thanks to me. He came on this trip into Cuba as a little boy, and he will now leave out a man. My mission is complete." Seb was happy with himself.

"I didn't know you had a mission. That means you can pack up your bags and go home now," I remarked.

"Are you crazy! I still haven't gotten laid!" He left back to his room, as quickly as he had entered with his new story. I was slowly waking up and decided to step outside before brushing my teeth or planning clothes for the day; the sun usually triggered my engine. I walked out to the sound of music in the air. It sounded like it was coming from the pool area. I continued in its direction, walking along the balcony, my right hand sliding along the white metal rail. It was the pool area. A rush of excited nerves tingled along my arms, made my hairs stand up, and goose bumps appear: This was the strange reaction I got from hearing amazing music. It was my natural high. Now I wanted to know who it was; I had never heard Spanish hip-hop. And, it wasn't pure hip-hop. It had that beautiful Latin sound, an organic mix of trumpets, trombones and congo drums, capturing the best it could the essence of "live," while fusing beautifully with the head-knocking power of deep bass and heavy beats characteristic of hip-hop. The rhythm of the MC pouring lyrics over the melody sounded great, though I couldn't understand the fast Cuban accent. The singer in the group powerfully rang out the hook. He had a clean, pure voice. I was thinking, "Hip-hop with a Buena Vista Social Club twist. Wow!"

Music was the one thing in the world that could send me traveling to the corners of the galaxy without leaving home. I overlooked the pool area. A worker was cleaning the pool. He was concentrating heavily on his task, carefully guiding the long metal pole and net, just skimming the top of the water for all the fragments of leaves and twigs left by a tall overhanging tree near the outer wall. The music was his theme song, accompanying his efforts. I admired his determination to rid the pool of every last floating speck; he even kneeled down to swipe a bug that had stubbornly escaped his net.

Today was big decision day. I wasn't thrilled about continuing towards Varadero, further down the coast. Our guidebook described it as a Mecca for European tourists on a cheap vacation package, which didn't coincide with my desire to immerse myself as much as possible into the real Cuba. I needed to talk with locals and blend in, see if I could borrow a pair of their prescription shades, see through to their world. This was hard to accomplish with a large group, especially since Seb and Roman stuck out like "Gringos." I remember hearing Leo explain that he wanted to travel further inland, maybe to Cienfuegos, but I thought Havana was overwhelming enough for a first trip and wanted to return as soon as possible. I wasn't going to travel all the way to Santiago with only a week left, Josh's objective, and I was sure Seb wanted to hit Varadero, where all the Italian girls were vacationing. I didn't know what Roman wanted; he didn't speak much in English.

I wondered if we would all be a group at the end of today. I was sure that everyone wanted to move at his own speed, in his own direction at this point. I was going to find out their reaction to my change in plans when we all met for brunch.

"You guys ready for Varadero?!" Seb sounded excited. No one answered. No one wanted to be the first person to break up the group. It was quiet for a few seconds.

"What's wrong?" Seb asked.

"Well I'm not sure about going to Varadero. Besides, it's just a bunch of tourists!" Leo answered.

"Yeah . . . I thought we would go to Santiago after here?" said Josh.

"No . . . that's too far for me. I want to head back to Havana. That's where the action is at," I said.

"Fine. You guys do what you want to do! I'm going to Varadero!" Seb seemed pissed. Roman didn't know what to say. He was happy to be out of the U.S. Plus, after last night's revelation, he felt different; he was a new man.

"I want to see that Cuban girl again from last night," said Roman.

"Well . . . it seems like everyone's doing their own thing," I said.

"I guess so," said Leo.

"Everyone has their plane tickets and times. See you in the airport. I'm off to Varadero," Seb said.

And that was that. Seb threw his bags over his shoulders and headed for the bus station, followed by Leo, followed by Josh, and eventually myself. I waved bye to Roman.

The bus ride wasn't very long and within hours I was back in Havana. I wanted to stay in the historic district, and find a "casa particular." There I would be able to live with a Cuban family and explore the city without the unneeded attention of four other traveling Americans. I was sure I would learn much more about the country this way. At the same time, I had my reservations traveling alone. The guys were fun to joke with and talk with, especially when strange occurrences arose, weird surrealisms that would never happen in the U.S. Every traveler runs into these situations where he thinks if only my friends back in my home country could see this, we would be rolling in laughter together. The crew was a source of entertainment, and having other people that you would continue to contact for the rest of your life to share these same experiences with was definitely valuable. But an instinct inside of me was changing with the coming of years. I, without consciously thinking about it, needed less and less to have company, a safety net for my life's experiences. As much as I wanted to count on people in this world, Maggie, my hometown friends and university friends, I was learning to count on myself, be just as happy without their company, as with. It didn't bother me so much that I was traveling Cuba alone or any place for that matter. I had even begun going to the movies alone back in Atlanta a couple of years back. When I wanted to do something, I was tired of waiting on my friends to find time or wait for Maggie to be in town. The hell with everyone else, I began to think. I'm not going to miss out on opportunities, because I don't want to be alone. The basic premise was becoming more and more ridiculous.

I first took a taxi to the El Floridita, the famous bar Ernest Hemingway, fifty years ago, frequented for his frozen daiquiris and mojitos. Not knowing it was such a posh bar, I lugged in my backpack to the stares of a clientele wanting to appear exclusive. I was discrediting their high society, I thought to myself as I walked in; I'm going to hold my head high, order the usual, whatever it is Hemingway drinks, and fight the stares. Anyways, I was used to this sort of environment back in Atlanta, going out for special Firm dinners. There everyone paced around stiffly, wine glass plastered to their chest like a permanent fixture. I still managed to have a little fun. Out of spite or bored rebellion, I would try my best to challenge their stiffness with dark, inappropriate humor. It was the only way for me to maintain any sanity. This place wasn't actually so bad, the more I thought of work events. A fancy band of violins and accordions was setting up in the corner, all in black tuxes. White tablecloths elegantly draped the small round tables in the dining area. I wasn't sure this bar had been this way during Hemingway's days. I always viewed him as the adventurer, the deep-sea fisherman, the bullfight aficionado. Of course, I was sure a writer shuttled between more than a few profiles. I pictured Ernest sitting across the shiny chrome bar, just the way I was in this very moment, in the back of his mind picking fun at the so called upper crust. I enjoyed a refreshing peach daiquiri and stepped back into the sun.

According to the map, if I walked down Obispo Street, I would be able to ask for private guest homes. I was not far down the street and already people were on me like leeches; they saw the backpack and immediately sensed a newcomer to the area. I was careful not to waste my time in fruitless conversations, and I waited until my instincts told me the person had some level of integrity. Later, I would find out how small La Habana Vieja district really was; I would find out that everyone knew someone that knew someone that knew something about someone. Word traveled at lightning speed.

A man in his late twenties seemed less desperate than the others. I could sense the honesty in his eyes, a steady look, like he had nothing to hide. He wanted kickbacks and tips, just like everyone else, but he seemed willing to lead me in the right direction without being too greedy. I followed him not far to Aguiar street, where he knocked a few times on someone's door. A man came out and said he didn't have any rooms available, but that he knew of someone else with rooms. I figured, great, now I will be going through two middlemen, not one. They were very secretive about this new option, and I was supposed to wait here, while they walked to confirm its availability. When the guy came back he told me to follow him, but that I needed to be quiet about the room, this guesthouse was unlicensed and the neighbors could blow the whistle if they found out. We walked over two blocks to Compostela Street. The guy didn't knock on the door at all, he led me directly inside. A lady in her mid-fifties stuck her head out to see if anyone was watching. I wondered why all the commotion—the neighbors would eventually see me. I had planned to be there at least a week. From the outside, only a massive building about three or four stories high could be seen filling the entire block. A few times, from the street, when a door had been carelessly left opened, I had been able to see directly through to the inside of these apartment blocks. Usually a long passage way, narrow and mysterious, seemed to penetrate deep into the old dusty buildings. I had felt each time like I was encroaching on people's privacy when I was able to look that far inward; kids were running around in open areas at the end of the hallways, and older Cubans were sitting, having private conversations. A whole microcosm of Havana life was playing out inside the dullness of the outer facades.

The guesthouse I had just entered didn't reach as far inward as the other portals, but I was still amazed at the inner complexity. Upon entering I was in the family room, then I walked through a narrow dining room, and walking even further placed me back outside again; the next door neighbor's home with all its windows open was the wall to this miniature courtyard. You could see everything that went on in the other apartment, like it was an extension of the family, a part of the same apartment. On the other side of this open space lay a kitchen with no doors. Stairways made of nothing more than shaky plywood rose before the kitchen on the right. I followed the lady upstairs to my room. But, before we walked up, she was careful to put her finger to her nose, signaling that I should be quiet. It was an odd arrangement. I felt like a fugitive running from the law, being harbored in a secret attic, careful not to break my cover. There were three rooms upstairs, two of them connected by a bathroom; these were for guests, and the family used a third room. I remembered passing a door to a fourth bedroom downstairs, next to the slender dining room.

Already, walking through the apartment, I had seen an older lady (maybe the grandmother), a little boy, a woman in her late twenties (maybe the mother of the boy), and the lady guiding me to my room who could easily be that woman's mother. I had counted four generations. Wow! Four generations living under one roof, and in a four-bedroom apartment at that. It was impressive. I wanted to put it all in a sitcom, somehow find perspective in the originality of the circumstance. So I brainstormed titles to my new sitcom. *One American meets over 80 years of Cuba.* No, I got it, even better, *The guest of four generations.*

The guest bedrooms upstairs were nice, complete with armoire and towels. The bathroom was useable, no complaints there. I went back downstairs, where the mother in her late twenties was preparing a meal. I thought, damn! I had forgotten to ask the price of the room. The lady said sternly fifteen dollars a night, twenty with two meals. That sounded reasonable enough to me, well within my budget. It was already too late to negotiate, considering I had put down my bags, and plus, what were all those hard working hours at the Firm for if I was going to worry about money while I was on vacation. I agreed to the two meals a day, and walked to the living room where the little boy was watching television. The family didn't seem so bad off, they even had a VCR. The little boy was watching music videos, none of which were Cuban. Beyonce came on and then Nelly. It wasn't MTV, and it occurred to me that the trade embargo had made it free for Cuban channels to pirate American videos, since doing business was outlawed—well, any business other than agriculture for cash. Rather than shunning our culture, Cubans seemed to be embracing anything American they could get their hands on.

A guy around the same age as the woman in her twenties, probably the boyfriend, entered the house and with him an adorable little baby girl. "Where did everyone sleep?" was the thought going through my mind. We all sat down for a nice chicken and rice dinner, and the whole time little kids were knocking on the door asking for these homemade versions of Popsicles. They had not one, but two little businesses going on. The little pop-ices were set in half-cut aluminum cans with broken wooden sticks. With one dip in a bucket of water, the aluminum can slid off nicely, the little kids handed over about fifteen cents each, and they walked away smiling. I was sure the pop-ice business was no more legal than the guesthouse business. Already, I was getting insight into Cuban capitalism at a grass roots level. These people had a desire to create a better life, a sustainable life for the family. Something strange was that the great grandmother and the grandmother appeared to be both single; the only man in the house was the father of the young boy and baby girl. I wondered what had happened to the older men. Still, they seemed to be doing just fine without them.

The family was rather quiet towards me, not really sure what to think of me at this point, not really big on welcoming a stranger in the house; it was just a money transaction, a room for a fee, nothing more. The little kids, though, were full of smiles and laughs. They still carried with them an innocence and naivety, not aware of their disadvantages, the everyday freedoms taken from them, or barriers to advancement, not aware of the problems humans create for themselves as they grow older. They weren't even born during the collapse of the Soviet Union. They were some of the fortunate ones, children benefiting from a double economy, the dollar and the peso.

The only man of the house was about my age. He was extremely reserved at first. I could sense him evaluating me, searching for any hidden agendas or bad intentions: was I a sincere guest, humble and understanding or was I going to use them, suck them dry of information, not reciprocate any knowledge or friendship? In the back of my mind, I wanted to absorb their daily routines, compare their efforts and progress to my ability, potential and successes thus far in life. I wanted to draw a better picture of human nature, see if—regardless of the circumstances one is dealt in life — there were commonalities, emotions felt at the same intensity among all human beings. Were levels of happiness or sadness really any different when all things weren't equal? Did the relatively poor feel love or hate, death or life any different than the rich? Were rich people happier in their marriages than the poor? Did poor people experience more boredom, because they didn't have an Xbox or Playstation or did they make up for it in ways? Were there enough other activities with equal excitement already out there, covered up in dust, hidden behind all the new exciting gadgets? Maybe I was never exposed to essential parts of life that may have been lost in the clutter of new age inventions. Who was mentally healthier, an American or a Cuban, a Brit or a Thai, Muslim or a Jew, a black person or an Asian? Were humans of all nationalities, ethnicities, and religions all just re-inventors of the wheel? Maybe Alberto, the man of the house, could lead me to these answers. I could tell just from the first hour, that he wasn't like the many hustlers flooding the Havana streets. He had strong principles and ethics. He was the type of person who treated others with respect, just as long as he received the same. The whole time at dinner, I watched and evaluated him just as he had evaluated me.

"What's there to do during the nights?" I tried to ask him. He understood my question and, not wasting any time or energy struggling to explain to someone who barely spoke Spanish, he threw on a t-shirt, opened the front door, and signaled for me to follow. It was now dark outside and the passing day cooled down to a refreshing temperature, perfect for a light shirt and shorts. I asked him what he did during the day. He explained that he was a professional dancer; he traveled with a dance company to many countries, like Canada and Mexico, to perform. I thought, "So, he leaves the country for work." Part of me wondered why he didn't defect. He also explained that now he was on a sort of vacation, because his dance company didn't begin practice for another few weeks and wouldn't leave the country again until summer time. I noticed a satisfaction and pleasure in his voice when he talked about his job; I was sure he was proud to be a dancer.

"What types of dancing do you do?" I asked. He mumbled a few words and I couldn't understand them. So, he stopped abruptly, in the middle of the street, stood directly up on his toes the way a ballet dancer would, spinning around two turns with his hands lifting gracefully to the sky. He was a ballet dancer. That was a little surprising.

Alberto maintained a hard, stoic expression most of the time, not what I had imagined from a ballet-dancing male. He didn't finish there; he began humming a salsa tune, and danced a *'one, two, three, four, five, six, seven, eight'* rhythm, right there in the middle of the street, while snapping his fingers and with not a bit of shame. He was smiling during this last performance, and I envied his confidence and the seeming fulfillment he got from it. He was a professional, not afraid to show the whole world his talents. I wondered what sort of response I would receive if I went around balancing liabilities and stockholder's equity to assets for random people in the streets. I would probably be pelted with large pieces of fruit.

We walked towards a few bars with live jazz bands, most of them playing "Buena Vista Social Club" songs. The small cafes were filled with people and music. He stopped near the front of the second bar, where a policeman was standing.

"This is my brother," he said.

It immediately occurred to me, "Maybe that's how they were able to run an illegal guesthouse and pop-ice business without problems." It made sense.

Nevertheless, Alberto stopped at the front of the bar and wouldn't go in. "I can't go in," he said.

I tried to ask, "Why not?" but he just kept saying he couldn't go in. I looked inside, and noticed the only Cubans were the bartenders and musicians; everyone else was a foreigner. It was strange knowing that Cubans weren't allowed to enjoy parts of their own country, and I remembered the Floridita being the same way, a bunch of snobby foreigners, maybe a couple of rich Cubans were scattered about. Still, the live horns I could hear inside grabbed me from the doorway of the bar. So, I said thanks to Alberto, shook his hand, waved goodbye, and went in for a mojito and live instruments.

The next few days Alberto and I walked all over the city. He had nothing to do during the day, when he wasn't helping take care of the kids, his mother and his mother's mother. And I sensed not too many foreigners of his age came around that were interested in him and his city, like I was. He had a lot of questions about America. He explained that his aunt was in Baltimore but couldn't come back to Cuba. He wanted to know what salaries people earned, what were the women like, and how did the people dance in America. He had heard that people drive big shiny trucks in America with huge rims that didn't stop spinning when the vehicle was parked. I told him that all of that was true. He lit up with excitement when we talked about the U.S., and he said that he one day wanted to move to my country. I asked him why he didn't defect when he was traveling as a dancer. He told me, "Cuba has no opportunities. But, I have a family here. I can't leave them." I told him that he would have no problems in America dancing the way he did. He grinned at my remark, seemed to grab comfort in those words, like for a brief moment his life's work made all the sense in the world.

He took me to the day markets, where they sold guanguay, dark wood statues with a sweet smell, and paintings. We walked through plazas and parks, and past national monuments, the capitol building, and the oldest cigar-making factory. Then he took me across the city to where his friend owned a dance studio built into a spacious colonial home, where large open windows circulated free flowing air. We walked up onto an old terrace, where the school held performances every Saturday night, and I fell in love with the view of Havana from so high up. The old grayish-white cement structures had a charm to them, when put together with a pristine blue skyline and ocean background. The outside was cheerfully sunny; kids were playing baseball across the street in an old cement basketball court, where the rims must have been yanked off years ago. The old man from downstairs came up to play Rhumba music for us and Alberto pushed me to learn a few steps of this dance with deep African roots. The old man watched in laughter as I tried stepping with my whole body to the music, but I was slowly picking it up. I watched Alberto as his left arm spanned outward like a flapping wing, while he stepped his right foot in the opposite direction. I envied their lifestyle in ways; these were people who, regardless of barriers, regardless of losses and struggle, continued to live passionately, full of vivacity. They didn't waste their life sitting and waiting for Fidel to smoke his last cigar or Communism to wither away. Time didn't stop for them; they were pushing forward with meaningful lives.

One night after dinner, Alberto and I walked through the Plaza de Armas at the end of the Malecon, where it passes a castle. A statue of Jesus can be seen looking down from a hill on the small island across from the tiny canal. The night was dark and transparent. The stars were sharply in focus like the planetariums I visited during school field trips as a kid. It seemed the perfect time to talk about everything that weighed down on my shoulders, and clouded my future. I told him about my job, and how it had so many benefits, like fancy dinners, trips to baseball games and concerts, and I was able to save enough money to start a mortgage on a condo downtown, a step towards one day achieving financial security. But something was wrong. I wasn't happy. I didn't feel myself at the job, and aside from finishing a hard day's work, I didn't feel like anything I had been doing was very fulfilling. Part of me felt guilty and selfish for talking about my problems to someone who didn't even have my choices in life, maybe he would kill to work as an accountant, to earn the kind of salary I was pulling in. He listened to me and tried to understand everything I was explaining to him; my Spanish had actually improved tremendously over the last few days, I started remembering many words and verbs that I hadn't used since my stay in Mexico. He listened carefully, made me repeat myself when he didn't understand, and then after all my worries were lifted off my shoulders for a brief moment and handed to him in the form of a puzzle, he just answered, "Why don't you search what makes you happy and do it? I'm doing what makes me happy." And, that was it.

During that night, I thought about all that Albert had told me, about how some of his family had made it out of Cuba, about how things had changed over the last two decades, how his family hardly had anything to eat after the Soviet Union collapsed. "We all lost weight during that period, I lost at least twenty pounds," he told me. He told me how he felt like a prisoner in his own country at times, that foreigners had more rights and advantages than him. If your skin is black and you are shabbily dressed, police ask you for your papers. He said regular Cubans weren't allowed in hotels unless they were workers; they weren't allowed in certain bars or certain beaches; they couldn't even get decent seats at National events, like the ballet. He told me his dream was to one-day sit front row at a National Ballet Performance: "Those seats are earmarked for foreigners, because us Cubans shouldn't have that kind of money earning our Socialist wage. If we have the money to pay for front row seats than we must have done something illegal." He told me that not only does the government restrict travel or movement to other countries, but even Cubans within their own borders are restricted. It's practically impossible to move into the city from surrounding areas. He told me there is this one joke that circulates

Havana: A Cuban child is asked,
"What do you want to be when you grow up, a doctor, pilot, lawyer, fireman?"
The child responds, "I want to be a foreigner."
That night I sat with my eyes open in my bed. I couldn't sleep. I did something that I hadn't done in years, something that only crossed my mind as a child. I began to pray. I prayed for Cuba and every citizen walking its land. I prayed that this beautiful Caribbean island would one day reach its great potential. I was saddened by the limitations and injustices felt by the people, something I thought no human being should have to live with. But deep down I was also optimistic about Cuba's future, especially after meeting Alberto. If there were more people like him, then I thought Cuba would be just fine. My mind was in one of those philosophical modes, where I thought too deeply, too poetically about things. It was all flowing out of me, so fluidly, everything I had read about Cuba, everything I was now witnessing firsthand:

> *Perhaps the tropical fortune inherited by this island forces its people into its rhythm, to flourish in its way, to reject ideologies thrust upon it, regardless of the benefits and costs. It was as impossible for the Spaniards to maintain a hold on this great island, as it had been for the U.S. to exploit its many resources and now a communist structure to shut off its natural borders. The place demands its freedom through every whiff of warm coastal air, every introspective view of never-ending ocean and taste of abundant rich earth. Perhaps there are places, environments, or destined circumstances on planet earth where life will continue to move and grow, regardless of the obstacles, just like organic vines tracing the man-made neighborhood walls of South England or tree roots piercing the endless stone ruins of Angkor Wat. If so, Cuba will forever be one of these places.*

I was living without many of these same obstacles to freedom. How could I make the best out of my life? Before finally dozing off to sleep I repeated to myself over and over, "You only live once, find your passion and live it!"

When the morning came, I realized I needed to find an internet café, and fast. What if Maggie had contacted me and was waiting on a reply, a confirmation? It was just a few more days until New Year's Eve, and I was anxious to know if she would actually make it. Would we be together again like last New Year's in London? Meeting her in other parts of the world was really the highlight of the last three years; it was always a flurry of passionate fun, and time usually whizzed right by us. We always talked about how we were hurrying to a quick death the more time we spent together.

But if she came (those words melted a sweet flavor in my mouth), what things would I need to prepare for? We weren't together for Christmas, so I would need to buy her a Christmas gift. And, it couldn't be just any gift; she was not an easy person to please, it needed to be something unique, with a lot of thought put into it, something from the heart. Damn it! It didn't occur to me. Where will we stay? I never even thought to ask Alberto and his family if they would mind her staying with me. Could they be strong religious types, maybe they would have a problem with us staying together, sleeping in the same bed, out of wedlock? I did see a crucifixion sealed behind a glass picture frame, hanging on the living room wall, right above the television. It was impossible to miss; no other decorations were hanging. "She is going to love it here!" I thought. "I know it! Warm coastal cities, moonlit bays and deep soulful music, those are her tastes, our tastes. I can take her for a late evening walk down Avenida del Puerto and the Malecon. We can have a nice Cuban dinner at the famous La Bodeguita on New Year's Eve, and I can reserve a table for the big New Year's bash in Plaza de la Catedral. We can smoke Cohibas and drink Cuban Ron, while they count down the New Year. All types of images were running through my head of how it would be, how it should be, if she were to make it to Havana for year-end. I knew I shouldn't hope and plan so much, not when I didn't know her situation. I was setting myself up for a long drop; all the subconscious expectations were sure to come crashing violently to the floor. But it was hard for me to see it any other way.

I ate breakfast with the family and walked a few blocks over to an internet café, crowded with foreigners. I paid money for a paper receipt with a code and special password, but the line was long, and I was stuck behind at least six other people. The hardest thing to do was have patience in a time like this; I wanted to know the verdict now, in this second. And the couple in front of me didn't help at all, the way they held each other, the smile in their gazes to each other, the way they blocked out the rest of the world; only their love mattered. All of this brought back memories of Maggie, because before her, I didn't understand "the look," that cheesy display of affection. It had been a long time since I'd felt that sensation and held true love in my arms. Finally, it was my turn in line. I typed in the password carefully. The computer was surprisingly fast, not what I had experienced back in the hotel the first day. My home page popped up and there was Maggie's name and Seb and Leo and Josh. Everyone had tried to contact me over the last few days. This time I clicked right into Maggie's email. I felt a silent yell leap out of me! She's coming! Ha haaa! She wrote: "Hey baby! I'm coming! Can you believe it! I don't have to work on New Year's anymore. My flight arrives in Havana New Year's eve early in the afternoon. Please send me an email confirming that you are still in Cuba and will be at the airport on time! Love you." Wow! She's coming! My baby's coming! I wanted to jump for joy. Then I read the guys' emails; they were all going to be back in Havana for New Year's Eve to celebrate. I didn't hear from Roman, he had probably fallen in love back in Playas del Este. New Year's was going to be a time I would never forget. I was so excited.

 The entire week I had heard that a big extravaganza would be thrown in Plaza de la Catedral to celebrate the coming of the New Year. There were supposed to be elegant white tablecloths set up over the bumpy cobblestones, a stage set up in front of the beautiful Cathedral for live entertainment, and even fireworks were to go off. I walked over to the plaza to buy tickets, one for Maggie, Alberto, and me. I thought it was the least I could do for Alberto, and I knew he wouldn't go to one of these on his own, with hardly any money. When I got to the plaza, the guy selling the tickets told me that the cheapest ticket was around fifty dollars. I was shocked. I only had a hundred dollars to spend on the tickets at tops, so I couldn't take Alberto. I walked back to the apartment with my good news about Maggie.

 "What do you normally do for New Years Eve?" I asked Alberto.

 "We have a big dinner of lobster, food we don't normally have the money to eat. Also, we open our windows and play music out into the streets, our neighbors and others passing by stop and dance, people are sharing alcohol; everyone is in better spirits, nicer than normal, people who don't speak, stop and have a short conversation. It's a joyous occasion. You're welcome to eat with us, you and Maggie," he said.

"Thanks. Can I help pay for the food?" I asked. It was the least I could do.

The next two days were spent anticipating New Year's. I asked the family a million questions, and I thought they could even be getting sick of me. I'm sure other foreign guests from the past hadn't latched on to them they way I had. I was becoming like part of the family: playing tops with the little boy, feeding the little girl from time to time, and Alberto and I were watching television a lot, much of it from the U.S. He loved the hip-hop and R&B music videos with all the beautiful women wearing hardly any clothes and dancing around. One channel played speeches of Fidel Castro almost all day. Alberto didn't waste anytime switching right past this channel.

I gave my address to the guys, so that they could find a "casa particular" close by when they arrived. The guys were returning the night before New Year's Eve. And I was sure they had their stories to tell.

A knock came on our door while most of the family was watching television and I was looking at school books with the little boy, who was excited he would be returning to school the next week. I could hear a loud booming voice and a little bit of snickering. When the grandmother of the little children opened the door, she probably thought it was another neighborhood kid asking for pop-ices, but Seb and Roman smiled into the apartment house.

"Is Chris here?" Seb asked? Roman was a step behind them, still seeming as timid as the first day.

"Those are my friends," I said to the grandmother.

"What's up guys? Come in. Where are your bags and things?" I asked.

"We found a 'casa' next door to you. When we were asking for the directions to this street, someone said they knew a place we could rent for a couple days nearby. It happened to be next door!" Seb said.

"Cool," I said.

"Dude we have so much to tell you! This one right here almost got himself married!" He pointed to Roman. "I practically had to fight him to leave. And the women in Varadero . . . unbelievable! You guys missed out. They were on me from the minute I got there. And, the Italians! Dog! We have to visit Italy one day. Do you know a good place to eat? I'm starving!" Seb continued.

"There are a few pizza joints a couple streets over," I suggested.

"Are you crazy? We've been eating pizza everyday. My stomach is out of balance from a diet of only cheese and bread. And Roman has gone on a hunger strike, because his money is running out. He only eats bread and drinks vodka and orange juice. Is there a place I can get a home cooked meal around here?" Seb asked.

"If you wait and chip in some money, I can ask the family if you can eat with us," I suggested.

"Yeah . . . I can wait. I'm dying for some real food," he said.

I turned to Roman, who looked sick. I asked, "How is it going?" He just nodded his head to say okay.

A few hours later Leo came knocking at the door. I knew it was him, because no one else beats down a door when they are seeing who is home. Leo was always very aggressive; he had an unrelenting energy and didn't have patience for waiting. He approached every step of his life, from finding jobs to seeking women to even smaller quests like ordering food at a restaurant, as if he was attacking a military target. This trait had served him well, made him successful early on in life. The negative effect at times, though, is to intimidate people he meets or piss them off, because some people don't want to be rushed. Two more heavy knocks hit again. I got up this time and walked behind Alberto, who was a little nervous.

"Don't worry. It's my friend Leo I was telling you about," I said. He still opened the door hesitantly.

"Hey! What's up!" Leo shouted. He still had his camping bag spraddled over his back.

"Do they know of a 'casa' around here with any rooms available? I need to drop this bag and take a shower. Tell him I'll take anything," Leo said. Sweat was dripping down his forehead and neck.

That night I heard everything, all the stories about the women they met, about the food they ate, where they slept, the crazy people they ran into, the guy who tried to pick pocket Leo and who, Leo said, "would think twice before trying it again with anyone else." I talked about Maggie coming, and they were happy for me, knowing that I would see her soon, and they hadn't seen her in over two years. Everyone wondered where Josh could be.

"Have you seen or heard from Josh?"

"No, I haven't, have you?"

"Well, he received the email with your address and to meet up for New Year's Eve. Didn't he?"

"Yeah, I sent him everything," I said. We all went back to the guesthouses and crashed early that night. We would need our energy the next day.

It was finally here, New Year's Eve. It was amazing how the year had flown by, days turning into nights, nights into days. Equally amazing was how fast time flew by and with it my vacation; in a couple more days I would be back slaving over white paper in a tiny box the size of one of those instant photo booths at the mall. But I wasn't going to worry about that too much. Maggie would fly back with me. At least I would have her around to wish me goodnight and make it so I would be late to work each day—and brain dead, unable to function from a lack of sleep. But I was young. I could handle it. When I become tired or exhausted, when the day is still not over and I have more to do, I always think of Seb's saying, "You have time to sleep when you die," and it usually brings me back to life. But enough of that, work was the last thing I wanted to be thinking about at a time like this. I forced those thoughts out of my head and walked downstairs for breakfast.

Dry rock-hard bread, dry lettuce and eggs. Good enough for me. Nothing could kill my good mood on a day like this; I would be picking up Maggie, the love of my life, at the airport in just a few hours and celebrating the New Year's with my buddies. The next few hours went by slowly. I had already bought Maggie a gift for Christmas, and I only needed to find a place that sold flowers, so that I could greet her the way I always did at the airport. I found a flower shop in Havana, near the expensive hotels. I settled for a bouquet of daisies, the closest to her favorite being big yellow sunflowers. I waved down a taxi and was on my way to the airport. It was shocking the difference in cab prices from when I rode across the city once with Alberto and shut my mouth the entire way as he told me; for about eight minutes I had been Cuban in the eyes of that Cab driver. Now I was a full on tourist riding through the city outskirts to pickup Maggie.

I was at least ten minutes early when I made it to the small airport. The place is small in comparison to Hartsfield Airport in Atlanta, and it didn't take me long to find where I would be meeting Maggie. So I waited ten minutes, then twenty minutes, then thirty. I walked to the Cubana Airline counter and asked about flight 456, when would it be arriving. The lady, looking like she had worked the night shift, told me that it would be late, at least forty more minutes I had to wait. An hour later a mass of people started bursting through the doors, but no Maggie. I waited and a few more people slowly filed out of the doors, being greeted by family members and friends. One guy must have been away a long time from Cuba, because after a woman, must have been his girlfriend or wife, met him with a warm hug, they didn't stop kissing for at least two minutes and their bodies never parted as they held one another walking out into the Havana sun. I was sure that is how Maggie and I would meet if she walked through those doors, but she wasn't walking through those doors. No one was anymore.

    I walked back to the counter, and got the attention of the lady, who seemed annoyed that I was returning to ask more questions. "Excuse me again. Was a Maggie... on that flight?" I asked, frustrated and in no mood for bad service.

    "I'm sorry sir. I can't tell you who was on the flight. It's against our procedures," she said.

    "I need to know if my girlfriend was on that flight. Has everyone left the customs area and baggage claim?" I was almost furious at this point and the attendant could see my fury, much more intense than her attitude.

    "I can have someone check for you. Just wait a moment." She got on the phone to somebody, waited about a minute; someone came back on the line and told her everyone had cleared both areas. "Sorry sir, no one else is back there," she said.

    I stood with my bouquet of flowers almost devastated. How could she do this to me? I had seen her miss flights in the past, so it could have been a missed flight. But, how could she miss this flight of all flights? My face was red, all blood from the other parts of my body was beating, all trying to find a space near my head. I felt my temples throbbing. I tried to cool down. I sat down on a small bench in the waiting area and put my head in my hands, tried to breathe deep breaths. I walked slowly out of the airport, empty and failed. I didn't want to wait another day, another hour. I was tired of being let down, over and over. For some reason this time was different. I wasn't in the right state to be making any concrete realizations, but I didn't know if I could forgive her this time, if I could keep going down this path of uncertainty. Whether she missed her plane by accident or intentionally, for whatever reason, I knew that it would happen again. I gave the flowers to an old lady and her grandson walking outside and jumped in a taxi back to the historic district.

"Cheer up dude." Seb was talking to me. It was hard to pay attention. My mind was flying back and forth from dreamland to reality. "Dude, forget about her. We're going to have a blast tonight. It's almost the New Year and we're in the middle of Havana. Snap out of this shit," he continued.

"I hear you," I said quietly, like I had been drained of life.

"We are going to get so fucked up tonight, you're not going to give a shit about anyone. Believe me dude," Seb said.

"Yeah, I know," I responded unconvincingly.

"Leave him alone dude. We'll put life back into him tonight," Leo chimed in. Alberto walked into the living room.

"Where is Maggie?" he asked.

"She didn't make it," I said, disappointed, feeling like somewhat of a fool.

"No?!" he questioned, surprised.

"You want to go to the New Year's Bash in Plaza de la Catedral this evening?" I asked. Now I had one ticket left over.

"I don't know. Didn't you say it was fifty dollars?" he asked.

"Don't worry about it. I bought two tickets," I said.

Leo jumped in, "Come on, you have to come, we're going to have a blast."

"Ok. I'll come," he said. The fact that Alberto was coming cheered me up a little.

We started drinking early that night. During dinner we were taking shots of Vodka that Roman had bought earlier in the day; the label on the bottle read Vodka from Poland and that was it. Roman had a special system for taking shots. He clenched one glass of straight Vodka halfway-filled in one hand, and another glass of orange juice half-way filled in the other hand. When he gulped the shot of Vodka, which was more like three bar-sized shots, he held his breath and soon after threw down the orange juice. He also had a theory on drinking that when a person drinks, the alcohol kills that person's weak brain cells, and the ones that survive are stronger, more dominant cells, allowing the person to think clearer. In my book, the guy wasn't past the first step to curing his problem, the denial stage. I wasn't sure that his scientific theory really wasn't a clever form of rationalization. Anyways, I felt better after each shot that went down. The dinner was fabulous and

I gave all the mothers in the house, and the children, great big hugs before leaving to the party. I was ready to bring the New Year in.

We made it to the plaza and found a nice table, in the center, not too far from the stage. As more people filed into the square, I began to notice, even considering that Cuba was itself more than seventy-percent black, Alberto, one-half of me, and one-half of Leo, were the only people of African descent among the celebrators. The only people that had any melatonin in their skin, other than us, were the waiters. The performances began and the only color of people on stage dancing and singing was black. I felt uneasy and uncomfortable with this reality.

The amount of alcohol on our table was ridiculous. We had a full bottle of dark aged Havana Club and two big bottles of champagne, and it occurred to me seeing all that alcohol on the table that I forgot to buy a nice Cohiba. The ones made in Cuba were hard to get in the U.S.

"No worries. We got you a cigar today, when you were away at the airport," Seb said. He pulled out a big fat Cohiba Robusto. My first instincts were to smell it. I wasn't a smoker, but I had told myself starting in Cuba, I would smoke a nice cigar for New Year's Eve as a tradition going forward, and where else to start than in Havana. Our table was filled with little partying gifts. Everyone had a mask, sort of like what the Lone Ranger wore and a fire sparkling stick which I hadn't seen since the Fourth of July years ago, when my uncle Big David and cousin Little David drove all the way across the Georgia-Tennessee border line to purchase fire crackers, because they were illegal in Georgia. We also each had the standard decorated birthday whistle to blow when the clock hit 12 midnight. We were prepared, and already the guys were talking to these cute Italian girls sitting at the table in front of us. The mom of one of them was there, and she was absolutely drunk, and we had at least an hour before 12 a.m. The square itself was of romance novels. The cobbled stones and balconies protruding from every building facing its squares gave it a medieval Gothic appearance, clearly, the influence of Colonial Spain. The light from the bell towers left a sort of eerie glow over the plaza and seeped out into the night sky, camouflaging itself among the guiding light of the stars and the moon's reflection. I felt regal sitting amongst the white cloth tables and the old fortress stones.

"It's been an exhausting year, guys. You ready to bring the New Year in right?!" Leo was talking drunk. That smile hadn't left his face since dinner. Roman was even talking up a storm, but in Russian and only to Seb.

"What is your New Year's resolution?" Leo asked everyone. "Alberto, you first."

I translated for him: "I want to move into an apartment for me, my wife and my kids."

Seb answered next, "I'm going to find a way to make more time for myself. I can't continue to give my whole life to this job."

Leo answered next, "I'm going to try and pick up a new hobby, like salsa. I'm tired of working and going to the gym, working and going to the gym. There has to be more to life." Then he said, "Roman, I'll answer your New Year's resolution for you. Stop drinking." Everyone laughed. And then Leo turned to me. The whole table stopped quiet for a "spot of time."

"What about you Chris? What is your New Year's Resolution?" Leo asked.

I paused for a few seconds, then answered, "I'm going to find what makes me happy in life." That thought filled my entire body, expanded my heart and soul, made me confident I had something to live for, something bigger than my current job and relationship. I had made a mission for myself. This year go and seek out myself, don't stop until I'm sure of following the right path, regardless of how many stones and horse carriages slow my pace, regardless of the fog limiting my visibility. I would shine a bright light through all that stood in my way. Twelve o'clock was approaching fast – 10, 9, 8, 7…3, 2, 1, HAPPY NEW YEAR!!! HAPPY NEW YEAR EVERYBODY!!!

BACK TO CORPORATE

Everybody's Gotta Learn Sometimes.
  -Beck

    As much as I dreaded my return to work, I was back. A month had gone by and the abuse I had known now for two years continued to be the easier option, the only real option I knew. This time my mental and physical health was probably at the worst it had been, ever. As much as I had disliked going to work before, and even with all the pains and emptiness that occurred during a passionate, long distance relationship, at least I had had the ease of knowing my relationship with Maggie was surviving, we were making it work, regardless of the distance complication. In the past, we were seeing each other at least every month, and we reciprocated a strong love over the phone lines and internet during our times apart. Now, ever since Cuba, uncertainty and an ever growing bitterness had crept into the relationship, and now, more than ever, I was experiencing headaches, strong piercing pains, that had the power of disabling my efforts at work. It was hard for me to sleep at night. I was taking sleeping pills in order to get at least a few hours of sleep, and sometimes the pills were so heavy that I couldn't wake up on time, making me late for work and increasing my stress levels even more. I had never known stress like this before. I felt like I was losing the only true love I had ever known, and all the realities of my relationship with Maggie, all the logical, clear signs that I couldn't fight the inevitable, were flying right by my consciousness. All I knew was I wanted to work this out. I had gone so long making sacrifices, compromises to my life in order to make it work out. What was I going to do if I lost Maggie? What were all the sacrifices worth, all the moments when we shared our life together? What was it all for? I would have to wait another lifetime to find a love as pure.
    Right after the Cuba trip, the first time I answered her call, I prepared myself to be calm, not lose myself in passion, in emotions. But her nonchalance and careless comments about what, I don't remember, infuriated me, and I lashed out at her through the phone lines. She had been put on the defensive. Her excuse for leaving me standing there at the airport for hours was she had been called by her modeling agent at the last minute to come to work that day for a new client, to

work a job that she didn't know much about, a job that didn't pay her much and benefited her with no real exposure or contacts. She even admitted to it without taking the blame, sliding the blame right to her agent, the same way people at my job did, sending me from department to department. I don't think she ever took responsibility for anything. "It was a stupid job. I need to find another agency, they're really fucking up!" she said simply as if she had no control over her work life. My suspicious mind wondered if it really was her job, the reason she didn't make the plane. That first argument was the beginning of a snowball that picked up more and more snow, continued to grow faster and colder, rolling out of control every time we spoke. A battle had emerged and the more we argued, the nastier and more disrespectful the arguments became. We were behaving like children, and both of us were too proud to give in. There was an element of insanity within it all. The more we argued, the more I wanted to get back on the phone with her and argue again, and the worse my days were becoming. My mood changed dramatically after each conversation and my red, fiery face showed it at work. Things weren't getting better, and my job wasn't getting any easier. Stress was coming from two directions; as soon as I got up from a beating at my job, my relationship was there to slam me right back on the floor.

It was now the middle of March and I held my head low at the same cubicle, the same solitary confinement that I had learned to call my home. Not long before I had had one of those conversations with Maggie over the cell phone, the same conversation that usually ended when one of us hung up in a violent huff. Ironically, I had become accustomed to feeling this way, depressed and enraged all in the same flurry, and continued working, using the little part left of my brain, not occupied by these debilitating emotions. My work phone was ringing. I thought to myself, it was probably Kumiko hammering me with another deadline or someone from the client finally responding to one of my voice mails. I looked at the caller ID. Someone was calling from the outside. It was Leo calling from San Francisco. What did he want? When I picked up the phone he sounded cheerful, so much that I thought I was talking to a different person for a moment, a slave freed from the corporate struggle.

"You're not going to believe what happened!" he said. His attitude and joy was that of someone who won the lottery or landed a job as the "Apprentice" beside Donald Trump. Or, knowing Leo, maybe he hooked up with a famous Brazilian model and was calling to brag about his recent success. He again asked me, "Guess what? You are not going to believe what happened to me?" I was already tired of the guessing game. Didn't he know it was 10 o'clock? I was four hours ahead of him and still fast at work. I had two overdue assignments floating in the pile of mess that was my cubicle, and I needed to leave before 12 tonight; I needed sleep.

"I have work to turn into my manager in the next hour. What? What? Tell me already for Gods' sake!" I said in an irritated voice.

"Okay. Okay. I've been laid off from work!" he said. There was a pause for a moment; his words continued to hang in the air like a paper plane over the airspace of my cubicle.

"But, why are you so happy? What happened?" I asked with even less patience.

"Ever since Cuba, people in my office have acted differently towards me. They weren't happy with me taking two weeks off during the holidays, one of the busiest times of the year." I could hear a deep sucking of air come through the receiver; in the excitement of explaining the story, he had forgotten to take a breath.

"Go on," I said.

"Apparently, all the managers gathered in the conference room and decided my fate before I came back from Cuba. But they wanted me to finish up my projects, and it took HR a while to complete all legal procedures and put my dismissal letter together. I knew something was wrong when I got back from Cuba, because the managers were all avoiding contact with me. They couldn't look me in the eyes. Those fucking cowards! Hahahahah!"

I was confused to say the least. He had just been fired from one of the top financial firms in the country. It was a job he had worked long and hard to secure, slaving through two long years in the finance programs at one of the most prestigious business schools in the world, NYU Stern, and now he had basically been fired and was overjoyed about it.

"Why in the world are you in such high spirits? You were just fired!" I asked in an excited, confused voice like I was asking a smiling serial killer why did he do it.

"You don't get it! I was hoping to get laid off! I'm free! I'm free from this corporate bullshit! I'm a free man! And the best part is, I can collect unemployment checks now!"

My focus and attention at work completely dropped. I had deadlines to worry and stress over and didn't want to feel Kumiko's wrath once again for missing them. But I didn't care.

"I'll call you in a second from my cell phone," I told Leo. I sat immobile for at least a few breaths; all kinds of thoughts were moving upwards like a tornado in my head, and as soon as one thought landed it was picked up again and twirled around. Leo was the first to break loose. I hadn't seen it coming, either; I envisioned Seb before anyone, he was more the rebel to me, the black sheep of the group. But with Leo, I was always learning something new and different; he was always reinventing himself, even from the first day we met. I saw him as a prep, a pretty boy only concerned with impressing the next official rung to his ladder; all the other sides, the adventurer, the womanizer, the hustler, exposed themselves later. It could very well be that I was a witness to those new sides blossoming, an accomplice even. I quietly rose from the clutter of paper and binders. I walked quickly past my manager's office, hoping she wouldn't have the time to stop me and ask if I'd finished the memo yet. Damn it! I thought. She had her door wide open.

"Chris!" A sharp harpoon voice caught me in the spine, reeling me back in.

"Yes Kumiko?" I said in a mocking voice. "Did you need me?" I said mechanically. I was already moving my lips silently to her next sentence, the way a ventriloquist would.

"Have you finished the memo? I do want to go home sometime tonight."

"I'm still working on it. It will be finished tonight," I responded, this time having entered her doorway with daggers shooting out of my eyes. She backed off a little. "I'm going to the bathroom now. Is that okay with you?" I finished.

"Okay, but . . . "

She was in the middle of her sentence when I walked out. Now was not the time to play her power game. I hurried to the stairs of the fire escape, where I always went to find peace and sometimes, not always, tend to personal matters. I knew the cubicle gossipers would have this conversation broadcasting live all over the office if I continued it there—anything to help their day go by faster or to bolster their ranking. Also, I knew the only time people ventured into the fire escape was when building management set off the fire alarms as a quarterly evacuation procedure. Although the building was on a hill, elevating its height and expanding its view to Downtown, we were, in actuality, only on the 4th floor. Still, my coworkers were too lazy to take the stairs. Their only exercise was a short walk to the elevators, to the parking lot, and from their home parking garage to their sofa. Sometimes I used the fire escape for quick lunches, a break from the monotony of three gray cubicle walls. This time I needed some privacy to phone Leo.

"Heyy-lo!" He was even more chipper.

"Tell me more! How are you getting unemployment?" I asked immediately.

"It's easy," he said, still taking his precious time as if he was on vacation.

"How then? How do you do it?" I demanded answers.

"All you need to do is show an official letter that you've been fired by your company. Send that to your local Department of Labor and they start sending you a check every week," he said. "It's that simple."

"You serious? That's . . . that's incredible!" I said, still in a state of shock, the good kind, like when something finally goes your way.

"But, the only thing is there is a catch," he said, cutting short my celebration. "You can't resign or do something defiant to get fired. You have to let them fire you on their own free will. You have to appear as if you're not fit for the job. They can't report that you didn't show up for work or you threatened one of your supervisors. You have to get yourself fired without them knowing you want to get fired," he said as if he, himself, worked in the unemployment office.

"Well, how much do they pay a week and for how long?" I asked.

"It's around five hundred dollars a week before taxes in San Fran. And, that's for six months," he answered.

"Are you serious?!" I thought to myself, that's two thousand dollars a month! Two thousand a month! That could free me up to do a lot of things. "You gotta be kidding me!" I said, wondering if he could be pulling a prank. But Leo wouldn't play around with something like this.

"No! Now you understand why I'm so happy! I can travel the world with this type of budget and not lose a step financially," he continued.

"We gotta tell Seb about this!" I said.

"I already did. I guarantee he's plotting a getaway plan as we speak. You gotta get fired too!" he said. It was strange hearing those words fly from his mouth, from anyone's mouth for that matter. "But remember, you can't make it obvious. They must think that you are one incompetent bastard!" he said, while chuckling under his breath. "I don't think that should be hard for you."

"Yeah, very funny," I said. "Listen I gotta go. I must begin my incompetence."

"Okay dude. Remember what I said," Leo said.

"Oh yeah, Leo, one more thing. What are you going to do with your free time now, now that you aren't working?" I asked knowing he had a plan.

"Remember that girl from Canada, we met at that 'paladare' in Old Habana?"

"Yeah, the one we said could have been a Brazilian model, who was with her mother?"

"Exactly!"

"But, you never got her number. Did you?"

"No, I didn't, but she remembered my name and the school I went to and somehow tracked me down. I bought a plane ticket to go see her. The plane leaves tonight."

"Damn! Small world," I said.

"Listen shoot me an email when you're out."

"All right, good luck on your trip."

"You will need the luck more than I do."

I hung up the phone, sat down on the stairs and looked out towards the city. I couldn't believe it. Maybe my prayers had been answered. I was more than ready to leave behind this misery of a life and get back out there to travel. But before, I didn't know how I could leave. I had learned so much during my travel to Cuba, and I was anxious to learn more. A yearning still burned inside of me to explore head-on what continued to play a mystery in my mind. Cuba had taught me many things, but the most important thing it taught me was freedom. I didn't need to work so many hours and days at a job that was so unfulfilling. I didn't live in a country that told me where to live, where to work, what I could eat and clothe myself with, and when, if ever, I could travel outside of its borders. Throughout most of my life, I was taught to earn a safe salary that would eventually allow me to retire in my fifties, so that I could then finally live life. But, that was absurd! Life was going on now. How was I guaranteed until my fifties? The reality was that no one was forcing me to work as an accountant. I was imprisoning myself. I had chosen to continue down a dead end road. I lifted myself out of the stairways and walked back to my cubicle. It was fast approaching 11 at night and still, a substantial part of the memo was missing. "How incompetent of me!" I said to myself.

The next morning I awoke feeling fresher and lighter. Less weight dragged my head and neck towards the frame of my shoulders, and not because of all the weight I had lost from stressing, not eating right. This time I didn't need to rely on the second and third alarms to go off; I was up and ready. Something animated my soul; it didn't want to waste another minute sleeping. It had to be alert, because something was out there for me waiting. I just needed to follow the signs. In the past, it was the dream world that needed its attention. I called the emergence of my mind from this world, the matrix. With everything that had been going on, I often wished that I never woke up into the matrix, but rather stayed in my coma, or even worse, because I didn't have the option of swallowing the blue pill over the red. After falling asleep on the couch one night in the middle of watching the *Matrix*, the only DVD in my apartment, I remembered waking up some mornings, finally escaping my condo to horrendous traffic, the whole time thinking that I was still living in the dream world. The helicopters hovering above traffic and buildings, the omnipresent eyes and ears of the city, were like scientists conducting lab research; all of us consumers, faithful workers, were its lab rats running the same circles. But today felt different; there was purpose in my every movement. I wanted to see the look on my manager's face as I for once did as I pleased, not flinching at her mountain of petty requests, not being sorry for turning in mistakes, those things humans are liable to make from time to time. Only, I would ensure that a mountain of mistakes would be made in the next few weeks. I needed to secure a ticket out of this joint.

As I sat in rush hour traffic this time, I observed the exhausted, agitated souls with a different perspective. I was like the guy in jail, who would be set free in only a week's time. The taste of freedom felt real to me. I had even found my old Bob Marley album hidden in the glove compartment behind the clutter of open letters, car manuals, and other sundries. I inserted it into the dash and chanted its lyrics live in concert, early in the morning for all those with their car windows down to enjoy:

> *Won't you help to sing,*
> *These songs of freedom*
> *Cause all I ever heard,*
> *Redemption songs*
> *Redemption songs.*

    For some reason when I entered the office building, this time, I felt compelled to dap up the receptionist before riding the elevators to the fourth floor, and I sparked up a conversation with people in the elevator like I was back in my hometown, the same friendly way the second floor workers from the marketing department always acted in the elevator to my usual cold stare; it felt good acting like those other humans. I burst out of the elevators and walked past the secretary towards my section of cubicles.
    "Good morning everyone!" I proclaimed, not knowing where all this positive energy was actually coming from, what had come over me. I scolded myself. Here was not the place. I had to shut this happiness off from my exterior; I was going to arouse suspicion among the others.
    "What's got into you? You sound unusually cheerful this morning," Todd said.
    "Well . . . nothing, I had a good night's sleep. That's all." I forced myself to shut-up and sit down. Todd flashed a skeptical look, but continued smashing into his keys with those fat heavy fingers, the way he always did.
    Uh-oh here it begins. I could hear the clacking heels of Kumikos's awkward walk approaching in the direction of my cubicle.
    "Good morning. Do you have what I asked you to finish last night?" She never wasted small talk on me, and I was thankful.
    "Yes I do," I said smiling. She looked at the binder a few seconds, flipping through pages in the front, then jumping to the back; her face the whole time was becoming bright red the way my Japanese friend Yosuke's did after only two beers, splotched with red marks. I waited for her to explode.
    "What the hell is this!" Kumiko exclaimed. "I told you to document the Cedar Rapids billing system, not the Charlotte Fixed Assets

System. And Ralph is waiting on this one before he can turn in the full report. Would you like to be the one to explain this to him?" She held onto the binder, and stormed off; I think I heard one of her heels break as she turned the corner.

Later in the day, I walked over to Tlou's cubicle. We hadn't spoken in over three days, and all day I had been in an unusual talkative mood. We talked about his family back in South Africa; he loved talking about the fact that his parents would soon have a house of their own with a three-car garage. He had prepared everything for them: he bought a large plot of land, he bought the blue prints for an architectural plan, he hired construction workers, and his brother was watching over the project, while he was gone away to America. For him, all the hard work and miserable hours were all worth the pain. He was helping his parents reach a living unheard of for many blacks back in his country.

Over the last two years he had opened his heart and soul to me, held back no secrets or any realities to this business. He told it to me the way it really was, the ins and outs to this game, no sugar coating. He was a veteran in this business, but unlike many other veterans, the ones that got greedier and greedier, it didn't change his heart. He was pure and nothing could ever change this. I wanted, in return, with all my heart to tell him what was really going on with me at this point; but I couldn't. He would find out first, but only after I was clear away from the firm, six months of paychecks cashed and reserved for my adventures abroad. I knew that even he could leak my schemes to someone who could eventually push it upwards in the hierarchy, blowing my entire exit strategy. As far as I was concerned I couldn't trust anyone for as long as it took. I would be walking a tight rope everyday that I was still on the firm's payroll. Tlou could sense something was different about me, something had changed, because my attitude and energy wasn't usually so optimistic and energetic. The weight of my thoughts usually kept me slumped and dragging, the same way most of my colleagues existed.

"You wake up on the right side of the bed this morning!? Something is different about you. What is it? What do you know that I don't know? Please, I want to lift up my spirits, too!" Tlou was smiling the entire time he was interrogating me, a sincere smile of, not only curiosity, but happiness for me. In some strange way, I think he knew what was happening to me, the way I was distancing myself from the lifelessness existing within the cloud that covered my job and coworkers. All the while, he knew that I wasn't cut in the same geometrical shape as most of my colleagues, and that I wouldn't last too long here. And not because I couldn't last, didn't have the ability or work ethic; university and two years of survival here had dispelled those theories. It was because my time in this world was better spent in other arenas. If only happiness and passion could be thrown in the mix of all that encompassed my efforts and potential in this world, then something great was bound to happen, the synergy of environment and purpose could then soar. I had learned a tremendous amount working, but I wasn't one of the ones who would stay and continue to make accounting my life, and Tlou accepted this reality. In some ways, whether he was fully aware of it, or not, he had been an agent for change in my life.

"I had a good night's rest, that's all," I answered Tlou.

The next week I completed only half of the work I normally finished, and Kumiko had left steaming off from my cubicle at least once a day. But still nothing. Nothing in the way of a special meeting, no calls from HR, or any higher ups calling for me to stop by their office. I was beginning to wonder what does one have to do in order to get fired around here? My theory that as long as I was filling out my time and expense report every two weeks with large blocks of worked hours and they continued getting paid by the client for exorbitant amounts of hours, then everything was fine and dandy, seemed to be ringing true. I needed another tactic. So, at the end of the two-week pay period, I filled out my time sheet with just enough hours so that I was barely over the standard forty hours a week, guaranteeing I received normal pay for those weeks. But, I didn't fill out the normal sixty to seventy hours a week. My firm didn't pay overtime, and wasn't required by law, since I was on salary. The next day I received a call from one of the partners. This was big. He called me into his office and told me to bring a copy of my last time sheet. I knew it.

He shook my hand first, then said, "Come sit down." I sat down in one of those subordinate's chairs that left you open and exposed, as if made to make you feel subordinate, while he faced me behind his dark, dominant walnut shield of a desk. He, then, motioned for me to slide the chair around and sit next to his desk; he had something to show me.

"We print out a summary analysis every pay period showing worked hours for each employee, and you stand out among all your other coworkers. Take a look right here. From the top of the list it shows for the two weeks just ended, 130 hours, 150 hours, 140, 140, 140, we go a little ways further down the list, the same, the same, then we come to you and 84 hours for the two-weeks ending. Can you explain what you have been doing everyday while sitting in the office?" he finished.

"Well sir, I thought long and hard about the number of hours I work here, and I just can't justify putting down seventy hours per week, when a large amount of the time I'm either waiting for the client to respond or hand in documents crucial to my tests or I'm waiting on the stupid printer to print-out my work." He was shocked. For a moment, I thought I saw his eyes, from the pupils to the outer layer turn dark red, while red horns popped up from the crowns of his head.

I waited for fire to spit out at me from his boiling saliva, but then he calmed down and in a diplomatic way said to me, "Well, what you are describing seems to me, to be normal occurrences in the daily job; and they should be factored into your time, all of them," he finished carefully.

"Well, I don't agree sir. I'm willing to put down the time I'm really working, but I can't ethically continue to put down hours I don't work," I said, without any hesitation.

"Well, with that said, maybe we need to not only review your time, but your performance here at the firm," he said, waiting for me to back down, reverse my already firm position.

"If you need to, sir. I can't budge on my morals," I said.

Then he said, as if I would pay for ever going against his wishes, "I don't think we have anymore to discuss. You may leave now!"

"Okay, thank you sir," I said, while closing the door of his office behind me. And that was that.

The next week I didn't hear from Kumiko all that much, and I suspected the process was under way. It was only a matter of time, before I received that *call*, the one I was naturally supposed to fear. Then on Thursday of the next week, it came. I was called to come into the main headquarters located in downtown Atlanta that following morning. I knew what that had to mean. As much as I wanted to be let go, still in the back of my mind, I wondered whether I was doing the right thing. Was leaving the firm, a job that had security and health benefits, a smart move or one I would regret later in life? I had my reservations, but I had to continue to believe that it was right, that my future had much more in store for me, much more than I could ever have realized by staying stationary in Atlanta.

    I didn't need to drive through rush hour madness on Friday morning. My condo was right downtown, only a few blocks from the modern day mammoth of a skyscraper where the firm's office was located. As much as I had prepared mentally for this meeting, I don't think it would ever have been enough for the psychological impact of having someone explain to you after two long hard years of sacrifice, working unpaid overtime every single week, growing and learning, melding your habits and everyday customs to be a part of this huge dynamic being, making friends, taking advice, sharing advice, living in this organism, this man-made womb; that, in the end, none of that matters to us anymore: your time is up, and with a few standard procedures—handing over the laptop, the credit card, the gate access badge, and handing you the dismissal letter, all nicely typed, official firm stamp slightly rising off the thickly textured vanilla paper, that was it.

    The HR lady responsible for canceling my membership looked directly through me as she spoke congenially. "There are headhunters you can contact," she said and with one hand showed me the door to her office. I walked out letter in hand. I'm sure her thoughts of my dismissal had flown right away with the same air that carried my body into her office, the same air carrying me out of the building, and her day continued with the same order it always had. She would probably make a few more phone calls, jot down a few reminder notes, then head to lunch early before the 12 o'clock rush. I didn't even receive notice from the managers that planned my exit; their daily lives had continued easier without confrontation. They were better off high up, not seeing the people destroyed by their commands, like so many soldiers sent off to war, never to return, so many civilians caught in the gunfire. One thing was for sure. I officially was a free man. The bright sunshine spraying its light all over the city sidewalks and streets felt nourishing; I had forgotten how much I truly loved soaking in all its glory. And a vision came to me; I could see a great forest devastated by fire, only a few charred remnants of trees still poking from its earth and with it a new sun, bigger and brighter, shone into the space that was old life. Already, new plants of a vibrant green sprouted up strong and proud, even more powerful than their ancestors, contrasting their new life with the black silt of old.

    I sent notice to Seb and Leo. Plans were in motion and we needed to coordinate. The next few weeks were not a time to relax.

I submitted all the right paperwork to the unemployment office. Through a good friend of mine, I found a wonderful, reliable couple to take over my condo for the next year or more. I dealt with all the junk that had built up over the last year, my taxes, any outstanding payments, and I backed out of my gym membership and cell phone contract. I sold off all the underperforming stock I had acquired over the years, collected my final paychecks, including the vacation time still owed to me, and transferred over my 401K, keeping it ready just in case. Luckily, I didn't have a car loan or other extremities to worry about. Seb was on a contract with his firm, and he was sure after all of the drama and conflicts he was experiencing at the firm that they weren't going to renew his contract. This meant that he would legally be able to receive unemployment from the government. The decision where to travel to next became much easier when Seb and Leo found a special program allowing them to both travel free to Israel, being that they were both Jewish, well Leo part-Jewish. Also, Seb had family living in Israel, not far from Tel Aviv; so I would have a place to stay while they were being escorted in and around Israel by bodyguards. In a short time after the Israel decision, we had charted out an intricate diagram for our next conquest. Our plan was to hit Israel first, then fly directly to Turkey where we would meet a friend in Istanbul, fly to the coast of Turkey, travel up the coast to the west from Ankara, fly back to Istanbul, spend some time there, fly to Bulgaria to meet a friend, then travel up to Romania and finally back to New York, before flying to the south of Spain for a year. Of course, we knew that plans do change and contingencies always arise.

    I stopped fighting what was happening to my relationship with Maggie. Communication had become impossible and we were talking less and less to each other. I finally told her about me leaving my job, and, as I expected, I was criticized and berated for it. I think in her mind, my job loss confirmed me as a failure in the eyes of her and her mother, and I noticed our communication dwindling even more from that point. Naturally, I would have flown over to Asia to stay with her, and try and make things work out, while seeking out opportunities on that end of the globe, but our relationship was so rocky and shaky, I thought it healthier to start over fresh, no job, no girlfriend, just me against the world. Unexpectedly, I received a call from Maggie a few days before leaving. I think the fact that I was going to be gone away for such a long time had finally sunk in, and she even asked me to come to Asia. But, by then, the coffin door had been shut, all nails hammered in, and it was too late. I had already purchased two round trip tickets, and I don't think she really believed whole-heartedly in what she was asking of me.

The few people that I informed about my future travels, all thought, either, "wow, you're not working that great job anymore" or "are you crazy for going to Israel at a time like this?" And maybe I was a little crazy. I saw the same images related to Israel that they had seen over the television of random violence, death, and destruction. Maybe I was taking on too many risks. Was it a result of all that had just happened to me: the loss of love and a secure job? Maybe in the back of my mind I had had a death wish coming to me? I had become careless with my life, not caring what would happen to me. But all my life, in ways, I had been a risk taker. So I had not really changed, but rather I now took on heavier risks. Besides all the dangers to physical health, Israel was an amazing society, rich in culture, the beginning of civilization according to the Bible. The three largest, most powerful religions of the world all considered the area their holy land. And it was possible that I would never have the opportunity in my life to visit this powerful country again. So, although the Palestinians and Israelis were both light years away from any real compromise or agreement, and no one could predict the site or time of the next bombing in Israel, though everyone knew it was only a matter of time, I had decided that now was as good a time to go as ever. I knew if I survived my visit to Israel, it would be an experience of a lifetime, one that would shape my being and my understanding of this world for an eternity. The only drawback to the whole plan was that it would probably shoot my mother's blood pressure sky high; because, like any loving mother, I knew that she would be worrying for my life and well being every hour that I was over there. When I talked to her, I tried my best to paint Israel as a different animal, not the ravishing beast that she and all of America had seen repeatedly over the television. And she never criticized my decision. Seb, Leo and I would soon be on an adventure that would change our lives forever.

ISRAEL

Writing is a discovery process.
—author unknown

Here I was, moments after take off, aboard the most passenger-scrutinizing and arguably the most secure airline in the world, El Al, heading for Tel Aviv, Israel. Finally it had all come to fruition: the month of planning a new beginning and direction in life. Early that day I'd said my goodbyes to my family and friends. For my mom and dad, it was a very emotional farewell. They didn't know the next time they would see their son, and how my life would change thereafter. My father, normally a very reserved man, not at all a hugger, gave me a quick hug, patting me on the back. With a large backpack, which would be my armoire, closet, dresser, desk, and bathroom cabinet for the next few months, I entered the Atlanta airport, checked in, boarded a cheap one-way flight to JFK in New York, and waited to embark on my flight to the Holy Land.

The almost sixty rows of seats, seeming to equal the number of stewards and stewardesses on board, elevated rapidly. The evidence shown in front of every passenger, an individual monitor, left nothing to imagination: 2000 feet, 3000 feet, 5000 feet, current time in NY 7:30 p.m. eastern, current time at destination 2:30 a.m., amount of time until arrival 11 hours 45 minutes. The massive Boeing elevated at a nerve-wracking, sharp lean, allowing me a direct view of the New York Harbor, where slender strips of land appeared as clouds in the middle of hazy, bluish grey water that was the same dreary color as the sky. It felt dreamy, like the way astronauts must feel, encountered with infinite space in all directions, not always certain what direction the aircraft is facing. The takeoff seemed to mirror the multitude of thoughts spiralling, tumbling, and flowing through my head. It was still hard to see a clear direction in my life; and at the same time, I felt as if I was ascending. I was taking great risks by flying to a country considered a danger zone by most of the world, especially the U.S. media. I would also be continuing to sacrifice financial wealth and stability by traveling later to Spain for an extended stay: there my plan was to pick up a second language and for the first time actually settle in another country. My friends, family, and the way of life I was beginning to understand and conquer in Atlanta were now taking the backseat to this instinct of mine, this dire need to occupy new comfort zones.

The paper of my life for the last three years, the blank sheet that had been scribbled on, smudged with lipstick, stained by coffee spills, covered with pictures, blood-soaked, littered with food crumbs and more recently dried of tears, was now being balled up and thrown into a waste basket. A new sheet now glided effortlessly along my table waiting to be used and adorned, in hopes that one day it would be elevated to art, not scorned and abandoned or rejected. I found peace in thinking about that blank sheet. It was the beautiful calm; a light breeze before a powerful storm. And I knew I had to enjoy this brief lapse in time while I prepared myself for the new things coming. But there was also another dynamic.

My brain was moving and turning in ways unfamiliar to me. I was opening the walls for a flow of new information to migrate in, near where old information still held claim to territory; and I could feel the vying for land and property taking place inside me: everything was still very much unsettled. During the elevation and when we had finally made it to a safe altitude, quick questions signalled this great internal struggle, flickering sporadically like a slide show of my abstract future. What had I really gotten myself into this time? Was I stuck in a spiderweb, each step binding me further in its sticky mess? Was I leaving at the wrong time in my life, acting out of an impulse, a kind of quarter-life crisis? Would this voyage give me new information, crucial to a more suitable path, the key being handed to me with a note? Would I be on a plane flight back home after a few months, drained financially and mentally, finally giving up, having failed myself and all the ones who cared for me? Would I ever find that *thing* that I was looking for; that something that I still couldn't put into words or describe? I was sure that *thing* was out there for me. I felt more alive than ever. I was reaching out and grabbing hold of that part of the human experience that speeds up knowledge gathering. In ways, I was reverting back to my adolescent years, because completely new worlds were opening up to me; only, this time, I carried a base of wisdom. I wouldn't let one drop of knowledge fall to the floor. I would taste the knowledge, touching the bottle to my lips.

It was just a few hours into the flight and a guy in his late twenties, sporting one of his spoils from an American discount outlet mall—a khaki hat from The Gap Store with tags still dangling from one of the ventilation holes proudly stating a final sale price of seventy-nine cents—typed feverishly on an IBM Think Pad, the whole time the tags on his hat dancing around like Milli Vanilli's hair. Another guy sat tensely by the window, his body upright while his head tilted pensively outward towards the glass bubble. Walls were built around his world as he searched the outside clouds. I noticed he was wearing one of those funny little waffle hats I had heard Seb call a kippot. It was discreetly secured by a hairpin the exact same color of his blackish-brown hair. Now, on the other side of the plane, a group of men began huddling in the open space near where the center of the plane was divided. I thought they were all waiting to use the bathroom, but more began gathering and then more until they were even flowing into the aisles. They wore dark suits and basic black hats and some had long locks of hair draping down by their ears. Not long after the brief silent huddle, as if they hadn't gathered there to socialize, they faced in the direction of the windows along the left aisle. And then suddenly, like a silent bell had gone off signaling them, and without synchronization, they bobbed their heads back and forth in a sort of trance; some grappled the Torah, others chanted prayers by heart. My instincts were to observe and try and absorb all of these intense movements unfolding every second in front of me. If I could have seen into the future, maybe I would have seen these intricate displays as a perfect prelude to Israel, because, even before crossing the border to this tiny country, even before smelling the air and sampling the soil, clues existed. I had already entered Israel when I stepped foot on the plane, and really even when I accepted the airline's meticulous interrogation process leaving practically nothing to concealment.

While in the airport, an hour before take-off, I had found myself exposing religious beliefs and short-term plans, answering character and personality questions—anything that would help me spill my whole life to them. And no one, not even Yahweh, escapes a thorough physical check behind closed curtains in a small booth. After all of the checks were done and El Al had exhausted every manner of retrieving information and distinguishing man-made items from flesh and blood, I was left feeling naked to the flight attendants and security specialists as I passed through the final check point. I handed over my last two possessions, identification and ticket, and walked the brief tunnel onto the plane, as nothing was left to mystery. My consolation for having passed through the equivalent of a mini-CIA check was a safe flight.

Now, the guy sitting next to me folded his laptop to a click and stored it in its case. He turned to me and asked with all directness, "Where are you from?"

I answered, "Georgia. I live in Atlanta." A curiosity flared within him and a strange joy erupted from that answer. Maybe he didn't fit me—my face or background—with the typical visitor or traveler to his country. He was probably used to the stream of American-Jews seeking out their roots; not many other travelers were daring the voyage, and Muslims were outright discouraged from flying the state-owned Israeli airlines. He seemed to find a joy and pride in welcoming me, the rare tourist, with all the interesting questions that someone like me unintentionally poses. This same peculiarity, along with my reason for traveling to Israel,—as I told El Al, "I'm here to meet up with friends"—made the airline's interrogation process all the more entertaining for the tough security specialists and exotic stewardesses.

"Is this your first trip?" the guy next to me asked.

"Yeah, my first time," I answered.

"Wow! You have so much to see! You will go to Jerusalem? Will you not?" he asked.

"Sure. I plan to take a tour there for one day. Maybe I will have other chances to go," I answered.

"So you will stay for awhile?" he asked, in a hopeful way. He seemed genuinely happy for me, happy that I would be experiencing his pride. It occurred to me for a second, while he was talking, that this is how the Israelis traveling in their large groups had been in Thailand: very talkative, direct and friendly. Soon the pensive guy sitting next to the window popped his head around and joined in the conversation, also seemingly excited for my visit to Israel, and also proud of what his country had to offer.

"Sure, Sure . . . make sure to visit the Golan Heights, Old Jerusalem and New Jerusalem . . . and make sure to visit the Dead Sea," he urged passionately. "This is the only water in the world, I think, that you can not drown in. You know why you cannot drown in this water?"

"Why?" I asked.

"The high concentration of salt and minerals makes the water dense and allows you to literally lie flat on top of the water. You float without doing anything!" But, then he went on to say, almost reconsidering his first statement, "The water is dangerous; . . . don't get it in your eyes or swallow, it can kill you. You understand?!"

Right away, many of the anxieties and negative perceptions I had carried with me—as this shield to the unknown, this mysterious Israel—were being washed away by my new unofficial hosts to the country. Suddenly, I was having a really good feeling about this whole trip and was ready to land as soon as possible. It seemed new, positive information was now colliding with the mountains of negative news I had received by television over the last ten years of my life, or whenever I had been first receptive to this country. I'm sure at some point back then, I was also guilty of blocking out this country like the majority of other Americans, and probably I had asked, "What does this country and its problems mean to me?" And, most probably in return, I answered, "nothing," wasting no more thoughts on this land beyond the ocean.

Upon entering the Ben Gurion Airport and passing through customs, I had this strange feeling of walking the red carpet at the Grammys or MTV Awards, because people seemed noticeably curious of my story. Who is this strange American kid? Two naturally beautiful customs agents sitting in their low booths both struck up conversations with me. They wanted to know where I would be staying and wanted to meet up either tonight or tomorrow night at some hip-hop club in Tel Aviv. They giggled back and forth to each other as we talked, and I was thinking the whole time, this doesn't happen anywhere else in the world. I took down their numbers and told them I would give them a call when I decided to come party in the city. As I walked away, I wasn't so sure that I would actually call. These were the first people I had met since the plane landed, and I technically hadn't even entered the country yet. I couldn't be making any promises at this point.

I grabbed my big backpack, the one that had helped me survive the trip in Southeast Asia, including the mountainous terrain of North Thailand and the wild jungle growth of Cambodia, and I walked out with sign in hand to a frantic airport lobby. I was instructed by Seb's parents to draw out a cardboard sign with the name Yakuv (Seb's last name), so that Greesha, Seb's first cousin, could easily spot me. I remembered thinking that day in Seb's house, when I spoke with his parents, that usually it's the person waiting at the airport who holds up the sign. But I didn't argue with Seb's parents: Seb even avoided their arguments.

I didn't really know who or what to expect. I had seen pictures of Seb's family in Israel, but they were all outdated pictures, as far back as when Seb and his cousin were still in Uzbekistan; they were only children then. Now, according to Seb, the same Greesha, only two years his elder, who used to stick by him as a little kid when they were jumped on for being Jews in a majority Muslim country—one of the Former Soviet Republics that waited desperately for a chance to break free from a highly repressive Soviet Union—was all grown up. Following in the steps of Bukharan tradition—a culture with a set of codes instilled and perfected over centuries and centuries, ever since this special sect of Sephardim Jews (Jews of pre-1492 Spanish origins) had fled Spain during the Inquisition to settle in Africa, the Middle East or as far away as Asia, Greesha had a wife, a little girl, and a newborn to look after. And according to tradition, Seb was supposed to be next; his entire family, all the older Bukharans, had started in their late teens and Seb's parents expected him to continue that cycle. In ways, I felt bad for Seb, because his pressures were heavy. He had the weight of not only his parents', but of a centuries-old lineage and cultural heritage. He could be disowned for playing outside of the rules. And he was already breaking some subtle rules. I could tell Seb was still not entirely accepting of his Bukharan fate, and something told me that this trip for Seb was in many ways a chance to make a burning decision that continued to follow and haunt him. I was sure that he wanted to seek out his childhood friend and cousin, to observe and witness firsthand, to see if this same path would be right for him in the near future, which in Bukharan terms really meant now.

Right away I caught sight of a tall, dramatic figure, waving in my direction, and walking directly towards me. He was alone.

"Hi. I'm Greesha."

"Hey. I'm Chris."

We each greeted the other with smiles and a sort of hope inside that the other didn't disappoint any expectations; him being an understanding host and myself a good flexible guest. The strange confrontation between two people thrown on each other by special circumstances always creates the unanswered questions: how does this person already perceive me? Even before he really gets to know me, what stereotypes or immediate first impressions will I have to dispel? I wanted to impress Greesha, whether or not he deserved it. I followed him outside to the parking lot; the whole time very much wide-eyed, taking in every little detail of the surroundings, already constructing opinions and populating this fresh template titled Israel. The large backpack began to make my shoulders and back slump forward, which didn't stop my head and neck moving in all directions trying to complete my panorama. I couldn't be ashamed to open myself up as a tourist, even though there was nothing very graceful or cool about it. Greesha had a sixth sense the whole time we were walking that my mind — ever since opening the doors to the main airport and Israel — had been working overtime, working out my new environment; and he didn't distract me with small talk, which would mean even more information to digest. We made it to his car, I filled up the backseat with my backpack, and he left me in the car to wait while he went to pay the parking ticket.

    I noticed the parking lot was rather boring with a collection of unimpressive cars. A few minutes passed, while I sat in the small four-door car, sheltered from the sun by the second floor garage. Suddenly, a strange, humorless face peeped around one of the larger vehicles parked in the next row of cars. He looked deliberately in all directions, inside of car windows and in open space. I wondered for a second if he could have been a carjacker or even some sort of terrorist. This guy was not a tourist. He wore an all black combat uniform and held one of the largest rifles I had ever seen in real life. It was almost the size of bazooka. Before it would dawn on me that he was airport security, he had already taken me in with his trained eyes, a quick flash of interrogation, absorbing as much information as needed and continued on slyly, maneuvering between vehicles.

    Greesha was now coming back to the car. We attempted to exit the parking garage, but the parking ticket, the one that streamsout at a push of a button upon entering, wasn't responding and the gates weren't opening for us to exit. I witnessed for the first time the fire from Greesha, as he backed up to a small lot, bolted from the car, and demanded that an attendant at the booth open the gates. When the gates finally opened and we were off cruising the glorious sunshine, Greesha's smile returned. I stuck my hand out through the passenger window and cusped the wind in my right palm; the breeze felt refreshing, like a gust of air conditioning. It hit me in that moment. I was actually here, traveling through the middle of Israel. The freshness and vitality in discovering with one's own eyes a new and mysterious place had to be up there in the same category as a runner's high.

    The topography of Israel was a surprising vastness; as soon as we entered the open highway I remember thinking how Georgia wasn't so much different along parts of I-75. Still, often I had the feeling here of driving through a large desert. Much of the vastness surrounding the highway was dead, brownish-red dirt, and the low-lying brush was the color of late autumn or mid-winter. I thought it was amazing how subdivisions of houses sprang out sporadically in the distance and how they weren't always connected to anything, as if the settlers had just haphazardly plotted on a piece of land with no rhyme or reason. I had to think maybe it was the same for early American pioneers moving out west, staking their claims. I had to remember Israel was only about fifty years old, and within that time period millions of immigrants had to be absorbed within its shallow depths. Just like in the rest of the world, if one looked closely, construction could be seen thriving in these random pockets. Off in the distance, the skeletons of cranes towered high in the sky, and many houses were still only dull gray cement blocks; not one of them was made out of wood.

We were only thirty minutes from the airport when Greesha got off the highway and found a lone curving road that took us to the base of a neighborhood perched at the sloping hilltops. The houses and apartments were spotless white cubes that gripped the slopes like staircases, sort of the way I had imagined small villages in Spain; and with the omnipresence of the sun, everything was vivid like the splashing of special studio light. It almost hurt my eyes to look around, like sneaking a peek at the sun. The neighborhood was quiet; hardly anyone was outside of their home—and of course, for good reason; it was midday, mid-summer. I had to repress my anxiety to see action; I had just arrived and would be on Greesha's timetable until I learned how to navigate Israel alone.

When we came through the doorway of his apartment, a little girl came running to greet Greesha; she grabbed onto one of Greesha's long legs with all her four little limbs and Greesha smiled as he walked into the living room, suddenly carrying this extra weight. An attractive dark-eyed, dark-haired lady, about half the size of Greesha, came out of the backroom hugging a little baby to her chest, swaying the little one back and forth. They were all so happy to see each other, like a great family reunion, their joy transcended even my welcoming. They were speaking a bit in Russian and then a bit in Hebrew.

Greesha turned to me and said, "I'm sorry but they can't speak English. My wife is learning to speak, but can't understand many words." As he said it, he turned to his wife who stood smiling innocently, not following at all our conversation. "I want to introduce you to my wife Natasha; this is little Isak, and this one," (he spoke quickly to the little girl; I think he was telling her to let go of his leg), "this one is Yafa." The little girl was actually very shy and almost refused to acknowledge me. "Follow me. I'll show you where you can put your stuff." We walked to the first room, across the small hallway, and right past the living room. "This is where Yafa normally sleeps. It's a small bed, but –"

I cut him off, "No. No. It's perfect. Thank you."

"Well, good. If you need to organize your things or take a nap you can do that. But tonight, we go to eat dinner with the rest of the family at my mother's house."

"Okay, thanks," I said, but I wasn't tired at all.

"Or, if you want we go to the beach for a few hours first?"

"That sounds good." I brushed my teeth and threw on my swimming trunks. The little girl was in an extra energetic mood. Her daddy was going to take her with us, while Mommy and her baby brother stayed behind. And she seemed to bask in the glory of a midafternoon outing. I had to admit, she was adorable. If I were to ever have a little girl, I would want her to be just as adorable and beautiful; and she seemed to yearn for her father's love and attention. Maybe, in some strange way, she had been jealous that I was distracting her father's attention, just by being here as the new guest. Maybe this time was usually reserved for her.

The beaches nearby Greesha's neighborhood did not impress me. They were not of white sand or graced with beautiful green palm trees. And the sunbathers and swimmers were made up mostly of families; little children were running around throwing sand and crying. But I had to continue being patient, because surely there were other beaches, more happening, and I would be in Israel for a few weeks. I had plenty of time to worry about those sorts of things, and any beach could be appreciated after living in the middle of Georgia for most of my life.

Yafa seemed bulletproof and tough for a little girl her age, but she wasn't fond of the water; she actually froze when she walked only a couple feet into the small fuzzy waves. Greesha said he needed to use the restroom and said to watch Yafa. (Israelis are very direct people; they usually don't ask, as much as they tell. Hebrew doesn't provide for all the meticulously polite gestures used in the English language).

And I naively agreed, not thinking how awkward and embarrassing it would be watching a girl on the verge of tears from the sight of water, considering the fact that I didn't speak Russian or Hebrew. When Greesha left, she continued to stand still scared in the water, almost paralyzed, as I jumped into the shallow water trying to show her how really harmless and fun it was. But she just continued to make a frown. I wanted to tell her that it was okay and not to be afraid, that I wouldn't let anything happen to her. And a few words even slipped out of my mouth to the same effect, until I realized that she couldn't understand me. She didn't speak English. And, to make matters worse, she began speaking to me for the first time, but in Hebrew, which I could not put into context. I was feeling just as paralyzed as she was, not knowing what I could do. On top of not knowing her language, I wasn't that good with children, mainly because I hadn't really been around many, at least, not since I myself had been a child. So, we just looked at each other; she stared at me from the top of the water and I stared at her sitting in the crests of the tiny waves.

    Finally, Greesha returned, and he seemed to scold her for not entering the water. He took her by the hand and walked her into the water, the whole time she held her other arm in front of her face and looked in the direction of the beach. And although she seemed to stand or sit like a dead log in the water, she didn't cry. That was probably my main fear: if I had guided her into the water, she would have cried and broken out into a hollering fuss. This is the same fear I had had with all little children and little babies: maybe, once they were under my supervision, I wouldn't be able to calm their eruptions. I hoped to get better at that sort of thing.

    Eventually, I floated out further into the mild Mediterranean Sea and decided to swim a few laps in its endless space. I did the breast stroke one way and then the front stroke the other, and then when I was tired and out of breath, I did a back float for awhile. There was always something meditative and therapeutic about floating on my back above calm water, having my ears submerged so that I'm cut off from all outside noise, with only a calm blue sky to backdrop whatever thoughts are floating in my mind. A silly thought occurred to me that only then, and also the few times when I had lain on my back to search the stars at night, was I completely focused outside of my world. An entire universe and galaxy out there hardly ever gets my attention.

    We all got washed up and ready to go out for dinner. Like

always after swimming, I was starving and wasn't too concerned with anything else. Natasha, Greesha's wife, had prepared a beautiful cake with white icing and another dish of rice with chic peas, along with Non bread. Everyone was dressed nicely, and the baby was snug in his carriage. We didn't have to walk far, because the rest of the family all lived in the same neighborhood, only four minutes from Greesha's place. As we walked, family and guest, towards the other house for dinner, the sun was near the end of its departure with all its reddish glow. I thought to myself, they have a perfect family: daughter, son, husband and wife. It was picture perfect; the only thing missing in my American world was a dog. But I couldn't even rule out that option for them; it was too early. Maybe Seb would find that it wasn't so bad after all, marrying and raising children right now, at his age. His cousin had a healthy, delightful family, something to be proud of; and in Seb's parents' eyes, Seb was wasting valuable family time. They were ready for grandchildren.

But the pressure wasn't only to have a family soon, but to find a wife, who was not only Jewish, but Bukharan-Jew. This meant that meeting a beautiful, intelligent woman at the local synagogue was not good enough. Apart from knowing the traditional Jewish religious customs, his wife had to know the Bukharan routine. Women had a defined role to play within this sub-culture: they needed to cook a certain way, stay home with the kids and always keep a sharp eye on their development, clean, and be a perfect domestic wife, while their husband made the money and supported the family financially. Not all Jewish women were up for this sort of lifetime commitment. And not only that, there was a sort of exclusiveness among the Bukharans. I couldn't grasp fully how love needed to appear in a certain form and ethnicity to be considered worthy. How could they uphold the mentality that other biological genes just weren't adequate enough to mix with their family? The thought baffled me. If I thought too long, it almost made me somewhat angry. So I didn't usually think too deeply. I just told myself, people are different, people have their own ideas and opinions, and none of their customs or exclusivity ever interfered with my life. Furthermore, right or wrong, it wasn't altogether a new principle or idea for me, that parents could be blind in accepting a mate for their children. My mom had gone through the same issues and dilemmas, when she began dating my father and later when she married him. I remember how she said her parents didn't totally accept my father until we came along, my brother and I. Somehow children had changed my grandparents' perspective towards a multi-racial family. Something similar had happened on my father's side.

When we entered the front corridor of the apartment, we were greeted by glowing personalities, wide open laughs, and warm energy that easily spilled over in hugs. Seb's uncle, standing behind his wife, flashed an inviting smile, and his gold tooth caught the reflection of the hallway light. Immediately I began to miss seeing my father's gold tooth (the one he always wished he hadn't gotten when in Vietnam), and the way he knows to be charming when he feels the mood or in the right environment. Family reunions were that environment. And not long ago, we would have been all together for July 4th; that's if, I hadn't just finished the job and committed myself to traveling. But even so, I remembered, even if I had the time, those reunions hadn't existed for years. Not since my first cousin, like a brother to me, ended up in and out of jail, and not since my great-grandmother died, eventually splitting the family over a silly "will." Today, at nightfall, marked the Sabbath, and most Israelis were in their homes feasting and sharing family moments. Seb's family was a moving machine with a beating heart. The men unfolded the long tables and connected them side-by-side, draped a beautiful white tablecloth, and searched for enough chairs to accommodate such a large gathering. Seb's aunt and uncle were there, his cousin and his family, another cousin and girlfriend, another aunt and uncle, and two other full families related to Seb's grandmother on his mom's side. And the machine continued to move along seamlessly.

The women had prepared mountains of food; I could see the clutter of platters and bowls covering every inch of the kitchen counters. I wondered what army would be showing up soon. Greesha's daughter ran into the other room to play with her cousin. And I waited while the table was set with the proper amount of plates and bowls. Already, Greesha was offering me Vodka shots, and I told him I had nothing to absorb the alcohol at this point. Finally, everyone had made it to the table. We started with a prayer. Then the first round of food began. I figured out that they didn't mix fish with other types of meat, there were religious reasons for this; we ate fish with the top layer of plates. Then, when the second round of food came, we had to discard the fishplates and use the next layer of plates. Between these courses was an ongoing toast. Greesha continued to fill my abnormally large shot glass to the rim, and before every shot, a new person had to propose a toast, and it was done in counter-clockwise order. I was hopeful I wouldn't have to talk, because of the fact that only two people at the table spoke English: Geesha and Namir, one of Seb's uncles. Meanwhile, the food just kept coming and coming and the shots of Vodka continued without rest. All of these shots were actually helping me to digest the massive concentration of food building up in my stomach. The variety of different recipes was pot luck brilliance, and everyone continued to eat, drink, and talk in the way great feasts are supposed to be lived out and celebrated. Seb's family warmed up to me fast. They were asking all types of questions, and they were not only curious about me, but they also wanted information on Seb, because they hadn't seen him in so long and I was an unfiltered connection. They were searching for the real Seb to come out in my stories; the one they didn't really know, and not the Seb they knew over the last years speaking to Seb's mom. The real Seb had another week traveling through Israel in a special convoy, full of other American-Jews seeking their roots, along with Leo, who skated by on a credible one-half. No one could deny Leo's last name as being Jewish, even though he still had to prove through family records that he was Jewish to be granted the free trip.

    The family asked me all types of questions, using Greesha as the English interpreter. They wanted to know where Seb and I had met. What was my family background? Seb's aunt said I was handsome, to the giggles and laughs of everyone at the table. She then asked did I have a girlfriend. I told Greesha how I had just ended a long relationship, and they joked that I needed to find a nice Bukharan woman to marry; how that would solve all my problems. I appreciated their attempt to welcome me in, even though deep down, according to what I had heard Seb say, I knew that they didn't truly believe in that statement. Then they asked me more details about Seb. Like who was he dating? And had he told me about any plans to settle down anytime soon? I knew if I answered any of these questions, especially the ones I myself didn't even know, that they would be on the phone with Seb's mom that same night. I just continued to plead the fifth or play dumb. It was clearly not my business, and Seb would have to deal with these questions in the form of family pressure when he finally made it from his excursions.

    The shots and speeches had made it to me, along the table, and I had realized now that they would probably want me to make a toast to the echo of Greesha in Hebrew. At this point, all the nervousness that I would normally have sober was gone, and I toasted to family unity and how they were accepting me into their home as a guest, and how I felt like part of the family. By the end of my drunken speech, I was talking about how I hoped the family lived on many more generations and continued to have these special dinners, where the whole family was united as one. And how I felt fortunate to have been a part of such a great family, even only if for one dinner, one Sabbath. At the end of my heartfelt speech, everyone blissfully threw up their shot glasses, the children and a couple of the women raised a cup of soda, and we all passionately clinked and clanged our glasses together.

The truth is there was something really special about their family. I could feel solidarity and loyalty; there was a smoothness and fluidity in their interactions with each other, and each member's role seemed clear and defined, polished and comfortable. The truth was as lovely as the family had been to me, and especially to each other; the intricacies of all the foods, the elaborate customs, special prayers, and how everyone knew when, what, and who should for each little thing to be done; all of this now made sense to me. I understood why Seb's parents didn't want Seb marrying a non-Bukharan. It could risk breaking all of these traditions, eschewing family unity and solidarity. These weren't fluke traditions made up at the last minute, either. Generations of Bukharans had kept these traditions alive, and I could now see first hand how delicate and precious this rhythm was. It occurred to me that maybe throwing a heavy electric guitar into a symphony orchestra was not the right mix and would damage any musical chemistry. Not that an electric guitar didn't create great music and harmony when it completed a sultry blues band or live-wired a rock band. And maybe that guitar could be strummed differently, with lighter strings, so that it could blend softly like a violin. But there was always that risk of destroying a solid music production.

Somehow I had become a believer in this Bukharan system. I appreciated it, and even wanted Seb to continue its flow and legacy. It really was a beautiful unity, not the stubborn arrogance I equated it with earlier. Seb had tough decisions to make in the future. It was hard enough for me to find a woman that I loved in a world full of nationalities and ethnicities, let alone if I had to narrow those options down to a few women scattered around the world. I was beginning to finally understand his dilemmas and pressures. The reality was that the days of Uzbekistani and Bukharan-Jews migrating in unified groups to the same country in order to settle together were over. While in the past this sect of Sephardim-Jews had all migrated to Uzbekistan in a unified cluster, now they were scattered in pockets all around the world, a large part of them being in the U.S. and Israel. If the culture's future to flourish with all its traditions and customs still intact wasn't doomed, I was sure it was heading for hard times. I wondered if keeping cultures as specific and exact as this one thriving in far away parts of the world was any different from trying to maintain a long-distance relationship, and I knew firsthand the result of the latter circumstance. I hoped the best for them.

Greesha and I took a walk through the neighborhood of Rosh Ha'Ayin to settle our stomachs and burn off a few of the extra pounds we had gained only a couple hours ago. The night was light and refreshing; the hilltops exposed us to a nice cool breeze, and spots of lights shone off in the valleys below. I could tell Greesha had already warmed up to me, at least enough to open up and talk. I had talked and opened up myself all that night at dinner. And I could sense he was even more eager to talk, now, not only because he trusted me more, but he normally didn't have an outlet, where men can be men, a moment of camaraderie to talk about hot ladies and all those other things that women have no use for in their conversations. We talked about traveling, and his face lit up like a burst of energy when describing his trip to Spain just a year ago—of course, with the family. He admitted wanting to take a trip somewhere faraway with only the fellows, maybe somewhere like Brazil (this had been a dream of his) and with open minded, free spirited friends, who knew how to travel without inhibitions.

"It's a different experience, when you have children and a wife to consider," he said.

"I can only imagine," I agreed, wanting truly to empathize with him.

He wanted to be free to follow his instincts and impulses, the way great adventurers like Ernest Hemingway and Marco Polo had done. At times, he admitted feeling trapped, like he was sacrificing some part of himself to this fate of his.

"You know, I'm only twenty-seven, and I often feel like I'm in this time bubble, where I've already lived my life and I'm looking backwards, feeling remorse over a time when I had options, when the entire world was at my finger tips; a time when I had the freedom to do anything I wanted," he said.

"But, you have a great family! I admire you in a lot of ways. You have an adorable little girl, a beautiful wife, and a little boy. And, everyone is healthy and happy. And, everyone looks up to you. You are this nucleus planet and everyone revolves around your orbit. And I'll admit that I never even considered having children or that I could even enjoy a family life up until now. You have something to come home to everyday and night; something to live for. In my eyes, you are living life to the fullest," I said.

"Thanks. Really, I would do anything for them," he said.

That night, I could feel the blood pumping through the veins in my forehead, my legs and my arms as I lay my head down in the tiny single-sized mattress to sleep. I tried to relax and calm myself, but I didn't know how to do it alone. I didn't have a routine for this sort of thing, like counting sheep, and I was done with the sleeping pills; I couldn't go back to those days again. But this time I couldn't fall asleep for a different reason; I wasn't depressed or stressed out. Rather, the contrary, I felt full of life. I didn't want to sleep another moment of my life away, in mourning of a dead soul. Suddenly, I couldn't just lie there pretending to sleep. I needed to do something. I had the inspiration to write; something I hadn't had the energy or motivation to do for a long time, not since high school when Juan, Alex and I would fill the entire basement with music that vibrated the whole house. I could still hear my mother's voice saying, "Turn down the music! I can't even hear myself think!" Too alert and too inspired to fully sit down, we would prop ourselves on the arms of the old black sofa, which had been demoted from our living room years ago. And we would write music lyrics, with this focus and concentration that couldn't be broken, at least not until one of us had to get up to carefully place the needle to the beginning of the wax instrumental.

I now had this burning desire to get everything down on paper. But with what? I didn't have a pen or paper, and I didn't want to go rummaging around in Greesha's house, especially not when they were trying to sleep. Then it occurred to me. Greesha had showed me how to use the Internet in the little study room. If it didn't make too much noise, I could type an email. I quietly tipped-toed to the end of the hall, opened the door slowly, as to avoid any creaking noises, and shut it carefully behind me. I didn't need to flip the light on, because the screensaver, little rectangular photos of the family flying around to all points of the screen, was my flashlight, my guiding light to find the chair. I sat down cautiously not to move the chair wheels too fast or squeak the metal shock below the seat cushion. I placed the mouse softly in the middle of the pad, and I double-clicked the Explorer icon. Then suddenly it was like all my careful silence had been for nothing: the "dial up" started screeching in high, torturous pitches for at least eight long seconds. Finally, I reached my Hotmail account.

I started typing. It was amazing how sharp and fluid my mind was at this late hour. (I had to consider that it was still about 9 p.m. back in Atlanta.) Words just seemed to spill out, effortlessly, onto the screen, filling it up with the same ease it would take to pour water into a glass jug. I wrote about everything: how I was feeling over the last week and especially today. I talked about all my fears and anxieties, all my relief and realizations. I talked about the plane ride over, the airport, and how warm and caring Seb's family had been. And as I wrote descriptions of places, I imagined myself to be a famous poet or Pulitzer/Nobel Prize winning author. When I was finished writing and releasing all that had been built up around my mind and soul for the last few days, maybe even the last few years, I felt lighter and calmer. It had been the exact medication I needed, and when I woke up the next day; I couldn't remember how I made it back to the tiny bed in the other room. I must already have been dreaming before I left the chair.

I spent more time with the family the following day. It was like I had been adopted. We woke up early with the sunrise, ate croissants and drank a quick coffee; Natasha, Geesha's wife, had prepared snacks, meals and drinks to carry with us. Today we would head north to the Sea of Galilee, where much of Israel was gathering to barbeque and lie out, after a hard week of prayer and fasting. Last night had admittedly caught up with me, and I tried to increase my levels to the unstoppable energy of Greesha's family. I tried sleeping in the car, which worked up until the moment we picked up the cousin of Yafa. The tranquil backseat that had served as a haven to recuperate from my restless last two days was now a playground to two of Israel's most adorable little girls. At first, they were wrestling with each other, the entire time giggling and shouting, pausing at moments when Greesha scolded them, and continuing again with goldfish-like memory. When they were bored playing with each other, I became their next target of entertainment.

Even though I hadn't really been able to fall asleep again, ever since they were reunited about an hour ago, I was still able to rest my eyes and let the side window and back cushion hold the weight of my head. Every minute of sleep was treasured like the final. But that pleasure soon came to an end, when I started feeling these tiny little fingers pulling my eyelids back, and this immediate laughter whenever I made the slightest motion signaling my waking. Soon, I began giving into the fact that sleep was not going to happen for me anytime soon, and each time I opened my eyes, the girls were holding each other trying to be scared, all the while laughing without inhibitions the way I had forgotten to, a long time ago. I rose from my awkward backseat slouch, announcing the end of our little peek-a-boo game with the tired stranger, and they had already found another game. They were now singing a Black Eyed Peas tune, the one Greesha played for me the first day he picked me up. How did they know that song?!

The open scenery changed often on the trip up to Galilee. Meadows closed into valleys, valleys rose sharply to dirt hills and mountainous terrain, land plateaued at points or fell back closer to sea level. It was much greener, this drive, versus the one I had taken from the airport; but like on that other drive, I noticed more development of houses, built out of the same strength of cement. Then, with another change in terrain, this time from valley to hilltop, I noticed something new, something I hadn't seen before, little minarets, the Muslim towers that, I had read, broadcast the Koran at least five times a day. The neighborhood houses were appalling, run down, covered with dirt, crumbling from the sides like pieces of eroded earth from the mountainside. Clothes draped any possible ridge. The land on which the houses sat seemed non-arable, too hilly and rocky for safely built structures. Greesha told me these were the Israeli-Arabs, who made up about fourteen percent of the population; they weren't considered Palestinians.

When we reached the Sea of Galilee, the same sea whose water Jesus was said to have walked on and calmed two thousand years ago, we were met by a traffic jam of people searching a spot along its banks. The best area along the banks, where the most comfortable sand lay, was fully occupied by cars and people, so we drove further until we could finally guarantee two spaces. We had been traveling as a caravan of two cars the whole time; the other family had trailed behind us all the way from Rosh Ha'Ayin in a Volkswagen. Along the banks, scores of people set up barbeque grills and some people had spent the night before in tents. We were lucky when we arrived to find shade under a fig tree; the Israeli sun was merciless. The sun was much lower in the midday sky than I was used to seeing it. I only remember Singapore being harsher. They unpacked the food, while I unfolded the new speaker set I had bought, along with my new baby, a 20GB iPod, fresh white pearl face, and shiny metallic backing, with not a single scratch aging its appearance. I played a little bit of Bob Marley and the Beatles while we sat on a blanket eating hummus and pita bread, red grapes and beer under a tree. The tree couldn't prevent the sun's blistering air seeping underneath, so we finally fought our summer laziness and walked down the bank for a refreshing dip.

Walking in the water was a mixed blessing; it was refreshing and cool, but below our feet the different sizes and shapes of pebbles and rocks were unpredictable. I didn't know if the next step would bloody my feet, and I found relief in those heavy smooth stones. I made it out a comfortable distance from the shore, and decided to finally relax, enjoy the water, and take in my surroundings. The Sea of Galilee is named as such, but I found out in reality it's a freshwater lake in a depression of the Jordan River. Imagining everything that these waters had witnessed over their lifetime was mind-boggling. Geesha pointed to the other side of the lake, where through either the heat fumes or the hot steam rising from the lake, I could see hazily a small city or village. It was extraordinary to think that one of Jesus' twelve disciples was born in that village along the shore. And, somewhere along the Jordan River connecting this lake, Jesus was baptized by John the Baptist. To think, two thousand years later, two billion Christians, followers of the world's largest religion, would still be reading and following this man's teachings was beyond my comprehension. I wanted to absorb the mystery and spirituality this place exuded, make it a part of my being, to cling onto these images and sensations until one day I would make it back.

It was partly a mystery, me coming here, to this intense holy core for most of the world. The last four years seemed to place me in a lot of bizarre places that left the hanging questions, how did this all come about, why was I here? As quickly as I was moving around the globe, in the process something in the way of an internal map, or biological glass compass, had broken, changing and opening my limited perspective on the world. Before Thailand and other countries on that side of the world, the thought of traveling to Asia had been like shuttling off to the moon or as far away as Mars; why go, and where and how would I leave? This was because, for most of my life, my perspective really revolved around the U.S., and not even the whole U.S., certain pockets of the U.S. I had conquered for the most part, Georgia, a speck of dust on the broader map. So, how had the chain of life events led me here? How had I built up the courage and enough curiosity to now be in Israel, floating in holy waters near the birthplaces of Jesus, Abraham, and even, Muhammad and Jacob?

My most recent life was characterized by a random series of rapidly moving events, each one pushing me further and further out into the world, and at breath taking speed. My car was flying down the highway and my brake pads were wearing to almost nothing. Yet the world that had once seemed like an overwhelming trigonometry algorithm was now becoming more manageable and comprehensible. I was beginning to see the world as consisting of a few larger, less chaotic chunks. My fear and ignorance were fading alarmingly fast. Somehow I had begun to find comfort in risk taking or maybe, if I could properly analyze my personality all the way from birth, I would know it was only a consistent trait taken to a different realm. I was engaged in solving a global jigsaw puzzle of extreme consequences and fewer solutions. The evolution of my travelling efforts was increasing my knowledge and understanding of what took place around the world double and triple fold each year, and with every trip I took. I had read the *Economist* and other magazines like the *National Geographic* in the past, but now I read them with newfound vigor and fulfilment, and for obvious reasons. Before, it was impenetrable information, inapplicable to my world, like spreading peanut butter over air. It was how most of university had been for me, mostly the ingestion of reading material that had no bearing on my reality. Chemistry class had nothing to do with hanging out in the school plaza chasing girls or when I was a computer lab monitor maintaining the sign-in log. In those days, the material that I read was chucked into some memory block in an obscure location in my brain, only to be discharged onto a final exam at the end of the semester. All of it was mostly meaningless bureaucracy (or at least I had thought), necessary in advancing to the next stage of whatever my life would become. The information was dead weight in my head; it never really lived. I had been given information in school that needed the miracle of life, and I wasn't God.

But now I had a different feeling about all this new information. I was receiving life when I searched out a new place or revisited an old. Every article on Asia, Europe, the Middle East, or Latin American countries, touched living emotions within me; there were flesh and blood humans behind each of those articles, unforgettable eyes of tragedy and resilience. I could also reflect more effectively on my life in the U.S., objectively analyze my experiences and progress, construe my old stubborn opinions and blind cultural norms as to how they related to human nature, to the larger community of human beings around the world.

But how did all this play a role in my purpose in life? Was it by accident that I had met Seb or Leo, whose need to explore was much like mine? I was addicted to travelling the world. I couldn't deny that. And, I had passed the tourist frontier, where the excitement of the *new*, without much further understanding, was typically sufficient. A large part of my life was increasingly falling into this realm of world exploration, and I was convinced it would end up playing a larger, more defined role in my future. But I didn't know how and in what form. I was following my instincts just as a dog chases a fugitive scent, and I hadn't a clue where it would lead me.

We passed the day swimming and munching, taking walks along the lakeshore and napping below the fig tree. I realized at times how much I missed family moments like these. My life lately had cast me in a starring role in this surreal movie where the plot of the protagonist was to integrate himself into foreign families, one after another, like an adopted child in a timeshare agreement. And considering I hadn't spent time with my real family for so long, I had to hold onto those moments now, when Seb's family struck some sort of familiarity, a kind of *déjà vu*. Like the moment near the water, where Greesha's daughter and her cousin, almost a sister to her, splashed water at each other at the edge of the Lake, while Geesha, who wasn't interested in the water sat along the shore watching and smiling. That moment brought back vivid memories of my brother and me, playing in the waters of Jekyll Island, off the coast of Georgia, where my father, even though he rejected the water (a side-effect of his Vietnam tour), sat back on the beach looking on with the same vicarious pleasure. How, when Natasha laid out our pita pockets and fruit nicely along paper napkins, her motions and motherly rhythm instantly reminded me of my mom's diligence and that period of only about a year when she bought most of her food, which included more exotic snacks like rice crisps and pita bread, from this co-op group, another one of her cost-saving gimmicks.

Towards the end of the day, I could feel the two-day train of practically no sleep, and the draining weight of a long day swimming and frolicking under the sun. The car ride back was sleep time for me, and the girls could open my eyelids as many times as they wanted; I hadn't the energy to budge, or defend myself. But Greesha, I was learning, had a restless energy. He was determined to make it to his Master's graduation party at some lounge bar, and he wanted me to meet everyone, all of his classmates, the ones he never really had time to talk to out of class. I grudgingly agreed to go with him and Natasha. Considering how hospitable and welcoming he and everyone had been, I didn't want to disappoint them. So I took a shower, threw on my versatile Abercrombie slacks, and plumped my body onto the couch, waiting for the signal. I tried sleeping even in the car, but I couldn't sleep, my body clock was damaged.

We drove up to Tel Aviv, and Greesha the whole time exuded this blast of newly found energy; he was speeding and changing lanes, and Natasha was scolding him, but giving in and laughing at times. Greesha had changed into a completely different person ever since he'd left the kids behind at his parents' house. He was like a high school kid on a Friday night, after having talked his parents into loaning him the car. We made it to Tel Aviv in no time and the city was streaming with electricity. The area that we were cruising through had cars parked everywhere, all over the curbs and side streets, and I was finding some emergency reserve of energy anticipating this new sparkle, seeing all the lounge lights and open restaurants with patrons still dining away towards the middle of the night, enjoying the night breeze. We were in a section of Tel Aviv called Herzelya Pituah.

The graduation party was at a trendy lounge spot, very modern and simplistic. Inside, the place was decorated entirely in light wood, which traced a geometric trail from front wall to back wall. The expanse of space was long and narrow, creating a very intimate, cozy atmosphere for everyone lining the low sofas and chairs. The modern furniture made the utter coziness bearable and deceivingly spacious. Though what gave the place its edge and spunk were the trippy lights and the people, crisp in swanky, up-to-the-minute wear. The deejay in the back corner was on top of the music, laying new cuts of chill-out and smooth hip-hop, artists I hadn't even heard yet or artists I had heard but not in these new cuts and mixes. It felt like being in New York, at a side-street lounge in East Soho. I didn't feel like I was in another country at all, other than for the abundance of Mediterranean goddesses, freshly tanned and sipping down cocktails. I had already caught the eye of a few girls sitting in the back lounge, where there were hardly any guys. Something about me grabbed at their attention, in a curious way, and suddenly I was the new cowboy walking the saloon; and the present thought circulating through everyone's mind was, "You ain't from around here, are ya?" Already my attention had left the realm of Greesha and his family. I found myself on a hunt, or not really on a hunt, more like in a harem. I was ready to meet girls, get back on the dating scene, get back that mo-jo I had suppressed over the last three years. But first I needed a drink. My rationalization: if Greesha could act a little crazy driving, I was going to drink vodka and Redbull the rest of the night, try and lose myself in the Tel Aviv scene. Who knows, maybe even get lost with one of these girls; I was ready to take on the city.

I've often been surprised and shocked at my spurts of aggressiveness. The group of girls in the lounge sofa sitting next to Greesha's little graduation party seemed to summon me in their eye language. And I didn't hesitate. I made them slide over a bit on the black sofa while I sat down, and I don't know what I was saying, or how it all started, but it was coming out of me and they were laughing and responding. For a brief moment, I looked back at Greesha and his wife, telling them in my expression, "Damn right I know how to pull women . . . .What did you think, Seb hung around a bunch of pacifists? Deep down I'm a hunter, baby!" I switched sofa seats a couple of times, toasting shots with Greesha, Natasha, and all his classmates; there were only about five more of them. Then I returned to the girls' table with the same cockiness and relearned arrogance I had had to use in the night scene, back during University. Girls back in Atlanta didn't respond to passivity; it always took effort, an extra push of courage somewhere inside. And back then, I didn't always have that courage; it flowed in and out of me capriciously. If I had it or I didn't have it, it always showed. Women could always read this courage and assertiveness, printed on my face in the form of what they perceived was self-confidence. And I wasn't always good at putting on a show like certain friends of mine. But tonight was my performance; the spot light seemed to follow me wherever I was, from table to table, from table to the bar, and from bar to the bathroom. I felt like everyone else could see this radiating light illuminating my every move and gesture. And I was enjoying my new popularity; if only for tonight. Or, maybe, the Redbulls and vodka constituted my reality. Either way, I was going to try and make the best of tonight.

The girls I had been talking to most of the night, the ones I had given the typical spiel: where I was from, why I was here—were ready to leave; they wanted to dance and they knew a hot hip-hop club. Greesha was a little surprised and not sure what to think; I had basically just arrived in the city, and I would be riding off with strangers (although, perfect strangers) without really knowing my way around. But he understood and told me how to get back in the house, and to call him if anything happened, if I needed help for any reason. I said my goodbyes and was off with the girls, all of them bursting with night energy, ready to get their *groove on* to hip-hop, and hopefully, show me a good time.

We drove further into the city, where blocks became tighter, store spaces tinier, and streets more cluttered. I was blindly depending on three ladies I had only known for two hours. Now I was a new member of the gang, ready to take on whatever they usually took on. We walked a few blocks from where the car was parked. That was normal enough. We passed a late night deli, and slid down a small alley to a side door, where an unusually laidback bouncer sat at the top of the steps on a wooden bar stool. The girls seemed to know him well enough; they flirted long enough to help me skirt paying any type of cover. After we passed the bouncer, a narrow, seemingly bottomless staircase suddenly led down into the madness, the way a basketball team enters a chaotic stadium. The entire flight down, we could hear the Pharrell and Neptunes joint, and already we were dancing, while trying not to slip on the narrow steps. Then, voila!

The place wasn't as chaotic as the stairway led me to believe, and preferably so. It was a healthy scene, not large like the mega-clubs back in Atlanta, rather cozy and intimate for a hip-hop club—more like the lounge spots in London and New York or even Hong Kong. A trace of fog lingered over the dance floor, and a bluish light hung on to those remaining clouds gusted out mechanically by the fog machine. The bar was to the right side of the entrance, and I didn't need another Redbull and vodka, but I didn't want to be distracted later, when we found a good space to dance. Furthermore, I knew how hard it was for me to stop dancing. One of the girls, Aleah, beat me to the bar, already offering the first round. I didn't turn her down. We found the perfect spot on the dance floor, right next to a side table for our drinks. I felt no barriers on the dance floor, polishing it with my contrived Airwalk, ripping a couple impetuous turns and spins, pulling moves out I didn't even know I had in me. I was impressed how well the girls moved; one of them did this hip and booty movement like Beyonce, and even bent over a little when she did it, as if she had lived in Atlanta. The way all four of us danced and shared each other, I had determined, was the way friends or lovers of years brushed up each other without restraint; we were one big dancing orgy. Freedom was in the air around Tel Aviv; and our gang paraded as stylish cool hippies of our own era, breathing, inhaling the music, curving our bodies instinctively to the rhythms. The peculiar strength in our cohesiveness as a group, and the fact that at different times during the night I had reciprocated some sort of dialogue with each of the girls, led me to believe all three were hitting on me. (I hadn't calculated in the consistent stream of Redbull vodkas on my perception.) I didn't know which girl to focus on. So, I decided to relax and let things play out the way they were supposed to, and if finally at the end of the night, nothing, then at least I had a great night to look back on. It wasn't everyday I was surrounded by so much of the right attention.

After a few hours, the girls were soaked in sweat and exhausted. We drove to a late night Falafel stand; and on the way there I had noticed Mariel, the slightly less talkative one out of the bunch, was falling comfortably in my arms, as we sat in the backseat. I had been given the definitive sign. I thought Aleah was much more fit, but I couldn't deny Mariel's attraction. She had beautiful rounded eyes, a healthy shape, and more noticeable were her lips, they seemed to glisten and swell a little, like peeled pink grapefruit of the ripe and juicy kind. After the late night snack, we all drove first to Mariel's car. She asked me if I needed a lift home, and I said yes.

The car ride back to my place was quiet, and mostly speechless. Every once in awhile, the silence was too much and one of us chimed in with a question or an observation from that night. The alcohol was beginning to wear off, and my brain damage was becoming more noticeable. I had the wits of a goldfish, and to keep from showing my foolishness, I just kept quiet and smiled; even though any effort seemed difficult. Before entering the main road to my neighborhood, we were stopped at a checkpoint; a booth stood to the side of the road, so discreetly, I hadn't noticed it during the day. A man walked out with a dark green uniform, and another man, maybe his assistant, stood alert and erect to the side of the barricade, blocking the street. A semi-automatic rifle dangled from shoulder straps, his hands milliseconds from the trigger. They asked a few questions to Mariel in Hebrew, and then the guy lifted the barricade the way clearance is given to enter a war camp. The Mash flashback that woke me out of my slumber hardly affected Mariel, who had probably seen these things all too often. When we finally made it into the neighborhood and back to Greesha's, I wrote down Mariel's mobile number, and thanked her for a wonderful night. And, in the midst of our final eye contact and the closeness spawning from our final whispers, we began kissing. At first, there didn't seem any other logical action or way of concluding the night. What seemed so harmless and light in concept, turned into something completely different. I lost myself in that kiss for a moment; because even through the drunkenness and loss of nerves, emotions and feelings surfaced that didn't have anything to do with Mariel. I closed my eyes and found myself in a dream of familiar emotions and awfully missed passion. Mariel was only a conduit of past memories, and I attached myself to those memories and that familiar warmth, trying to suck every living ounce out of its pleasure. Maybe Mariel was attaching herself to something as well. We held that kiss, passionate and mouthwatering; we held it to ourselves, selfishly, afraid to look up for even a second, afraid to lose the moment and return to our realities. We held on insistently for one powerful spot of time, until the magic lifted and left our sad hearts lingering. I had to leave the car. I softly closed the door. When I turned around, I couldn't look back. I heard Mariel's car drive off in the distance, back to her home, back to her own sanity.

    The next morning I awoke suddenly when Greesha opened the front door. He was on his way to work, and it just occurred to me that I hadn't made it inside the apartment yet. I had fallen asleep on the front steps to his door, afraid to wake him up at five a.m., knowing he would have to leave for work at seven; that would just cut into his already short sleep, and I was trying to fulfil my end of the bargain: be a flexible house guest. He stood dazed for a second, while I got myself together and climbed into the apartment. His look of disbelief had to be shared with Natasha, so he stepped back into the living room and put his hands outward like a cross, palms facing upward to dramatize his reaction to Natasha. We all three laughed for a moment, and then Greesha said excitedly, "You have to tell me everything what happened when I get back later . . . okay?" And he walked out the door.

I was dead. I hadn't partied like that in a long time. I couldn't remember the last time I had had a night out that was so lively and continuous, all the way to wee hours of the morning. But I knew I would pay for it all today, because not only had I drunk alcohol and partied all night, I hadn't really slept well in three days. The irony was that that I left the U.S. thinking that my time away from corporate slavery would mean reasonable hours of sleep every night, no more fighting for short power naps during the day. I was going to normalize my life in some aspects, live healthier. I had eaten those words over the last three days, even though I enjoyed every conscious waking second.

Today was spent sleeping and eating, sleeping and eating, more sleeping and eating. I didn't have the energy for anything else. But I forced myself to call the tour companies I had written down off the Internet. Tomorrow I would begin my lone exploration; I had three more days until Seb and Leo would come walking back into the picture, carrying their dynamics. I booked tours for the following days, and then went back to sleep.

The next day I awoke bright and early like I had weathered a storm. Greesha agreed to take me to a hotel in Tel Aviv on his way to work. It was a pickup point for tour passengers. That morning I had seen graphically on the television a scene of terrorist violence that had occurred while I was sleeping the day away. Yesterday, during the late afternoon, when people were rushing home from work, after a long day of keeping the faulty gears of Israel oiled and moving, a suicide bomb attack blew half a bus into shatters. Most of the people inside that bus perished with the attack, Greesha translated for me, while I cautiously tipped down a scorching hot coffee. Even though I wouldn't be going to Tel Aviv until later in the week, the news shook me. It was a vision of the exact nightmare I had tried to ignore, somehow shut out of my mind, though now it was too strong an image, too probable a reality. Geesha didn't talk much about those images and realities; it was just assumed that I knew, and there was no sugar coating the facts in Israel. It was true. If you rode a city bus, walked into a bar or restaurant or store or anywhere other people, other Israelis, frequented, you were running a risk of being blown up. This was a country still very much at war, much different from the fading revolution that Castro tried to perpetuate in the minds of everyday Cubans. Israel was a fifty-year-old country, still expanding and contracting its territory, still fighting and defending its right to exist, and consequently still paying for its mistakes and misdeeds.

But it was too late for turning back now; I had made the decision to explore Israel with as little fear as possible, and to venture as far as its boundaries would take me. And that meant I wasn't going to miss the heart of Israel and the center of religion for three of the world's greatest faiths. My first stop would be Jerusalem. The name still sparked mystery and wonderment when I heard it. Pilgrims, Jews, and Muslims travel from all over the world to praise and worship their god here, and many great holy wars have been fought over this land and this city, even still today. I, too, yearned to be a part of its great history, discover its otherworldly magic.

Greesha placed me in front of the Dan Panorama Hotel, told me to stay safe, and sped off to work. The tour company had told me over the phone the tour would probably be at most six other people, and I couldn't tell if the few people waiting the inside lobby were part of the tour or just random hotel occupants. I wondered if I was in the right place, whether to wait in the lobby or stand outside for whatever, whoever would be picking me up. Anxious nerves controlled my thoughts; I didn't know if I was in the right place. I asked the front desk and they were sure that tours came through the hotel, but never heard of my tour company. So I waited. I sat inside for a while and then walked outside, afraid the van or bus would see no one standing and just pass right by. I was beginning to realize how much I hated waiting. Because before the age of sixteen, I always waited, ready to leave the house, depending on my friends, the older ones that had cars. And I vowed never to wait again once I passed my driver's exams and talked my parents out of the old Civic hatchback.

A blue van, the extended version, finally showed up with the tour name written on the side in hot red paint. No one followed me into the van. While hunching my back over to climb into the last bench of cushion, I greeted the other passengers, who hardly stared back. And it caught me off guard when the tour operator began speaking loudly through a microphone, his voice amplified from all directions in the vehicle.

"And where are you from?" he asked, in a raspy voice.

"U.S.," I answered.

"Now, we have U.S., France, and Germany," he said, repeating two more times, in two other languages. "Well, that's everyone," he said, while finishing the round about, and pulling back onto the main street. I expected more people, a larger van, maybe a bus even, but then Greesha's words appeared in my head, him telling me this morning how the endless suicide attacks in Tel Aviv and Jerusalem, the country's most important tourist attractions, had continued to push the tourist industry flat on its back, year after year, like the strength of a big bully constantly watching, waiting for its victim to stand up again. Not long into our ride, I had already separated the two groups, the French couple, who couldn't keep their hands off each other, sat directly in front of me and the German family, mother, father and daughter, sat stiffly and quietly in the first row; they hadn't even bent their necks to notice me as I entered the van.

On the ride over to the Holy City, the tour guide pointed out landmarks and cities off in the distance and explained bits of trivia or history about those places. But every time he spoke, I had the strange feeling that he was cutting short his English translated explanations. The long-winded sentences that seemed more like a conversation often ended up in just two or three words when he finally made it to my native tongue. And when I asked him questions, he was short with me, usually a yes or a no. I wondered if one English speaker wasn't as important as two French or three German speakers. Only ten minutes into the drive, and I already had a bad feeling about this guy. Every once in a while I could catch a glance of his face through the rearview mirror. I noticed the way wrinkles formed his face and forehead, like that of someone who frowned or had tensed up in anger a lot. His hair was thinning in odd places, and was left loose and wild in some places like it hadn't been combed in weeks. I wondered how many days and hours he baked under the harsh Israeli sun, because dark sunspots dotted those places not covered by hair. I had a sixth sense about this guy. Some instinct within me, some ancient ability to read character told me this guy was of the shady kind. It was the same gut feeling that I had used in Cuba, discerning the hustlers from good businessmen and good-hearted people. Even when I didn't follow my instincts, I could always look back to those first moments when it was crystal clear and the signs were in front of me. Spotting a hustler was something I had learned as early as middle school and high school, where good friends of mine had been hustlers and cheaters. And with their guards down to me, I would watch as they manipulated others, the more sheltered kids at my school and in my neighborhood. The guide had a hard and worn appearance like veteran taxi drivers in New York. The closer I watched his cold movements and the more I listened to his lifeless voice, the real voice behind the expensive audio equipment, the more I felt I was studying a tainted spirit. Maybe, in his time, he had seen something that changed him, been privy to a tragedy, something that tinged every innocent bone in his body, forever. As many questions as his existence prompted, I didn't want to know why he was this way, I plain didn't want to know him. I was sure with as much pain and struggle as someone like him had faced, he had in turn dished out his fair share of misery and pain. I didn't trust him. And it bothered me that I wasn't receiving the full treatment, like the others, how I was being ignored and slighted. It wasn't the same Israeli treatment I was getting used to ever since my plane flight into the country. In my mind, he was wasting my time and money. If I ever had to name a pet peeve, it would be the withholding of information and unanswered questions—it was the perpetual periodista in me. I tried to suppress my annoyance. There was no use getting too worked up over it. I had made my judgment. I focused more on the surrounding scenery, as we drove to our destination.

On our way to Jerusalem, we passed a forest full of pine and cedars perfectly planted and aligned in rows and columns. As far as the eye could see, trees reached outward and over the hilltops. According to our Mister Guide, who suddenly had more to say in his explanations, each one of the four and half million pine trees planted represented an adult Jew killed during the Holocaust, while each one of the million cypress trees represented a child killed during the monstrosity. It was right that we all stayed quiet and reflective in the van. The trees and what they symbolized seemed to reach out to our souls with despairing, bony waving arms and eternal voices crying out to each of us, one by one. A sadness gripped me as I sat dazedly in the backseat trapped in a nightmare; involuntarily my eyes searched for every single tree, even if there were too many trees to acknowledge. I admired the undertaking of such a massive project and was hopeful for a future rich in the green life stretched out over the valley and beyond the hilltops, like risen bodies. From the time we entered the area, to the time we passed the last row of trees, there had been an indescribable energy felt as if we were passing through a time warp. And only later, miles further down the road, did my uneasiness begin to dissipate.

Our path to Jerusalem wound through mountains, where dynamite had broken through hard earth and rock. As we entered the outer layers of Jerusalem, the city appeared extremely calm. Maybe too calm. People were patiently waiting at the bus stop, Muslims and Jews and hip teenagers with skateboard shoes and baseball caps. The few surrounding buildings, at first, gave a feeling of passing through a redbrick college campus. And before we drove too far inwards, the van found an inclining street leading upwards beside the elevated Hebrew University, and our guide pulled over to a lookout point, where the land drops off. From here, we were to take photos. I took expansive panoramic pictures of the Mount of Olives and the old city of Jerusalem. What I noticed was that all the buildings and gates, everything, was built of solid stone, a material plentiful in the surrounding mountains. It occurred to me that even cities risking natural disasters, like earthquakes and hurricanes, or even tsunamis, weren't built this sturdy. Here in Israel, a wooden house would be like a cardboard box in the street or a trailer home. Then again, how could someone even think to throw up a wooden house next to thousands-of-years-old Roman structures? The holy people of Jerusalem had built these places to last an eternity.

We got back into the van and headed down toward the old gates of Jaffa, the western entrance into the old city of Jerusalem. "5,000 years old! The city is 5,000 years old!"—the guide's last words still rang in my head. It was hard to fathom. The oldest city in the U.S. couldn't have been more than a few centuries old, and here I was about to walk the same land Canaanites had settled around 3,000 B.C.E., the same land where the Israelites had roamed in 1,000 B.C.E., and where the Babylonians destroyed and conquered in 596 B.C.E., later succumbing to a Persian Kingdom. Jerusalem had been the center of the earth for humanity's three greatest religions, a sacred land, constantly fought over like a gigantic precious stone. Something evident weaved in and out of its long torturous history, and the anticipation of finally witnessing with my own eyes why for so long, so much of humanity had been so fixated over this tiny plot of land was heating me up. The van parked not far outside the old city walls. From this point on, we would be on foot. I kept thinking how incredibly old and stony everything was. The streets were built of bruised white stone, the buildings, the gates, the small tunnels, the houses and the churches. Our guide explained the city in four parts: an Armenian Quarter, a Christian Quarter, a Jewish Quarter, and the non-stop pace of the Muslim Quarter. But still he seemed to short change me on certain information along the tour. I found comfort in the smells of the fresh ka'ak bread with sesame dip, and I marveled in the panorama of street views, archways and tunnels, elevations of stones and structures and lived-in apartment homes all amalgamating into this edgy, flourishing Jerusalem that couldn't be described or explained; a person had to be there to understand.

During our tour, I had been especially touched by the Via Dolorosa, the site of the treacherous stony walk Jesus struggled mercilessly along for the last time, before his crucifixion. There were fifteen stations marked off in Roman numerals along the buildings crowding the narrow streets, each point a momentous scene along Jesus' walk. The streets themselves, along with the eerie feeling that Jesus had walked the very steps I was taking, haunted and humbled me. Nothing was beautiful or pleasant about them. They were composed of bulging stones, uneven and protruding like stacked piles of raw meat. The path led all the way to the Church of the Holy Sepulchre, the final station, the site of the Crucifixion after which Jesus was said to have risen from the dead. Apparently, an extreme Christian or an extremely devout Christian (depending on one's interpretation) could pay money to re-enact the very path of Jesus with a replica crucifix strapped to the back. I thought the idea was tacky and absurd, although I didn't know where that placed me. We visited the Western Wall, the holiest place on earth in the Jewish Religion, and the oldest place, built in the first century B.C. by King Herod. Not far from the Western Wall, over on the other side, in the Muslim Quarter, stood the Temple Mount and the Dome of the Rock, arguably the second most revered monument in the Muslim Religion. This is where Muhammad was said to have risen into heaven. We even visited the site of The Last Supper.

Strangely, I had a feeling of everything, all the history and religion, not having sunk in yet. Maybe it was too much to digest all in one day. Or maybe I was too hungry to think. We were now walking to a group of street corner restaurants, and our guide directed us to sit and eat at a particular spot among the many; it seemed he knew the owners. "Aha!" I thought to myself. "I know this game. Lead the naïve, helpless tourists to some restaurant where you can charge them exorbitant prices, and reap a commission on the side." Well, it didn't affect me, because I had brought my own lunch of hummus and pita, an apple and water. He wasn't going to get over on me. But then, as I pulled my food out to eat, while the others ordered from the menu, he had the nerve to ask me to eat somewhere else after he obligated the entire group to sit here. An explosive anger stirred inside of me. It wasn't his business to tell me where I should eat. If the owners or waiters wanted me to leave, that was for them to say, not him. It was obvious to me that his only problem was the commission he would be missing out on from me. Even the Germans, who before had been rather expressionless and speechless, spoke out in disbelief towards his comment. I was equally surprised that all this time they knew English. I wanted to lash out at the guide, but I found some inner strength of calm, knowing that it was dangerous for me to get to that point. I was a speeding bullet when I reached that point. So I saved my words and anger and walked out to the hot, shadow-less curb, and ate my lunch. Even though the sun battered me, I felt better after the meal. Next door was a gift shop that our guide wanted us to visit. It would be another stop on our tour. Inside the shop, he haggled with the French couple and Germans, trying to pressure them into buying one of the cheap-quality religious gifts. It was a pathetic and most despicable display. Then, he walked up to me, making his religious rounds, as I was looking through one of the glass cases of Crosses and Star of David pendants.

And, he asked me, "What is your faith?" I looked at him blankly. He continued, "I'm sure you're mother would love one of these …"

Before he could even finish his sentence, I stopped him, and, spilling out of my depths came, "Are you crazy?" And, then the gates of the damn broke open. I couldn't stop how I felt about him at this point, how he was taking a good place, a holy place, and exploiting it without rules for his own financial gains. I wondered how many tourists who had flown from across the world in order to enrich their lives spiritually had fallen into the swindling trap of this freak. "Have you lost your mind?!" My voice got louder. "Do you think for a second, that I believe any of your nonsense? That I don't know what you're truly after. You don't give a damn about any of our family and friends. Be honest! You want a commission! Simple and plain! And, look at these prices! One hundred dollars for a cheap silver cross! Have you lost your mind! Has the owner lost his mind! I wouldn't buy these cheap imitations of spirituality, even if they were on sale! And I wouldn't put any more money in your pockets either!" And then it was over; the floodgates closed back, and I walked outside, done with the petty shop.

Almost immediately, I felt better. I finally was able to let go of all the negative energy that had built up ever since I stepped into the van. And I was happy to see that the other five people, after they heard my frustration, decided against buying anything in the gift shop. What struck me out of all of this about Jerusalem was that religion was big business for them. Something about that didn't sit well with me. I began thinking about how religion was exploited all over the world, not only for money but also for power. And I began to think of all the governments that used religion to justify so many abuses and laws. There were clearly two kinds of people in my book, when it came to religion, those who use it to better the lives of others, and those who exploit it selfishly to the detriment of others. I was sure the guide was in this latter group. Luckily, our tour was basically over. We had the holocaust museum left, and we would be on our own during that time. I just hoped he didn't try to leave me, because I hadn't a clue how to make it back to Tel Aviv, where Greesha would be picking me up.

On the way back from the museum to Tel Aviv, I gave Greesha a call on the cell he was loaning me during my time here in Israel. I suspected it was Natasha's cell. The whole time I had been here, I continued to be pleasantly surprised by his hospitality.

Greesha answered in a stressed voice, "Hello."

"Hi. It's Chris. I'm just calling to let you know I should be back in thirty or so minutes, back in front of the Hotel."

"Chris. Something happened at work. Listen, I won't be able to pick you up anytime soon."

"Oh . . . okay."

"You will need to take the bus. Do you have a pen or something to write with?"

"Um, yeah, I have a pen right here."

"You need to find Bus 51 DAN at the station. That will take you out of Tel Aviv to the city of Rosh Ha`Ayin. Take it all the way to the bus station. From there take Bus 17 DAN to my neighbourhood. Do you remember the street and address?"

"It's . . . " I said, trying to sound comfortable with the whole idea.

"Yes. Okay," he sounded halfway in our conversation, the whole time as if he was focused on two things at once. "I have to get back. You have the cell phone. Make sure to call me if anything strange happens. Seb's mom will kill me if anything . . . . Okay I gotta go." And, he hung up.

I was a bit stunned. I held his directions in front of me, but I was sure there was something he left out or something I hadn't asked. And I would be on my own in the middle of Tel Aviv. I had my reservations about asking Mister Guide anything, but I didn't know where any bus stations were, and I wasn't even sure what part of the city I had been dropped off at early this morning.

Then it hit me. I was going to have to catch a bus! In my mind, stepping onto a Tel Aviv bus was the same as trying for a losing lottery ticket. The winners, to me, were the ones that didn't play the game. And the very real thought of stepping onto the losing bus made my body shiver. Because, ever since this morning, after seeing the charred bloodied remains of victims blown up on a bus, in the very city that I was now en route to, I had continued to play those graphic images over and over again in my mind. All day, I remembered feeling completely different about suicide attacks than I had witnessing them from the eleven o'clock news back home in Atlanta. Because, back there, thousands of miles away across the Atlantic Ocean, it had always been "think and forget." Those news briefs on Israel that usually stopped me for a few seconds at night before I tried getting sleep, or paused an otherwise meaningless conversation during another firm-sponsored not-so-much-happy-hour, forcing my head up towards the small television behind the bartender, all of these briefings, were like watching another Steven Segal movie. And even though, in the back of my mind, I knew it was real, somehow it was easy to detach myself from the mortal consequences, the real loss of life, the families on both sides of the attack devastated and changed forever. Those thoughts as if placing tissue over bullet wounds, barely gripped the images I had seen on television over the last years.

Now, it was different. I was very close to these harsh realities, not even twenty-four hours away from them, and I had never once taken a bus in Tel Aviv. Where to get off? Where to begin? Were there dangerous areas to this city? Areas that didn't welcome foreigners or even normal Israelis? I knew places like that back in the States. I had to calm down. I took a deep breath. I had to think optimistically. I talked to myself: "People take buses everyday. It's not something odd or new." And I fought back thoughts of the article I had read about that one couple that vowed never to take another bus again, after their neighbor had passed away; I didn't want to focus too deeply on the fact that there were normal Israelis who didn't even take the bus for calamitous reasons. I looked at the time on the cell phone. For some reason I didn't have my wristwatch on; I couldn't remember if I had packed it or not. It was only about 3 o'clock, and I wondered what I would do with the rest of my day, that's if I survived the bus first. I wanted to hit myself for thinking that way, but I couldn't block away those thoughts.

I talked to Mister Guide, who had held a noticeable grudge towards me, ever since our gift shop incident. I knew that asking him for directions was the stupidest thing I could have done, but I didn't want to ride all the way to the opposite side of Tel Aviv, if the bus station wasn't there.

"Bus station," he said, in an argumentative tone. "You don't need a bus station. You just need to find the right bus stop. I'll tell you where to get off, when we reach the city." He said it as if to also tell me at the same time to sit back down. Now I had even more apprehension, knowing that I would be at the whim of wherever maniac Guide sought fit to put me out. It didn't matter, I told myself, not believing in my words. "I could find myself in the right direction. I just need to get out of this god-awful van." We drove a fair distance into the city before Mister Guide pulled over to the curb and dropped me off. He told me it would be somewhere around here, my stop, and before I climbed down from the steps and onto the sidewalk, I did notice a cluster of bus stops, a little ways down the street, before the intersection. Maybe he would set things straight by putting me off in the right place. Soon, his engine roared again and I was out walking in a strange, new place.

The bus stops down the street, come to find out, weren't the right ones. But suddenly I didn't care. I immediately found myself wrapped up in my new scenery with the new people walking around me all in one big hurry, all with serious metropolitan faces, the way afternoon walks in downtown Atlanta had been during the work week as if no one had time to be sociable humans, unless you considered those stressful hand gestures over the mobile phone as friendly. And something else had happened ever since I left the van: the black and white photo that I had stored in my mind's periphery as a headshot of Israel had changed quite a bit. I was now in a world of many ethnicities, all different shades and physical make-ups. An African man crossed me on the street with a kippot on his head; he looked like many of my Ethiopian and Eritrean friends back in Atlanta, that same young unblemished skin and curly hair. A thought crossed my mind. Were some of these people Palestinians? Until now, I thought Palestinians would stand out like sore thumbs amongst the crowd of Jewish Israelis. I still had a particular stereotype of an Israeli from the majority of people I had met since coming here, but that image of dark hair and olive-white skin was fading fast.

I felt much more comfortable with Tel Aviv, after being plunged into its core, the way a skydiver must feel in the air after passing the most difficult part, jumping out of the plane. Now I had a decision to make. I could continue to search for a bus back to Greesha's or I could explore Tel Aviv during the day. As far as I was concerned that drunken night out in the Tel Aviv club scene hadn't counted; that night I felt more like I was partying somewhere in New York than in the Middle East. I stopped a harmless looking girl on the street. She was waiting at a bus stop and wasn't part of the river rapids of people flowing through the sidewalks.

"Excuse me. Where is the center of Tel Aviv? I mean, where are the main attractions?" I asked.

"What do you want to see? You could go to Dizengoff Square, where all the high fashion and trendy kids go shopping and eating. Or, you could go to the beach. There are shops and bars and restaurants there. You should go to Allenby Street. Everything is walking distance from there."

"Okay. How do I get there?"

"Well, the bus I'm waiting for goes to Allenby Street. I can show you where to get off. And don't worry, I know what it's like," she finished. Her last comment lost me.

"You know what it's like?" I repeated in a confused voice.

"You're American, aren't you?"

I nodded my head yes, not sure where this was going.

"I was there just last year, and I remember having to ask people for directions, not always sure where to go."

"Ohh, right," I responded, "Where were you in the U.S.?"

"New York."

I thought to myself, it figures. Atlanta was over four million people, and I had never met an Israeli there. I figured they all had to be in New York or maybe California.

"I'm from Georgia. I live in Atlanta."

"Oh, yeah! I always wondered what that was like."

"It's a great city." I wanted to say more about Atlanta, but I didn't know where to start. What I did know was that the world was much smaller than I could have ever imagined.

The bus came to a stop. It was our bus and immediately I felt tense, somewhat nervous. All I could think about was the bus on the television this morning. And I began staring, analyzing each and every person to see if they fit any profiles or to look for anything suspicious, as we found two adjoining seats in the back of the bus. I wondered if this is how it was everyday for Israelis riding the bus. Instead of contemplating the meeting you had that day at work or the special planned dinner you had for that night with family or friends, was the mind always preoccupied with what-ifs, and who is that strange guy with the large backpack? These thoughts kept circulating my mind, and soon I had brought up my concerns and curiosity with Rayna not even thinking to sugar coat the questions, as they escaped my mouth.

"Well, I can tell. I know when I look into someone's eyes if they have evil intentions. I've walked off buses in the past when I got a bad vibe," she said.

"But how do you know?"

"I just know. If you live here long enough, you can spot trouble."

Her answers weren't good enough for me, because even on our bus, there were all races and social levels. It would be impossible to pick someone out of all these different people. "Do you know anyone who has died in a suicide attack?"

"Sure, a friend I grew up with died in a street café, when a suicide bomber just casually walked in with explosives strapped to his back. And some kids from my school died. I'm lucky no one from my family. Really, I think everyone in Israel has been touched, by someone they knew."

As she tried to finish her last sentence, a loud crash shook the bus, and in the exact same moment, everyone from the back of the bus where we were sitting started screaming and panicking. Chaos ensued. Everyone from the back was trying to run to the front, but the doors of the bus weren't opening. So people were being pushed over and into the other people frightened from the sudden blasting noise. I was in shock. I tried to run with the crowd, at the same time looking back to see what had happened. I was sure that a bomb or something had gone off. All I really knew was the back window of the bus had completely shattered and part of the window was hanging in clumps; the left side of the bus was badly bent. I could see into another bus, right behind our bus. Maybe the bomb had gone off in the other bus. No one knew the answer.

People were screaming and gasping, clinging to the sides of the bus for some form of shelter. I wanted off of the bus, but I was also somewhat debilitated by the suddenness of everything. My body wasn't ready to beat down the doors for a fast exit. Then, everything calmed down. People stopped screaming and panicking and started walking back to their seats. The bus driver told people it was all right, they could go back to their seats. And when we sat back down, it was all clear to me. The bus behind us had run into the back of our bus, shattering the entire back window and damaging the frame. It was an odd coincidence.

I was still a bit shaken by all the commotion. My heart was pounding out of my chest, and I found myself trying to maintain my composure in front of the Israeli girl and everyone else, act like I had it all under control. A woman who was closest to the back window was crying, her emotions having been overwhelmed by this freak accident. I thought, "What are the chances?" I had received the lottery ticket with all the right numbers, all except the last digit, just barely keeping me away from the losing ticket. I still wanted off this bus, but I held myself together and rode out my emotions and nerves, waiting for Allenby Street. The bus driver didn't bother to wait for another bus or try and inspect the damage; he just continued on his route as if nothing had happened. "What a day," I thought, and it still wasn't over.

"The next stop is Allenby," she said.

As I was getting up, I said, "Thanks for everything. I hope the rest of your day is less turbulent than this bus ride!"

"No need to thank me. Enjoy the city. Make sure to walk down near the coast. And be careful."

"Okay. Maybe I will see you around." She waved bye to me, and again through the window, as the bus was pulling off.

There was this energy in Israel that kept everyone moving, a constant unquiet. I had seen it on the plane, and I could feel it like the passing wind of people swarming the street of Ben Yehuda, the street intersecting Allenby Street. I was now in my second day in Tel Aviv during the day. Yesterday, I had left not long after arriving to Allenby

Street, because for one, I realized how exhausted I had been after an entire day of incidents, and secondly, I wanted enough time to find my bus home in the day light. I had never felt so cautious in my life. That night when I returned home, after having taken two buses more than I needed to finally reach Greesha's place, I had called the tour company to complain about Mister Guide and his conniving ways, and luckily the company had offered me a second tour half-price off to the Dead Sea and Masada, which would begin two days later on Thursday. That was perfect, because the following day, on Friday, Seb and Leo would be arriving. And I was sure they had seen their share of tours; this was my only chance.

So, today was a free day. I was beginning to get over my fear of buses, and the graphic images of the terrorist bombs began fading away, replaced by more immediate images. Like everywhere I went, now, I noticed soldiers walking the street and riding the bus. Greesha had explained to me that every boy has to serve three years in the Israeli Army and girls two years, once they turn eighteen years old. "There is no escaping the draft!" he said. It was peculiar to me seeing teenagers walking casually on every street corner, with large semi-automatic rifles strapped around their shoulders, some of them being absolutely gorgeous girls in green uniforms. And, ironically, I felt a little safer knowing there were so many soldiers. Though it was a strange safe. Last night, I had decided to do more research on Israel and Tel Aviv, revisit the Palestinian conflict and search for more information regarding terrorist attacks and where they occurred. I always did it that way. A normal person would probably do the research before flying across the world, but I always needed to associate words with real human beings and physical landmarks. What struck me the most were the articles on Palestinians and Israelis, and their ongoing conflict, a conflict that seemed to be getting worse and worse, year after year. And standing in the heart of Tel Aviv now, on a Wednesday, in the middle of a busy week, I was affected by those articles on Palestinians and my understanding of how the city and much of its surroundings had come to be. Imagining how this area might have looked only fifty-odd years ago, or how it might have looked today, intrigued me and bothered me all in the same moment.

I loved Tel Aviv. It was a beautiful city with absolutely beautiful people. Yet, beyond the Dolce & Gabana glasses and BMWs, there was something rotten in the air of Israel. As much at home as I felt around the Israeli people, and as much as I truly deep down felt camaraderie and love for every person I had met thus far, except for that tour guide, of course, something didn't sit right with me. There was something missing, like an endangered species, from my surroundings here, and what was missing seemed to lurk like a secret whisper behind every corner and every new high-rise building. Thousands of years of history had placed different religions and kingdoms at the helm of this intense land; and never without first sacrificing the blood of others. The Israelis were only the next in a long lineage to wash that human blood from their clothes and skin, hoping in time, after future generations, the blood stains of man could be cleaned from their memory, hoping that their weak moment in history would never come again. I wanted to understand this warring country better, hear the right answers, justify why it should have happened this way, or not. I wasn't dealing with balance sheets and income statements that made sleeping at night so much easier after Mr. Benton's Accounting 101 class. I wanted to have an opinion, clearly explain with objectivity what was the right thing for both sides to do. But the more I talked with Israelis, the more I read others' opinions on both sides and heard why "the other side" should be condemned for the actions of a few and the hate of many, the more confused and lost I had become within this crisis. There didn't seem to be clear answers or answers at all. All I knew was an entire body of people had been virtually wiped away from these streets, sectioned off as in Indian reservations or concentration camps, cleansed from the active life in Tel Aviv or in Jerusalem or at the Sea of Galilee. Knowing that the demographic of these lands had been dramatically different only fifty or more years ago, imagining families and traditions that now hardly existed along this sacred soil, didn't settle properly in my mind.

    Those broken branches of thoughts seemed to get caught and tangled on other thoughts, also revolving in my head: like the grievances of Jews over years and years of oppression and struggle within Western society. For them, it had always been about survival, finding a place safe for their kids to grow up and feeling as part of a broader community. Israel was that saving grace for many Jews threatened in their homelands, like in former republics of Soviet Russia, and most famously Germany. After centuries of movement all over the world, they were running out of countries and regions to migrate to. And Israel was an answer for many of them, the best option. Still, creating a narrow nation in the midst of other families and communities was the great sacrifice to finding a home. I was peering over this great spectacle with only limited insight and vision, which was making my analysis even cloudier. I had heard that Israelis had legally purchased much of the land from Palestinians and it was true that the Palestinians had been uncompromising in respect to any final deal, which would have divided land and permitted an Israeli state. Also, Palestinians could have remained under Ottoman control, if it weren't for WWI, which involved the help of other European nations and the help of many Jewish fighters, alongside Palestinians, who both had an interest in opening this land to a future nation. But the Palestinians, did they have a right after being liberated from Ottoman rule, to say, this is still our land? To say, we still have the right to use it as we please, to reject anyone from laying claim to any part of it, or reject sharing it if we don't want to, regardless of the reason? I couldn't answer these questions with a razor sharp decisiveness. The best way I knew how to view the situation was with what could be done now to help smooth has to keep pushing forward in life, regardless of the pain. I kept pushing forward in the hot sun.

I wanted to see the coast of Tel Aviv, stop at the beach, maybe even take a swim. I didn't know if summer days held magical powers, but I always brightened up on a bright sunny day. Today was no different. The closer I got to the beach, the darker olive the bodies, and it seemed, I'm not kidding, the larger the breasts. It occurred to me walking down the street that at least nine out of ten girls were well-bosomed. I don't know if that was an Israeli trait, but it was more than noticeable, and none of the women were too shy in sharing them for the world. Israeli women were quite beautiful with their dark curly flowing hair, and their sunglasses large enough for scuba diving. "Wow!" I thought. "The last girl I just passed was too much! Real model chic! Slim, tall and curvy; ready for the beach." I had to catch myself from staring. I had noticed one thing. My mind had become more and more preoccupied with women lately. I analyzed them a lot. And I could be fooling myself, but I think I appreciated them much more. I mean my tastes in women had blossomed, opened up to the world. I was a lot more curious these days, and I found myself infatuated with the new, exotic and mysterious.

Maybe I had always been that way. I couldn't remember. What I did remember is how much I was dying to see Maggie. But I couldn't go back to those days. I had left that life behind, along with the other prisons. It occurred to me that I hadn't been with a woman since Maggie; more than a half a year. Damn! That probably answered my preoccupation with women. I had even passed up the chance, at least a couple times, since being here. I kept forgetting that I was a free man, officially. Somehow Maggie continued to stay by my side as if a ghost or some sort of guardian angel. "But," I said to myself, "what am I thinking? She's probably off doing her *thing*, could even have a steady boyfriend by now. I'm such a fool. Of course, she has a new boyfriend." Models don't live a minute without someone they can call their own, someone they can love and show off to their gay hairstylists. Sometimes it seemed like I hadn't really moved on. And maybe it wasn't my time. The truth, I didn't feel in any rush. In many ways, I was happy being single. But, I wouldn't turn down one of these exotic beauties, if she were the right person, at the right place and time. Something hadn't frozen me with the other girls I had met, since being in Israel. Something was missing in our chemistry. I could hear my friends back in Georgia saying, "What are you waiting for! Stop being so picky!"' And they would probably be right. I needed to snap out of this zone, this locked gate to everyone I met.

  I reached the small plaza before the beach at the end of Allenby. I walked left on the promenade towards the small huts on the beaches. I had a taste for a slushy, refreshing drink like a Daiquiri. I sat down under an umbrella and looked out towards the Mediterranean sea, remembering again how calming and therapeutic was the sound of rolling waves, the familiar smell of salt in the air that never let me down. Only good memories attached themselves to simple waves. Today I was going to take it easy, not hurry myself with sight seeing. I had even brought a book to read when I was tired of drinking and watching eye candy on the beach. I hadn't done this in years. Let me correct that, ever. It was like being in retirement or something: I wanted to laugh at my fickle life, thinking of how crazy it had been only a couple of months ago. I wondered if my ex-colleagues were struggling this very second trying to make some urgent, life or death, deadline. It was baffling, what I had gone through. And now, all of it seemed so irrelevant. I had buried the profession, said my farewells. I wasn't in any hurry to breathe new life into any of those old memories. But what was I going to do when the traveling got old? I still hadn't figured that out.

  The rest of the day was spent lounging on the beach, marveling in the author's wordplay, the way I could see myself in his characters, how he placed me at the scene of his crimes as if I was helping to solve them or if I felt rebellious enough, fleeing from my unjust accusers to a better hideout. It was great. I hadn't picked up a book for fun in years. Maybe even since university. It was incredible finding that I had the motivation and willpower to pick up the book at all. I remember as a child chunking the thousands of books that my mother always pushed down my throat into the back of my closet or under my bed. She bought them as birthday gifts, as Christmas gifts, and even sometimes for no reason at all. I used to watch her stay up at night in our living room with a coffee or sometimes a beer next to her on the short bookshelf and a persistent purring cat on her lap, and the way she could just devour books. Finish whole books in two days, even a day if she really lost herself. I used to think how boring she was for giving up her free time to a couple hundred pages and a cardboard backing. There was so much to see outside in the world, and she was trapped up in the house reading, quietly. It never dawned on me at that time that one could travel across the world by the flick of a thumb, and, of course, the patience of an adult. Back then, I would rather go outside or have a sleep over at a friend's house. And during the summer, when kids checked out books from the library, so that they could win special awards, determined on how many books they read, I could have cared less. I had backyard basketball games to attend with Edgar or Mario, neighborhood mischievousness to explore with Derek or Jarrel or video games to challenge Teddy at or even a forest behind Jermaine's house to get lost in, passing the same tree stump for hours. My disdain for books lasted all the way to university, and even then I never picked up a book unless it meant passing an exam. But now I was swept away by this book. It was an unbelievable experience to follow with suspense a character so humanly real, you could shake that person's hand or hug them as if you had already met. I wondered what it took to write a book, what kind of personality created this amazing story I was reading. I lay down by the beach after finishing a quarter of the book, before deciding to go back to Greesha's. The sun was draining and I knew I would be in the sun all day tomorrow. Then, Seb and Leo would be arriving the next day. That was going to change the entire pace and attitude of the trip. I had to admit, I missed the guys. I was looking forward to catching up on all the time we missed. And this time would be as if we were back in Thailand, no job, and no imminent job curfew; just two long years to look back on, so that we never got bored or forgot how to appreciate our time traveling.

I woke up the next day as early as Greesha. We did our usual, coffee and a croissant, morning news, and then, off into the Tel Aviv traffic. He was to drop me in front of that same hotel, Dan Panorama. This time the tour company promised me a top rate guide, one of their best. And they were right. Only a couple minutes into the drive, from when the tour van picked me up, and already I liked the guy. He was a straight shooter kind of person that looked you in the eyes, and seemed to genuinely enjoy his job. He had an open, honest face, a large forehead, and he combed his hair back, not to hide a single facial expression. Furthermore, everyone spoke English on this trip. I didn't have to deal with communication lapses and blank stares. I had a great feeling about this one. I was psyched and anxious to walk on water (well, at least float without effort). The ride, once we escaped the hustle and bustle of the city, spread out infinitely. I marveled in the subtleties of vast countryside. We passed a watermelon patch, the size of at least ten football fields, and I sat in awe at the thousands, if not millions of ripe watermelons bubbling from the earth, like hot lava stones. The vastness closed in when we passed the West Bank settlements, and an unsightly cement wall, the controversial wall separating Palestinian territory from Israel, protruded from the hilly terrain and was hard to distinguish from it, winding upwards and downwards as if a thick gray ribbon placed on its side. And not all the way finished either. It was cut short at one end, exposing settlements and dusty, non-arable land. A brief fear ripped through me as we passed through what technically was Palestinian territory, knowing how close I was to the desperation. Much of the ride had been spent avoiding this territory, circumscribing around its southern tip so that we could reach around to the Dead Sea on the other side.

Once through the Palestinian area, our ride had the feeling at times of traveling to the end of the earth or even outer space, because the land, with all its creases and cliffs, erosion and dryness, seemed like how the moon might appear during sunlight. We were declining steadily through lines in the valleys and in between mountains that appeared like gigantic ant mounds, as seen from the tops. We were above them as if the cascade of summits were reddish-brown stairways, and we were descending to the depths of a grand canyon.

Someone asked, "What are the black dusty tents doing off in the distance?" At brief plateaus along the mountain slopes could be seen long rectangular tents, supported on the sides by tree limbs.

Our guide answered, "Bedouin settlements. Bedouins are an ancient community of nomads inhabiting these lands, a culture dating back to biblical times."

At a flat landing next to the roadside, a car was stopped. A little girl nervously sat astride a camel that still hadn't found the strength to lift itself up onto its toothpick legs. A middle-aged Bedouin with dark sun-baked skin, wearing all white fabric to reflect the sun and a bundle of white fabric wrapped neatly around his head, pulled vigorously at the reins trying to motivate the camel, but the camel was clearly taking its time. As we cautiously stopped to the side of the road to take a better look, the camel finally rose, pushing from its back knees clumsily upwards, and then managing to find its front legs. The little girl seemed frightened at first, not sure what to think about her new adventure, but after the camel found level ground and caught a slow steady stride, the little girl was ecstatic and giggling with all her might the way only children know how to do. I felt sorry for the camel, not because of the ride or the scorching heat, but because he had no choice in his wardrobe. A stylist at a circus must have dressed him in the rainbow of clown colors covering his back bumps and the pink headdress holding his reins, a blaring contrast to the desert colors encrusting the mountains. The camel seemed to hold an expression of reluctant compliance to his owner's wishes; because, of course, he had no choice.

We were now back on the road and dropping steadily in altitude. Signs reminded us along the way how far we had descended: 100 meters below sea level, then 200 meters, and then 300 meters. And it continued like this until we reached about 400 meters below sea level, at which point the land stretched out flat in front of us, and we were no longer driving downwards with the change in topography. We stayed constant, while only the mountains surrounding us off in the distance moved nervously from peak to valley. And it dawned on me, today would be my last moment of peace before a storm of adventure, when the three musketeers would unite in arms and cast out over the Middle East and Eastern Europe in pursuit of more foreign territory, more harmless spoils. I wondered where Seb's and Leo's Israeli excursions had taken them, when had they passed through on this long, flat road I was now speeding down. I wondered what it was like for them, traveling for almost a week now throughout Israel, all expenses paid and sharing experiences together with other Jews. Then, I thought of Leo and his mixed background, part German-Jew, part African-American, and I wondered if it was a bit of a shock to the other American Jews on the trip. I could even picture the scene when everyone had to introduce themselves and where they were from. The other Jews in the group all staring at Leo, somewhat dumbfounded, "Is he one of us? He must just be a friend of that other guy, the baldheaded one who's always talking and grinning. I'm sure that other guy must be a Jew; he has our nose." (Of course, they would be speaking of Seb.) Then, I can see Leo, standing up when it's his turn to introduce himself, first saying his last name, which is clearly Jewish, "My name is Leo Himmelreich," and then announcing, "I'm a German Jew from New York." And the whole crowd becoming quieter, quieter than they already had been when he started talking, the whole time thinking to themselves, "It can't be. How could a Jew of Western European origin have brown skin? We have blonde hair and blue eyes. How is it possible?" And, then when Leo is done speaking and carrying on the way only Leo knows how, comfortable, confident, and decisive, always commanding his audience in a persuasive and charismatic manner, he just sits down. And when everyone has almost lost their mind in bafflement, the jovial, prankster deep down inside Leo stands back up and says, "Oh yeah, I forgot to mention, my mother is African-American and my dad is German-Jew," to the relief and ethnic reconfirmation of the others. I found myself laughing in the backseat as we continued to span the long road, reaching to a now visible coastline of the Dead Sea.

    I had to admit. I missed the other guys' company. Not that I didn't appreciate my own personal time, but it was great having friends to share adventures with, someone to later recall memories that could have fallen into that dark abyss of memory. Friends don't let you forget; and especially not those most embarrassing moments, that would have been better lost in that abyss. Seb and Leo still won't let me forget the famous Swedish Lotion incident in Koh Phan Ghan, or the "Elephant Doodoo" incident in the northern Thai Jungle. And I would never let Leo forget the "Head" incident in Bangkok or Seb the "$300 fridge" incident in Cuba.

    The road we were on eventually faced head on to the coastline, forcing us either left or right. We continued to the right passing near a "kibbutz" settlement and stopping at a small convenience store or beauty products factory, where mud from the Dead Sea was bottled for use in cosmetics, as a facemask or wherever someone needed skin revitalizing or protective maintenance. Apparently, the Dead Sea had a high concentration of minerals helpful to the skin's vivacity. What amazed me was that someone actually found a way to exploit the Dead Sea, other than through tourism, considering that only eleven types of bacteria have been known to survive in its salty depths. The road we were on was quite far from the coastline, and our guide explained that even the road we were on had at one time in history been buried under the sea. And he went on to explain that technically this sea was a lake situated between Jordan and Israel, because it only connected with water from the Jordan River and underground water sources from the surrounding desert. And now the sea was being drastically reduced, due to irrigation efforts in Jordan and an intense water-evaporating sun. The desert encapsulating the Dead Sea wasn't what I imagined a desert to be like; large massive cliffs and mountainside hung over us like great gods. And the sea itself could be mistaken as an oasis, until its lifelessness is further explored.

Our first mission was a visit to Masada. Being somewhat unprepared, as usual, I hadn't a clue what "a mission to Masada" really meant until we ventured down a lonely off-road leading to the highest mountain cliff in the area. Then I realized we might have to ascend this colossal-sized cliff, after my eyes followed a ski lift carrying people upwards vertically from its base. I suddenly had second thoughts about the excursion, watching the ski lift contraption sway back and forth as it moved upward. I wondered what was so important up on the top; clearly one couldn't ski such sheerness and surely nothing could live above what looked like an enormous crumbling redbrick.

I'm afraid of heights. Not that it's stopped me from meddling with nature, because I once rock climbed near Toccoa, Georgia, and even more frightening, I had to rappel the side of a high-hanging cliff. I get dizzy from those heights. But I learned a valuable lesson, long ago. Once past the initial jump or climb up, I'm in heaven; I could rappel Mt. Everest with the reserve tank of freedom and confidence I exude after I'm suspended in mid-air. That's what I kept telling myself as the lift, large enough to hold about ten people, wobbled upwards and the view of people on the ground below shrank to the size of pebbles. Eventually, I got over the initial fright and began to take pleasure in my new found height. I couldn't tire of looking off in the great hollow of distance. I could have stood there wide-eyed and dreamy for days, even months, just as I had seen in the expressions of quiet from the people riding the lift earlier. I had not realized how immense and measureless the Dead Sea area was until now.

We reached the top of the giant cliff. And a whole ancient city had been awaiting us. Of course, now the city was only a bunch of stone and dirt ruins, but to imagine that some guy named King Herod had the wherewithal to build an entire citadel at this distance from the ground, equipped with two palaces, baths, villas, and a great cistern and aqueduct system, and all built before 70 B.C.E. was remarkable. People lived and flourished up here. Up at this height, the already intense Israeli heat was magnified, and I didn't even care if I was the only one walking the tour with my shirt off. In fact, at this height, a lot of man-made realities seemed insignificant. I was gazing out towards an overwhelming world that swallowed me in its depths.

I hadn't really grasped the meaning of sublime until I was perched at this distance, in the midst of this sweeping magnitude. And I thought that maybe the definition of sublime couldn't capture the essence of how little and secondary I felt to what I was now facing. I felt at any moment, I could have been picked up and thrown into the heaping dust of this desert monolith by some higher being, never to be seen or heard of again in the history of planet earth. That's how insignificant mankind now seemed to me, because man didn't have the power to build mountains like the mass I was presently standing on, and man couldn't fathom the power of something so great as to rip a breathtaking sea into the rippling winding geography. All of this was beyond our control and out of our reach as humans.

What struck me atop Masada was my mortality. At that moment, I was made to respect my limits as a human and appreciate more the power of the world around me. Because, in a special way, I was a part of something much bigger than me, and was fortunate enough to realize this gift of life and opportunity I had been given. I could easily be just one of the specks of earth, dry and motionless before my eyes. I wondered if this mountain-top panorama, maybe, had given the community of Jews back in 66 B.C.E. the courage to fight off an army of Romans, seven times the size of theirs, for freedom, and ultimately risk their mortal physical lives. Then it struck me. I hadn't felt especially spiritual during my time in Jerusalem, where the great religions of the world supposedly collide and prosper. Maybe I had been looking too hard for it there, or not enough. But here I felt it. Here in the middle of forever, every step reminded me that there is a God, someone or something everlasting. I could see and feel with my own eyes and body this force that had been here thousands and millions of centuries before me, and that wouldn't miss a beat even when I had packed my things and finally left. Somehow, considering myself in the scheme of such power and infiniteness didn't scare me or defeat me. Rather the opposite, I felt proud and forever thankful to be a part of this world, this universe, this eternal kingdom of God.

After Masada, I had the feeling of cruising on a big, puffy floating cloud. We made it to the Dead Sea and the lowest point on planet earth, 412 meters below sea level. The atmosphere's heavy pressure at this depth, along with an Israeli sun, cooks you on high. Luckily, the sea lake was nearby for cooling off. I still didn't fully believe what seemed like another tourist gimmick, when the guy on the plane told me about floating effortlessly in the Dead Sea or when Greesha told me this morning that you could lie and read a newspaper while floating on your back. But it was absolutely true. The water wasted no time in propelling your entire body to the surface and holding it there. This novelty so amazed me that I began rolling my hoisted body in the water. I stopped on my side for awhile, twisting my arms and legs in the air at the same time, to see if it was really true, my virtual inability to sink. I wondered if it was really a miracle when Jesus walked on water. Maybe the Bible had gotten it all wrong; maybe, it wasn't the Sea of Galilee where he walked on water. I mean, both bodies of water had been wrongly named Seas when all along they were lakes.

Today few people were out floating these waters, and calmness extended outwards. The only ripples on the waters were from six of us floating on our backs or covering ourselves with black slimy mud; the rest of the waters and far off scenery carried the stigma placed when Christian monks had long ago given these waters the morbid moniker Dead Sea. The lake could easily be considered the world's largest natural spa; the stillness and vastness of the water was therapeutic, and the rich content of minerals making up the water and mud had the power to strengthen and bring youth to the skin. The only discomforting caveat was the risk of swallowing or touching even a single drop of the saline water to the eyes. There was definitely a reason why only special strands of bacteria had the chance to endure life here. Still, the utter serenity perpetuated my puffy cloud, which continued to support me as I floated on my back; it supported me effortlessly as I got up to change and even when I made it all the way back to Greesha's house. I didn't have a stressed bone in my body.

That night, I felt lit with inspiration, as I hovered over the computer keyboard again, pouring out my adventures effortlessly. Sometimes, a down pour of words dropped through my fingertips, creating a backup of water or a mental bottle neck as my fingers couldn't handle the amount of words and sentences draining out through them. I shocked myself with all that had been locked up inside of me, never before having had a chance to free itself. I wondered how long this urge to write had existed in me and where I had gathered the bits of wit and prose, because I was never able to speak so freely and expressively. Luckily, I didn't ponder over this love that was building inside of me, but rather continued to give it wings. I wrote about the frustrating, though fascinating tour in Jerusalem, and about the bomb scare. I wrote passionately about the inner struggle that still carried on in my heart over the Palestinian-Israeli conflict. I laughed and felt spirited writing about my exploits today; in my own way, I prayed and worshiped when I wrote about the godliness of all that confronted me and engulfed me. That night, the cloud that I had floated on throughout the day, that had carried me safely back to Rosh Ha'Ayin, comforted me as I finally dozed off to sleep, feeling as if someone had tucked me in; it was the real calm before a great storm.

"Wake up! Wake your ass up! Stop wasting away the day! Look at him, all curled up and sleeping like a baby...hahahaha!" These were the words of Leo and Seb, the first words to pierce the thin veil of sleep, the first words of my waking.

"Huh," I said, grumbling.

"Dude! We made it! Get your lazy ass up! There's no time to sleep!" they persisted.

"Huh...all right," I grumbled again. I was awake. I just didn't want to be rushed back to reality so quickly.

"Seb, leave him alone, dude. Let him finish waking up," Leo said with new found valiance. "We'll be in the kitchen, dude; Natasha's cooking a big breakfast for us. You chauvinistic Bukharans," Leo said jokingly to Seb as they both walked back out to the living room.

The fun was beginning. The thought of breakfast was the last straw. I threw on my clothes and entered the living room.

"What's up guys!" We slapped handshakes, snapping at the end, the way we always did.

"Dog, we gotta bring you up to speed. We've been all over Israel," Seb started.

Then, Leo popped in. "Seb already has a steady girlfriend. Just two weeks into leaving the country and he's fallen in love. Can you believe it?" Leo said in disbelief.

"You gotta meet her, dog. She has the most beautiful eyes and the nicest titties I've ever kissed," Seb continued.

I broke out in laughter. I had forgotten how much of a riot the old gang was. "You guys are trippin!" I said, egging the conversation on.

"Dude, they were holding hands through most of our trip. And you should have seen Seb almost crying when he had to leave her," Leo said, teasingly. He could be cruel sometimes.

"Where did she go?" I asked, clearly void of a few background points.

Leo quickly answered for Seb, "She went back to Atlanta."

The whole time Seb sat there smiling, sort of soaking in the abuse, but not really disagreeing or ashamed. I could tell everything Leo said was true, because Seb wasn't fighting it. But, what could I say? I had met a love that lasted about three years from my traveling in Thailand with the guys. They put up with my distractions and the divergence my relationship had caused, so I had to keep my mouth shut on this one. Plus, who knew the next time I would run into that special someone, tightening the love lasso around my neck and spinning me around in that obnoxious lover's world, where the rest of the watching public, especially your closest buddies, want to puke all over you both, for your cheesy actions. You couldn't predict or shield from things like that.

I kept my mouth closed and waited for breakfast. It was Friday. And Greesha managed to get the full day off, in part because we were so close to the Sabbath. We were all one big happy crowded family in the palace of Greesha. Seb was already playing and carrying on with Yafa and I wondered how he pulled it off. It took me a week before she really warmed up to me. Greesha was huddled with Seb, as well, and Seb was delineating his stories of the week, work in New York, and his family. Basically, they had a lot of catching up to do. Leo and I talked about Israel thus far, and talked about our planned trips to Turkey and Bulgaria and Romania. Even plans to study Spanish in Spain after our adventures were over. Of course, that would be an adventure all in itself, one that was too overwhelming to even really think about at this point. Leo was psyched about going to Tel Aviv and told me how boring at times it had been on the excursions with Seb. Because, little did he know that the Jewish field trip to the holy land was geared towards Russian-Jews, and all the tours were in Russian and everyone spoke in Russian most of the time. He said Seb had to translate to English everything that was going on, but that his translation service was cut short when Seb ran into his new girlfriend on the trip, Sasha, and as Leo put it, "floated off into some fairyland." The guys were back! And nothing had changed; still, not a boring day went by in the Seb-Leo camp. We didn't even go outside, but still the day went by unnoticed. There were too many stories to tell and too many unanswered questions. Not even a week could really have been enough time.

Before dinner, Seb whispered in my ear, a bit nervously, "Don't bring up Sasha to them. She's not Bukharan Jew and I know they will ask. I already told Leo to keep a seal on it."

"I wouldn't bring her up, you know me better than that," I said, feeling underestimated. It's funny how we are as humans, always reconfirming in words what we already knew. Seb had been with me long enough to know that I wouldn't share new information with his family. That was his responsibility. Furthermore, certain codes were learned amongst friends I grew up with; that is you don't divulge information to others that isn't already common knowledge. Unfortunately, the root of this philosophy was that my friends were always covering up for things they did or didn't do and girls they were dating or cheating on. Somewhere along the way, I had learned that sharing information on someone else's life could end up ruining their manipulative plans. I was always finding ways to plead the fifth with my friends' parents as a kid or with their girlfriends or anyone who knew their girlfriend. That's just the way it was. (Now, having said this, I've probably broken a few codes telling this story, but people will just have to forgive me this time). The fact was Seb was going to be put to the test over the next few days, and the face-off of the first round would start in just about two hours, when we sat down to feast another glorious Sabbath dinner. I had to admit. This was what I liked the most about Bukharan-Jews: they threw-down on Friday night dinners, which was probably true for all Jews. If Seb had to keep the tradition alive, just to continue these special dinners, I was in full support; as long as he kept inviting me, of course.

I was feeling like part of the family. They always welcomed me with open arms, and this time, walking in with Seb was like walking the red carpet behind a superstar. For them it was an emotional moment, hugging Seb and looking him up and down from head to toe, the way grandmothers and aunts always do. They were studying Seb as if he had just stepped out of his mother's womb, holding him with loving arms and admiring him. Seb's grandmother was even tearing at the eyes with overwhelming emotions. I could tell they were proud to see little Seb, the skinny frail-looking kid from back in Uzbekistan, not little or skinny anymore; on the contrary, muscular and healthy, a normal height for a young man. And I was sure they had heard of all his accomplishments: the young kid, whose parents didn't have a cent to their name when they entered the U.S., Seb being a freshman in highschool at that time. Eventually, Seb making it to NYU and entering the business world as a Wall Street Banker. He was already practically a legend in the family. And this was the more reason they were probably going to ask him, why did you quit to start traveling with these two knuckleheads, and why haven't you found a Bukharan wife like your cousin Greesha, who is really like a brother to you? I even wondered myself sometimes. But it wasn't any of my business.

Besides the few tears sliding down the cheeks of Seb's grandmother, I was in the midst of a jubilant family reunion. They placed Seb right smack in the middle of the dining room tables, joined together, and Leo and I were on either sides of him, his partners in crime. It even felt like the dining room lights had a weird way of shining a more powerful, and more focused beam of light around the silhouette of Seb. He was the main attraction this night. I had been the main attraction last week and didn't miss it at all. Every imaginable question was being thrown in Seb's direction, and although Leo and I couldn't comprehend Russian, we knew they were digging deep, not leaving any stone unturned. I was even wondering had any of them worked or gained any experience at an auditing firm similar to the one I left recently. They would have made great auditors, in my opinion.

The questioning seemed to slow down a bit, after the probably sixth or seventh round of vodka shots, and now, according to Seb, they had begun reminiscing on the past. And Seb, hoping to deflect attention from himself, brought up the time when I had eaten dinner at his parents' house back in Atlanta and the special Bukharan meal that day had been P'lov, a mix of tender cuts of beef and exotic spices, and a rare yellow rice called dagzire, supposedly grown in Uzbekistan and only sold in New York, mixed with tender cuts of beef and exotic spices. Well, there was only one obstacle to this meal; traditionally Bukharans didn't use eating utensils to carry it from plate to mouth and everyone ate from the same bowl. This was a specially shaped bowl, needing an equally special hand technique to grab at the food, which meant digging the fingers down into the bowl, cuffing the hands in a "u" shape, so that the food pressed into the top crevices of the palms. There was also a special way of guaranteeing that the food didn't drop onto the table when finally placed into the mouth. (I never learned the last part of the technique; my place mat had gathered enough rice and meat to feed a small kid).

Well, that day, Seb and his family, including his sister, never mentioned that I should be careful not to place my hands too far back into the bowl, because that part could be flaming with heat. And I, with my eyes that are bigger than my stomach, and hands that were having way too much fun grabbing at food on the table, I reached towards the middle of the bowl for an extra big serving. And a second later when the food was already in mid-air and my brain had finally received the message that my hand was now burning through the skin, I let go of the entire handful of food, which flew into the air and onto the lap of Seb's mother. Luckily, she and the whole family found my antics to be more than hilarious, and the whole family was crying laughing at my expense. Now, Seb's family in Israel was also laughing and I had to succumb to a few laughs, although I remember that day, when my hand was so charred, I couldn't even pick up a pen to write my own name. I was happy that the special rice and beef dish wasn't being served tonight. We continued to feast on the endless rounds of food, and take vodka shots, which I realized had the effect of freeing space in my stomach so that I could eat even more food. We all needed a night-walk with Greesha, after that meal.

The next night, to my surprise, was another great feast, and this time another of Seb's cousins had come to celebrate Seb's arrival to Israel. This cousin presented a different side of the family, and not because he was a bad guy or criminal, but because he seemed to breathe rebellion. He had gaudy glasses and his hair had been shaped into so many designs it was hard to keep track. He even had patterns cut into his beard and side burns. It sort of shocked me, seeing as this was Seb's cousin, a Bukharan Jew still connected to the family, not yet exiled; because I was sure that Seb's parents would have had Seb pulled apart by his limbs. But what was more interesting than his cousin's appearance was the background information on his cousin's absolutely stunning girlfriend for three years. She spoke Russian and was Jewish, but she wasn't Bukharan-Jew. I thought to myself, there's an infiltrator in the family. But she was not only beautiful, she was extremely nice and generous. I observed as she tried to lend a hand in the kitchen, tried to help carry out the plates of food, and was constantly being thrown out of the way as if entering the eye of a tornado only to soon be funneled out. I noticed their subtle ways of rejecting her help, not allowing her a brief moment to be accepted or learn the Bukharan system. My heart went out to her, because she obviously wanted into the secret society of Bukharan customs and traditions, guaranteeing a future role as wife to Seb's cousin. But more remarkable than that was the fact that she had been allowed to feast with the entire family. They didn't accept her, but Igor, Seb's other cousin, hadn't been ousted from the family, and he had even found a way to slide his loving girlfriend into at least a front row seat to view the Bukharan machine. They weren't happy with their infiltrator, but they weren't completely heartless, either. I began to create new ideas for Seb and his situation, and wondered how this recent news flash was affecting Seb's mind. Not that he wanted to upset the order, but he had to know if he did, he wouldn't have been the first. Some level of tolerance was being exhibited at the Seb family reunion, and windows of opportunity were being offered, even if silently. Of course, Seb ultimately had his parents to confer with. I hoped the best for Seb. He had some serious decisions to make in his future.

After dinner, Seb, Greesha, Greesha's wife, Igor, Igor's girlfriend, Leo and I packed up in Igor's utility vehicle and headed for the lights and glitter of Israel's city that never sleeps, Tel Aviv. This time we were headed to a different night scene than the one I had visited last weekend. It was amazing. I had already spent more than a week in Israel. And I wondered if the rest of my travels would continue to fly by so quickly. I hoped not before I figured out what I was going to do with the rest of my life.

Igor bulldozed the sidewalk to show off his monstrous four-wheel-drive while finding parking in a crowded offshore area of Tel

Aviv. I sensed a bit of pride coming from Igor, his 4WD having the right of way to the city. Then I thought, his Nissan Panther would have been crushed in a city like Atlanta where tiny females drive vehicles the size of cargo trucks. But, nevertheless, at this time, it was an impressive size for Tel Aviv. The streets were becoming more familiar to me the further we walked. I realized I had been over here during the day. We reached a small tile gazebo next to the beach, and I was sure that the street running directly into us from the east was Allenby Street. I was always entranced with nightlife along a beach or river or lake, really anywhere, where nature collided with the wild fruit of city life. At night this part of Tel Aviv blossomed into something magical. Clubs, bars, and restaurants lined the beach promenade like flames from colossal candles. I plunged myself into the flow of unique characters out reveling in the scene, and secretly wished, if only for brief moments, I could act in their play. There were strange religious hippies drumming conga drums; they took turns passing out special Judeo booklets to the passersby. A teenage boy with long rock star hair stood boldly, strumming an acoustical guitar and singing his heart out in a brief plaza, before the beginning of the beach sand.

  I was still in awe at the beauty of what seemed more and more like the prototype Israeli femme. They showed me that even the sun's descent wasn't reason enough to forego sunglasses, even if they shielded most of the face; these accessories seemed more like permanent facial features. A little further down, at least fifteen kids illicitly huddled together, not far from the sidewalk. You could hear the sound of rubber snapping back and what sounded like gas stuffing a balloon full of helium. The kids, all of them, were laughing hysterically. They were bold to be inhaling so close to high traffic. But, this was Tel Aviv, the heart of Israel's rebellion, a place condemned by the likes of Ultra-Orthodox Jews and coveted by the country's soul-searching artist population. A place where much of secular Israel parties on until wee hours of the morning, including sacred Sabbaths. Tel Aviv was very much a modern-day cosmopolitan city, a complex, sparkling diamond nestled in the throes of today's dominant religions, a beacon of Western society.

  We began the night at a super-trendy open-air club, along the promenade. Igor didn't hesitate in the least when heading directly for this club; he seemed to be on a mission the whole time, not wasting a glimpse at the other clubs hugging the coastal artery. And I admired his taste as we headed into the flashing glamour of lights. The club was named E! like the channel. I wondered, had I missed the episode of "Wild On E!" where Brooke Burke flies off to the Eastern Mediterranean Sea to party the night away in Tel Aviv. The club was definitely worthy of international acclaim. If I could compare it to anything in the U.S., it would have to be the lights and open flamboyancy of Miami. The club was painted in all white, emphasizing a high tech light system; and in some ironic way, the pure white walls, climbing high into the night sky, created a feeling of serenity as if stepping into the clouds of heaven. Only the Angels here tonight weren't dressed in all white, and the ones draped in white were Gucci Angels, wearing devilish belts and heels. An enormous cinema-sized projection screen on the back wall of the club towered over the room, challenging all that strolled the promenade to enter the club. And, fitting to a club named after a channel ripe in fashion, the screen projected models parading the catwalk in all modes of skimpy dress. I was missing my white linen suit at the moment. But some things had to be compromised on this trip. I had worn my all-purpose kakis and baby blue v-neck instead. We entered the club, walked to the top level and seated ourselves at one of the round tables, overlooking the deejay and the dance floor. A waitress came around to our table and everyone ordered Redbull-vodkas (I still hadn't learned my lesson). Igor ordered a Nargalay pipe (Hooka as many Westerners called it) and hors d'oeuvres. House music persisted to bounce off the white walls and off into the night. A Nargalay pipe with elaborate etchings in shiny silver was placed in the middle of our table, and the waitress lit the fragrant tobacco before we passed the long colorful tubes around. I didn't feel a buzz or anything, but there was definitely something relaxing and soothing about breathing in the soft flavorful smoke. I quaffed my drink unknowingly and was surprised that I could even touch food again, after such a large feast early that night.

Finally, the house music that seemed to inspire the models walking the enormous projector screen changed to hip-hop, and I was once again reminded how the world could be brought together by my favorite mode of communication, a melodic medium. Music was what people all around the world had in common. If only it could be used to avert wars and injustices. Involuntarily, everyone at our table, including Greesha and Natasha, began bouncing and swaying along the circular lounge sofa, catching whatever part of the beat suited their own bodily instincts. And, once again, I was taken back at how pervasive the genre hip-hop is. I didn't know whether to take their sudden fixation on me as a compliment. I must have fit some stereotype of what an aficionado in American hip-hop should look like. I often thought the salsa club back in Atlanta treated the Cubans the same way. And the worst was when I was profiled as a Cuban in a salsa club, because, when I finally had the nerve to make a fool out of myself on the dance floor, all dancing expectations following me into the club were destroyed. For Cubans themselves, this had to be positive racial profiling.

The music animated me from my seat and animated Leo, too. We decided to take a run at the dance floor, see if this posh club had any spice, could the women in here dance as good as they dressed.

"Damn!" I turned to Leo, "That's that Usher, Lil John, and Ludacris joint."

"Small, world man," Leo answered.

It was nice to be taken back home to Atlanta for one song. Then the deejay played 50 Cent's blockbuster summer hit. That's when Leo and I eased ourselves into the center of the floor. Leo quickly courted some girl out on the dance floor, even pulled one of her legs up in the air, while he was dancing. That was Leo for sure, always pushing the limits, never wasting any time. I began my signature moves, eventually being sandwiched in between two girls. Once again, the Israeli girls proved to be "bout it." Our routine consisted of dancing two or three songs, going back up to smoke the Nargalay and drink vodka, then come back down and dance again. Seb was spending quality time with the family. Leo and I were getting bored with the club. I had spoken with a French girl who easily could have been a model, but my interest was waning every minute of the conversation. I wondered what was wrong with me. What would it take for me to put my undivided attention towards a girl? Surely, I couldn't start and stop talking to every girl I met during the trip. Maybe there was something I was looking for in the women, and the first sign that I wouldn't find it, had me running for the door? I needed to begin acting like the reality I carried; I didn't have a girlfriend anymore. Maggie was history. I would never meet another, if I continued to reject the ones I met. Leo and I were both bored watching the all but married couples at our table, and we decided to leave Seb and his family behind while we investigated more the beach promenade.

The night had almost passed us. It was late, and I could feel my energy evaporating. Still, as men not giving up, not relinquishing the hunt, we pushed forward in search of new territory and more opportunities. Something was forcing us away from another dance club. It seemed that part of the night had come and passed; now, we searched along the beach for a more relaxed ambience. Somewhere we could hear ourselves talk, as my mom would say. Not far from the E! Club, a sparse line of bars along the beach spread out in the darkness. One in particular emitted special warmth, more fitting to the background of Mediterranean waves calmly ebbing and flowing. Tall candles set clumsily in the sand cast small jittery shadows and emanated a warm inviting glow around the bar's circumference. The interior of the place was visible from the outside, as well. But the inside light never overpowered the atmosphere; on the contrary, it seemed subordinate to the glowing astrology: the sand candles appeared like little ground stars. We took a seat in the chairs just right inside the candles, where we could face the waves. Probably like any single man at this time of night, we scanned the few people lounging before the waves like we were, to see if there was any potential. Nothing. The few women sitting were coupled off. It was that time of night. So we decided to get a couple of beers to mark the declining hours of the night and just to enjoy the rhythmic powers of the Sea. I fantasized I was looking to Spain or Italy, because the bluish-black world of the Mediterranean Sea mixed in the infinitude of the night sky, and I knew the sharp focus of my eyes was blazing a direct path to Europe. The stillness and the depth of the sea brought back flashes from my trips to the Dead Sea and Masada, places where the world never ceased to overwhelm the human eye.

Our waitress walked over with cat-like precision.

"Gentleman," she said, like she had been standing there for a while as we lost ourselves to the dark sea. She startled us, caught us both by surprise. And not only because of her abruptness, but because she stood over us like a precious gem goddess. Leo gave me that look, the one he always gives when he sees something he likes, and I concurred in my facial response. He would go in for the kill like the Lion of the Jungle he was; I just knew it. And it began, the charm, the assertiveness, the confidence and persistence. He asked questions to keep her talking. He announced his city, New York, and continued to pry for any useful information that would help him captivate and capture her interest. The U.S. and New York topic sparked a twinkle in her beautiful brown eyes; but, she still resisted.

Seeing opportunities to speak, I would butt in at times with light jokes; I found some of her comments easy to bounce off of, and I wasn't sure that Leo was winning her over with his current spiel. But if passiveness was a hindrance, I was sure to lose this game. I never had the energy to compete with Leo or Seb; they were both forever more talkative than me. I usually resigned myself to private, individual encounters; that's where I could advance the conversation at my own pace. But somehow in the midst of my remarks, and the full blown conversation that Leo had taken on, the dialogue was slowly moving in my direction, and I could sense much of the eye contact, playful, but not too suggestive, connecting with my line of sight. The waitress, the exotic beauty standing before us, was giving me subtle signals. I knew those signals, and neither Leo nor I could deny them.

When she walked away to get out beers and help other customers, Leo turned to me and said, "I think you need to pick this one up. I could see it in her eyes the way she looked at you and studied you, like she wanted to rip your pants off. It's all yours man, when she comes back."

"Thanks dog." I appreciated his honesty. Leo was confident in that way, he knew there would always be other opportunities. Each time she returned, our conversation became warmer, and it even seemed like she was hanging around our table a more than inordinate amount.

This time, when she left, Leo commented, "You have to get her number before you leave here. Go in for the kill. She's taken the bait, and now she's dangling from your hook." I listened to him; though I had planned to get her number, I was just slower about it than normal. For me, getting the number from a girl who captivated me, a striking beauty inside and out, was the finale that usually shook at my nerves. I always put off the number asking until the last moment. It was like the salesman spinning the most beautiful sales pitch imaginable and at the end, asking for the actual sale, the signing of a contract or striking a verbal agreement. That was what the hour of convincing a potential customer and skillful use of words were for, only a couple seconds of time, long enough for the person to either accept or flat out reject. In my case, the waitress could either say yes, I'll find a bar napkin to write that down for you or I'm sorry, I would, but I already have a boyfriend, and walk off as if the flirting and eye contact never existed, only in my mind. We had stuck around that night for quite some time, late in the morning, until no more customers were sitting, drinking, and at the point when the waiters were leaving for the night, one by one. Yael, that was her name, said she had to help clean up, it was her night to sweep the floors, blow out the candles and stack the chairs, and at that point, I just went for it.

"What are you doing this week? Will you be free anytime this week? Because, we should go for a drink or hang out at the beach, of course, not at your job, but somewhere else." I was now rambling. She stopped me before I made too much of a fool of myself.

"Here take my number down. I'm off all day tomorrow." And as she was talking, she pulled out her trusty pen, tore off a slip of paper from the tablet she took orders from and wrote down her number, her name and a little smiley face at the bottom, folded it up nicely and handed it to me. "I gotta go now. You guys have a safe night," she said in a soft voice.

"Thanks. You too." And as we walked away from the bar, I wondered why did everyone in Israel always leave you with a "be careful'" or "be safe," something to that effect. Otherwise, I was happy to be ending the night with a little bit of success. And not that a night without scoring a number was a failure. But, then again, who was I kidding.

Yael loved to sing and write songs. But performing was her passion. Singing in front of a packed audience was her addiction, the drug that she never could get enough of. She even did free shows, once in a while, just because she couldn't stand going a week without communicating with a live audience, as she described it, finding herself in this world between god and earth. Come to find out, Yael had a few years on me. I would never have thought it from her smooth baby skin and her wide brown eyes. At the same time, a tempered wisdom radiated within her, the way she looked off in the distance at times seemed as if she were looking towards the future, and her opinions on the world and her life were based on experience, things that worked and things she knew couldn't work anymore. Her heart was in music; and even though a lot of obstacles stood in her way, like her family obligations and the distance from here to the U.S., she talked as if none of it could stop her, none of it could deter the goals and progress she made thus far. Yael's skin tone was like the honeycomb seen through swirling honey. I told her that she would be taken for Dominican or Puerto Rican back in the states or even mixed-race, African-American and Caucasian, like myself. She told me, I, too, could pass for Israeli. And then, I remembered her telling Leo and me last night that she had lived in New York for a couple of years.

"What did you do while in New York?" I asked.

"I worked a bar at night and in the day time I worked on music, but I hooked up with the wrong people. I learned what not to do while I was in NY. The music business is really shady," she said, nodding her head in disgust and dimpling the side of her lips at one corner. I wasn't so sure I wanted to know who the "wrong people" were, but I asked anyway.

"The wrong people?"

"Well, it's a long story. But, basically I got in a lot of arguments with the guitar player and he ran off with my songs."

"Okay," I said, not knowing what to say, or even where to begin. There was obviously information left out.

"But, that's New York for you. You can't trust anybody over there," she said, as if her two years made her an expert on the city. "But, I love New York," she continued. "As soon as I can earn enough money and figure out how to renew my visa, I'm going back. Things just haven't been the same here, since I returned to Tel Aviv. I feel in ways, I've outgrown the city. But my family is here. My sister needs help, and its hard being away from my dad for too long. The truth is I'm kind of torn between both places. And then there is the music. I can't make any real money over here. I need to go to America to make it big." And she was right. If you made it big in the U.S., then you could be guaranteed success all over the world. American fame was like a virus that spreads throughout humanity. The previous night, I probably heard more American artists than any other, and that had been true practically anywhere I traveled around the world. I wondered what it was I could achieve in the U.S. that would spread itself to other countries. It seemed obvious that I needed the U.S. as a platform to produce and promote my success. But what could I do? What did I have to offer that the rest of the world wanted? It was a burning thought, but as hard as I pushed for ideas, nothing sprouted; I was brainstorming a drought.

It was nice having her soft skin melt beside me on the beach towel as we chatted about life. I realized the calming effect that sea waves have on conversation, how they seem to help you reflect on life without the adverse effect of becoming stressed or worried. The Sea had a way of saying everything would be all right; if nothing else, you have me to talk to, you have my body and soul to swallow your loneliness or worries. We lay like this for much of the afternoon, slowly finding comfort and trust in the other. I wondered if she could hear my heart beating when she pressed up against my chest, and, at times, I could feel her soft melodic words vibrate through my body. I wanted to lie like this on the sand in front of the water, our bodies connecting together as one, for an eternity; it seemed equilibrium had been reached between my mind, heart, and soul. And not until later would I look back on this moment as another "spot of time."

A beautiful sunset was the encore after a full day's performance. We were both starving at this point and so decided to wash up and change before walking to a suitable restaurant. I was on Yael's turf, and she had good restaurants in mind. After changing, we crossed over the promenade and Herbert Samuel Street and walked to the left. One thing hadn't changed during my time being here. Still, teenagers roamed the streets strapped with rifles. I was even beginning to get used to it, only I wondered was it safe for the same soldiers to be drinking and socializing like civilians in a bar. I looked at Yael and pointed inside Mike's Place, to the soldiers casually hanging out and listening to some band performing onstage, a bar completely open from the front.

"Is it okay for soldiers to be in a bar?" I asked, arching my eyebrows in disbelief.

"Oh . . . I perform in that bar on Thursday nights," she said, as if the soldiers weren't very important to the topic of Mike's Place.

"We'll come back here after dinner," she said, in a bit of excitement.

"But, the soldiers," I repeated. I wasn't sure I wanted to mingle with armed teenagers, toasting it up at a bar. It reminded me of the Old Western movies, where everyone is drinking and carrying on at the old saloon in the center of town, when two cowboys get in a dispute over something silly, and one of them challenges the other to a shoot out.

"Oh . . . the soldiers," she said. "The thing is only a year ago, a suicide bomber walked right into the middle of the bar and blew himself up. Six people died. Ever since then, there has been high security. You see that guy at the front, checking everyone who comes in. He's responsible for stopping a bomber before they get too far."

Wow. I thought to myself. It was hard to imagine that in such a small bar like this one, and all the chaos that had to have ensued, the screams and destruction. It was hard to believe that all that happened right here, a few feet away from where I was standing.

We walked further down the street, where we passed tons of little restaurants, and eventually stopped at a place where immediately the waitress working recognized her. The waitress saw me and immediately winked at Yael to show her approval, and she pointed to a table just being cleaned off and reset, a nice corner table peering out towards the street and promenade.

"When will I get to hear you perform?" I asked, while I devoured a flavorful couscous.

"This Wednesday at the Camelot I'm performing with my band. You have to be there. You will be the person I pour my heart out to when I'm on stage. I won't take my eyes off of you the whole time," she said as if reciting a romantic poem. It sounded great. I was excited to be the focus of someone's passion. I wanted to see her flying in that space between earth and god, maybe even join that special world of hers. But there was only one problem. I was leaving on Wednesday. I'd already paid for a plane ticket, and I couldn't leave the fellows again, not on this trip. I had done the same thing in Thailand, even though we met back up periodically. But this time it was different. We weren't traveling through only one country. And I had to know this time, life was this way; I was exploring, and I needed to continue to see as much of the world as possible. It was important. I needed to find that thing I was looking for, and I couldn't stop until I did, not even if a beautiful warm heart stood in my way. But it was hard to tell Yael I would be leaving so soon. We hardly talked about when I would be leaving, because it did seem entirely too sudden.

The next few days made leaving Israel and Yael even harder to stand. We did harbor something special; it was becoming more and more obvious. But she understood that I wasn't stable at the moment. I had a mission to complete, more soul searching and exploring to do. I could never be happy if I didn't do what deep down my instincts had been telling me was the right thing. She could relate, because there were still things pulling her away, sending her back to the U.S. But we were determined to meet again somewhere, maybe New York, or maybe even Rio where she had dreamed of seeing the Carnival. We agreed that the world had so much waiting for us if we just continued to follow our dreams. I didn't tell her that I was still trying to figure out exactly what was my dream.

The morning of Wednesday, before Seb and Leo had risen and after Greesha had already headed off for work, I returned with a burning desire to write. I wanted to somehow sum up this trip in Israel by writing another journal entry that would reach my mother, and if it wasn't too personal and intimate, I would send it out to more people that I knew. I started writing about the last days' events, going to dinner with Seb's family two nights in a row, meeting Yael, and everything that I had realized and learned from roaming the city with her, and observing other Israelis. I finished by trying to sum up my experience in Israel, the people and how they cope with everyday life, how they react to atrocities going on around them on both sides of the separation wall. I even tried to compare my experience with what I had learned from being in Cuba for weeks. It seemed that in Cuba there was the oppression of lack of freedom, not being able to leave the country or even a region of Cuba to travel, not being able to create a million dollar idea and start a company, lacking in many products and services that the first world had enjoyed for decades. Different from Cuba, in Israel there seemed to be the fear of death, the feeling of constantly living in a war zone, not knowing when the next confrontation would arise, constantly being reminded of the present conflict by helicopters flying above or the endless amount of teenagers uniformed and carrying massive weapons, the roadblocks, the baggage checks, car checks, the armed guards at every restaurant and bar, and even in McDonalds. Also, there was the moral dilemma of having a conflict as complex and deeply rooted as the one facing both Palestinians and Israelis. And what I realized out of all this was that life doesn't stop. The majority of Israelis deal with their present situation and keep pushing forward. Kids still need to go to school; people still celebrate birthdays, weddings, Sabbaths, Bar Mitzvahs; politics still are being fought out domestically within the complexity of a nation of diverse Jews: Ashkenazi, Sephardim, Heradim, Russians, Oriental Jews from Arabic and African countries, European Jews, secular Jews. People still go to the beach, still populate the same clubs previously bombed, still go to the banks, still attend university and research. People still choose to live as normal a life as possible, along side the terror and the neglect. For me, it was harder and harder to be fearful walking through Tel Aviv or Israel, when the Israelis themselves chose to live without fear, continued to move freely, not staying at home or avoiding the bus. On the contrary, buses were jam-packed with people. Immigrants were still shaping the hills and valleys of Israel, developments of new buildings and houses were continuing, and neighborhoods, as if rings of tree growth, reflected the migration of different ethnicities and nationalities: you had the Ethiopian neighborhoods, the Russian neighborhoods, and even the old Yemenite neighborhoods, where Yael grew up, before moving to her apartment in Tel Aviv. Israel was a multi-culture within a culture. One that refuses to live scared. And then I remembered what the pensive guy sitting to the window had said on the plane, and it kind of described Israel for me in a lot of ways:

"Sure, Sure . . . make sure to visit the Golan Heights, Old Jerusalem and New Jerusalem . . . and make sure to visit the Dead Sea," he stated passionately. "This is the only water in the world, I think, that you can not drown in. You know why you cannot drown in this water?"
"Why?" I asked.
"The high concentration of salt and minerals makes the water dense and allows you to literally lie flat on top of the water. You float without doing anything!" But then he went on to say, almost reconsidering his first statement, "The water is dangerous . . . don't get it in your eyes or swallow, it can kill you. You understand!"

TURKEY

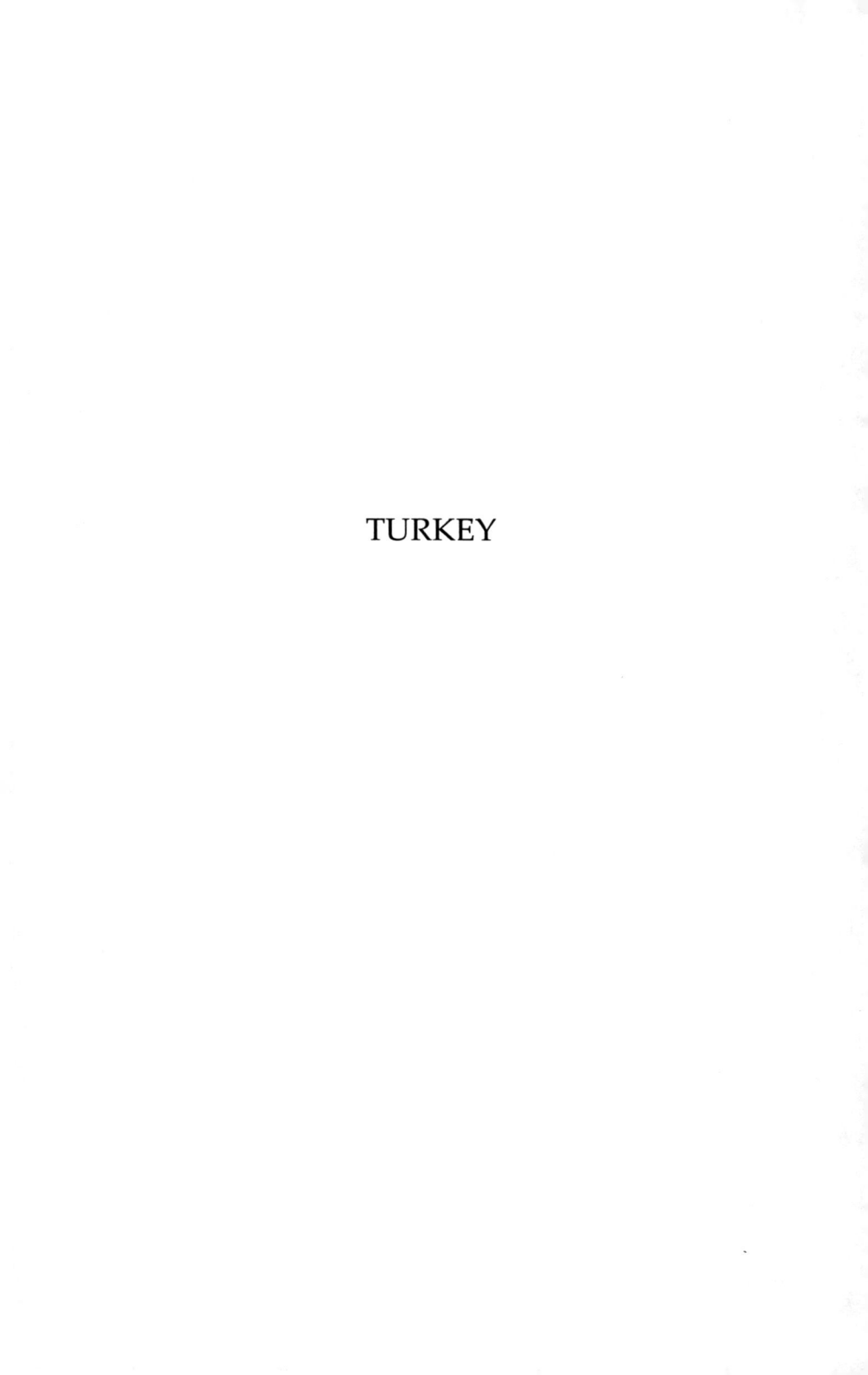

> "The World...an illusion that had to be reinvented everyday."
> -Paul Auster

    I could try to describe that gust of wind pushing at the backs of Seb, Leo and me as we once again joined the ranks, this time with brotherhood and adventure painted like war paint all over our minds and bodies. But the feeling was too elemental to reconstruct in words. And where would I start? We knew better how to milk the most out of our travels, not necessarily what to expect, but the spirit and flexibility from which to receive the unexpected. At this point, we were comfortable with each other's experience level as competent travel colleagues. All three of us had been through so much together, good and bad, that we were living testament to a spirit of survival, the attitude of never giving up. None of us could have foreseen when traveling through Thailand, squeezing in those last few months of freedom before the end of our lives, that we would again have the opportunity to explore the world freely in Cuba. And to be together again, pushing forward as a team to Turkey, was the surprise of our lives. How does one put together in words the energy and emotion on the plane flight from Tel Aviv to Istanbul, the Three Musketeers, back again for another sequel, another forbidden adventure?

    We had been to Buddhist Thailand, to Catholic Cuba, Jewish Israel, and now we were headed for Muslim-dominated Turkto ey, the kingdom of the fabled Ottoman Empire, the first frontier of democratic Islam.

We three corporate survivors (or corporate dead men, however you chose to view it) had experienced love and heartbreak, the corporate cycle of conquest and relinquishment. Our fraternal bond had innumerable fibers, and we had been through unique trials. We were off to continue our legend, back to fight another day. We hadn't given up our quest for the unknown and journey to fulfill our destiny. As a matter of fact, our successes and failures had made us more charged and powerful, more secure and determined that our day would finally come. Maybe we would find out later on in life that that day had already arrived, gaping at us with open eyes. It had been months since the ending of my accounting career, and by now, my mind was overwhelmed with answers and questions. I needed badly to link those two floating columns, as if they were columns on a school exam. This linkage, I was more than sure, would be the key to understanding a longer life's vision, crucial to focusing my path. I knew it was only a matter of time.

Wham! Wham! Crack! A sequence of staccato thuds, and a composed flight captain is speaking over chaotic noises and vibrations, as if none of those noises meant anything, as if he were a conductor of an orchestra calmly introducing the next piece.

The speaking in Hebrew finishes, and another voice much shakier and slower, repeats in English as if the speaker were reading from a piece of paper: "The captain asks that you please fasten your seatbelt. We are heading toward heavy clouds and rain and the captain asks that you please not be alarmed. We will be experiencing turbulence for the remainder of the flight." More bumps and thuds. I can hear the chassis of the plane creak and shake, not like a plane should, more like a rollercoaster, the old Scream Machine at Six Flags over Georgia. I look over to Seb and Leo. They're sitting quietly, holding onto their armrests, not amused at all.

Flying is the only weakness of a traveler, where he has no control, only dependence and prayer. In a plane there is no such thing as defensive driving or critical selection; in a taxi, if a driver appears drunk or incapable, you just wave down another. Not the case on a plane, and, even worse, any mistake is likely a deadly one. That's why a part of me always freaks out a little bit at the sound of any strange noises or erratic movements. And this time wasn't any different. Earlier, I'd fought for and won the window seat, on an instinct I carried forward from those "ride shotgun" wars with my brother in the Civic Hatchback as a child. Looking now through the foggy window, I saw the bright sunny cloudlessness that we had left Israel with had dramatically changed to darkness. We were riding a storm cloud. It's funny how no one really speaks on a plane during heavy turbulence. Mouths are open and eye contact is abundant. But the mood is mute and pensive. And I think the thoughts and images are usually "what if?" or "remember that plane crash earlier this year?" I wondered if people were going through last wishes and saying mental goodbyes to loved ones. As I said, only a part of me freaks out; the other part waits for it all to be over, my life in a sort of dramatic pause until the conductor brings down his baton yet again and the plane finally lands. And dramatic finale was an understatement; after three hovering circles above the old Ottoman capital, resulting from an aerial traffic jam, El Al Airlines landed safely. We hurried from the plane to the bus and into the airport. We scurried past a frantic and distracted Customs Check point, not at all critical or suspecting. We were supposed to meet a guy named Jeff. And none of us, including Seb, who'd made the contact through a Wall Street buddy, Damyan, knew what this guy looked like. He would be waiting in the café, outside in one of the airport lobbies.

There was only one café inside the airport. A blonde-haired guy, masculine and privileged, wearing dapper slacks and a sharp, pointed collar, perfectly bowing out at the corners and three quarters of the way unbuttoned to show his equally blonde chest hairs, sat down at the table. Immediately, he recognized us as the three backpackers who Damyan probably had described in some detail; it wasn't hard to spot us. He stood up and smiled as a confirmation. He had this Fabio quality to him, like a Roman statue, bold and proud. He had a seamlessly cut beard, exactly the same consistency and length all the way around his face and a flawless line contoured upwards into his sideburns. I had to admit it. I was slightly intimidated by this guy. When we got there, a large beer mug fresh with condensation stood on the table. It was clear that he was in no hurry, so we put our bags down and he offered us all beer. Seb and Leo turned him down, and I nodded thanks, I'll have the same thing you're having. Jeff was supposed to show us around the city, put us up for a week or so. But something told me that he didn't have those same intentions. First, he began complaining about his family being in town, not much room in his house and tensions were high enough between the normal deliberations of nagging and family expectations. Next, he told us that the weather had just turned nasty beginning today and that it would be rainy and unbearable like this for the next two weeks. We had landed during an inopportune time, when Jeff's family and greater Istanbul were experiencing an unusually high rainfall for summer weather.

So, with this new information, decisions had to be made. Jeff told us that the south of Turkey was warm and dry, and much of Istanbul would probably be traveling there to escape the weather. But he couldn't. Business was a bit shaky and he must stay and work. Our plans had changed instantly. We walked to the Turkish Airlines counter and bought one-way tickets directly to Antalya, all the way on the southern coast. That way we could wait out the weather, circle the Mediterranean and Aegean coasts until we reached back to Istanbul, not missing a step, and still get to see the great city. We waited another hour. I drank another beer, and we boarded our flight.

If you connected the dots between Tel Aviv, Istanbul, and Antalya, it would look sort of like a narrow obtuse triangle. We were flying almost three times the distance between Tel Aviv and Antalya. But you can't predict these sorts of things when you book a flight months in advance. The best thing you can do is to remain flexible. So, we said goodbye to Jeff and Istanbul just as fast as we made hello, and we were off again, back in bad weather.

The bumpiness in the plane had abated for a while now; it hadn't occurred to me that we were now away from God's wrath and heading towards a happier side of Turkey. We disembarked from the plane, caught a taxi and pulled out our Lonely Planet guides. We needed to find a hostel to stay for the night. It was already dark outside, and on the ride towards the town, nothing seemed to be open; all stores were closed, and Antalya appeared to be fast asleep. It had been a long day, full of airplanes and airports, and the stillness at this moment, seemed to be a bit disappointing, a final cap to the uneventful. We found the hostel from the guidebook. Someone luckily was awake to check us in, and we settled our things, showered and fell off to sleep.

The next day we awoke to black olives, bits of cucumber, one hard-boiled egg (poached) each, a small dry piece of bread, jelly and a coffee—not my idea of a good start, but this wasn't the Ritz and we weren't in Vegas. Our instincts were to find the beach, so we set off for the center of town, where all the buses made their rounds. Now, exposed by the sunshine, our side of town was charming; old stones, slick and weathered by centuries of local movement, flowed over into the old brick-stone buildings. Along our walk, remnants left over by the Romans camouflaged themselves near corner walkways and old city embankments. Vendors lined the street, selling all sorts of curiousities unique to Turkey, like simit, circular bread rolls and marble chessboards made the Turkish way. I passed what arguably could be the most quaintly romantic hideaway in the back alleys of the world. A multi-toned brick wall, possibly meant to delude passersby about its internal treasure, faced the street. Ivy overhung two arched entryways, making it difficult to peer inside. I pushed a couple of vines to the side, and what I witnessed would be the only reason to ever return to Antalya: a garden oasis and pool sunk deep into the courtyard. A few lucky souls lounged beside the pool, breathing in the green oxygen and reading books. It was a small bed and breakfast establishment, and the exclusivity in numbers made it a perfect getaway spot for couples. I had to remember that my current group didn't provide the ambience for a romantic journey and to reserve the image for future recollection.

    To find the beaches, a bus had to be taken beyond the outskirts of town; and when we reached the beaches, it was hard to know where to finally tell the bus driver to stop. The beaches were perfectly flat, a far distance from the road, and they seemed to stretch forever. Restaurant bars had strangely sectioned off massive stretches of the beach into rectangular blocks, like some sort of planned offering from the government, and the effect was everything appeared the same. In short, the beaches were deficient of any personality. Seb wanted to get off here, though he hadn't a reason; and neither Leo or I had a complaint. We walked the long reach from the road to the beach, bought ice creams, chatted pointlessly with the bartenders for a while, who were mostly interested in practicing their English. And then we walked along the beach. I soon realized that walking without flip-flops was a challenge. The sand looked like sand, but felt like sharp rocks. Still, I continued walking, out of boredom. On our way back from walking the infinite coastline, we saw two older ladies dressed in full clothing—layers of long grey shirts and head wraps, both fairly obese, who rolled around in the water near where the shore meets. I thought Leo's comparison to two humpback whales caught at the shoreline by a low tide was a bit crude and tasteless, and I still feel a bit of guilt for laughing at his joke. Nevertheless, it had been obvious ever since we stepped off the bus that we were in the wrong place, around the wrong vibe, and it was time to find the nearest bus station and keep it moving cross-country. And that's exactly what we did. The next morning we would be off to Olympos, further down the Mediterranean coast. I thought, "Please let us hit the tourist jackpot this time."

We woke up early in the morning, ate our cucumber breakfast and found the bus station. The bus was not very big, more like a large van, with people crammed snuggly into the seats. And my heart dropped as I fixated on a dark-eyed beauty. I saw something in her that reminded me entirely too much of a past love. I wanted to dismiss the thoughts, the random coincidence and physical similarities, but just as I pushed it behind me, miles into our journey, pushed it behind the breathtaking views of mountainous cliffs upon clear azure ocean, Seb nudged me. He pointed with his eyes in her direction.

"That girl in the front looks just like Maggie."

"I know, I saw her." My voice went weak as I said that; it was as if the sound was still trapped inside of me, muffled, not able to fully escape. Seb was listening from the outside of a dark cave, and I hoped he didn't search any deeper.

"I remember when you guys first met. Remember that? It was outside of a Burger King. You were afraid to step to her at first." For some reason, my silence wasn't good enough for him. He just had to keep on digging. "Where is she at now? Do you know?"

"Shanghai, the last I heard."

"You haven't gotten over her yet have you?" A bit of a pause. "I understand. But, there are too many hot women out in the world. All different kinds, too. I never look back on relationships. Once they're over, they're over. You gotta know where to cut your losses or gains. Hehehe."

"Yeah." I wasn't really listening to him. I was back to fixating on this girl in the front. Her charcoal black hair and slender face. Her delicate shoulders. She really had a lot in common with Maggie. It was powerful. I had an urge to go over and hug her, a person I didn't even know. I wanted to feel the warmth again, whisper I still love you and how my heart hasn't been the same, ever since. But, she wasn't

Maggie, and she wouldn't understand. Furthermore, the guy she cuddled up to when she wasn't peering off into the rocky landscape, he probably wouldn't be very understanding either. I finally focused again on the scenery.

Everything close whizzed by us in the van. Through the window, roadside trees flew by in dashes of greens and browns, wild flowers in yellows and purples traced lovely lines in the forest, and every once in a while a great clearing would expose vast ocean. The water and cliffs were steady focal points, not jittery and fickle like the forest. I had never seen such persistent mountainous coastline, and every few hundred yards was a new surprise. Small coves hid between mountain ridges. Sheer cliffs, littered with boulders and rocks, suddenly sprouted bushes and trees, or a bare dusty gray slope would bear beautiful wild flowers, gleaming, vibrantly reflecting the sun. Unlike Antalya where beaches were flat and lonely, this part of the Mediterranean exuded personality and grandeur. How could I ever get bored looking out towards such a decorated and celebrated coastline?

Our drive entered a patch of forest, where the coast was completely hidden. My internal compass told me we were heading inland, away from the coast. The most unpredictable mode of travel within countries had to be the bus. The ticket always had a destination, and regardless of whatever the person behind glass told you at the booth in the station, what you could expect was an improvisation of bus changes, pickup points and delays. We soon stopped on a dirt embankment in front of a shed. People were waiting outside, and also a large van. I asked the person in front of me where we were, and he explained that we should get off now and change to the van. I wondered how he knew so well, because we weren't instructed at the station. Changing from the bus to the van was like moving from first class to a propeller seat. The van didn't have enough seats for the passengers traveling on to Olympos, and I ended up sandwiched between two strangers, my thighs and ankles glued symmetrically, my knees massaging the spine of the lady sitting ahead of me, and my back forced forward at an incline. At least I had a window view. This lasted for another hour when the van finally ventured onto a dirt road. We were close.

At the first site of accommodations, the first drop off point for passengers to Olympos, Leo just climbed out of the van. At first, it seemed he was making room for others getting off, but then, a tout with a heavy Australian accent walked up to him proclaiming the overall greatness of his cabin community, and Leo was sold. Meanwhile, Seb and I both were a bit puzzled and taken off guard. It was unlike any of us to jump on the first offer. We knew there were other options and wanted to weigh those accordingly. But Leo would prove stubborn. He wasn't getting back on the van.

"I'm getting off here guys, the place looks okay," Leo said.

"Let's check out the others before making a decision," I said.

"You guys go ahead. This place is good enough for me." And, that was that. The van had a schedule to make, the sliding doors slammed closed and we continued down the dirt road. I could see Leo through the back window, still talking to the tout. They both walked into the front cabin constructed in mahogany logs. I didn't really have time to study the place, but something was strange and chaotic about it, something of a backpackers' anarchy.

"What's up with Leo?" I asked Seb.

"I don't know. He's acting a little weird." But we didn't put much thought into it. For a second, I wondered if we would see him again. We were riding down a long dirt road, and I had no idea how many pensions were available, how large this place or city or village was. The guidebook didn't mention that. What it did say was that Olympos was famous for its Tree Houses.

The somewhat narrow dirt road opened up wide, and soon tree houses and cabins popped up all over the place. A small embankment put on a pedestal all life situated right of the dirt road—a much livelier scene, with pool tables planted outside on the grassy dirt, and a ping-pong table. There were long wooden tables and benches, the kind that blend with the forest, rough and splintered, built to last in the harsh outdoors. Some people were sitting, eating lunch, gulping down a few mid-day beers, while many people were filing out down the road, with beach towels and bathing suits already on. Good, I thought, that means a beach is not far. The left side of the road was teaming with pensions, but the scene was a bit more secluded and intimate. Forest naturally partitioned the tree houses and cabins like picket fences. Suddenly we had a world of options. Even some of the names listed in the guidebook appeared. Seb and I got off and walked to the left. We were sure this was the right area. We found a charming pension, family-owned and run. They had cozily built platform decks, raised a few feet in the air and supported by large pine trees, with the dual purpose of providing shade while lifting people from the ground level nuisances. The wooden platforms were cushioned by an array of pillows, different sizes and colors, the way Moroccan Tea houses are decorated. Here you could read a book, chat or eat dinner. Only one tree house stood in the front, to the side of the small restaurant-bar. Below the tree house was another wooden deck, though smaller and more closed off. This was where it seemed every generation of the owning family lived out their forest paradise. A grandmother smiled pleasantly as we walked by, entering the complex. An equally pleasant lady greeted us from behind the bar. She had a warm plump face, two little dimples contracted in, waiting for their moment. But she wasn't overly inviting. She had seen every traveling personality walk through her compound, even the schizophrenic type, and I could envisage her bursting with kindness when the time came. She just needed confirmation and trust. She wouldn't waste herself on just anyone.

The offers were two meals, breakfast and dinner, ten dollars a night in the small cabins and seven dollars a night for the tree houses. Who turns down two meals and a tree bed for seven dollars? I could live here for years off my savings. Furthermore, how could I live with myself knowing I turned down a chance to live out a childhood fantasy? Still, we went to inspect first, before making any commitments. A star rating hadn't yet been available for tree house accommodations, and we didn't want to live on top of a bush. The tree houses were further in the back, beyond the restaurant-bar, behind the cabin with internet and books, and the laundry house. In the back, near the outhouses and outdoor shower stalls was a whole complex of neatly aligned cabins and sparsely built tree houses. Fortunately, only adequate clusters of trees were chosen for this housing feat. We quickly found our haven and I was the first one to walk up the raggedy planks of wood. Every step I took, the ladder and the house shook and screeched. The entire time I was dubious of the experiment. What if this house actually fell apart while I was inside, and I came tumbling down, planks and nails? Or even while walking these steps, maybe I wouldn't make it to the top. I pushed down the slab of wood, hitched with one lonely nail, the only means of securing the door from weather or theft. Later, when I would think back to this experiment, I don't think I would have trusted all my stuff, months' worth of luggage, to a flimsy tree house with no means of locking it. The thought was a bit insane, and stupid. But, we were backpacking it, and the rest of the travelers were in the same predicament; some special silent community agreement had been made, that if you stay away from my stuff, I will also respect your belongings.

When I opened the door, bent over not to bump my forehead, and climbed in, I could feel the house move a little to the right, along with the slope of the hill. Although I felt a little nervous at first, the house a disaster waiting for the first strong gale to blow, it also imbued my spirit with something liberating. It was exciting letting go, and trusting nature and fate. This tree house had probably held a thousand people before in its past. And why should I be the first one to suffer its mortality? I plopped down irresponsibly on my new bed, not at all concerned about the movement. It was like lying on one of those waterbeds, only less claustrophobic and back damaging. Well, I would have to wait and see about the back damage.

Seb yelled from below: "Is it safe to come up?"

"Yeah. You're going to trip. This thing could fall any second. And a few boards are missing on the sides. If one of us has a girl up here, the neighbors could sit outside and eat popcorn."

"I'm coming up, dude." As he walked up I could hear and feel every step, even seconds afterwards. It was an insane arrangement, but I was sold. It fit perfectly the mood and backpacker scene. "This is crazy!" Seb said, with his famous nervous face of fear and excitement, as he peered in. In Seb language, "crazy" meant he liked it too.

We took some photos of the tree houses and the pension for later memories, got changed, and headed for the beach. The beach was in walking distance, just a straight path down the dirt road and through a national conservatory. What we didn't realize until we got near a toll-booth was that we needed to pay to get in if we weren't Turkish. Seb had the smart idea of walking around the last remaining pension, before the park began. And I still feel guilty for our breaking and entering, but the name of the travel game was to save money at any opportunity, not knowing when those few dollars would come in handy later, and deferring any Karma tax. We darted through shrubs and tall weeds, eventually joining the rest of the travelers walking the dirt road. The day was brilliantly sunny, and every step made you even happier to be heading towards the sea. That day, everyone seemed light on their feet. People weren't walking anymore; they were prancing and skipping. We eventually found ourselves walking just a few feet behind a fluttering young twenty-something. Something about her captured Seb's and my attention immediately. She had an untamed exuberance, unashamedly young and free-spirited, and naughtiness escaped her movements and gestures. She was the person many Hollywood actresses aim to portray, if only on screen, most of them failing miserably, not having purely escaped all the baggage and tribulations from off-screen reality. But this girl fluttered her wings with the wind, like a ray of light bouncing (and landing) from one point to the next, too quick and unpredictable to catch. I wondered if the girl was another foreigner escaping the societal confines of her native land, far enough away so that she could finally be accepted for who she was and not sandwiched between the laundry list of accusations and past experiences, character plots that some people have forever defined her with, including her own mother. Every once in a while she waved about two silky fabric strings with silk butterflies at each end. It had a circus quality, and the full motion of the butterflies tumbling and rising in circles struck me as the flapping of angel wings. An innocence still prevailed in her spirit, a rarity for someone probably in her mid to late twenties. I found this spirit to be encouraging, even motivating. I caught her glancing tauntingly in my direction a couple of times (maybe towards Seb, I couldn't really tell), not long enough to make any commitments, but some sort of invitation to try my luck, see if I have what it takes to please a flower child, like herself. Seb dared me to walk over to her and ask to use her butterfly contraption. I didn't like Seb trying to plan out my own attack, but his dare was probably what I needed to break free from my shyness, the sidetrack excuse to approach her.

    I walked up beside her. She smiled flirtatiously, and the first thing I asked was to try the butterfly thing-a-ma-jig. Immediately, I realized she didn't speak English, or maybe that was one of her little games, to pretend she could only communicate physically. But, she understood my arm movements reaching for her butterfly toy. I tried flinging the things backward in the air, almost slapping another pedestrian in the face, which she found to be hilariously funny. She was enjoying me making a fool out of myself. I couldn't manage to keep a steady rhythm and allow for the two butterflies to move in tandem; they kept cross cutting each other, ending in a tangling mess. The beautiful Turkish girl smiled while she took them out of my hands and then gave them a twirl again to show me what I was doing wrong. We hadn't spoken the whole time we exchanged butterfly contraptions back and forth, not until she vocalized what sounded a lot like beer, while pointing to a little vendor stand. She gave me back the butterfly contraption and skipped off to the stand.

Seb had been close behind us the whole time. "I think she's a freak. She might be the story that goes down in the history books. Keep working on her."

"She doesn't speak any English."

"You serious! Hahahaha. All the better." Seb had become more and more cynical and crude, to say the least, over the last two years. I was sure his Wall Street banking experience had changed him this way. He had stories, of all the fights and women, the lavish spending of money, fast cars and trips away with his bosses. All of these experiences had molded Seb in some ways. We were no longer the naïve graduates fresh out of university. Every day was making this clearer to me.

She returned with two bottles of beer, one for each of us, one of her ways of communicating. I said thanks, and then introduced myself by saying my name and placing my hand to my chest. She tried repeating, but was unable to pronounce my name well. Then, she pointed to herself, saying "Leila." It was a beautiful name. I tried to introduce her to Seb, and even that was a little difficult. So Seb took it on himself to give each of us Muslim names. My name was now Mustafah and Seb's was Alibaba. She really got a kick out of that gesture, continuing to laugh, as all three of us were now hopping along, sharing cold beer. Our path led us through a valley between two stony mountains. The mountains were toweringly close, and some people were braving to climb parts of the mountain, free-handed. To some travelers (probably Aussies) it was worth the risk of falling, if you could make it to the cave half-way up and pose for photos as if the cave was the mountain's swallowing mouth.

The brief clearing beyond the tollbooth and ending after the last vendor stand, converted to a line of trees on both sides hanging over a small creek with wobbly cobblestones, used as a makeshift bridge. It was almost better to slip into the tiny creek to feel the cold mountain water refresh your ankles than to skillfully tread the slippery stones. A beginning slope of a mountain erratically rose upwards on our left, and crumbled stone, the remnants of ancient structures, was sprinkled about. I understood better why this was named an archaeological site, protected by the government. The beautiful ruins we had come upon were from Roman times, almost two thousand years ago. The ruins were scattered further up the mountainside, but we were determined to make it to the refreshing sea. So we kept our pace and were rewarded when the path finally opened up to a large cove, beautiful white sand,

and a frolicking microcosm of people. Quickly Leila pulled me by my arm to follow her, while Seb trailed closely behind. She seemed to have a special spot in mind, or maybe she was meeting friends. That's it. She wasn't really alone the whole time; her friends must have been waiting for her all along. I knew a girl like herself had to have a following. Instead of walking around, we crossed through a small pond of water that must have been trapped here when the tide fell. It was freezing cold when I stepped in. On the other hand, I thought, maybe it was being fed by mountain water somehow. After crossing the pond, she ran to her friends who were sitting down under small swooping trees and brush. They seemed to make up two couples, all were very friendly, and one of them even spoke a little English.

After we introduced ourselves with our new Turkish names to the laughs of everyone, one of the guys asked, "Would you like beer?" I wasn't too keen on dismissing invitations, not while traveling, so I agreed and so did Seb this time. He translated to Leila, and she bounced to the edge of the freezing cold pond and pulled out three beers from its depth. By this time, Seb and I were completely starving. We were also curious if Leo was frolicking somewhere on the beach. So, we left Leila and her friends and said we would be back later with more beer. They pointed us left where we could find restaurants, and we moved on, this time avoiding the arctic pond. We walked past the entrance where we'd first encountered the beach and walked the fluffy sand around the curve of the mountainside. Again the beach opened up, but this time much wider. In fact the sand went back a few hundred yards, inclining with the sudden topography. A marvelous showing of wooden yachts parked not far from the shore, where people were employing the steep planks of the boats as diving platforms; every so often was a swan dive, but mostly from that height, people just held their nose, lifted their free arm to the wind and plunged feet first. The lengths of the drops were commendable. And just like anywhere in the world where good sand and summer sun meet, an occupation of tan lovers existed on the outer edges of the tide, some daringly dormant, and others squinting to read. For the most part, this was a young backpackers' scene, free of many families.

We strolled in search of food. A couple of restaurants could be seen up ahead, perched on a brief plateau at the mountain's foot. But unbeknownst to us, a little white dog, with brown spots, much nimbler on the sand than we, had been following us for some time. And yet not following us: the mixed-breed dog had been walking with us, just at the distance of our blind spots. Gradually and with the utmost diplomacy, he had managed to walk with us side by side, man to man. It was a brave and dignified approach, if not absurd, for a dog to have put together. And he earned our immediate respect up front since, for at least a few hundred paces, the dog never even asked for approval to join the ranks; he just continued along, head straight and tail arched upwards as if waving a battle flag, never giving the slightest thought to rejection from the brotherhood. The act was audacious. And for a dog to have mustered it up, well, it was hard to believe. So there it was; in less than two minutes we had been offered a proposal, all considerations for admission had been deemed irrefutably sufficient on the grounds of powerful first impressions, and approval had been granted, instant membership into our secret society. Of course, a mixed-breed like myself had to be somewhat biased in his final decision, but we had never considered over the past years of traveling the addition of a traveling dog. A sort of traveling mascot, if you will. This may have been the missing ingredient. Anyhow, not too much had changed. The dog was one of those more self-sufficient breeds; he had too much pride to beg for attention and affection. He didn't need our pity or any affirmations of his self-worth. He merely needed a crew to run with, like-minded companions, whom he could confront the world with, while still maintaining his autonomy and independence. And for a nomad, a stray dog, he had done well for himself. He appeared healthy. His fur was relatively clean, aside from the two genetic spots on his back and side belly. He appeared to maintain psychological stability; unless his erect posture was all another one of his ploys, a clever lie, he held a good self-esteem. He was comfortable with himself and knew his limitations as a canine in this human world.

    We all three walked the hill to the restaurant and found a nice outside picnic table that allowed a clear view of the sea, Seb and I seated at opposite benches and the dog seated on an earthly throne.

    That's when Seb started again: "We have to give the dog a name. What do you think?"

    "How about Chie," I said.

    "Nooo. If he's going to fit in our group, he needs a name fit for an adventure, a world traveler. Someone like Marco Polo or Ernest Hemingway."

    I immediately laughed and said, "You're trippin'. What about

Marcus Hemingway?"

"Hmmm," Seb said, stroking his chin as if threading the absent hairs and then said, "I like it. But, he's a Turkish dog. He needs a Turkish name. He can't stray too far from his roots."

"All right, how about the Sultan Marcala Hemingway or Muhammed Marco." I paused for a minute, staring wistfully into mid-air. "No. How about Marco Muhammed Hemingway."

"That's it! Marco Muhammed Hemingway!" Seb pronounced. We both looked at the dog, who stayed close but continued to look off in the distance, and Seb said, "He has no idea, what we are saying. We just gave him a leader's name. An international pimp certificate to roam beaches all over the world, banging bitches."

"Seb, you're taking this too far."

"I wonder if he knew we were heading for the restaurant and expects a few culinary treats to celebrate his admission into the gang."

"Nahh. We were too far away from the restaurant for him to know. If he's that smart, the dog deserves to be fed." And, clever he must have been, because toward the end of the meal, I threw him a few pieces of freshly baked bread from the basket, some left over cucumbers (I think Turkey must be the leader in cucumber production) and lamb meat from my kebab.

Before we paid the bill, thoughts of Leo came up. "I wonder what he's up to. That was strange of him to jump off the van like that. Something's up with Leo. He's acting really strange recently."

"You're right. I wonder what got into him. I noticed even from this morning that his mind was somewhere else." Little did we know at that time, all of us would go through our delusional moments, where we didn't act ourselves, off in our own world—and not long after making those comments.

"Speaking of the devil. Is that Leo walking down the plank of that yacht over there?"

"Where?"

"Over there!" I said, pointing at about two o'clock. The dog also followed my hand movements, but I don't know if he truly understood.

"I can't tell," Seb said.

"That has to be him," I said. "How many brothers could there be in Olympos?" It was true. Among the Turks and the foreigners, Leo and I were the only persons with much skin melatonin. And Leo could have easily been mistaken as having both parents of African descent. "How did Leo get up there?" I said, sort of baffled. It seemed to me at the time the yachts were private boats. But the truth was it didn't surprise me that Leo had found a way onto the boat. Leo was one of those people that could find his way into any situation he desired. And at this point, we both noticed him walking back down the plank, almost as if first inspecting the jump.

"What is he doing?" Seb said, "Is he going to jump or what?"

"It looks as though he's going to run and jump."

That was Leo, all right. Always the over-achiever. He could never just do the normal thing that everyone else commits; he forever needs to go above and beyond, set himself apart from the rest. And that's exactly what he did. He convinced the other anxious boat jumpers to move back at a good enough distance. He then began running down the plank, picking up speed in the process, and right at the end of the plank, he jumped into the air, rolling into a ball, triple flipping in mid-air, and landed gracefully in a dive. Seb and I almost broke out into hand clapping. Leo had managed to impress us, once again. It was great to see a fellow society member triumph as such, and it was enough of a daring feat to make old Marco Muhammed Hemingway proud. I was almost sure that Marco had seen the entire spectacle unfold.

We paid the bill and moved down the beach to see if we could catch up with Leo. He was still swimming around when we made it down to him.

"Leo, your ass is crazy! Where did you learn to flip like that?" I asked.

"Learned it during high school. I was lifeguard at a city pool and when no one was in the pool, the other lifeguards and I used to compete for best dive. Over the summers, I just got better and better, until I was winning all the contests." He never ceased to amaze us. "Who is this little mutt?" said Leo, now looking down at the dog. Marco looked away, trying to ignore him and his little remark.

"Hey! Don't talk to one of your fellow brothers that way. He's officially part of the society. He proved himself early on with the utmost courage and stateliness," said Seb.

"What did he do?" Leo asked.

"The truth is he just came up and started walking with us, like he didn't really give a fuck! Kind of caught us off guard. That deserves something," Seb finished.

"Whatever, man," Leo finished, not giving that last comment any attention.

"Oh, shit," I said.

"What?"

"I forgot the beers. I'm going to run back and get them. Wait here."

I returned with the beers, and we walked back to where Leila and her friends were sitting. They were happy to see us, or maybe it was the beers. I introduced Leo, who was knighted with the new name, Aladin. We drank down a beer and talked. Apparently, they were all from Istanbul, down here to escape the weather and have fun (whatever that meant). We told them about flying to Istanbul first, and the bad weather and our change of plans, and the fact that we still wanted to go there, but probably at the end of the trip. They welcomed us to stay with them when the time came or at least go out to some bars and clubs. At this point Leila wanted to go for a swim.

We walked towards the water's edge. I could tell Leo and Seb were plotting something, not only because of the devilish gaze coming from their eyes as they watched a frolicking Leila, but because I knew them and what inhabited their minds ninety percent of the time. And maybe they were right. This girl had no other means of communicating, other than smiling, gesturing, and touching. Was she up for a Woodstock, free love experience? All the signs were leading in that direction. It was possible enough. The atmosphere was a perfect stage for casting these types of scenes, and all the characters were a bit out of their minds. There was an obvious limitation to our relationship with Leila, considering the language barrier. And yet we had communicated brilliantly thus far. I couldn't be held responsible for what was about to take place. If you were placed in these circumstances with the peer pressure of a special brotherhood, the absence of witnesses, the liberty of Sun and clear blue Mediterranean Sea, the tropical temperatures, and add to it how we were just exiting our careers and how nothing completely made sense to us anymore—. Our world had been turned upside down. What would anyone our age with these sorts of circumstances do?

Leila pranced off playfully towards the open sea, lightly kicking up sand and waving her arms back and forth with the loose rhythm of her legs and feet. Seb, Leo, Marco and I followed behind her with our tails wagging. When we reached the surf, Leila was already frolicking about, swimming back floats and breaststrokes, kicking and throwing up water in a lively manner, every few seconds gazing in my direction and then turning her attention else where, the way a feline orchestrates its prey.

"Go out there man. What are you waiting for dude?" Leo said.

"I think she's up for some kinky shit. Put in a word for us while you're out there, dog." Seb was laughing, but I knew he wasn't completely joking.

"She doesn't speak English, you dumbass!" Leo said to Seb. Then Seb started using sign language to prove his point that it was possible, using his three fingers to represent us, and then, one finger to represent her, and by that time, I dove into the water. Immediately, the water held me cold and stiff as the mountain pond we walked through earlier. I could barely feel my body as I was swimming. Then after a few strokes, and once I had gotten a good distance from the shore, a warm current grabbed me, the way a cozy log cabin with a fireplace would greet a winter guest. I reached Leila, who had distanced herself well away from the shoreline at this point.

Out here, the surrounding sea had an intimate way of closing off the rest of the world, secluding us in the relaxing sounds of open sea and changing our visual perspective from that of land-walking mammals to that of lily pads. I felt alone with Leila here in the water. An abandoned floating device, the long ribbed kind, with built-in pillow, usually made in bright florescent colors, floated by us. This one was a florescent yellow. We both used it as our crutch. Then she let go of the float, at the same time holding onto me in the water, clutching onto my shoulders for relief, and wrapping her legs around my waist. With equal agility and continuity, she un-strapped her bikini top, leaving it to float freely with the calm motions of the sea. Desire and heat poured out of her body; the playfulness she exuded earlier had changed into intense passion, impossible for me to deny. Her language was gripping and persuasive. I understood beautifully every vowel and consonant, every syllable and accent mark, the brief commas and close connecting hyphenations of every silent adverb, adjective, noun and verb flowing from her being. We spoke universally, free from any foreign accent or lisp, closing the gaps to this small world of ours, building a bridge between her and me, a connection secure enough for all of humanity.

We explored the sea's warm depths in that moment, swimming with its warm Mediterranean currents, using our bodies as human pitch forks, trembling and vibrating in the resonating tones of those sultry sub-dialects, a subtle completion and finessing touch to every pungent word expressed through our silent tongues, gaping mouths, and life-filled bodies.

And then, almost suddenly, the bridge between us abated, melted away, until the waves of the beautiful turquoise-blue surface were ever so gently massaging the sides of our faces, and our eyes opened to our bobbing heads, the water and panoramic vistas from sea level. I could see an audience along the curving cove, arranged as if seated in an amphitheater, and Seb, Leo and Marco in their front row seats gazing in enjoyable disbelief. The other humans were sneaking peaks, satisfying their voyeur impulses, but not committing to the public perversion. Although, considering the waters' natural veiling, their minds played out their own versions of our enactment. Because, really, the only clues given had been facial expressions, body proximity, and a floating bikini. And, at that very moment, the bikini was making its way towards the sand, the waves slowly carrying it further towards the beach as if sand settling in an hourglass, the universe's way of saying Scene I had come to an end, now wait intermission. Something was very teasing in her actions, and though she ended Scene I of our act in time-breaking speed, leaving my conflict unresolved and me as a puppet dangling by a string until the next act, her playfulness and lightheartedness is what I would continue to remember for the months and years to come. For her, it was exactly that, a play. And she was definitely the protagonist, improvising each one of her lines, as I countered her passionate performance.

Her eyes glittered and taunted me in those last moments, and as fast as our eyes had opened she swam off towards the beach, leaving me to find that cool mountain current in which to cool off and also fend for the abducted floating device. I decided to relinquish the float and swim back to shore.

For a while, we all played a game on the water's edge. Leila had initiated it. She carefully stacked at least five stones one on top of the other, gradually getting smaller towards the top, until a tiny pebble crowned the makeshift tower. The object of the game was simple: knock off the top stone without touching the other stones beneath it. And we took turns in a row, starting with Leo, then going clockwise, from Seb to Leila (excluding Marco, of course), and the last one to throw, myself. This petty game actually went on for about an hour, until we were just pelting the stones with all our strength, having forfeited any skill or accuracy. Then suddenly, Leila pushed Leo in the chest and ran off into the water, sort of taunting him to follow her in. And that's exactly what he did. Seb turned in my direction and I to him, and from that point on we knew what had started. Leila had introduced new characters into her play; that's the way she liked it, always keeping the audience at the edge of their seats, until the curtains go down. After Scene II, I walked with Leila back to the pension, and up into my tree house. The plan was that Seb and Leo were supposed to trail behind not too long afterwards. Only, as I would find out later, they had been delayed by two other Turkish girls, both from Istanbul, one married and on vacation, the other here by herself on vacation. They were both seated at one of the platforms in the front area. They lived in our pension, and, apparently, Leo and Seb had found their eye contact irresistible. By the time Seb and Leo finally came shaking the tree house down with every quaking step and opening the tattered wooden door, the show was over and Leila decided that Scene IV would have to wait until later. I walked her out to near where the bar was located, we borrowed a pen and swiped a business card of the pension, and she wrote her pension address and number down. And, in a flutter of sign language and finger counting, we planned to meet here at my pension later tonight, around ten or eleven, sometime after dinner.

    When I returned to the tree house, a sort of home base hideout for the crew, Marco was waiting watchdog at the bottom of the steps. I wonder if he was smart enough as an Olympos dog to stay away from dilapidated tree houses that were on the verge of falling any second. Maybe his last home was a tree house. I gave him a quick pat and shuttled up the stairs. When I got up the stairs, the guys were talking about the girls they had met. Leo was going on about his girl being married, but the ironic flirting that accompanied her words as if daring him to make a move. "I've never been with a married woman before," Leo said. Typical Leo talk. When those words flew out of his mouth with the sweet scent of appetite and craving, I knew what he was up to. Seb talked about the sophistication and elegance of the girl he met, and how if his parents found out he even made the slightest move on a Muslim girl, they would ban him from the family forever. His father, he said, would probably kill him. But all of this didn't seem to deter his desire and interest. Seb was in an experimental stage. Those long hours burning the midnight oil all over Manhattan, working his life away, had turned him into a wild animal once he broke his cage. All his restrictions and cultural confines had been broken along with those chains. And probably, these same Muslim women would be exiled from their community back in Istanbul, if word had gotten out that they were using nonverbal language with three Americans, including two Jews and a Christian.

As I would find out later, Istanbul was at the core of Turkey's conflict, and these women were pioneers in a newly developing and nouveau riche Turkish cultural revolution, where women were exercising their rights as a liberated people. These girls' actions were enough to have them pelted to death by mobs in most other Islamic countries. Later I would also learn about the courage and forward thinking on the part of a man named Mustafa Kemal "Ataturk," the founding father of modern day Turkey, who bravely instituted, for the first time in an Islamic country, the separation of religion and state, the right of women to vote and serve parliament, and the addition of last names, changing him to "Father Ataturk." After WWI, and not long after the fall of the last Ottoman Installations, he saw the need for the once dominant, thriving Muslim culture to make much needed reforms in order to compete with a fast advancing Western Society, for Turkey not to be left behind in an obsolete dust. Nevertheless, the last thing on the minds of Seb, Leo, Marco, and me was the history and culture of Muslim civilization. We had more urgent human issues to deal with. Leo was garnering his wits and Seb was battling his convictions. It was their turn to put on a show for me. I had started this freaking ball moving, and I wanted to see it continue to roll.

After dinner, we all had our plans. The truth is I don't know where Marco had gone for all that night (maybe to some sort of late night doggy hangout), but after dinner and our brotherly love at the dinner table to save him bits of leftover food from our plates (he was lucky that the Pension serves an "all you can eat" buffet) we wouldn't see him until the next morning. Seb hung back with Uzge, his new Turkish princess, and Leo and I walked with our dates up to his pension house. Before we left, Seb was going over his typical spiel to Uzge about how he came to America when he was only eleven years old from the Muslim country of Uzbekistan, where he didn't know a lick of English, only Russian and a little bit of Farsi, and how he learned his way upwards through the American system, etc., etc.

    The walk to Leo's pension was a bit like walking through the countryside after dark, because the only lights helping us along were from other pensions and for most of the walk only trees and bushes lined the dirt road. It reminded me a lot of that walk we took at night from our bungalows along the coast of Ko Phan Gan to another side of the Thai island, where the full moon party existed. The forest noises here in Turkey weren't as complex as those in Thailand, though. Plus, the air was cooler and less humid. Then, suddenly I was overwhelmed by what appeared when the trees abated, exposing the narrow valley we had been cautiously trotting. The way a tree shades sun, a glowing moon had been obscured and was finally able to shed its borrowed rays, providing us with a guiding source of light. But what captivated me so sublimely hadn't been the emergence of light, but the way at nighttime, the mountains of Olympos seem to hover so closely in the background as if they were gigantic waves in the Pacific waiting to break. The proximity and darkness of these massive mountain waves towering over my every step struck awe and respect in me. I couldn't force my head back down from its upward tilt. Once I had caught sight of this natural wonder, I didn't want to stop looking and soaking it in. Add to that the silence and peace emanating from the seclusion of these two parallel mountains built side to side like apartment buildings in Old Spanish cities. It was magical. Olympos was nature's way of erecting marvelous stone palaces, constructing valley fortresses and prime seaside real estate. No wonder so many ancient civilizations—like the Romans, Venetians, Genoese and Rhodians—had tried one by one to inhabit the security of its natural barriers, only to be exhausted finally by a relentless tide of pirate ships. Pirates were those ancient peoples with no laws or god, and this organic outcrop of ingenuity had been abandoned for centuries.

    I finally pulled my head out of the sky, when we reached Kadir's Yoruk Treehouses. The place was much different from the low-key setup of my treehouse. The place was huge and complicated, strange to look at. Walking into this sort of compound was like walking into a surreal dream, similar to the wooden ghetto in that Leonardo DiCaprio movie, *The Gangsters of New York*. And it had that pirate feel to it, too. The first bar was a riot of drunken backpackers, all ages and ethnicities, a strange mixture of lonely travelers, odd honey-mooners, and college graduates. We didn't waste our time in there. They were all drunk and chanting obscenities. We walked left to this one club on the premises. It was of a funny design, sort of like a mini-Roman amphitheater, but made out of wooden planks; everything here was made out of dark ragged wooden planks, the bar, the club, the pensions, everything. In the very center of the small amphitheatre, lay a full flaming bon fire, with small chars of the wood flying upwards every so often. I was sure the connected rows of benches, curving in a three-quarters circle, had been used to seat a performance of some kind in the past. At this time, people were sitting down drinking. Those who weren't drinking were up dancing on all the other floor space not engulfed in flames. At the top of all that seating was a bar, and we walked directly to that bar upon entering.

     Leo's girl was enjoying her act of defiance. But something told me she was holding back, that maybe she didn't really want to go through with it all, though I was sure Leo would push her limits. The music that night was a random mix of everything in the world, and after more and more drinks, we didn't care what was playing. Leila, I found out, was a decent dancer, but something very hippie struck me in her moves. She danced around like a fairy with wings, just letting her entire body go to the music, no method to her madness. Leo had learned salsa dancing in San Fran, and was showing off as usual; he had the same salsa disease as Seb. Only, the disk jockey never bothered to play Latin music, other than maybe one Ricky Martin tune, and that wasn't salsa. Still, Leo couldn't resist spinning his date around in a complicated mix of turns, where more than once, they had become entangled; maybe that was his plan, to entangle. Meanwhile, I was getting drunker and drunker, and Leila was getting drunker and drunker, and Leo had had his share of Vodka Redbulls; but his date was composing herself quite well. And then with the changing in wind direction, Leo's date got a phone call on her cell phone. I didn't even know people could get reception out here, nestled between mountains and hidden in the forest, but she did, and after the phone call, which we all assumed was a certain someone, she decided she had had enough for the night and walked back to her treehouse. She wasn't completely alone in that tree house. Her friend had also gone on vacation with her, only wasn't a night owl like the rest of us. Anyways, when Leo's date left, that was when the real party started. Leila who had snuggled up to me most of the night was now showing Leo the same amount of attention, if not more. It was all a part of her play. Scene IV was about to begin and she needed to prep the characters, give them their parts, maybe even do a little rehearsal, before the intermission ended. By this time, we had gone a whole day communicating with Leila, and I could count on my two hands how many words were spoken, most of them when the characters were given their new Turkish names.

Eventually, the club wasn't interesting enough for the three of us. And we slipped away to Leo's humble abode still gripping our drinks. Leo hadn't told me this beforehand, but somehow he ended up with a roommate, who was sort of sleeping when we entered his small pension. I felt bad for the guy when Leo kicked him out. The next hour or so was probably the funniest scene to the play. And I can't explain why. But the bottom line is Leo and Leila and I would take with us to the grave a most hedonistic experience. Nothing too crazy, but definitely not something that happens everyday. Scene IV ends to the applause of everyone, and after the curtains closed and reopened, a brief encore.

The next day I walked back to my treehouse to change and shower. And Marco was waiting at the steps. Gradually, Marco was opening up and becoming friendlier. Or maybe he was in a good mood. Something good must have happened at the doggy hangout the night before. Anyways, Marco gave out a joyous bark when I greeted him, patting his impressively clean fur. Of course, beach dogs have an ocean to bath in. I think he was happy to see me. Seb wasn't in the tree house when I arrived, which could only mean one thing. Yahweh, please forgive him as he has sinned. Or maybe he hadn't gone all the way. Only Seb holds these truths. After finishing the necessities, I walked back down with Marco to breakfast, where Seb and his new friend were already eating. I sat on the far end of the platform this time, to conceal Marco from the owners of the pension, considering we didn't pay for three "all-you-can-eat" buffets. Seb had seen signs posted about white water rafting excursions somewhere nearby, and Uzge was excited to be joining us. Leo came around a little later, and after we joked about the night before and filled Seb in on everything, the conversation turned to that yacht Leo had triple dived from the day before.

"By the way, how did you manage to get on the boat to dive yesterday? Wasn't it private?" I asked.

"Yeah, it's private; but anybody can get on if you purchase a ticket. It's like a mini-cruise. The boats travel all around the coast, stopping at all the top places. Called the Blue Voyage. You can cruise

for three nights, four nights. Depending how far you want to go."
"Is that right! How much does it cost and where do you buy these tickets?" Seb asked.
"That I don't know. We can ask, when we check out the white water rafting. But I don't think they are very expensive, the tickets."
So, we had our objectives. Today would be book rafting and book Blue Voyage day. And the day flew by fast. We decided to take it in early, because the next morning at around eight a.m., we had to grab a quick breakfast so we could be out front waiting at 8:30 a.m. for the van that would take us to the river.
The next morning began rather chaotic and seeming to set the tone for the rest of the day. We were supposed to leave at 8:30 from the pensions, but didn't end up leaving until 9:30 a.m., and about thirty minutes into the bus ride on the way to the river, some girl realized she forgot her passport, which turned her hysterical because she wouldn't be returning to Olympos, she was to be dropped off in another town after the rafting trip. This put us another hour behind. To make up time, the bus driver drove like a maniac through windy, narrow roads, circling through mountains and valleys; add to this the blasting of Turkish music, his sort of theme music manifested, and I wasn't so sure that we would make it to our destination. The winding and breaking, curving and passing other vehicles, must have been too much for one of the girls riding in the back. She became nauseous and soon we were pulled over to the side of the country road, she wasting her guts all over the peaceful meadow. And she was not the only one; another girl got motion sickness, causing us to stop yet again.
Finally, after a chaotic three-hour drive to the Dalaman river, we hurried to throw on our life jackets and rush down the dirt hill to the embankment of the river where our raft had probably been waiting at least two hours, though you wouldn't be able to decipher all of this from our guides, who seemed very relaxed at that moment. There were probably fourteen of us, which meant we needed to be split into two rafts. Our first run at the rafts was a tortuous upstream battle towards a cave at the foot of the mountain. Up until then, none of us, including Seb, Leo, myself and the others had stepped foot in the water. The mountain cave was one of the sources of water filling the rapidly flowing river. We all climbed the rocky mountainside to the opening of the cave, when our guide flicked a hand full of water over us. The water was the equivalent of liquid ice. I could feel every single drop of

icy water sting my skin, the after chill from those drops lasting seconds almost minutes. It was absolutely mind-boggling the contrast in the hot summer sun and the freezing cold mountain water. A few people sipped the mountain water before we left, and, just like the guide said, I'm sure it was of the purest water. But, after my Thailand experience, I had vowed never to drink water not properly sealed in a bottle. One week of severe diarrhea was enough to write-off water all together, that's if it hadn't been vital to my life. Before returning the rafts, the guide who was guiding the other raft put on a show by swimming to the other riverbank (swimming the water was impressive enough), climbing the steep cliff, and diving—what seemed to be slow motion—into the water, swan style and then swimming against the current back to our side of the riverbank. In that quick feat of courage and exhibition, it was evident to me that he was the daredevil type, spontaneous and proud and, maybe, even stubbornly proud. He would be our new guide, helping us make the bulk of the journey, which was all the way downstream. The only problem was our first guide directed us fluidly through his command of the English language, but the new guide only spoke Turkish. And though there were three other Turks on the raft, Uzge (Seb's new fling), a Turkish guy, and another much softer-spoken Turkish girl, who we would only get to know that day on the raft, the Turkish guy didn't speak English and Uzge and the other girl were dreadful translators.

    Our new guide was not only a daredevil, but he was the competitive type. He wasn't happy when we weren't in the lead, and the other boat was quickly learning the downstream course, honing their skills rapidly. Our problem was a simple lack of communication. And, there weren't any major problems when the boat was going directly ahead, not needing to turn with the cutting curves of the river and most importantly when we weren't headed for a major rapids. During the calmer points of the river, the guide would give us a command, telling the left side of the boat to paddle harder or don't paddle at all or paddle in the other direction to counteract the river's pulling force to one side of the embankment or everyone paddle hard to catch up with the other boat or even to pass it a couple of times. These were translated by either Uzge or the other Turkish girl with ease, not under pressure or with time running out. And even then, we had made a few mistakes not acting at the time the guide wanted. But our guide was patient with us in those moments. We could still easily make up for our mistakes. We had all the time in the world. But, when river rapids were fast approaching, and we needed to be in a specific point of the rapid in order to run the rapid freely and safely, the translations weren't fast or decisive enough. This incited an explosive fire within our Turkish guide. And after our first rapid, where we nearly tipped over because we unintentionally paddled too far to the left, taking us over protruding boulders from the river floor, he nearly blew his top. And it seemed that even our little mistakes, thereafter, were each little fires lighting inside of him, and he was becoming more and more frustrated. The other boat was beginning to leave our range of sight, we were so behind. And our guide, a daredevil pro like himself, doesn't lose to competition easily, and he sure as hell doesn't get blown out, where his competition can't even be seen anymore.

I had no clue what was going on. He would speak, and seconds later Uzge or the other girl would echo in English, or they would speak at the same time in their heavy Turkish accents, so that neither Seb, Leo or I could understand a word. And we were the muscles behind this boat, the sheer force that moved us along during the calming of the river, the heavy arms that helped to steer the boat when the river's force pushed our boat towards the river bank or rocks. If we didn't understand the commands, then the boat had problems, and even worse, when we understood different things, the boat had the potential of floating completely out of control throwing us completely off course. And this occurred at least twice. The tension on that boat had been increasing rapidly, and the temper sparked in our guide must have prompted him to say something disgusting or offensive to Uzge, because after our last rapid where I was almost sure the boat had capsized, the pounding of our boat sideways on the thrusting water as we landed awkwardly almost throwing us all out, the two them would not stop exchanging words. And those words were not kind words. Uzge was absolutely furious, and the guide's face had become fire tomato red as if it could explode any minute. We tried to calm them both down, but as soon as the argument stopped, another one ensued, and eventually, the guide couldn't take this attack on his pride anymore and raised his hand as to hit Uzge. Leo jumped up, as to try and say whoa, you don't hit girls, and especially don't hit girls in the middle of an ice-cold rapidly moving river. It occurred to me that we were sort of innocent bystanders aboard this raft, we didn't speak the language, and we weren't a part of their argument; if something went terribly wrong, what control did we have over the situation? This was his river, he was skilled in its survival. We didn't want to fight; we just wanted to make it safely back to dry ground.

Another thought crossed my mind at that moment, maybe ridiculous, but you have to understand my impulse to always analyze each and every Turk I encountered as if conducting an anthropological study. I wondered if the guide was accustomed to women, his native Muslim sisters, arguing or contesting him. He was a river boy, probably didn't live too far from here in some small Muslim village, while Uzge was a city girl, open and liberal, at the heart of Turkey's change. He probably was appalled and felt disrespected. He was probably thinking to himself, "Who is this little girl to be arguing with me, her elder, the leader and provider within the hierarchy between woman and man?" Whatever his reasons for finally igniting into flames, erupting the volcano inside of him, when he was pushed to his limits, he pushed Uzge with an angry force, and not only Uzge fell into the water. Seb was sitting beside her in the raft, and when she fell back, Seb had been the only object that her little hands could grab on to try and catch herself before falling. Instead of catching her fall, she pushed Seb into the water with her. We were furious, Leo and I, and if it hadn't been for the urgent need to paddle the boat to the side and try to catch Seb and Uzge before the boat floated too far downstream — because already the images of them were becoming smaller and smaller behind our raft — to try to give them an object to climb upon, so that their bodies didn't stay emerged in the icy water for too long, we would have both rushed that guide, Leo and I, giving him a little taste of that icy cold water. But it was all too risky. We still needed him to guide us out of this winding mess, and we needed his help to rescue Seb and Uzge. And at first, he even seemed as if he wanted to keep going. So we yelled at him, threatening him to do something, and quick.

We were able to position the boat so that when they came floating down the river, we could intercept their bodies, lifting them back onto the boat. It was one of the craziest situations I could remember having been in. It was almost like pissing off the flight captain who you owe your life to while in mid-air. When Seb and Uzge finally made it back on board, their skin looked pale and they were shivering all over. The first thing Seb said was, "I can't feel my nuts!" I will never forget those first words, because here Leo and I were furious, still with thoughts of throwing the guide overboard, while Seb is the one who actually went overboard, and instead of being angry, he makes a joke. Leo and I couldn't help but start laughing. "Serious guys, I think I lost one of them," Seb continued. Maybe he wasn't kidding, but it came out as comedy. Later that day, Seb would explain to us that Uzge thought he had jumped overboard to save her. He explained that if she hadn't grabbed onto his lifejacket as she fell backwards, he would never have jumped in. "Are you crazy! The water is ice cold! I wasn't going to jump in after her!" But Uzge didn't know that. Seb had become her hero, her knight in shining armor for the remainder of our time in Olympos. There was no doubt about that. She clung to him like the shirt on his back for the next few days, before we were to board that Blue Voyage.

That night, after the van ride home from the river, and a little bit after another dinner buffet, I walked into the small computer room set up in our pension. I walked in with inspiration pulsing through the veins below my skin. Turkey had provided a lot of information. I wrote about the first day discovering Olympos and night with Leila. I wrote about our new mascot Marco and his unexpected emergence into the brotherhood. I talked about the breathtaking vistas in the mountainside, and I was anxious to tell the rafting story of today. Something was happening while I was explaining my experiences, placing my words together carefully and passionately. The story was the meat of the equation, but also important was the delivery of my experiences, the emphasis I placed on more important parts of the story and characters, the building of my stories into the proper climax, not sparing the emotional side, the most powerful side. These were all powerful details within the writing process, and even though I was merely sending emails, I took pride and fulfillment in the completion of each of those emails. It was important to me that the person reading was able to live vicariously through my encounters. I knew that many of the people I was writing to would never have a chance to fly halfway around the world to visit Turkey. It would never be possible for many of my friends and family, especially those that had little children of their own. But if I could free them from the quotidian stresses of daily life, even if for a few minutes, take them away from their realities and provide some sort of relief to their day, then every word that I wrote, every sentence and paragraph was critical, and deserved the utmost care. One thing that I was discovering was that I enjoyed writing.

We had spent three more days lounging on the beach, partying the night away with Leila and Uzge. The married girl told Leo that she started to have doubts and couldn't go through with it any longer; she had to stop talking to him. But that didn't stop his fun. There was enough of Leila to go around; she had become like our silent buddy on the tree house infested grounds of Olympos. Wherever she went, we would go; and wherever we decided to venture off to, she was right behind us. And, to top things off, Marco was still officially our travel mascot; well, as long as the buffets didn't run dry. Life here was great. Olympos turned out to be a very tantalizing place, and it would have been easy to spend the rest of the summer lounging in its depths. But time was essential, and a large part of Turkey and ourselves remained to be discovered. We had put our deposit money down for the cruise ship the same day as we booked the rafting excursion, and this morning was our time to pack all of our things and bid farewell to this mountain escape along the Mediterranean Sea.

    Leo walked up right after breakfast. I knew from the minute I saw him that something was wrong. But it didn't occur to either Seb or me what it could be. Why was Leo in such a stressed and angry mood? He walked up to us in a huff. "Guys, I have to go home," he said.

    "What do you mean you have to go home?" Seb said, shocked.

    "I have to go home," he repeated.

    "Where? Back to the States? Are you crazy? We're about to board the ship and you already put down your deposit," Seb continued.

    I was too shocked to even respond to Leo. It was the most unexpected comment that could come out of his mouth in this moment, completely from left field, with no warning whatsoever. We were supposed to be a team, travel the length of Turkey, and not only Turkey, we had two more countries scheduled, and even after those two countries we had Spain for as long as it took to learn Castellano. What was he saying that he had to leave in a huff, that he couldn't continue with us to the cruise?

    "Look guys. Something came up. Most of my money is tied up in used cars back in the states, and my business partner was supposed to sell them, but he's having trouble getting rid of them. They need to be sold as soon as possible, or I'm screwed out of a lot of money. And right now, that money from those cars should be in my bank account, but it's not. I barely have enough to make it back to the States, if I take that cruise with you guys, I would be risking a lot," Leo said, almost out of breath.

"So what are you going to do about the deposit money you put down?" I said. I didn't want to stress the poor guy anymore than was possible, but he could potentially be forfeiting a substantial sum of money.

"I'm going to demand my money back when the guy comes. Say that a family crisis came up and I need that money to return to my country," Leo said.

"Damn dude. It's not going to be the same without you, Leo. But, you gotta do what you gotta do," I said.

That sounded so clichéd, but at that moment, I was still in shock. I didn't really know what to say or think. The trip had made a dramatic turn. The third part of the brotherhood was about to dissolve. Now it would be Seb and me taking on Turkey. We could handle it by ourselves, but it wouldn't be the same. Each of us brought a special element to the team, and Leo was no exception. He really was like a brother to me, to both Seb and me. We had been through a lot together.

Leo said, "I'm going to get my money back, and try and meet you guys somewhere, maybe in Bulgaria, maybe I'll have to wait until Spain."

But something told me that the odds of him buying another plane ticket were slim. I don't know what made me think in this way. But I had the feeling that once he made it back to the States and back to the rat race, that we probably would not see Leo again, not for a long time at least. When the van finally pulled up, Leo used his investment banking skills to talk the guy out of keeping his deposit. And when it was time to load up our backpacks and get into the van, after we both gave Leo farewell handshakes and hugs, a part of me seemed empty. Leo was standing at the edge of the road with Marco standing to the side of his feet, both watching us get into the van, both longing to join us for the rest of the trip. But, then the van door slid shut, the engine revved, and we were off back down the same dusty road that had brought us to this backpackers' delight. We were off to sail the Mediterranean, and though Leo wasn't physically with us anymore, his presence wouldn't be forgotten on the open sea. Many moments would arise where either Seb or I would say, what would Leo do in this situation? Leo had left his legacy.

The ride a couple hours away to the dock where we were to board our vessel was somewhat gloomy. And understandably. We had left a member of the team behind. But, we were just resting as always happens between storms, passively taking in the scenery as background during a brief alone time. There was no talking or planning between Seb and me. Enough planning had been done; we'd bought the tickets. And now wasn't a time to arouse emotions or expend any energy. We were existing in a sort of black hole between events—a beautiful black hole with a lucid blue sea to our left, and impressive cliffs with a road that often bordered those cliffs with such uncomfortable proximity to the point only hill and water could be seen, but nevertheless a black hole. One filled with empty vegetable thoughts. A chance for the brain to cool and rejuvenate for another adventure. We needed the downtime, because we were just about to walk into another illusion, a fairy tale of sorts. Our boat, as we would soon find out, was not your typical yacht; and the captain wasn't your typical run of the mill captain. He was built for the open sea. And his vessel was the organ keeping him alive, the wooden crutch supporting his weight, even an extension of one of his arms.

The little fishing boat rocked back and forth ever so gently, colliding with an algae infested wood post jutting out of the water. A short, sun-baked man with even darker hair and two inches from official dwarfism, reached out, one foot planted on the dock, the other foot moving whimsically with the boat and tide. One by one, the first load of people very cautiously handed him their luggage, somewhat fearful that the ragged water could claim their prized possessions. Seb and I, gentlemen as such, waited for the second load. I stood at the dock's edge wistfully. There were two yachts: one was freshly painted white with bold blue letters, proudly stating, "The Odyssey," and the other was of lackluster dark and light brown wood and black letters too difficult to read from this far. I hoped for the "The Odyssey"; it was larger, friendlier and safer looking. And, of course, the little fishing boat passed right by "The Odyssey" straight towards our dodgy pirate ship. That figures, I murmured to myself.

I wasn't disappointed though. Who really knew what would await us? The most important thing was that the boat moved without sinking and the beautiful Turkey coastline stayed its pleasant color and temperature. I was already keen for a swim. The sun was beating down strong enough to guarantee a refreshing dip. But I would have all the time in the world for that. This cruise was scheduled for four days and three nights. We were going to hug the Mediterranean coast northwestwards, all the way until its illustrious moniker didn't suit anymore, where letters are knocked off and added, turning the same mass of molecules into the Aegean Sea.

As we approached the wooden yacht with all our stuff packed tightly in the tiny boat, and our crewmember dwarf standing in the back between our bags, guiding the lawnmower sized motor connected to underwater propellers, I was finally able to make out the black letters painted on the boat's hull. It read, "Mr. Hook." "What a strange title," I murmured. Traveling often caused me to talk to myself. What if the captain was like that fairy tale character in the Peter Pan story; a real life pirate of sorts? I couldn't relate such a title to anything else. The little fishing boat rocked against the hull of the ship, and, one by one, we grabbed a hold of the wobbly metal ladder attached only at the top of the boat's plank and boosted ourselves upward onto the deck of the boat. That is when we entered our real life fairy tale.

I'm ashamed to say this, but I felt awkward at first. How did I greet the captain without staring at his missing arm? He had to be used to the stares and first impressions by now, but I didn't want to be one of those ignorant fools who preoccupied their minds so intensely with superficial thoughts. The fact that he only had one arm—well sort of an arm and a half—was utterly insignificant. But I couldn't force those thoughts out of my mind. And when I tried harder to rid my brain of such superficial nonsense, this only helped to preoccupy an even larger portion of my current thoughts. It wasn't that I thought negatively of the captain in any way whatsoever, it was more that I hated myself for concentrating so much on his nub arm. I wanted more than anything to appear sincere when we met. I tried to smile normally and think of how it had been for every other person I had met for the first time. Act just in that way, not giving him any more or less than what most of my acquaintances can expect the first meeting. But I found myself staring at the arm, and smiling more deeply than usual, a pitiful grin. And it didn't help when he introduced himself as Captain Hook. My thoughts were immediately taken over by that arm after that comment. It was a cowardly move, but when I found the first opportunity, I quickly ventured away to put up my bags, to find a brief exit somewhere fast in order to collect myself.

    We had a cabin reserved on the floor of the boat. I had been on a cruise before, but only through Carnival Cruise Lines, those small floating cities, where rooms are set up like in hotels. In contrast, our room beneath the deck of this boat was a walk-in closet with only one bed. I was happy to hear that people normally sleep up on the deck at night. Our cabin was equipped with an airplane-sized compartment, where one could literally defecate, shower, and brush his teeth all in the same motion. I checked the water pressure and found it leaked out instead of spraying. No biggie. Already, people aboard my boat were jumping off into the transparent sea. A couple of Italian boys were playing basketball above the main deck. A small goal was attached to one of the large metal beams supporting the sails. The penalty for an unrecoverable missed shot was a dive into the sea. I had pieced together the crew and passengers aboard this trip. They were not at all the unruly spring break crowd of traveling Europeans and Turks that I had envisioned from observing all the boats floating along the Olympos beach. But it was probably for the best. After a full week of partying and carrying out the hedonism of my mid-twenties, a few days of rest and moral sanity was exactly what my body and soul needed. Here, aside from the Spanish girl who never left the sight of her boyfriend or husband, there were no real female distractions. And, consequently, no real reason to drink alcohol. For the next four days, I would have the opportunity to swim as much as my heart desired, eat three full meals a day, soak up vitamins from the sun, soak in the beautiful scenery, and swim some more. There was nothing to complain about. There were two Italian families aboard the boat, including two little boys, a little girl, two mothers, and one father. Aside from the kids, the parents were to themselves most of the time. There was a German couple, consisting of that attractive Spanish Senorita and a German man. They were extremely quiet most of the time, although they observed Seb and me as we ran around the boats socializing with whoever had ears and playing basketball with the children. I could tell they wanted to join in but were too shy. I could have been imagining things, but the Spanish girl couldn't seem to take her eyes off of me most of the time. I wasn't sure what it meant. Also aboard the ship were two Turkish women, a Turkish doctor, a German woman who couldn't shut up once in the most mundane conversation, and lastly a Kiwi and his Norwegian girlfriend. There were two crewmembers who almost looked like twins and of course the captain. Seventeen in total; nineteen including us. These were the people that would catch a glimpse into the life of two fledgling Americans traveling the planet without too many rules.

The day went according to plan. I got to see how the layer of coastline closest to the shore, the shallow part, appeared in a turquoise glow and how the deep center was the bluest of blues from afar. I also had a chance to study all those mountains jutting up randomly along the coast, and the sparseness of its vegetation from afar. From our distance, the slopes were pale thinning heads of forest hair, the vanilla soil dotted sparsely by green shrubs and trees. But the lack of lushness wasn't ugly at all; it was fascinating to watch, a landscape livened with wisdom and character. The first few hours I found myself sitting at the table near the captain's wheel, where the Italians were engaged in a game of backgammon. Later, I perched above the mats, all the way on the other end, near the front corner of the boat. The breeze was even more intense at that point. There the three Germans, the Kiwi and Norwegian were lying back enjoying a perfectly sunny day. It was dangerous to shoot hoops while the boat was moving, because the ball could be left behind, so the kids were often downstairs watching television in the inside lounge or listening to music. When I had had enough sun, I would pop my head downstairs and engage them in their Italian language, which usually made no sense to me, but every once in a while I could catch a few words that sounded similar to Spanish words and link the meanings in an attempt to understand the context of what they were saying. Plus, I never tired of the long drawn accent. It sounded as if they sang their words.

The boat pulled up near a dock, where we would rest the first night, and where other yachts were parked as well. I had heard that tonight all the passengers from all the neighboring boats were to party at the bar not far from the dock. I really had no intentions of going. The entire day, when we were not moving, I had swum and soaked up sun. I was exhausted. All I wanted to do was eat dinner, hang out on deck for a little while my food digested, and conk out. Before dinner, I remember joking with the crewmembers about the funny white liquid they were drinking. Apparently it was a special Turkish concoction of liquor and milk. They talked me into taking a shot and the taste of it was disgusting. I hadn't yet eaten dinner, and I could feel the shot slither down my throat and slowly into my empty stomach. It was the most unpleasant feeling. And I had sworn off Turkish liquor afterwards. The dinner was very healthy and abundant; I had left feeling completely full, and was pleased with the service of the ship, thus far. For the money we spent, this cruise was an absolute steal in my mind. After dinner, the German pulled out a Scrabble board and invited everyone to the table to play. We had mustered a good game, and even had teams representing different countries. There was a German team, a Kiwi team, and an American team. Of course, we won in the end. Although Russian was Seb's native tongue, he had only to assist my flourishing lexicon.

Towards the end of the game, I noticed my stomach bubbling and moving around. It wasn't a good sign, but it also wasn't any reason for alarm. All the elements of my life had dramatically changed today; from the food, to the exercise, to the motion of the ocean, I had basically altered lifestyles in the matter of one day. So it was normal that my stomach would be a little off kilter. Nothing, though, prepared me for how I would feel over the next few hours. I decided my stomach was telling me to go use the restroom, as crude as it sounds. So I walked down to my closet cabin to handle my business. At this point, the party at the little port we docked at was beginning to blast its music, signaling everyone to disembark and come drink and spend more money. When I reached the inside of my cabin, it was as if I had walked into the very speaker box amplifying music from the club, the acoustics of all that cabin wood somehow trapped in the pounding bass, and I could even hear the trebled voices of the singers. They were playing all the 80's hits, like Madonna and Duran Duran. In the meantime my stomach was not getting any better, and on top of it I couldn't use the restroom. It was as if the food was stuck somewhere in between my stomach and throat. So, I decided to just lie down on the bed and wait it out. Eventually chills reverberated through my body; at the same time I started to sweat. And not a little sweat—beads of water were rolling from the top of my forehead slowly down my cheeks and ears. But at this point, I had become too weak to even wipe off the sweat. It was all over my body, and I can remember the t-shirt and shorts I wore were soaking wet, my legs and the sheets below my legs were wet. I wondered what was happening to me. I had never felt such sickness fall over me. I didn't have the energy to do anything. And the whole time, I could hear the people on the top of my boat and from the club, yelling and laughing; they were probably drinking and dancing around. I wondered if anyone noticed my disappearance, and would someone find me here and help me, explain to me this illness that had swept my entire body.

Finally, I mustered up enough energy to roll over. I thought that maybe I could throw-up, get the sickness out of me that way, but nothing came out. Whatever it was, it continued to hover in that unreachable spot, away from any contractible muscles. Meanwhile, the music continued to pound and I continued to be forgotten. The smell from the cabin I found out by being there long enough, reeked of something old and wet, which just made me feel even more nauseous. The only thing comparable to what I was feeling at this moment, was a terrible drunkenness, where you lose control of your head, and it starts spinning out of control. But I hadn't drunk anything. Well, only that milky liquor, but it was only a shot. That's it, I thought. It had to have been the shot. What was really in that shit? The thought just angered me, but I was too weak to be angry. The most important thing was that whatever was happening to me would pass. I even wondered if it could have been a form of seasickness. But even that didn't make logical sense. I was perfectly fine the entire time the boat moved. And it was long after the boat stopped that I had the slightest symptom. The pain in my head, the dizziness, the stomach and chest ache, the overwhelming weakness, all of it lasted for most of the night, about three or four hours. And not once did anyone come down to check up on me. I was that tree in the forest that falls, when nobody's around. I could have passed away stuck in the basement of an old wooden boat, and nobody would be around to witness it. It was a hopeless, helpless feeling.

I don't remember at what point my body decided it had the energy and will to rise from that stinky bed. I honestly don't remember getting up or even taking the steps to reach the sink. All I can remember is that when I coughed up all of the day's goods, it was as if performing an exorcism on myself; demons and goblins were being forced out who never wanted to leave my exhausted body. By the time I finished, the cabin sink was full all the way to the top. The vision and smell of that filthy sink still haunts me to this day. And, I didn't finish there. I let the goods out the other end as well. My body was literally an empty hull of a skeleton. It wasn't possible for me to have the slightest foreign substance floating around in my body. All of it was evacuated out in two monstrous pushes. As grotesque as all of this sounds, it was a hell of an experience, one that moved my existence. I had never felt that overcome by mortality ever in my life. The remarkable thing was as soon as I had left the bathroom, of course, after brushing my teeth, the sweat abated, my head reverted back to normal—somewhat numb, but normal—and, my stomach while still a bit weak, recovered. I wasn't experiencing any of the choking pains I had felt less than two minutes ago. It was the oddest and most rapid recovery in my life. Still, I was exhausted from the whole experience, and when I walked the narrow stairs out to the deck, I had forgotten about the beautiful surprise still left. The next morning would be the shock of Seb's life. But when I walked onto the deck of the boat, the night was amazing. I felt I had risen from the depths of hell into heaven. The sky was clear, and the stars were more vivid than I had seen in Israel. Everyone by this time had found a space on one of the mats and seemed to have fallen asleep under the stars. The temperature of the night had cooled significantly from the Mediterranean day, and as I lay down on the last free mat, a slight humidity, and an even slighter breeze seemed to cover my body gently with the comfort and lightness of a thin cotton sheet. My body was exhausted, and there would be no energy for any tossing and turning this night. I was a dead log with a face. I could still hear what seemed like a boat of Brits off in the distance chuckling and talking, but it couldn't distract me from the calmness and peacefulness of such a still night. I searched the constellations before closing my eyes.

    I awoke to the ship jerking awkwardly, in a cross between a back and forth, side to side movement. Each powerful wave that we conquered seemed to push us back a little before we could advance further. My body and brain weren't ready for the day, but I was being forcibly shaken to wake up by the ocean's ferocity. Eventually I had no choice but to accept the facts and find peace in the morning dawn. Already, the sun was coming up over the horizon. There is nothing like watching a round blooming of reddish-orange light slowing gaining its spherical form from underneath the sea's surface. The captain and his crew were wide awake. A glint of power and introspection seemed to gleam from Mr. Hook, a sort of charisma and fulfillment as he turned the large steering wheel with one hand. It had to be something else to wake up almost everyday of the year with the most global of forces, the Sun and the Sea. I reveled in the Captain's movements. One thrusting swing to the right and the wheel glided effortlessly, listening to his commands; a sudden stop with his left arm, a fast push in the other direction, and he was in charge, steering the boat steadily. He was the ruler of his own empire out there in the sea. He owned the boat and paid the crew. All laws passed aboard this ship were of his creation, subject to his internal vetoing procedures. I admired the fate he constructed for himself. He wasn't sitting around the house feeling pity for himself, or out on the streets making others feel sorry for a few coins here and there. He was out here living it. Taking his life into his one hand. No one had to feel anything for him, they could either love him or hate him. He would continue to make the best out of life with whatever resources he had available. A person like that had to be respected and admired. Sure he was an eccentric character, both a bit loony at times and outlandish. I had spoken with him the day before after I came to terms with my absurd behavior and finally conquered my uneasiness. He explained to me after his brief denunciation of the American government and his new nickname for us Americans on board—he now called us the Yankees, of course with a friendly smile—that if Turkey were to succumb to the European Union, he was going to sell his boat, take the money to Indonesia, build a house and live there for the rest of his life. He didn't think Turkey should have anything to do with, as he put it, Europe's or otherwise Western Society's corrupting political and economical system. He said he wasn't going to sit and watch while Turkey sold the rest of its soul to the West. He was very adamant about this belief. And although I didn't know him that well, I could picture him cashing out at the bank, packing up a few possessions and fleeing to the Southeast of Asia. With him it seemed a perfectly outlandish and normal action.

    I decided that I wasn't going to fall back to sleep anymore. I had adjusted to the violent rocking and now had the bright idea of climbing onto this hammock the Captain had suspended from ropes at the bottom of the mast. This hammock was above the back section of mats where people lay who miraculously hadn't snapped out of their sleep yet. I wasn't able to lie in the hammock earlier, as it had been prime real estate when the yacht was casually cruising along the coast. I liked our boat. There were fun trappings all over, enough to never get bored. I found the balance to lie in the hammock after about two attempts. The constant rocking of the boat made opening it hard to do, without stepping on people sleeping below. But I was finally successful. I was surprised the Captain never objected; I was sure he and his crew were watching me try and tame the riotous hammock the entire time. The hammock rocked back and forth with my body in it, almost like the pirate ship ride you can find at any state fair or theme park. It was not at all relaxing, but still the movement of the hammock, often against the swaying of the boat's direction was thrilling and entertaining.

The boat seemed to pick up steam, while the sea's force rocked the boat even more violently. I found my entire body being thrown back and forth. What I didn't realize was that the ropes used to support the hammock and myself had been rubbing abrasively against the metal poles holding up the sails the whole time. I could hear the screeching and clanking sounds with the rhythm of my rock, but they didn't alarm me at all. Furthermore, I was almost positive the Captain and his crew had to be watching the entire folly, from beginning to end. I was sure they would have warned me if maybe the hammock wouldn't be able to support both my weight and a fast fidgety moving boat. Finally, the ropes couldn't take the gnawing and wearing down by the metal beam anymore, and they completely snapped, sending me flying through the air and finally landing on the talkative German lady. She immediately woke up with something to talk about, and it seemed everyone else was now awake and staring at the half-hanging hammock and my body flagrantly atop a grumpy German. I looked backwards and the Captain was laughing his head off, and his crew were also amused by the morning disaster. I looked around to everyone now wide-awake and said, "Good morning." It was the only comment I could think to say.

I observed an overwhelming happiness characterize everyone's actions aboard the boat during the day, the crewmembers and the captain included. Smiles, laughter, and full of life gestures animated even the German couple aboard the boat. Something very healthy and soothing comes from the sea, its breeze, and its overlooking sun. Happiness seems to pervade human behavior in surroundings like these. I didn't know if there was scientific evidence to prove it, but I was sure these waters were holistic medicine. When you're out cruising the open sea, the minutest occurrences seem to fascinate the mind and cause wonderment. Like the large sea turtle we saw skim the surface of the clear blue, before scurrying off into its depths. Or even when the captain parked the boat in the open water to serve lunch, and fish for dinner's main entrée. Watching him and his crew fish, I found, was a delight. Their bait was simply bread from the pantry. They tied it to a fishing line, not even using a pole. And, with a few light tugs to simulate a fishes' movements, they would bring up sizeable fish, big enough to eat. He and his crew wasted no longer than thirty minutes stuffing bait, dropping it, and tugging it back to the surface, before they had caught enough to satisfy our hunger. Other varieties of fish were eventually attracted by the smaller, more vulnerable fish. Large monstrous fish too large for the thin nylon wire and scrawny bait hung around, either checking out all the commotion or spying on the smaller bite-size fish. I even saw eels swimming around in the madness. Later, after lunch, we visited landmarks along the coast, like secret caves and coves and a rope swing hanging from a tree, perched on a small bank. The Italian kids had to finally be convinced to abandon the excitement of the swings.

Another part of the coast was a testament to ancient civilizations. Kekova, an old Lycian City, dating back to the 5th century B.C. could be seen buried under the clear water; archaic steps leading nowhere and rustic columns made from stone were still standing visible, just under the tide. Also, opulent tombs could be seen implanted into small mountain caves, where they were said to be elevated to a height above and beyond the reach of the unscrupulous pirates. Inevitably these tombs had been raided, though luckily not completely destroyed. Fill in the rest of that day with loads of jumping from the deck or plank, back floats and front strokes, a few basketball shootouts, and the Captain and his crew restraining Seb, so that the Captain could fit his nub arm in Seb's ear to make it look like his hand was touching Seb's brain. Day two had raced by us, and it was already night. Another Olympic Scrabble match ensued, and afterwards everyone plopped their limp bodies down on the mats. I could never get tired of watching the stars before falling to sleep. It was almost like having my own personal planetarium on my bedroom ceiling. It was difficult not to feel the romantic nature of such a private cruise, as the one I was on. Maybe, I even wished that Maggie was still with me; the ambience was the perfect backdrop to love. Love . . . that powerful word. It continued to haunt me. I had come to grips with the fact that I was still in love with Maggie, and it was becoming evident that I might never shake it. Not that I wanted to shake it, but it had a way of haunting me, where I continued to feel as though part of me was lost, something missing. Maybe I would find that other part of me with someone else. I really hoped so. Or else, I would look hopelessly for the rest of my life for that missing puzzle piece, never to find it again. But I knew it would be wrong to continue in life putting such tough requirements on every woman I met. That was unfair, and I was even sure that I had committed such an offense in some slight way towards the couple of girls I had met thus far. It wasn't their fault. They were just being themselves. How were they to know that I was comparing them so rigidly to a past love, and really dismissing any long-term visions from the start. I thought to myself, eyes still open, searching the lights, that I just needed more time. Eventually I would stop comparing, stop accusing unsuspecting lovers for being everything they were not. That's it. I would just need more time.

    Today was going to be one to remember. Seb and I had done our Lonely Planet homework. Aside from the Dan Brown book that was being read in three different languages aboard the boat, our guidebook was the only other option. Apparently, the very beach of Oludeniz we would be approaching today was famous all over the world for its perfect paragliding conditions; second in the world to be exact, right behind somewhere in Brazil. I had always wanted to experience skydiving, and this was a close second. A small fishing boat arrived at our yacht to pick up Seb and me; none of the other passengers had it in them to jump. Daring thrills were not their objectives, they only wanted to lounge around, eat well, and look at the Sea. Seb and I hardly ever pass up a challenge, and our general philosophy is always try at least once, whatever a particular region is famous for. If you're in Naples, Italy, you eat pizza. When in Valencia, Spain, it's paella, so on and so on. The amazing sight from sea level was the colorful display of kites littering the clear blue sky. It seemed as if paper confetti were being dropped from the mountains over Oludeniz. That would be us in less than hour: soaring eagles hovering in the mid-day sky. Oludeniz has all the elements for a thrilling paraglide: tall mountains, warm temperatures, and an abundance of stable wind gusts. These are crucial to guarantee a safe return to earth. If the wind gusts aren't constant enough, you could jump off the mountain into nothingness; and if the kite doesn't catch the proper wind direction, it will flop and people die. Also, hot temperatures help enhance the flight, because every hot air current crossed in the sky can help to push the kite upwards again. As long as these heat gusts are manipulated correctly, it's possible to paraglide all day, or as many hours as the person can endure. And, naturally, high mountain peaks provide more air distance than low mountain peaks. The mountain of choice for paraglide jumps peaks at around seven thousand feet in altitude. Skydiving out of an airplane is even possible at this height.

We made it to the paraglide company office in the middle of town, paid our seventy dollars each, and now awaited a vehicle to carry us up the mountain. A jeep truck with two benches running the length of the cabin appeared, and in it three guides. These were the people we would trust our lives to in the middle of the air. Though I had silly, irrelevant preferences. I noticed that there were two guys and one very attractive lady awaiting us in the truck, and it wasn't because she was attractive necessarily that my instincts were to risk my life with the lady. Tandem paragliding works where the professional guide sits on top of the other person from behind, basically body to body. If it so happened that my jump wasn't successful, which means death, then I wanted to go out with a female strapped to my body, not the receiving end of a male. It was a ridiculous, and probably ignorant, form of reasoning, but I was determined to go with my instincts on this one. So, immediately, before Seb had any idea what was going on, I sat as close as possible to the lady glider on the truck bench. I was going to somehow manipulate a pairing with her.

The mood was a bit somber aboard the jeep. Only one of the guides appeared friendly or the least bit talkative, the others sort of ignored any confrontation of the social kind. And that included a forty-minute ride up a steep, dusty mountain. Their sour moods just helped to increase my anxiety levels and fear. It would have been nice to have gotten to know the guides a little better, do a quick psychoanalysis and affirm their sanity. I was going to be jumping into mid-air with one of these guys, most likely the girl, and I wanted to know that they or she hadn't gone through a recent heart-breaking divorce, that one of their family members or friends hadn't just died or that she didn't abuse depressive drugs. But, forty minutes wasn't a whole lot of time, and they continued to sulk the entire trip upwards. I was sure something was up between them. Maybe it was the girl and that guy sitting the other bench. They were the ones who couldn't look each other in the eye. They seemed disgusted with one another. Our drive was an adventure in itself. The old jeep truck seemed to struggle on certain steep hills, at some points kicking up dust and swerving a little. And other trucks climbing the same mountain road hadn't the slightest bit of pity or respect. If their trucks were more powerful and faster, they passed right by us, kicking up big clouds of dust and gravel, making it impossible for us to see ahead. I was sure they had taken this climb a thousand times already, but it still wasn't comforting. The vegetation near the top rung of the mountain changed to only pine trees, the only trees able to survive this altitude. I knew we had to be getting close.

Finally we reached the top of the mountain. The dirt road led us to the jump-off spot. We now had to put on bulky wind suits and a helmet, just in case the landing was rough. The girl told me we would be jumping together, and I almost wished the happy, saner looking guy had chosen me, instead. But, it was too late to turn back now. We waited in line after another pair of jumpers. Seb and his guide were one step ahead of me in another column. He was holding the digital camera. I decided I wanted to snap with my mechanical Nikon SLR. In no more than five minutes, Seb and his guide had unrolled their kite out of a large bag, placing it horizontally on the mountain. Strings were attached to the kite and had to be placed in a line ahead of the kite. Seb and his guide climbed into a special harness, attached themselves to the strings and without any hesitation began running down the peak of the mountain at full speed. Before they reached the bottom, the kite had thrust them up into the air.

Meanwhile, the girl I was to jump with and some random guy, who hadn't come in the truck with us, began to argue about who knows what in Turkish. I hadn't a clue what was going on, but it didn't sound pleasant. In my mind, it was the most inopportune time to be arguing and becoming emotional. I needed that her undivided attention was with me and the wind; nothing more. But she persisted to rebut his every comment. Something I would normally shy away from is getting in the middle of someone else's argument, especially strangers; but this time I told the guy to fuck off. This wasn't the time to be arguing. My nerves were being tested to the limit. I had to fight the initial fear of heights; and the fact that this wasn't mountain climbing or rappelling, and I didn't have a rope attaching me to solid ground, made me even more nervous than usual. And on top of all that, I had to calm down my guide. He then told me that I needed to report my guide to her boss, for flying too close to the mountain peak after jumping. Apparently, this was an argument stemming from one of her last jumps. I immediately told her not to worry about him and to just concentrate on our jump. I wasn't going to report her to anyone. How could I even think of betraying the person who holds my life dangling in her hands? That was the most ridiculous thing I had ever heard. Part of me wanted to punch that stupid-idiot for inciting these emotions in her. The other part of me wondered, if she had made mistakes before, could she make even graver mistakes with me? But I tried not to think so negatively.

It was now our turn to jump. The windsocks were blowing in the direction of the sea. After we were both in the harness, she told me in the corner of my ear, "Whatever you do, don't stop running! If you stop running, I won't be able to pick you and I both up, and we could go tumbling down the side of the mountain." It was a very sobering thought and warning. I felt like my life was on the line, and I just needed to run a straight line, until the kite pulled us both up into the air. My only worry was that I didn't trip and fall. The jump off was a dusty mound with broken bits of gravel strewn all over. The thought occurred to me, what if I slip on one of those stones? I had to be prepared for any possible contingency. The time came when we were called to run, and all I remember is the guide yelling loudly, "Run. Run. Run," and, me thinking to myself, "pick up my feet, pick up my feet." And then the chaos of the shouting stopped, and the noisy ground and rocks abated, and with one powerful tug of a solid wind gust, all sound stopped as if hitting a vacuum. A couple seconds later the guide pushed a seat built into the harness under my butt and told me to lean back. I could feel air covering the contours of my body, but not the slightest bit of noise. It was just utter peace in all acoustical directions. The view was overwhelming from this height. For a few minutes I had forgotten to take out my camera to take photos. It was amazing the depth of topography that could be seen from this distance. Our kite hadn't really descended much yet. She had glided further outwards, but hadn't come down even a meter yet. I was looking down onto mountains the way people peer into geography books or over plastic miniature models of mountains.

The mountains didn't seem like the same ones I had seen from the boat, those monstrous bodies ascending sharply. The mountains from this perspective appeared as though someone had flattened them. The anarchy of jutting topography seen from sea level now could be viewed as an orderly structure of ragged stone. A brilliant pattern could be seen, where glaciers had shaped these mountains long ago. Ridges move from center to mountain border in rows. The sea was a different experience as well; its shallow parts were color coded in light turquoise, while its deeper parts were a prominent sapphire. And the beautiful white sand meandered between the mountainside and coast like rapid, cutting rivers of pale milk. At this height and with this shared freedom, a minority in a bird's world, I couldn't have a worry in the world. No earthly issue had any priority out here. I only hoped that the flight would take forever; nothing inside of me wanted this feeling with the wind to fade away. I felt so small in reference to the infinite landscape, yet I felt so powerful for having such oversight. I nervously pulled out my camera from its case. The entire time it had been in my wind suit. I snapped in all directions, trying to create panoramas of the mountain coastal terrain. I hoped I would be able to piece those photos side by side to help me recreate these images and feelings later, when I would have no hope of traveling and soaring the planet.

We stayed suspended in the air for at least thirty minutes, if not more. We could have stayed up there even longer. I was sure my guide needed those thirty minutes more than me to help her forget about the pettiness of human behavior. She even seemed to smile after we finally landed, a pleasantness I hadn't seen from the time we met in the old jeep.

Everyone has their mediums of therapy and relaxation, those events that help the soul to breathe. For some people, it's going to the beach, listening to the waves, and soaking through the serenity of all the blue vastness. For others it's paragliding. For me, I thought, writing was my escape from the world, a way to relax and ease the daily noise. If only I could make writing a career. Then I would have found my calling. Only writing is a pipe dream. How many people actually make it writing books? Anyway, it's one thing to write email diaries to friends and family, or the occasional poem or song, and a whole other cookie to even attempt a full novel. But that was where the money was. I was almost sure of it. Look at Dan Brown or Ernest Hemingway or even Paulo Coehlo. Have you read *The Davinci Code*? Have you read *The Davinci Code*? Have you read *The Davinci Code*? I must have heard that question a million times. I had seen three different books from Dan Brown, translated in three distinctly different languages aboard the cruise yacht. Three books out of sixteen passengers. That's a ratio of about 1/5 or twenty percent of the passengers. Now, considering our boat had representatives from four continents, North America, Europe, Asia, and Australia/New Zealand, Dan Brown had managed to infiltrate a large percentage of the human community on planet earth. It seemed inconceivable the breadth of his success. A literary Bill Gates, if you will. If only I could be so fortunate as to push out a two to three hundred page masterpiece. That would definitely be the day.

Those wishful thoughts faded away fast. We had now made it back on the wooden yacht and were off again to find a quiet coordinate to rest the boat for our last night. Tonight would be my last night sleeping under the carpet of stars. This trip had been for the most part very easy on the spirit. A very healthy getaway: we ate a lot of veggies and fish and it was clear that swimming was the best exercise for the body. I had lost all the right weight and could even see my abdominals peeking through a little bit. I felt good. The next day we would be back to backpacking and exploring on our own. No more grand chauffeur of the sea to haul our lazy butts around. It was back to foot and bus. And I didn't mind the change of pace; I had rested well over the last three days. It was time to move on.

The next couple of days flew by in a flurry of old rocks and stones, the only remnants durable enough to survive thousands of years. According to the guidebook, some of the most intact spectacles from the Roman Empire and before were scattered in the ancient city of Ephesus. So, we headed northwards inland by bus from Fethiye, the last stop on our cruise. This old city was probably worth the cramped bus ride. The most important feature according to books is the Great Amphitheater, reconstructed by the Romans to seat 25,000 attendants almost two thousand years ago. I marveled more at a library façade still standing after almost two millennia. The penetration of clear blue sky through openings between its chipped and weathered stone columns begged which camera, the digital or Nikon SLR. We opted for both. I wasn't exactly sure who created the list, "Seven Wonders of the World," but the credential instinctively obligates a person to visit if anywhere in the neighborhood. And so Seb and I walked up the road outside of the old city to where only one lonely column of the Temple of Artemis still stood. I actually thought we were in the wrong place at first. How could one standing column and a few scattered carvings of white stone be considered a Wonder of the World? The surrounding meadows and hills were pleasant enough to see, but the temple was definitely not wonderful. I guess I was supposed to imagine how great it had been during the time of Alexander the Great. But too many missing dots were yet to be connected. Meanwhile, Seb got ripped off buying a replica of a thousand year-old coin, soiled and beaten to look ancient. Seb still thinks it's real to this day. And I should know better than shining light into blind dreams.

Our next "Great Wonder" was located along the Aegean Coast in Bodrum. We took another bus and arrived there at nighttime, just in time to find a hole-in-the-wall hotel with money-starved owners. When the morning arrived, we set out for the Mausoleum, the tomb of a great ruler. Only our friendly pirates had looted and ransacked the place centuries ago, and probably the most fascinating remnants were sitting all the way in London, in the British Museum. If I was ever to continue along my path to viewing the Great Wonders of the World, I had probably begun at the wrong place. But, nevertheless, the mental images were stored for safekeeping, and I remained open to the possibility that one day they would have aged in my mind the way of fine wines and cheeses. We were now ready to take on Istanbul.

All emails and phone calls were placed for a proper welcoming into the old city. Apparently, Uzge had sent more than one romantic love letter to Seb, while he was away at sea. She wanted us to crash at her apartment, and she had a car to pick us up from the airport and chauffeur us around the city. Have to give credit to Seb. He hooked it up. If he hadn't risked his life jumping off that raft, we might have been living in and out of hostels, taking the metro and bus everywhere. When we flew into the airport, the weather wasn't rainy and hostile as before. Uzge was her usual half-sarcastic self when we met her at the airport, a very modern woman in many respects: worked in the information technology industry, had a well-paying job complete with benefits, a car and sundry stipends, and her company had a network of international customers allowing her to travel various places around the world. Not at all a person behind the times or veiled away for much of her life. On the other hand, as I would soon find out, her roommate hadn't ever left the country; and according to Uzge, although she was a young energetic student at the University, her life was on a one-way road to domestication, the wife with kids scenario and a financially supportive husband; the typical Muslim family hierarchy. She hadn't known anything else in her life. Although she was in a modern Muslim city, abundant with enough contrast and contradictions to pose options for a more progressive mode of life, she wasn't particularly interested in the lifestyle of her avant-garde peers. The way things were and how they had always been suited her just fine. Putting us up would present an interesting conundrum for a young woman like herself, drilled in tradition and Islamic culture norms. Her idea of being rebellious or adventurous was to listen every once in a while to MTV videos and even attempt singing along to the blasphemous lyrics, when no one was around.

So, when a love-struck Uzge presented her with the proposal of two young males living in the house for a couple of weeks, two American males, she had to be thoroughly convinced. Of course, Uzge was in love, and she wasn't the only person living there, and of course, we were respectful young gentlemen with an appetite for culture and sophisticated worldly things, the kind that wore wire-rim spectacles, tucked our polo oxford shirts in tightly, never repeated profanities, and would be virgins until after the proper marriage ceremony. The truth was Uzge's roommate was scared. She didn't have a problem with males of our caliber, as described by Uzge, crashing the couch for a little while. That would give her an opportunity to improve her English she had studied for so many years. Furthermore, she had heard so much about us through Uzge, and even sensed a bit of enlightenment in Uzge's. And Uzge had been smart to arouse her girlish curiosities. She had presented us as handsome young men, exotic and unattainable on this side of the world. And what was the harm in getting to know a few pleasant faces walking around her apartment and to interact with people she had only really seen a glimpse of on TV? This would be an educational visit, a sort of foreign exchange if you will. None of that is what scared her. She was afraid of what everyone else would think. Uzge explained that their pocket of the city was known as being home to extremist Muslim groups. She was afraid of what her neighbors would think, and how they would treat them if it were known that two young unmarried Muslim women were housing two unrelated American males. Then there was the landlord. If he caught wind of our stay, all four of us would be thrown out on the streets, in rapid time. The third dilemma, a more personal, and far more real, problem was what would her boyfriend think? At this time, he was halfway around the world on a business trip to Hong Kong helping his company find manufacturers for cellular casing and other low-tech parts for their new line of mobile technology. He would be back at the end of this week, and according to customs and traditions, he wouldn't be happy at all with us staying over, especially considering he himself hadn't even slept over once, since the start of a two-year relationship. He was saving those glorious days until after the wedding. But, in the end, Uzge's roommate, being the softhearted individual, always putting her friends first, and noting the benefits of our stay, how they outweighed the negatives, agreed to let us visit for a while. She had even determined that her boyfriend didn't really have to know about us staying over, until he returned. Anyway, his company had made a habit of keeping him on business trips longer than projected, and maybe, he would never really have to know we ever stayed. So, after much ado, Uzge, Seb, and I were driving through the old megalopolis called Istanbul en route to our new home, for as long as we weren't thrown out.

It was becoming dark on our arrival to the neighborhood. Already, it appeared stores were shutting down. Some had locked down their garage gates, though small corner restaurants and convenience shops still had their lights beaming. The neighborhood had an eerie feel to it. The few people walking the streets seemed to be looking for shelter or trouble. We found a parallel parking spot, gathered our stuff and followed Uzge up the steps into her apartment building. Uzge and her roommate lived a college lifestyle, clothes hanging up over living room furniture, just a few items sprawled out, a small television set, a few magazines, just enough to prove residence. I was happy to see that the couch was long and its cushions sturdy. I loathed the sofas that sort of hug and pull you in as you surrender to them. This would be my bed for the next few days, and if the last couple of months had taught me anything, I knew the importance of a good night's sleep and a healthy back. I was still paying for the nights spent in the tree house. "Let me go find Logan and introduce you," Uzge said, excited, and left to knock on her bedroom door. It was a curious thing that she hadn't come out to meet us already. But Uzge told us that she was a shy girl, and a very talkative person once she finally warmed to you.

"Seb, Chris . . . this is Logan," Uzge said.

"Hey, Hi!" we greeted. Logan struck me as a simple girl. She wore regular loose fitting jeans and a white t-shirt with Turkish words printed in red. Her hair was pulled up in a ponytail, so that it didn't fall down near her face; she was a very practical girl, not at all concerned with fashion or appearing sexy. She smiled pleasantly when she spoke, but not at all keeping eye contact. She seemed a bit timid and unsure of herself, as if she wondered the whole time how we would view her. We asked her a few questions, tried to crack a few jokes, and she laughed but never continued the conversation or answered our questions with more than a yes or no or "I'm from Istanbul" or "I'm twenty-two." What struck me the most was her natural beauty. She had those exotic Arabic eyes, mysterious and private, and her smile, although somewhat insecure, glittered with innocence. For a while she clasped her hands together, swaying them back and forth unconsciously, and as soon as she found an exit, she returned to her room. Soon after, Seb retired into Uzge's room, and I just perused the Istanbul section in the Lonely Planet. Then, I set up my iPod and speaker set and put on Otis Redding. Finally, I took a shower, brushed my teeth, and eventually forced myself to sleep.

The next day Uzge and her roommate wanted to show us around the city. We got dressed, ate a couple slices of bread with jelly and Nescafe and were all ready to go. Uzge told us to walk ahead of them and they would exit the building a couple minutes later. It was important that we weren't seen leaving together as if we had spent the night. I thought the whole idea was a bit extreme, but I respected their decision and didn't ask any questions. When we reached the car, which was parked a few blocks over, Uzge and Seb sat the front and Logan and I sat the back. I noticed she wore a light jacket, open a bit in the front with a loose pair of jeans. During the ride towards the old part of the city (everything seemed old in the city), she looked at me from time to time, sneaking quick peeks that if she looked enough times would eventually add to a longer more intense examination. I found talking to her was a lot of fun. For one, she laughed at my jokes. I think my sarcasm and bluntness about things in life was refreshing and bold to her. I could tell she wasn't used to discussing anything outside of school and religion by the reaction I received; she would blush and become slightly embarrassed. And part of me fed off of that innocence. I found myself saying anything and everything just to see that cute little blush and look of surprise one more time. It was very addictive.

We were on the European side of the Bosporus, and it didn't take too long until we reached the southern side of the Golden Horn, where the Old City stood. We found parking on a street curve and walked until we reached the entrance of the Grand Bazaar. This place was an overwhelming maze of fast talking vendors and special bread and candy stands. A person could easily get lost in the tons of extravagant silk fabrics, ornate Aladdin shoes and mystical headdresses. There were around four thousand shops to choose from, and many of them appeared to create the same illusion, almost like entering that crazy house at the fair with all those mirrors. The girls thought it funny when we dressed up like Arabic princes or pampered Sultans, and we convinced them to act as our mistresses or concubines by wrapping themselves in thin silky veils and moving hypnotically to our imaginary flutes as if mysterious belly dancers. Later after we left the Bazaar, we found a typical Turkish restaurant, where they served us kebabs on a stick and we drank Ayran, a salty yoghurt drink, perfect for hot weather, though an acquired taste.

That same day we took a ride up to the University, where probably the most beautiful views of the Bosporus Strait and the Asian Continent could be seen from hilltop. The winding of the strait and the lush vegetation on either side combined with views of towering minarets sprouting out of the ground and into the horizon like enormous cypress trees, and the descent of houses like amphitheatre seats off in the distance, all made for an indelible stillness implanted deep in my psyche. All I wanted for those forty odd minutes up on the lookout was to soak in the ideal of human civilization. Istanbul hadn't prospered for over three thousand years along this juncture of water for nothing. The strategic location of a city connecting two continents and supported by an artery of life-giving water was enough to attract not one or two great colonizing empires but three, the Byzantines, the Romans, and the Ottomans. Looking down into the valley of this great natural phenomenon while it glistened with light inflections created by passing ships and boats was a powerful experience. The University was vacant of student life when we entered its plazas and courtyards. However, cats were literally everywhere, at every turn, at every flight of stone steps, behind bushes and plastered to windowsills. Some of them were sociable felines, following in their surreptitious manner (lurking, stopping, and angling elsewhere) for some time until we had passed through their patch of invisible territory. It was a surreal site to see so many cats, all different colors and sizes, in one place. Some of the cats I noticed had pure white fur with eyes two different colors, one blue, one yellow. In some odd way, cats seemed to fit well in a campus environment. Maybe it was a reflection of my mother and her love for felines, and the connection between this place and her teaching at a university that legitimized this island of college cats. I found myself taking lots of photos. Cats are very posy creatures, when they aren't pretending to ignore.

Next we decided to traverse the bridge connecting Asia with Europe. It was a limited objective, and a fair distance to accomplish, but in the end just being able to say we crossed over continents with one span of a bridge was worth the absurdity. We turned right back around when we reached the other side.

Over the next few days, I found myself falling more and more in fascination with Logan. She was a good girl, but I also began to see this different side to her, this yearning to break free, shed her cultural confines, and enjoy being in her twenties. She was this flower waiting to open up to the world and bloom. All she needed was that one thing to push her out of her shell, to open the tide gates. Because the need to explore ourselves and our sensuality is in all of us. I was afraid she would never have that chance at the rate of her domestication. She had been suppressing her natural urges for so long, and was becoming used to her fate. But all that was changing now, she was getting a taste of the outside world and freedom. Her behavior had changed dramatically from the first couple of days of our stay, when she would lock herself in her room all the time, scared and deprived of life. She still ambled around the apartment shyly, only a spark in her eye seemed to exist now that wasn't there before. And she wasn't afraid to walk around in her nightgown with her hair down. One day when Seb and Uzge were locked in their room, I helped her while she prepared dinner. I sat my iPod in the kitchen, and we sang along together to an old Jacksons Five song. She had a beautiful voice, sheltered and honest. I was watching this Plain Jane caterpillar metamorphosing into this beautiful butterfly, everyday becoming more courageous and wonderful. The scales tipped a little when Uzge talked her into going with us to Club Laila. This was a club that had stuck in my memory banks ever since Atlanta when a friend of mine told me he and his girlfriend had been to Istanbul and that if I didn't do anything else I had to party one night at Club Laila. It was the most amazing club they had ever been in, and they had traveled the world over. So, I was psyched about going, which made Seb psyched. And, knowing Seb was psyched, Uzge was determined to go, finally finishing with Logan's confirmation. Only she had nothing to wear to an event like this. She had never gone out to a nightclub. Of course, she had partied before, but only at house parties with close friends and family. There she learned how to move her hips and belly, but under wraps and supervision. Never was she able to unwind with the night, dance her heart out, and indulge in anonymity. So, we had to go to the mall to find her an outfit for the night.

It was a Friday, and all day I could sense this overwhelming energy just springing from her spirits. She bounced around the apartment in a gleeful way. We all accompanied her to the mall that day. And of course, we were also interested in purchasing something of fashion from Turkey, something native and unique. I had made a habit ever since my trip in Thailand to complicate my wardrobe with bits and pieces from around the world. It was and still persists to be a vain attempt to hold on to those places. Anyway, Uzge spotted a stylish women's boutique, complete with dinner dresses, sexy skirts, and all types of accessories. We entered this boutique, and it almost seemed we didn't belong there, well at least Logan didn't belong. She was somewhat of a fashion dud. There was no rhythm to the way she dressed or carried herself, no flavor in her monotony. That's when Uzge handed her this one-piece dress, dark black with a few streaks of red. The dress was too contracted for me to really make any sort of assessment in that moment, but it very well could have been a thin blouse. Seb and I waited in the lobby of the dressing room, bored, sitting on the little bench. They cluttered around in there for at least a couple of minutes; I could hear a belt buckle jingling and hitting the floor, then a few hangers clanking back and forth, probably left by the last person who had changed in there. Then, I heard a few gasps of air, something like a light shrill, a lot of quick chatter and giggles, a little bit of silence, then the door opened. When Seb and I looked up, our jaws both dropped. I wasn't even sure that I was looking at the same person anymore. If it wasn't for the fact that the room only had one door, and that I knew only two people had entered before, Uzge and Logan, I might not have believed the person I was now looking at with such amazement. Logan was absolutely smoking hot! I don't even think she recognized the person in the large mirror facing the dressing rooms and directly behind the bench we were sitting on. She was nothing like that girl in loose fitting jeans and baggy shirts. She had transformed into a woman; a hot and sexy woman, one with curves, voluptuous curves and cleavage. That dress fit her like a glove. Her hair was left to run over her shoulders and down her back, and her eyes were more pronounced than ever. Most importantly, she stood erect with her head facing forward. Not the usual slumping of the shoulders and hiding of her eyes. She looked outwards with confidence and flare. She shined brightly like a jewel emerging from the dusty depths of the earth, gleaming with all its raw brilliance. And the way she had exited the dressing room was like a bolt of lightning striking, shocking both Seb and me, and paralyzing our expressions for a "spot of time." When my wits finally returned to me, I immediately took out my digital camera and started snapping photos. She posed for the camera with great grandeur and dazzling elegance as if pausing for a few seconds at the head of a catwalk to the glittering of flashes. And for the moment, she was that model. It was almost a shame that such beauty had been hidden under lazy garments for so long. She was a beautiful individual from the inside, and now I was discovering how beautiful she was on the outside. It was now time for us to take the city by storm. We were ready for the night.

I put on my best slacks, shirt, and shoes. Club Laila was known the world over and you had to dress to impress. They wouldn't let you in if you didn't blend with their elitist image. I wasn't sure what the fuss was about, but I was going to find out. The valet parked Uzge's car, and we gave a red carpet stride up to the entrance of the club. We paid fifteen dollars to get in, a sum I wouldn't pay back in Atlanta. But, every once in awhile a person has to invest to have a rich experience. Walking into the club was like walking back outside. The club hadn't a roof. At first the options of what section to enter were a bit confusing; we accidentally entered a restaurant section and were instantly directed outwards. I counted four distinct sections; a restaurant, a central bar with room to mingle or dance, an upper section above the bar and a restaurant outside of the main area to the right, and a VIP section facing the Bosporus Strait. We were planning to go all out tonight, so we tiptoed into VIP. This section was furnished with luxurious lounge sofas and coffee tables to each sofa. In order to be in VIP you had to pay for what complemented each sofa, a huge silver platter of fruits, champagne, and if you were even more ambitious, it could include a few Cuban cigars. We all decided from the beginning to split whatever the bill came out to be, and surprisingly it wasn't completely outrageous. Though I think the waiters don't expect a VIP member to stop with the platter, we were going to make the platter last as long as possible. Uzge and Logan were extra giggly tonight. Logan didn't drink, but she was making an exception because of the spontaneity and rarity of the situation. Looking around I considered the Laila to be one of the top clubs I had ever set foot in, in my life.

We were along the harbor of the Bosporus Strait, exposed to fresh, open air. At this close proximity, I could see the force of the water as it raced by. Except for the dim lights emitting from the club and reflecting off its rapid currents, it was dark and gloomy out there, a very powerful backdrop. And on the other side of this violent channel of water was the continent of Asia. In the simple affair of indulging a Friday night, we were also Westerners peering over into the Far East. But what skyrocketed the club to number one on my list of world-class clubs was how the high-rollers approached a night out on the town. We had had our car valet parked. Meanwhile, the real "ballas" were arriving in yachts, right outside of the very VIP section we were sitting in. It was unreal. The club was elevated a good ten or fifteen feet from the water. So, when private yachts pulled up, the only things that could be seen were the tops of the boats swaying back and forth and high-rollers wearing dinner jackets and tuxedos stepping onto the club dock. I had seen nothing like it.

    The club played a mix of popular Turkish music, house, and occasionally an R&B song from someone like R-Kelly or Craig Davis. All four of us were enjoying every minute of our night out. If we weren't considering whether the guys in black suits were escorts or not, or trying to land grapes in each other's mouths, we were up dancing near our sofas. We had actually been the first people up to dance, starting a wave of dancers. And when I pulled Logan in to dance close to an R&B song, something magical seemed to be happening. She didn't get scared or sit down, we danced together, bodies both moving to the rhythm, her chin resting on my chest, looking up every once in awhile to smile, and for those five minutes or so, it was if she had forgotten about the limitations of her life. Another smooth, melodic song came on and we danced again. I remember her warmth and gentleness; she was sensual and soft. When Turkish songs came on, Uzge and Logan tried to show us how to pop our shoulders front to back to the rhythm. And when Seb heard the slightest bit of Latin melody reverberating from any song, he would spin Uzge around in a series of arm loops and turns.

    At the end of the night, when we made it back to the apartment, everyone took their showers, brushed their teeth, and dressed for bed. Seb and Uzge said goodnight and retired to her room, Logan said goodnight and walked to her room, and I lay down on the couch. A minute later, Logan appeared from the darkness; she was standing in a long t-shirt at the doorway.

    "Chris," she called my name.

    I leaned my head forward to see her better. "Yes," I said.

    She was standing with her right hand wrapped around the side of the living room wall, her right side facing me. "Can I give you a kiss?" she whispered.

It was so low and thick with Turkish accent I didn't understand her the first time. I sat up on the couch to understand her better. "What?" I said.

She whispered louder. "Can I give you a goodnight kiss?" she said again.

It was so innocent the way she expressed herself. Her words were delicate and pure. I stood up slowly and walked over to the doorway until we were face-to-face, lips inches from each other. For a moment, we looked each other in the eyes without moving. We wanted to know that this moment was real, and that it didn't fly by in a hurry. Slowly she reached her head in, her soft lips pushing into mine, and we held a delicate kiss, only our lips slipping in between the openings of our mouths. And then she lightly withdrew her kiss while her eyes were closed, and slowly opening. She didn't say a word, just walked back in her room and quietly shut the door. I walked to the sofa, and after my heartbeat slowed to a relaxing pace, I fell asleep. Looking back I think it was her way of thanking me for everything, for taking her out on the town, discovering her sensuality, and respecting her as a lady. I wanted to think that I helped her have a night that she would never forget; a moment of freedom and spontaneity that she otherwise wouldn't have been able to experience, had I never showed up.

The next day her boyfriend was due back, and it didn't look like he was being extended for any longer in Asia. He was up in the air, soaring above the clouds, probably reading the Airline News or searching their sundry catalogue of gifts, on his way back, as we all were waking up, and having breakfast. It was again beginning to dawn on Logan that her boyfriend was going to flip if he knew we had been spending the night. So in the end, to avoid the head ache of an angry boyfriend both for us and for Logan, we decided it would be best to leave and find a hostel. The last thing we needed was to be running for our lives in the middle of Istanbul. For all we knew, her boyfriend could call up his family or even go completely haywire, leaving us to fend for our bags and of course ourselves. It was better if we left. Furthermore, the neighbors were becoming suspicious. We had heard knocking at the door, when Uzge and Logan had left out for the store once. Some strange guy stood on the other side of the peephole with intolerable eyes. Plus, the girls' paranoia and assiduous caution was beginning to corrupt my sense of safety. I began to formulate what-if scenarios, and the whole thing about being in a Muslim country and the Afghanistan War and the Iraq War and the Muslim extremists living around the corner—it was enough to make you crazy, if you thought about it for too long. We were in an apartment with two lovely ladies that wanted to us to be there, who seemed more than comfortable with us prowling around in our boxers, hanging up our clothes, and sharing meals with them in front of the small television set. While the entire time, the outside public was condemning our every action, waiting to pelt us with stones and paint us blood red as witches and devils. It was a lot like living in the eye of a hurricane.

Our goodbye was sort of emotional. We had only been roomies for a week, but the transformations and changes we had gone through in that week felt like much longer. Seb and I packed our things neatly in the car. Logan wasn't going with us this time, there was hardly enough room for the three of us. She stood at the cement corner with both hands at her chin, gazing patiently and melancholy. I walked to the curb, not really sure what to say or not to say. So, instead of talking, I planted a soft kiss on the mouth of Logan; nothing slobbery or overly passionate, just a simple statement. It was my answer to last night. And before I could turn around and walk away, a tear rolled down her cheek. It was a minute drop of eye fluid, but it had an effect on me. And if I hadn't turned around and gotten in that car, I would have been forced to do the same. I had felt an emotional connection with her, too, and I wasn't completely ready to leave yet. But we were leaving, Seb and I, and we were moving on like we had done so many other times along the trip. It was ultimately the downfall to traveling, making real life, flesh and blood connections only to leave in the midst of their blossoming or cultivation. It was something I never fully came to grips with, or desensitized myself from. I was human just like the rest of them. And I continued to carry those emotional ties with me, even years after their dissolution. These were the extra bags that travelers carried with them, invisible to the eye, but so heavy on the mind. That's why it was so important to pack light from the beginning.

We drove off, stopped at the traffic light, and right before turning the corner, I took a look back to see if Logan was still watching, waiting there until the last possible second, but she wasn't, she had returned to her apartment with all her things and her daily routine. Seb was busy looking up hostels on the guidebook. Our plan was to live in the Sultanahment area of Istanbul, right below the Golden Horn, and in the center of a big tourist trap. There we would find the great mosques of Istanbul and all the glorious landmarks that had lasted centuries. We weren't that excited about the whole hostel bit, sharing our space and risking our stuff with any random backpacking tourist off the streets, but it was invariably a part of traveling. Plus, who had the money to stay in luxurious hotels? We had retired at too young of an age to be living that sort of treatment. More countries were up ahead, yet to be discovered and lavished with our meager foreign dollars. We needed to be ready for contingencies that could arise.

We were lucky to find a hostel in the heart of the Old City, close to all the sites, though not burdened by a busy street. We gave our passports to the guy at the front desk to place in a locked safe, and we settled into our room. Our life had reverted back to backpacker tourist, and we had a list of objectives: take the cameras, take the map, and scour the city. We had been interrupted various times before by the "call to prayer" emanating from overlooking minarets. They were active at least five times a day, and the shrilling sound of the person singing or chanting was unmistakable. But nowhere in Turkey had it been more obvious, this prayer to Mohammed, than in this area of Istanbul. Prayers seemed to be chanted almost every hour. In reality, it wasn't this way, but the frequency of the prayers was constant. Also, in this part of the city, there were numerous mosques and minarets, and they weren't timed to start at the same time or to chant the same words. At times it almost seemed as if the people singing prayers were battling other minarets in the area. I suppose a person could even get used to the constant distractions, if they lived here long enough. I noticed that the "born and bred" Turks didn't skip a beat when the "call to prayer" was sung out:

Allah u Akbar, Allah u Akbar
(Allah is Great, Allah is Great)
Ash-hadu al-la Ilaha ill Allah - Ash-hadu al-la Ilaha ill Allah
(I bear witness that there is no divinty but Allah)
Ash-hadu anna Muhammadan Rasulullaah
(I bear witness that Muhammad is Allah's Messenger)

The shrilling oscillations and dramatic extensions of notes had no effect on a street conversation or a mobile phone argument. People carried on with their daily business. No time was lost. Seb and I, on the other hand, couldn't think clearly when the minarets burst into life. If we were looking at a map, we had to put it down momentarily or if we were in conversation, we paused for a couple minutes or changed our topic to Islamic prayer. I wasn't able to escape its reach. I had been around church bells before, that monotonic booming, consistent and precise, but these sad, eerie prayers, sung with so much devoutness and faith, were impossible to hide from. They stung you wherever you stood, made it clear where you were walking and who could be watching. It was a constant reminder.

Seb and I spent the rest of the day in and out of mosques. We visited first the Blue Mosque, built by Sultan Ahmet I during the 1600s. It was admittedly one of the most impressive showings of architecture I had ever encountered in my life. It was a succession of little tiled domes gradually climbing to a massive bulb of a dome in the center. At least six minarets, tall and stately, bordered neatly the great dome cluster. The mosque was surrounded by lush, thickly leafed trees, and adjacent to the mosque was a beautiful garden park with fountains. The mosque itself seemed to rise up from the surrounding landscape as if an exotic botanic centerpiece, a majestic Asiatic tree rising to the skyline. Before entering we had to leave our shoes in a box at the entrance. If we hadn't been wearing jeans, we would have had to cover up our legs. The inside of the mosque was like stepping into a magical palace. The dome was hollow and vast, still every inch of its interior was intricately decorated in a complex pattern of mosaic tiles. Tiny lights draped all the way from the tops of the ceiling, touching just far enough to be unreachable. Lengthy black wires connected them in such abundance that a virtual ceiling of lights had been created above our heads. The wires had the effect of filtering the light in the vast air beneath the domes, like elaborate circus nets. People were praying when we entered, bobbing their bodies back and forth and kneeling. It was a very powerful image.

We visited probably the most famous mosque, the Aya Sofia, next, then we visited an underground aqueduct system, called the Basilica Cistern. It was a maze of underground columns and archways dimly lit to reflect the shallow water below. A few Roman remnants of carved columns attracted pauses from the visitors at the back sections. The day went by relatively fast in the process of viewing these attractions. We had to save the Topkapi Palace and the Harem for the following day.

The next day flew by with a flurry of tourist stops. While touring the opulent Topkapi palace, home to a succession of powerful Sultans, and now museum to an impressive collection of jewels and all sorts of artifacts, I encountered deeply unsettling images of women, dressed in all black robes and black veils covering every part of their face except the eyes. In many cases, even the eyes were hidden behind glasses or thin veils. It was a depressing sight. It was as if these women were walking zombies, erased without a name or description, unknown and irrelevant to the rest of the world. Up until now, I hadn't fixated on this strict Islamic attire, but when I did, it moved and frightened me. So many questions ran through my head: Who were these women? What did they look like on the other side of that black fabric? How did they feel? What mood were they in? Did they notice my stares? And, if so, how did that make them feel? Were they sad or happy? Were they hiding something? Did they want to live differently? How did they view the other women walking around? Were these women heathens or enviable?

What visually struck me in that moment were the contrasts and contradictions revolving throughout Turkey. This was a country and culture internally faced with extremely differing views on how to go about daily life. You had the orthodox Muslims who were well-defined carbon copies of the Koran and its teachings. They followed every religious custom and cultural obligation placed on them, not veering in the slightest way. Then, you had the diversified Muslims who embraced Western culture and ideologies and expressed bluntly their contempt for conservative Islam. They wore the latest fashion, listened to MTV music videos, drank alcohol, and partied all night long. The women on this side of the country's cultural divide weren't afraid to look sexy, to work a challenging job, and even partake in politics, whether only in friendly debates or actually running for public office. In short, Turkey was a visible clash of cultures. The West versus classic Islam.

Of course, most people had a little bit of both cultures running through their veins. And Logan was a perfect example of this evolution. She was a young girl strongly influenced by her family's way of life and her most likely suitor, though constantly confronted with this new world of global media, internet and television. She was introduced to many more dynamics than her parents had ever been. She was the first girl to make it to University. That's where she had met Uzge. And fate, in turn, had introduced her to Seb and me, giving her even more information and insight into the broader world. She was in many ways at the frontline in Turkey's cultural civil war. And I was sure that her life would never be the same after meeting us; that's what new knowledge does to a person. It broadens your perspective, and in turn, changes your way of life. I wondered, watching the fully clothed and veiled Muslim women walking through the palace, if they were an endangered species around these parts. Would I one day return to Turkey, let's say in ten years, to the absence of these hidden souls or would conservative Islam have pushed on with the same oppressive intensity? As open-minded and non-judging as I would like to be, deep down in my heart I hoped these societal customs for women would pass. Those images of women hidden behind black robes in Topkapi Palace would continue to haunt me and beg a million questions.

After we visited the Palace and the Harem and shifted through a few gift shops, it occurred to me that I hadn't even thought to give Leila a call. Part of me was a little hesitant to go that route, considering how wild she had been in Olympos, but Seb and I were becoming bored with the tourist trap and were itching to find a little trouble. And, that's exactly what we found, when I called Leila. She was so excited when I called. She couldn't understand a thing I said, and passed the phone off to her best friend, someone who hadn't gone with her down to Olympos. I told them what hostel Seb and I were staying at, and they immediately invited us out for a night on the town. They would come by to pick us up at 11 o'clock. I didn't really know what to expect with Leila. She was a very unpredictable personality. As a matter of fact, she seemed to thrive on catching people off-guard, so much so that I decided to just sit back, hold on, and enjoy the ride.

We waited outside the hostel around 11 p.m. There were three small tables, only big enough to sit two people at a time. The hostel provided the extra service of selling beers and wine and snacks. Seb and I decided on Efes Pilsen Beer. Then, a slash between a van and car drove up with its lights blaring and stopped strangely, almost perpendicular to the normal flow of traffic. I couldn't see who was in the car because it was dark outside and the windows appeared tinted, but I figured it must have been Leila and her friend. I waited and the window rolled down smoothly, automatically. Immediately the concert happening inside the car was now open to the public, an unrecognizable face poked out smiling hysterically and then the driver leaned over and waved frantically. It was Leila. Seb and I chugged the rest of our beers down and walked over. I sort of sensed that the girls were high on something. I had seen those silly facial expressions before, and they were a result of either delusional eccentricity or substance use. In this case, both were plausible conclusions. Seb looked a little worried, but I wasn't. I was along for the ride, and if fate didn't steer me safely, than it probably meant I was doomed in whatever decision I made. We shut the doors and sped off. It all made sense to me. I had fallen into a sort of déjà vu back to my high school days. I remembered these settings quite well, the fast car, the loud music, the "fuck it" attitude that there is only one life to live, and tonight could be the last night, so you better live freely and have as much fun as you can, and not worry about tomorrow or any consequences. I had been in this environment too many times to remember. I probably had even been the catalyst for these "sort of night outs" because I was the one with a set of wheels back in those days.

Leila's friend caught Seb and me by surprise. She spoke very good English, and was very talkative. "Hellow. My name is Bahar. It means springtime in Arabic," she started off, like some language tape. There was a lot I still didn't know about Leila. Her life was mostly a mystery to me. Her friends back in Olympos didn't speak very good English, and they were too preoccupied with each other to give much background information about Leila. And the need for those details seemed to escalate into a desire over time. Questions, having been built up for so long, burst out of me. I didn't waste any time.

"What does she do to make money?" I asked.

"She owns a clothing manufacturing business," the friend explained. Her answer sort of shocked me. I had expected her to say a waitress, painter, or a student, anything else but a responsible business owner. Turkey, I had heard, was well known for its textile industry, so at least that made sense.

"How old is she?" I asked.

"She's twenty-nine," Bahar said. That wasn't shocking at all after the business owner answer, but she looked so much younger than twenty-nine.

"How do you know English and she doesn't?" I asked.

"I studied in England for a year, but I probably learned from watching movies and listening to music," she said.

Her English was commendable I thought, it even had that proper English tone to it. But something was kooky about this girl.

She was too high energy, too animated and excited when she spoke. I could smell a thin trace of marijuana in the air, but even that wasn't enough to cause her to turn into a cartoon character. Another thing I couldn't help but notice every time she turned her head and shoulders all the way around like an owl to speak with us was that the side of her lip had a deep scar, as if someone had caught her by the hook of a fishing pole and reeled her in. It was a cruel thought to think, but I can't always control my thoughts. Inevitably, Seb gave her the name Hook, which I was glad he didn't say too loud. It was an insensitive use of name calling, but we were reliving our high school days, and kids can be cruel. Can't they?

We were on our way to meet the rest of the crew at some bar. The bar was nothing special; it was the second floor of some city building. We ordered drinks, toasted to the night, and danced around awhile. Leila and Bahar were a crazy duo; they danced together most of the time, wobbling their bodies around in a bohemian manner. Their friends came a little later. They were the ones from the beach and were happy to see that we actually made it to Istanbul. We were meeting for the second time, which caused them to be more talkative than before; the "small world" circumstances had created a sort of extra bond. The girls were dancing even crazier by now, and one of the guys—maybe because he was a little embarrassed for their behavior—slipped that Bahar had traveled to Mexico for over a year, and when she finally returned to Istanbul she hadn't been the same. I didn't know what "she hadn't been the same" meant exactly, but when he said that she had smoked peyote somewhere far in the countryside away from Mexico City, and afterwards how she had lost control and gone crazy for about two weeks, roaming even further into rustic valleys and mountains and other small pueblos, finally returning to her senses and back to Mexico City, I sort of put it all together. After a few hours of drinking and watching the girls fall all over the place dancing, we decided to go back to Leila's house. Apparently, everyone lived in the same neighborhood, the same street even in Istanbul, and it was normal to go back and have small house parties, inviting the other neighbors over as well. So that's what we did.

Leila's condo was an impressive place. It sat on the top floor over looking a slope of other residential buildings, falling sporadically towards the Bosporus Strait. A beautiful full moon was out this night, and the living room also had a glowing full moon in the form of a white globe lantern placed right smack in its center. Everyone sat around the dining room table or lounged on the sofa, smoking joints or drinking whiskey, telling old stories or bragging about the different countries they had visited. There were actually two conversations flowing about the entire time, the one spoken in Turkish and the one understood by Seb and me in English. But never once had the situation been a burden or drag on the night, and there were other universal modes of communication floating the room, like the brief spurt of dancing, incited by Bahar, and the crowd response to Tracy Chapman later on when the night calmed down a bit. Around 4 o'clock in the morning everyone had ventured back to their flats, down the street or downstairs, and all who were left consisted of Leila, Seb, and me. I almost think she had planned it this way. Once again she was engineering her own sort of Broadway play and we were cast as her protagonists. Act Scene V was titled, Turkey's Hippie Free Love Revolution.

When I awoke, Seb was lying on the other side of the king size mattress, only Leila had vanished from between us. I nudged Seb, who was smiling in his sleep and having a good dream. "Where did she go?" I asked. He was pulling his head forward and propping himself on his elbows.

"I don't know. I never saw her leave," Seb said. Seb looked around the room, readjusting to what had only been darkness and a large bed last night. Now, new details abounded. Seb gasped, sort of startled.

"What?" I asked, spooked from his reaction.

"This photo, l-l-look it's flipped over." He was gripping a small picture frame, the kind with no hinges, built in one L-shaped piece. An attractive woman smiled out at us from the photo. She had long flowing hair; everything looked different except the face and bone structure. It was that of Leila. And that's not all. A second person was in the picture, a man with dark features and a burly neck, and a dark, thick mustache like that of Saddam Hussein. His face cuddled hers, almost as if turning for a kiss. They seemed to be a couple happy and in love. Then the thought occurred to me. What if they were still together? But then why wasn't he here?

"Maybe they're not still together," I told Seb, who was pissing his pants.

"Look at this guy. He doesn't look like he bullshits around." Seb pulled out the nightstand drawer and pushed a few of her things around. Another picture. This time only of the guy. It was a full body picture of him wearing big black boots with shiny metal straps, the kind Harley bikers wear. He wore black jeans and a tiny black t-shirt. Well, it wasn't tiny, but it looked like it on him. His whole outfit was dark black, coordinating with his dark bushy eyebrows and long charcoal black hair tied in a ponytail. He was a rather large and muscular man, and his mustache was that final sinister touch. He was this Gothic Arab Hells Angel. Not the kind of person you crossed paths with and lived to tell about it. Seb's eyes were wide-open and alert now. We walked out of the bedroom into the living room. There was another picture on the wall behind the sofa. And yet another in the kitchen on the refrigerator. How could I have missed all of this last night!

"Why didn't she tell us?" I shouted out.

"She couldn't, she can't speak English," Seb remarked.

"Well why didn't someone tell us, anyone!" I said. Seb walked into the closet. It was separate from the bedroom and living room, a whole other room.

"Chris! Come in here and look at this!" Seb said with urgency. I could tell he was really beginning to worry, at this point. When I walked into the closet Seb was pressing a humungous dress shirt from Zara to his chest. The shirt swallowed him like a nightgown. "This guy is a monster! Can you believe this?! Look at this!" he said. "And, these boots! These boots were . . . (we said the next part at this same time) in the photo!"

"Jesus!" I said. "Shaquil O'Neal could fit in these boots!"

"We gotta get out of here," Seb said. We both hurried to find our jeans and shirts and socks and shoes, all of which had been scattered around the apartment last night. Furthermore, with so much adrenaline running, I was getting tangled in my pants. Seb wasn't even fully dressed when he leaped towards the door, his shirt still hanging off one shoulder. "Oh shit! How do we get out? The door," he said, struggling to pull it open, "It won't budge. It's dead-bolted. She locked us in! We're stuck!" Seb was panicking.

Quickly I ran to the window, hoping to find a new exit strategy. The window was open and I leaped across the room, almost flying out of it, stopping myself just in time with my arms on the frame of the window. I stuck my head and shoulders out, and suddenly felt a case of dizziness. Chills went through my body. It was too high for me. "We're too high up to jump!" I said.

Still, Seb wasn't ready to give up. He looked out the window in all directions like a crazy person, someone with no other choices, a person trapped in burning building. Seb said, "What if we tie blankets and sheets together and . . . ."

Before he could finish, I said, "Are you crazy! That shit only works in the movies! We'll be two scrambled eggs on the pavement!" It might have worked, but I was too afraid of heights to ever go through with it.

"What are we supposed to do then?! Wait on our killer to open the door and trap us in here, until he slaughters us with his bare hands? And, what are we supposed to say when we're caught trespassing on his territory? That we made a mistake, took a wrong turn and landed in his wife's bed!" Seb was losing it.

"Relax. Who said he was a killer and how do we even know he is her husband? He could be an old boyfriend or something."

"An old boyfriend! Old boyfriends don't appear in photos all over someone else's apartment. And the clothes and boots. What explains that?!" As soon as Seb said that a key started turning in the lock. I could hear the threads of the key slither into place, and then the deadbolt began screeching slowly and loudly.

"Quick. Hide!" I whispered. Seb ran into the kitchen. I ran into the bathroom. It's funny how unorganized something as simple as finding the right hiding place can be when adrenaline takes over the mind. My heart was thundering. It was all Seb's fault putting these sinister scenarios in my head. But, What if it was him? What if he finds us both hiding in his apartment? What will he think? Maybe that we are robbers that broke in? Or, will he think that we slept with his wife? Either way, I thought, he's going to kill us! Neither scenario is friendly. I could now hear the door creak open, slowly, like in those Alfred Hitchcock movies. Then, I thought about O.J. Simpson and Nicole and Ron Goldman. And, what if? My friends back home, they would have been right. I can hear them now, " . . . how is he going to go all the way over to Turkey, on foreign territory, in an all Muslim country, while America is still in Afghanistan and still at war in Iraq and the whole Israel-Palestinian conflict. What did he expect? And, to top it all off he gets caught in another man's house. Now that is asking for it." Then I thought, what if they never find me. What if I went missing, never to be discovered again. The mystery of Chris, what's his name, it would be all over the news. Two Americans last seen in

Istanbul, partying the night away with two crazy Turkish girls. There was alcohol involved, and one of the girls had a hooked lip. I could see it now. Then, I heard someone speaking in the other room.

"Hello. Hello." It was a soft voice. It was a woman's voice. I took a deep breath. I pulled the curtains back and stepped over the side of the bathtub and peeked my head out of the bathroom, around the corner.

"Oh. Hi," I said, regaining myself, somewhat embarrassed at the peculiarity of the scene. It must have appeared a little strange, me popping out of the bathroom so cautiously and Seb from behind the kitchen counters.

"What are you guys doing?" she asked.

"We didn't know who it was," Seb said. Then, Seb pointed to the picture on the fridge. "We thought maybe you were him," he said.

"Hahaha! . . . " she thought his comment was funny, but we weren't laughing. She changed the subject. "Leila had to work early this morning. She threw her keys on my balcony this morning. And told me to let you out of the apartment, when you guys woke up," she said.

"Oh . . . heheheh." Seb and I looked at each other. It started to dawn on us how silly we had been, reacting.

Then I asked, "But, who is this guy? He's everywhere. The photos. His clothes and his boots." She didn't say anything. "Is Leila married to this guy?" I asked.

A couple of seconds went by, before she smiled and said, "Yes. But, he won't be back today."

And she left it at that. Seb and I gladly exited the apartment, swiftly headed down the stairs and escaped into the translucent sunshine of a midsummer's day. A little while later, when we had found the right direction to walk in, that would take us to the Bosporus and back to our hostel, Seb said, "And to think all this time, Leo had wanted to sleep with a married woman, and he had the whole time. He just didn't know it. Wait until he hears this. He's going to flip." Another few seconds went by, while we continued to walk along.

"Ahhh . . . this world never ceases to amaze me. This one's going down in the history book," I said. We found our way back to the Bosporus, the blood of the city.

BULGARIA

> *Let us live while we can, speak while we may,*
> *and at present pursue our journey.*
> Miguel de Cervantes,
> Don Quixote

"I'm not kidding! Our bus is called the Camel Cock!" Seb said.

"What are you talking about?" I said. I wasn't sure what type of joke he was pulling this time. But his face was clearly telling a joke. It was the words that didn't register anything of any relevance to our situation at hand. That is, a bus station, and two exhausted Americans, ready to shed the role as foreigner in Turkey, and regain that coat in other lands.

"Well, it's not spelled with a 'k' on the end, but it's Camel Coç!" Seb repeated, smirking. He was right. Our bus, the one with a direct route to Plovdiv, Bulgaria, was clearly spelled Camel Coç. But Seb was pulling my leg. He knew better than anyone that a "c" with a little squiggly line wagging its tail was pronounced differently (its correct pronunciation is Camel Coach). But how could Camel Coç buses make a mistake like that? I was sure someone, somewhere down the business channel, between the bankers, the investors, the bus painters, the owners, for heaven's sake, at least the rich little bastard who had probably been shipped off to the U.S. to attend university or in London, at least he would have told Daddy what his line of buses sounded like to the masses of English speaking society. Who in their right mind wants to ride a Camel Coç?!

    We paid our bus tickets with literally the last Turkish lira in all of our pockets. Our bus was scheduled an hour later, and after about thirty minutes, the jugs of bottled water we had been drinking to battle dehydration and the orange juice from the hostel that morning were knocking at our stomach doors. What we didn't prepare for was the toilet cover charge one had to pay before entering the bathroom. And as Seb and I found out, no expression of pain could convince the attendant otherwise. It was a tricky situation. We could be on a shaky bus for Bulgaria with minimal stops or no stops at all, and already before stepping foot on the bus, our bladders were asking us, "Are we there yet?" Our other option was to find a nice plot of outside land somewhere to handle our business, of course, one of the advantages bestowed on the male genome. But taking a piss anywhere in the vicinity of Istanbul's bus station was like trying to find a low-traffic area at Hartsfield Airport in Atlanta to do your business without being hauled off by Homeland Security. It was virtually impossible. The one lone option of distance away from the public as in contrast to privacy, called for climbing a steep slope behind the parking lot of buses. That means that buses full of passengers had only to look out their windows to follow your heroic trail upwards for the couple of sparse bushes somehow still hanging from the eroding soil. Up there, behind all the madness of buses leaving and coming was your burning bush of glory and justice. That's if you could make it. And time was running out for us. Seb and I had to make a decision. Risk the climb or suffer for god knows how many hours. Of course, we risked the climb, and I have to say it was the most disgusting display of courage and survival I had seen in my life. Apparently, we hadn't been the first ones to save a few lira, and I won't go into what I saw up there. I'll just say the soil should have been rich enough to plant more than a couple of bushes.

    We finally made it on our bus. And it turned out that ride from Turkey to Bulgaria happened to be the best bus ride of my life. I mean the Camel Coç was more comfortable than first class on Delta. For the first time in my life, I was being served drinks and snacks and the bus steward sustained a perpetual smile the entire ride as if he gained fulfillment in our happiness. It was a surreal bus ride, one I hadn't been expecting. Seb still laughs about waking up and seeing me with my feet up, head leaned back, munching on snacks and smiling uncontrollably. And how could I not be, it's not everyday a person rides the Camel Coç.

    If you needed to put Seb in a box, some categorical description to distinguish him from the roles of others, he's a talker. He has almost perfected the oratorical art of talking himself in and out of situations. His renowned specialty is women. He can talk a woman into the comfort of his bed, while talking her into relinquishing her heart, where at this point he talks to her heart until it beats to his rhythm, becoming so attached to Seb's bodily harmony, that when he finally detaches his pacemaker, and has traveled clear across one of the Seven Seas, this heart inevitably stops working. Later, to prove his mouth has a reviving miracle and can coach broken hearts into functioning again, he has been known to reengage dialogue, jump-starting the heart in question, and even succeeding to convince the heart and its owner to forgive him and love him even more, for sweeping through their life with wind gust precision. Seb is a talker. He talks to people until they decide to do things they don't normally do, like give him jobs, free accommodations, or once in a lifetime opportunities. His oratory is packaged with the most indelible charm. People who come under his spell want only to serve his interests; they would do anything to please him. So, knowing Seb is a talker and hearing him talk about his buddy Ivan from Bulgaria, and how he's going to take care of us when we reach Plovdiv, and how we would be set for the next week or so, I didn't really know how to translate. Because, being a talker also implies a life long pursuit of sugarcoating and exaggerating, and although Seb means well most of the time, some of what he's said in the past sounded great and fancy, while not ever panning out. For Seb his mouth is a gift as well as a disease, and I normally wait things out to see if it's sick Seb talking or magician Seb. I was delighted when magician Seb rescued us the night of our bus ride into Plovdiv.

    Ivan picked us up from the bus station at about the time when older generations were secure in their homes and the younger crowd was out surfing the local clubs. Right away Ivan struck me as a clever and very much alert personality. He sat upright in his seat, made witty remarks at any pause in conversation directed his way. Seb was already going over our previous adventure before we slid into the luxury sedan. Seb told him about the unexpected absence of Leo, and some highlights of the different characters along the trip. With everything Seb was describing and highlighting, it seemed as if he was almost challenging Ivan to show and prove, take our adventures to higher plateaus. Because, after all the summaries and boasting, Seb asked Ivan, "So Ivan . . . what is the plan?"

Ivan was a goodhearted, jovial fireball of energy, wide-eyed and always seconds ahead. I wondered if he and Seb were direct animals of the Wall Street routine. Ivan, I noticed, had that same unrelenting charm and creativeness when he spoke as Seb; only with Ivan, it appeared with a touch of innocence and naivety, a person still oblivious to the high-crime on Wall Street, still untainted by the horrors of life and the desperation of struggle. That was not to say that Ivan was a slacker or had an easy life. The exact opposite. He showed up at the steps of NYU Stern as a foreigner, a non-native speaker of the English language. This is where he and Seb had first met. He proved that obstacles as tough as language and culture could be overstepped with persistence and a merciless consistency. He worked himself from University to Wall Street in a flash of unbroken light, saving all his school vacations, summer breaks and rare-to-extinct firm sabbaticals, depositing them in the First Bank of the "Belly of the Beast" to gain the most unfathomable interest as a hotshot banker. Maybe he had always been destined to turn a fortune, with the blood of Bulgarian elitism running through his lineage. But no one would ever be able to deny him of his natural resolve to create wealth out of sheer hard work and ability. He had clearly climbed the ranks of upward rising New Yorkers, start-from-scratch immigrants, and diehard go-getters; and all of this, without too much help from his family, hidden nicely in the small home country of Bulgaria like royal constituents of a faraway kingdom. Ivan was the closest I would ever come to meeting flagrantly connected wealth. After getting to know Ivan and his family background, I had somehow likened him to the role of Eddie Murphy, when he played a prince in *Coming to America*. Ivan was wealth incarnate, but you would never know it from his humble outward qualities. Ivan was the modern day good guy.

By the time we finally made it to Plovdiv, Bulgaria, it was already late on a Friday night. Bulgaria in this way was no different from the rest of the world, because clubs and bars were filled to the rim with weekend party-goers. And of course, considering it was our first night in Bulgaria, Ivan wanted to show us the night scene. There are some places in the world where the abundance of beautiful women flows naturally into certain corners like the rising water from hot springs. Plovdiv was only a small representative of this country, and yet when we walked in the Palmas Dance Club, it seemed we were entering a private women's club. I didn't know places like this existed. And to say I was considered exotic and unique in Israel, because of anything demographically related, would be to completely downplay my demand and how I must have been perceived in Plovdiv, Bulgaria. I had only to open my eyes to attract responses from women, and though Seb wasn't palpably different from the Bulgarian males, he hadn't needed to open his mouth. As modest and humbling as it may sound, we were virtual human magnets. Women were everywhere and I couldn't help but to think how ladies night at the best club in Atlanta couldn't achieve this disproportion. Women were dancing around the circular bar island, on the platform steps leading from the dance floor upwards towards the fluorescent window pains, in the strange dark corner by the black shiny tables, lined on the edges with tacky chrome plating, below the deejay booth and of course on the dance floor. Behind the bar, the waitresses wore Gothic beach attire. Over the next few nights, Ivan, Seb, and I did what most men our ages with so many options would do: we flirted and partied, laughed and never complained. Not even once. And Seb had been precisely right when he said Ivan would look after us during this trip. The first night we checked right into the best hotel in town, a huge contrast to the backpacking and sleeping on couches we had grown accustomed to over the last months. I had forgotten what it felt like to get a goodnight's sleep and wake up without at least a couple kinks in the neck or back. Our beds were large, firm and flowing with feather downy comforters. In just a day's trip across country borders, we had dramatically changed our lifestyle.

Someone had pimped our ride. Ivan's parents loaned the BMW M5 for our stay in the country. We visited Ivan's parents and their meat processing plant before deciding to take a road trip across the country to the Black Sea. If you were Bulgarian and possessed any carnivorous attributes, then you were probably affected by Ivan's family. They owned the largest Meat Processing and Distribution Company in the country, and before speeding off into the countryside, we were invited to take a brief tour through chicken guts and styrofoam wrapping. Walking into the plant was like inspecting nuclear uranium. We were slapped with white robes, hairnets, plastic shoe covers and rubber gloves. They ran a tight, respectable ship, and still, with all of the precautions and good practices, I wanted my vegetables even more.

We were to meet up with Ivan's parents again later and also other members of his family, when we reached Sofia. His parents were proletarian in comparison to his infamous Uncle Damyan and we had no idea how much so until later in the trip. So, with a turbo-charged sedan, we took to the open highway running the vast countryside of Bulgaria. We witnessed our first bout of corruption in the car ride to the Black Sea, the after effects of being a Soviet satellite. Going about 240 kilometers, the equivalent of 150 miles per hour we flashed by a couple of cops sitting outside their white jalopy of a car and immediately saw them waving us down with all arms from the side of the highway. I didn't think Ivan was going to stop. The funny thing is the policemen didn't even bother to jump in their cars, knowing they would have no chance of ever catching up with us. But Ivan, being the good citizen of Bulgaria, brought the car to a screeching halt and began backing up until we were in walking distance of the cops.

"What are you doing?!" Seb said, seemingly baffled at Ivan's actions. "We can take these guys! They have no chance on the open road!"

"Don't worry. I'll handle this. Just watch. I'll show you how we do things over here," Ivan said, with an open smile. He was showing off.

Before he got out of the car, he pulled out a few notes of currency from his pocket and folded it up neatly into his palm. Then he walked back towards the policemen. If you were an eyewitness to these events, the first and only thing surfacing in your thoughts would be, wow, these three guys, the two policemen in uniforms and Ivan were the best of friends, high-school classmates or something. Because they must have chatted for at least ten minutes, and during that time, nothing but smiles and pats on the back. I was certain if it had happened back in the U.S., Ivan would be almost locked up for driving as fast as he did. But not here. When Ivan returned to the car after his barroom chat, he told us to look back and wave. And surely enough, the cops were waving at us, the way a returning astronaut or royal family member would be treated.

"What happened back there?" I asked.

"I told them all about you guys, your visit to Bulgaria from New York. And, they wished us a good time," Ivan responded.

"And how much did you give them?" Seb asked.

"I gave them the equivalent of about fifteen American dollars. I could have given them less," Ivan said.

"Are you kidding me! You guys were carrying on like old friends. Do you know them?" I asked.

"No, the police are friendly around here. The truth is they aren't paid very well as police, so they have to find other ways to make money. Bribes are like a second income for them. Welcome to Bulgaria guys!" Ivan smiled his signature smile, large and wide-eyed.

"Damn! Let me drive this time. I want to get pulled over too! We should get this on camera! This is fucking great!" Seb said in excitement. We all laughed together.

The drive towards the Black Sea was evocative of *On The Road* by Jack Kerouac, only because I envisioned Route 66 just as sparse, vast, and never-ending. However, we were finally, after a few hours of passing cars and blasting every music CD available in Seb's collection, in front of flat, darkish-blue mountains, Stara Planina (translation Old Mountain), part of the Balkans. Off in the distance they lingered just out of reach, the way rainbows forever end and how desert oases never materialize. But we could see them, crackled and corrugated. They seemed unimpressive while holding my attention just the same. At this point, Seb was busy snapping photos of any weed or outgrowth jutting from the meadows, and I have to admit he was getting the hang of creating artsy vistas out of the common man's boredom, the way a writer brainstorms a new scene or an artist changes a white canvas. Then he turned to us, making us his focal points. He snapped a shot of Ivan turning his head to the right, smiling largely with his arm resting the top center of the steering as he drove along, and then with a technique representative of the digital age, Seb held the camera out by the windshield capturing all of us, including himself. We tried at least three times for a good picture, but every time at least one of us held a serious face, while the others contrived crazy circus faces. Then Seb broke the silence with a "just in" news flash.

"Guys, you know my birthday is coming up in two days."

"Dude . . . you shouldn't have told me that! We're going to have to do something to celebrate! Let me think it out. I'm going to make your birthday one to remember."

I had the thought that it couldn't get much better than the simple reality of traveling Eastern Europe in style. We would be hard pressed to top what had been for at least a few months, one large birthday party. Every day was like being born all over again. But it was equally hard not to empathize with Ivan, who had been working Wall Street over these last months and was on a limited holiday to his homeland. He would be back working in only a week's time and wanted to indulge every minute of freedom. And he wasn't completely in holiday mode. He had business meetings with his uncle. They were in preparations to start a bank, specializing in real estate, and, as Seb and I were finding out slowly in the car, Ivan wanted Seb to help build the entity. I couldn't completely grasp the magnitude of this project, until Ivan explained that as long as his uncle could put up twenty million to initially fund the bank, the Bulgarian government and council of the EU would match a whopping eighty million! There was no doubt our carefree sabbatical was turning into something different. After hearing those numbers, I had even offered to help, in whatever capacity.

"Guys . . . I have already told my uncle so much about you," said Ivan. I didn't expect that Ivan really mentioned my name to his uncle, but these were the beginnings of a merger between Ivan and the brotherhood, and he couldn't very well leave me out. "He's going to want to see for himself how serious you are. You have to make a good impression when he meets you."

"I didn't know we were meeting him," remarked Seb.

"Well, yeah. I made an appointment with him, five days from now. He's flying down from Monaco to meet with us. And, I'm telling you, it's big when he makes the decision to meet. He'll probably have his bodyguards with him. But don't be intimidated; he's really a nice guy. Though he might test you at first."

"Bodyguards?" I said, surprised.

"Yeah. Well, he's a really powerful man here in Bulgaria. And when you're in his type of business, you have your share of enemies. He was shot at last year. So, now he doesn't go anywhere without them." Ivan had a way of making the most incredible and sinister statements sound as if he was discussing recipe tips with his grandmother.

Seb was very calm and quiet when Ivan made these statements. I wondered why he wasn't asking more questions, why he didn't act more enthusiastic about the opportunity. He carried on as if he hadn't even heard Ivan speak.

"What you guys want to hear? Buena Vista Social Club? What

about the Dirty Dancing 2 soundtrack?" Seb remarked, only seconds after Ivan's topic. I was enthralled by the idea of meeting Ivan's uncle and observing his infamous ways, while Seb carried on, oblivious.

We drove all the way to Sunny Beach on the coast of the Black Sea. It was a resort town, not very distinctive from the rest, but it did have the best restaurant in the world, as far as I was concerned. It put Hooters in the U.S. to shame. The women were all extremely fit and instead of those hideous orange shorts forced onto the Hooters girls, they wore all orange, scattered with dark streaks for the shirt, so you had no chance of missing them. The outfit was as skimpy as lingerie. And the food was so hearty and tasty, a blind man would be just as happy. And that was exactly the name of the restaurant: Happy Bar and Restaurant. Happy Bar and Restaurant on Sunny Beach, Bulgaria (research it, if you don't believe me!). And, the first night on Sunny Beach was preplanned debauchery. We all knew it, without having to agree upon it. It was our destiny.

"I've just seen the most beautiful brown-skinned girl upstairs. Her skin wasn't even brown; it was like the color of gold, almost caramel. And she had this long amazing curly hair."

"You didn't say anything to her?" Seb remarked, as if to say don't waste your time talking about it to me, be a man of action.

"I couldn't. She was talking to some young punk-looking dude. But she stopped in mid-sentence when I passed her. And we locked eyes. I'm going to wait and see if she comes down here."

"I haven't heard you talk like this in a long time, she must be hot! But don't waste your time waiting. Let's get on the dance floor and show these fools what's up."

"Let's get another shot first." Shots were extremely cheap at this club. I thought the bartender had made a mistake after the first round of shots. We asked for something with Vodka in it, two shots each and the price came up to about four dollars. Furthermore, Ivan wouldn't let us even think of buying drinks, or buying anything for that matter. He was taking hospitality to the ultimate level, and I was determined to return the favor one day. So when I turned my attention and direction from the dance floor to the bar, he immediately asked like an involuntary reflex, "What do you guys want to drink?"

The club was a reflection of the resort town. Ivan knew we probably wanted to be around wild, crazy women and this resort was the European's cheap package tour haven, attracting a bunch of young, hedonistic Brits and Scandinavians, proficient online, who wanted nice sandy beaches somewhere faraway from their respective homeland and a few clubs to get sloppy wasted in every night. It wasn't quite the authentic Bulgarian experience we had made a practice of seeking out in other countries, but at this point in our travels it was probably the perfect choice. We had been immersing ourselves, absorbing new culture and living organic for the last two to three months and it was refreshing in a way to be getting dumb drunk, having a comfortable hotel bed to look forward to and saying the hell with culture, I just want to meet some crazy freak, get drunk and smash. That's what visiting too many Roman ruins does to a person; after a while you amalgamate into the same self-destructive, indulgent tyranny that eventually led to their collapse.

Tonight we were hell on wheels. All of us. We strutted to the dance floor with attitude and slight arrogance. We had a lot to be proud of at this point, and of course, the vodka and occasional Redbull can make most men believe in their predominance, especially when the music being played in a faraway country has the ingredients of mama's famous casserole. Even though it may have been farther from the truth, I had the feeling that Bill Gates probably has walking into an international technology summit in China. Every flinch and gesticulation to the music being played was some hereditary instinct. My mom breastfed me to the roots of this music; my dad sang to me while I was still in the womb; my uncles draped fat gold ropes over my neck and force fed me Slick Rick and Run DMC. But the reality—hip-hop was just as much a part of me as it was of everyone else. The Brits had created a taut breakdance circle in the middle of the floor, showing off their moves and fashion. I had never mastered b-boy dance, and wasn't sure my body would be capable at this point. But that didn't stop us from showing our moves and pairing up with daring females already shaking it on the dance floor. I had concocted my own signature move over the years, a cross between the air walk and my slow, clumsy feet, and the move didn't look half-bad. I danced with a gorgeous Bosnian blond for at least three dances and then went for more drinks. When I was walking away from the bar, I noticed that golden bombshell, ambling her way down the stairs. My mouth watered at the sight of her. She embodied exotic beauty, the kind found deep in deserted Pacific-islands. Her skin was cocoa butter soft and her hair had the ability to mummify her if wrapped around enough times. But her eyes. They were of a transparency and light-brown similar to that of a condensed-block of lacquer. Those eyes carried the mystique of a mood ring and the power of a crystal ball. We locked eyes once again as she sprung her last step from the staircase. That same blonde girl I had danced with in tango-precision to modern music was now talking to her. They were friends. So I grabbed Seb who was talking with Ivan at the bar.

"That's her."

"What?" I could tell the alcoholic shots were having an effect on Seb, slowing his comprehension.

"That's the girl I was telling you about earlier."

"Yeah . . . she's beautiful. Definitely your type." He was referring to her physique. Ironically, Seb, the Jew, was always after ghetto booty, while I usually went for the slim and petite. It wasn't a rule, though.

"She's talking to that girl I just danced with. Listen, you gotta do me a favor. Go over and dance with the girl I just danced with, that blonde girl with the Beyonce booty, and I'll take my girl on the floor for a spin."

"All right. Let's do it," Seb said. Ivan was laughing. He saw us pointing over in the directions of the girls, and I could tell he was having just as good a time carousing around, as he was knowing we were having so much fun.

Wow! That's the only description appropriate when two souls meet with the passion and sensuality of nature. We were taking ownership of the small corner, near to the bar, and right below the deejay booth. Dancing with her made it difficult to do spins or turn around for even a second, because her beauty was so captivating, and holding her in my arms sparked the epiphany that two bodies could be built for each other; that destiny truly has its roots. And I didn't know anything about the girl. Oh, and alcohol does have a way of heightening emotions. But I wasn't inebriated beyond real perception. We danced it amazing for at least five songs.

I wanted to know more about her, though it didn't seem the

right timing to be having tea talk. Plus, she walked off with one of her girls. They were enjoying the attention of a million drunken guys and weren't going to merge all of their energy towards one person just yet. But I knew this game, and just played it patiently.

That night I lost sight of my fascination, and could only hope to find my mystery girl the next day or even the day after that when Seb crossed off another year in his life. I was hopeful I hadn't yet lost her. Her friend mentioned being on vacation here at Sunny Beach for a full week, and the beach wasn't that big. Plus, I knew that Seb was equally on the trail of that Bosnian Blonde, and he had the luck of Hugh Hefner on his side.

We ran into the girls again the next night. They were just as fun and full of energy as the night before and admitted missing our company on the dance floor. They struck me as being much more down to earth and humble than the night before, and real conversation was imminent, now that we had known each other for a couple nights now.

"I never caught your name," I said to the caramel princess.

"Soheila." She had a frank way of talking, sensual but very much to the point.

"Beautiful name."

"What?" she said. We had to talk over the music.

"I said that's a beautiful name, it's unique. Where are you from?"

"Guess." She gave me a view from her profile and threw her hair back, jokingly as to model quickly.

"All right . . . I would say . . . I have no idea!" She frowned at me. "Okay, okay . . . you look mulatto, a mix between Arabic and American Indian."

"What!" she said laughing, "I've never heard that before. My parents are Persian from Iran, but I've lived in Sweden all my life."

"Wow! That's a story."

"And what about you? You look Cuban, Brazilian or something. I mean you talk like an American."

"Yeah, my mom is of Swedish blood and my pops is African-American. I even have distant relatives in Sweden. I'm American."

"Well, you have to come visit me, if you're ever in Sweden."

"Definitely. Sounds like a trip I have to take. Let's take shots!"

We danced for awhile. Ivan was now flirting with the Blonde Bosnian bombshell, while Seb had somehow attracted another friend of theirs. We had been rotating through the circle of friends, unknowingly, and they had no objections, not territorial at all. Plus, the other girl Seb was concerning himself with presently had a plumper buttock.

"So what's your thang?" I asked Soheila.

"My thang?" I knew she would react confoundedly, and she did frown up in a cute way.

"I mean, what gets you going, what's your passion?" I wasn't sure what to expect from this question, maybe she wasn't passionate about anything, only just floating around.

"I love to write." She caught me off guard by her response. It was like in the movies, when two strangers meet and so happen to have the same exact interests.

"Damn! You're kidding. That's my passion." I had decided by this point that writing was a passion for me. Not that I expected any rewards or income from it, but I was sure of the fulfillment it provided. "What sort of stuff do you write?"

"Mostly poetry. I write songs as well." She hadn't told how beautiful her voice was. She remained modest about actually singing, until one of her friends blurted out that she was destined for stardom. Whether this was true or not, she definitely possessed the talent and in my opinion an interesting background story.

That next day Seb, Ivan, myself and all the girls, five of them in all, sat around the beach soaking up the sun and listening to my iPod sound system. We had grown into one happy clan in a short time. Things had gone extremely well for us all. Soheila now lay in my arms as we listened to a little Mos Def, then a little Dweli, then a little Otis Redding. She knew by memory the lyrics to almost every song, and I finally got a taste of her voice. It was untainted and angelic like her appearance. And I had a realization out there on the sand. As much as I had felt at home with all the people met along the way, nothing compared to my time with Soheila. She excited my passions and captivated me visually. But more than that, I felt one-hundred percent at ease with her. Our time together reminded me of being back home in Georgia, and not that she resembled any one particular person. She was clearly different than anyone I had met. But when she talked, I always had the feeling of knowing her for a lifetime. With Soheila, I had the best of both worlds, femininity in the purest form, and at the same time a buddy that could share my interests and talk with ease about them.

Today was Seb's birthday. Ivan and I plotted on what we could possibly do to make it at all special, considering the already festive atmosphere. That afternoon, when we all huddled on the beach, and while Seb was napping and getting rubbed down with sunblock by Ravan, his new fling, Ivan silently signaled for me to follow his lead.

"Chris. Let's go up to the bar and get drinks to bring back."

"Yeah . . . good idea." I turned to Soheila, "Want anything, sweetheart?"

"Ladies, anything in particular you want, or should I decide on your behalf?"

"Well I would like to contain myself until tonight, so nothing with alcohol, Ivan," said Ravan.

"I'll take water, Ivan, sweety," Bosnian Bombshell said.

"Okay, I'll get water for everyone," said Ivan. I don't think Seb or anyone else was really listening, so we plopped back through the flour-soft sand in our flip-flops towards the bars. They weren't far. When we arrived, Ivan ordered waters for everyone and two Rakias for us at the bar.

"So, what do you think we should do for Seb's birthday?" Ivan asked.

"Well . . . we could throw him a small party and invite the girls. But that's kind of what we've been doing all along."

"I know what! We could throw him a surprise party in the hotel room!"

"Well, yeah . . . but we need some sort of twist."

"I'll order a cake from the restaurant with candles. And we could buy champagne and hors d'oeuvres to soak up the alcohol. And . . ."

"I got it. Why don't we make it a sort of slumber party. I mean like a lingerie or beach party! That would definitely surprise Seb, and it wouldn't make it just your typical surprise party."

"That's a great idea! If we can convince the girls to dressing up . . . I mean down." Ivan laughed at his joke.

"I'm sure the girls would have no problems. I mean . . . look at them on the beach." We could see them from the bar. It was an outside bar. A basic straw canopy protruding outward over the bar counter.

"They are perfectly comfortable with their sexuality."

"Okay we have to find a way to slip it to the girls, without Seb knowing. How are we going to surprise Seb?"

"Well we could get Ravan to take him for dinner, while we hook-up the hotel room and get the girls ready. Then when he returns, surprise him!"

"But, he would want Ravan to be dressed in slumber. Wouldn't he?"

"We could take him to dinner, but one of us has to slide out to get everything ready and get the girls into the room."

"Okay. I'll do that. But, you have to keep him busy for at least an hour."

"No problems. I'll get him reminiscing old times. He won't stop talking . . . believe me."

"Cool. You ready?" Ivan paid the bar tab, and we walked back, our arms clumsily cradling bottles of water. The plan was set.

"Surprise!!!!!!" everyone shouted. The girls threw Seb on the bed and stripped him down to his boxers, taking his shoes off and throwing them across the room, while the whole time laughing. I picked up the bottle of champagne and shook it violently. Then, I suddenly remembered my iPod and speakers, and quickly covered them in a towel. Now, hoping not to waste any champagne, I quickly unwrapped the tin foiling, and untwisted the metal wire (I should have shook the bottle last), and released the cork with my thumb, spraying the bottle up into the air, but mainly at Soheila and the other girls. Everyone started jumping on the bed and wrestling. For at least ten whole minutes, total pandemonium erupted, with pillows flying in all directions and bodies flopping, jiggling, and bouncing around. It was the closest my friends would get to the Playboy mansion. And we enjoyed every second of it. Finally, everyone was exhausted from horsing around. We drank the remaining amount of the champagne bottle. Quietly the Blonde Bosnian Bombshell nudged Ivan, saying "the cake."

"Ohhh . . . yeah," he said outloud by accident. He went into the bathroom and called the Blonde Bosnian Bombshell in there, too. I was wondering what was up.

Then they returned with a round cake with chocolate icing and a few candles burning brightly. I ran to turn off the lights, and Ivan placed the cake on the small nightstand in between the two beds. We all huddled around Seb, sitting precariously the sides and corners of both beds.

I started off singing the happy birthday song, and in the middle of it the girls started the Swedish version to the same tune.

> *Ja, må du leva, Ja, må du leva,*
> (Yes, may you live, Yes, may you live)
>
> *Ja, må du leva uti hundrade år*
> (Yes, may you live for a hundred years)

We couldn't finish it without laughing most of the way through.

"Make a wish," said Ravan. I thought she may have hoped for Seb to somehow include her in the wish. And, with one deep breath, an inhalation the size of a yoga mediation, Seb exhaled with a forceful blow, managing to out every candle on the round cake in one circular motion of the head.

Two days from Seb's birthday and we were still all one big happy family. I had really drawn close to Soheila during the week, and even when I promised myself to tread lightly. I found it humanly impossible to deny what was blaringly clear. We were easy together. We shared together a formula for success. And though I didn't know where in the world we would meet again, I did know that I couldn't let go of this girl easy. All the relationships in my past led me to appreciate our time together, because now I realized how couples should function: in a supportive manner, without communication blockage, or doubts. I had no doubts with Soheila, and I had only really known her for a week. But, life has a lot to do with preparing you for a particular moment. All the experiments and struggles, failures and small successes are only really leading up to a quick painless resolution. I had been let down enough in my life, so not to be crushed by any one event. But, I was sure of our compatibility, and I would do whatever it was in my power to see us face to face again. The guys and I had business to handle. Uncle Damyan would be flying into the Bulgarian capital any second. We had packed up our stuff, and were ready to drive out of Sunny Beach towards Sofia any second. I wanted to give Soheila something. Not only so she could remember me, but something I could slyly ask back, a reason to see her again. I had received a million and one compliments over the last few months about a basic trucker hat, with plain brown padding in the front and a solid brownish-green color mesh around the sides and back. It had truly been a sort of icon or symbol of this trip, as much as Seb shaving his head bald had been, and I had worn it in well, better than any pair of jeans I had ever owned. It fit my head impeccably. Soheila had worn it on her head at every chance, and I knew it would be put to use, once in her possession. The last thing I wanted was my brown hat, like a pet animal to me, to be thrown in solitary confinement, somewhere in the corner of a lone Swedish closest. As simple as a brown hat appears, it was a part of me and I wanted to sacrifice something of myself, so that maybe one day it would reappear attached to a beautiful caramel goddess.

Soheila and I sat in the stairwell of my hotel. We didn't really say anything to each other. I just held her in my arms and put the hat on her head. I believe she was crying, but my eyes were closed; her little head was cuddling my chest. Then, after about ten minutes, I took her by the hand and we walked outside to the circular entryway in front of the resort. Seb and Ivan were getting their last kisses in and saying their goodbyes. I kissed Soheila one last time, jumped in the backseat of the Beamer and we drove off.

We were all somewhat void of interaction for at least a few hours during that drive. It was taking a toll on us, befriending places and people and leaving, befriending and leaving. We were no healthier than a tree with its roots chopped up and scattered in different soil. But we couldn't stop now. We were about to meet the infamous tycoon of Bulgaria and hopefully procure some type of opportunity. At least, understand a little more how a man with so much power and money operates and moves. We drove down country roads connected to highway and back onto one-lane streets again. Two lightly brown-skinned women stood at the end of one adjoining dirt road, wearing short colorful dresses, almost as if someone stitched together the most beautiful scraps of a textile factory. Seb instinctively wanted to stop and say something, but Ivan explained they were young Gypsy prostitutes. We moved on. Later, when everyone had had their share of peace and quiet (riding old country roads is very therapeutic and, in some instances, melancholic), Ivan began briefing us for our meeting. I thought it amazing the magnitude of the project and the ease of Ivan's oratory. To even mention the consideration of such an undertaking back in the States would be met with the most condescending laughs, and to hear Ivan shoot off the new business entity without a single doubt in the world was refreshing. It made all of my past ideas seem very feasible, like a walk in the park, and I immediately knew I would need to reevaluate my doubts on a lot of things after our conversation and meeting with his uncle. I was witnessing the power of action without nerves. While I was sure the new bank would be well thought out, I also knew that time wasn't wasted ruminating on any limitations. Of course, when you are as connected as Ivan's uncle, the word *limitation* tends to translate as if from an obscure foreign language.

According to Ivan, his uncle Damyan had begun the cigarette trade, his main revenue stream, while Bulgaria had still been under Communist control. The idea presented itself one day when he was traveling back into the country from Turkey as a medical student. (In those days, only the few lucky privileged ones had the freedom to go in and out of the country like free human beings. Bulgaria had needed good healthcare as much as any country, and that was especially true for anyone fortunate enough to be working in government, so Damyan was privileged to travel.) Earlier, in the train station, while waiting on the ticket cue, only minutes before stepping foot on a train that would lead upwards from Istanbul through the Bulgarian border and on to Sofia, Ivan's uncle Damyan had noticed a tall, slender man further up in the cue. Initially attracting Damyan's attention was the surety and fluidity of his movements; he was immediately inquisitive due to the flawlessness of the man's western suit, the subtle embroidery in his French cuff. He sensed superiority in the stranger's calmness and distant glances, signaling his long-term thoughts. Damyan was a young man, sure in his predestined success, but more enthusiastically a man searching out tools for prosperity and the mentors holding these indispensable traits. In Damyan's opinion, this man was definitely a mirror of prosperity.

As ambitious and aggressive as he was, he would have never dreamed of approaching such an intimidating man. That is, not until the man extracted a beautiful white and red cardboard box from his inner pocket, and slipped a small white stick out of its depth, a perfectly round and tapered object. It was clear what this object held; it was far more advanced than the hand-rolled sephia-colored papers he had seen fumbled around awkwardly. Damyan watched as the guy elegantly trapped the symmetrical object between his middle fingers, effortlessly firing it with a match, breathing in as if sucking in a cloud, and evenly dissipating the stick, while smoke seductively reached towards the hollows of the station ceiling. It intrigued him, watching that man with his perfect little stick, effortlessly puffing and blowing out until he finally flicked the little nub to the ground and decisively stamped it out. Until this point, Damyan had only really seen messy tobacco pouches accompanied by clumsy pipes and time-consuming rolling papers. How perfectly convenient it would be if more people in his country were able to light little sticks of tobacco, smoke them and carry on virtually without any interruption to their daily lives.

So with the desire and passion of discovery, Damyan watched as the gentleman with creased suit exited the line with boarding pass in hand, then gracefully slipped into the train five carriages back. He lost him in that swift second. But Damyan was a determined young man. He knew that the best things in life were not gained in the time a man could flick off a cigarette and stump out the flame. So, once his train ticket was in hand, he found his cabin in the eleventh carriage, unloaded his belongings and raced through the carriages towards the front, opening and shutting carriage doors, opening and shutting doors, all while the train chugged and choo-chooed, beginning its journey through the open countryside. He finally reached the fifth train car and found out all the cabin doors had been shut closed. There were no windows or nameplates, so he started one by one knocking persistently at each of the cabin doors, until someone finally opened up and he could peek his head inside. In those days, during Communist times, people weren't as obliging and courteous as peaceful times afforded; these were hard times, and everyone had experienced friends or family mysteriously disappearing. So one can imagine his reception, as he knocked door after door to the absence of the gentleman in western attire. People scowled at him and slammed doors. Finally, after four cabins, closer to the sixth carriage, he spotted the man. He was wistfully looking out towards the surrounding meadows. There were only two occupants, he and another very skeptical guy, not as friendly.

"I must to speak with that man," Damyan insisted to the scowling man.

"I . . . I don't . . . " the man waited for any connection between the two men, before slamming the door.

"Excuse me sir!" Damyan yelled to the man over the roaring of the wheels and engine.

"Please, come and sit," the slender gentleman said with all calm and clarity. The cabin consisted modestly of two benches facing each other and perpendicular to the window. "May I ask why I should be so fortunate to make your company?" (Back in those days, gentlemen all over the world spoke with a long-winded politeness.)

"Sir. I must ask you where if possible would someone be so fortunate as to find those delightful sticks of smoke you were just ten minutes ago indulging?"

"Ohh," the gentleman started a brief chuckle, "I can tell you the exact location where I purchased these cigarettes."

"Excuse me sir. What was the name of these wonderful contraptions?"

"Cigarettes. A special brand of them imported all the way from America. First you must know what they are and why someone would squander their time, fooling with them."

"They have tobacco in them, sir?"

"Yes. They are fabricated with the most flavorful tobacco and pull with the ease of a sleeping breath. These happen to be no risk to your health, as they have a tiny filter placed in the front. Here ..." at which point, the guy pulled out the remarkable box from his coat pocket and majestically slid out a cigarette, "I will spare one. But you must learn how to smoke it properly. Once you have found a means of fire, you must lightly suck on this side of the cigarette, while barely touching the flame. Finally, you mustn't rush. Cigarettes are meant to be relaxing. The address in Istanbul for the shop is 9 Adan street, on the south side of the Golden Horn."

"Thank you sir," responded Damyan, and he returned to his cabin.

Damyan was a very clever and intuitive businessman. He had first made his profession as a doctor, knowing the future power it would afford him under a suppressive Communist regime. If he could make a name for himself as a doctor, since he knew the only concern mighty enough to cause fear in a dictator of Soviet proportions was the vulnerability to disease and immortality provided all humans, he was sure this role would guarantee him the better fruits of Communist assignment. While Communism may have been strictly principled on equal sharing among all members of the human race, because we all should be considered equal, he also knew that what it really meant was anyone without substantial inroads to the powerful government would be forced to survive on whatever scraps weren't already voraciously consumed by the government's bureaucratic appetite. And, while government appointment was an equally appealing endeavor, doctors were usually the ones spared during war times.

Even as an astute medical student, he wasn't privy to the health risks involved when one makes a career of breathing in tobacco fumes. He should have been skeptical, for the drug was as addictive as vodka. Still, it didn't cause men to abuse their wives and children or cause regrettable pub fights. Already as a thriving medical student, only months away from graduating, he had made valued connections with bourgeois Bulgarians, government officials, army generals, and the sons of army generals. He knew right away their appetite for such exotic goods as tobacco, and accordingly knew the great demand such an item as convenient disposable sticks of tobacco would have. So, the next time in Turkey, he searched for 9 Adan street, on the south side of the Golden Horn, somewhere in the back alleys of Istanbul, and found that special store selling those magical sticks. It was exactly where the spindly gentleman with the western suit had directed. And he purchased as many boxes as his budget would allow him.

It had already been a year, and already Damyan had managed a thriving cigarette operation in and out of the country. He had such great demand that his bourgeois contacts found ways to send him back and forth to Turkey, even long after his official studies as a medical student abated. He was so successful, he hadn't even needed to begin his career as a medical doctor to Communism. Ironically, his trade placed him on the other side of medicine. He was making enough in profits and political favors to stay well afloat for years. So, when Bulgaria finally defeated Communism (not corruption) and opened up to the rest of the world, he was already deeply involved in lucrative foreign trade. In 1990, Bulgaria had their first parliament elections after the fall of Communism, making them a multi-party, democratic republic—incidentally electing back into power a pseudo-communist party. At which point, Ivan's uncle increased his business, setting up new trucking routes of cigarette importation from the northern border, as well as seeking out factories manufacturing cheap, off-brand cigarettes. The demand for cigarettes had grown exponentially ever since the common man found means to buy these highly addictive sticks. And he had made all the right connections in the government, resulting in an almost monopolistic control over the country's supply of cigarettes. Of course, eventually there were competitors in the market, but none of those competitors had the loyalty and friendship of the most dignified Head of Customs, who could forget about that 300% import tax as truck after truck holding close to five-hundred thousand dollars worth of cigarettes rolled, day-in, day-out.

Now, Ivan's uncle being the shrewd businessman and unrelenting opportunist, had decided to further extend his empire and diversify his revenue streams with the establishment of a powerful new bank. And he was already guaranteed ample real estate from his circle of cronies, those fat cats who trade business and contacts in the exclusive whirlpool of the rich, hardly ever letting a drop of the dirty water fall over the side. Really he didn't need any connections as long as he could get the bank up and operating. Bulgaria was only two years away from official EU membership, when the flood of foreign investment would make even the simple shoemaker on the neighborhood corner a gazillionaire. We were witnessing a financial revolution in modern day Bulgaria, and every one of us in that fancy car riding down the rustic countryside wanted to be a part of it.

When Ivan finished the story of his uncle and the new banking venture, I was speechless in the backseat. If Ivan could have seen my face while he steered the car calmly down the road, he would have seen frank astonishment. I thought this stuff only happened to people in the movies.

The day of reckoning. All of us were at one of Ivan's family's apartments in the city of Sofia. We were trying to get dressed and ready for our lunch meeting with Ivan's uncle. Only we had nothing very formal to wear. I had to resort to khaki pants and a polo shirt, and Seb had a linen shirt and pants, his most formal attire.

"Guys! That's fine, we're only meeting for lunch." Ivan was rushing us out the apartment, so not to be late. "I know my uncle. He'll be there on time with all his bodyguards waiting outside."

So we got dressed quickly and sped off to one of Sofia's most lavish restaurants. We approached a black wrought iron gate arching upwards to a sharp pinnacle, at the exact point where the gate parts to open. Light posts, in the same gothic style as the gate, outlined a careening driveway, passing us through a wooded area of old lurching willows. I considered for a moment the spookiness of such a place, if seen during the night. Outside, the restaurant looked like a small mansion, complete with narrow stained glass windows, and a large arching door, carved with the most elaborate detail. Five burly guys in black suits congregated outside, two of them smoking cigarettes, the other three very attentive to any outside anomalies. Of course, we were with Ivan, so as soon as we got out of the car, one of them valeted the car, two of them ushered us into the restaurant, while the other two stood watch. The restaurant was just what you would expect; it was adorned in old classic paintings and tapestries, white embroidered silk draped angularly along large round tables, and miniature chandeliers hung right and center above each table. A larger chandelier, a complicated labyrinth of thousands of tiny crystals and lights, greeted us as we entered the front lobby.

  We walked around the reception area, following a sloping pathway until we reached a large backroom naturally lit by an amazing wall of glass windows. From this backroom, a mind-blowing panorama of lower Sofia could be seen stretched off in the distance. And right outside the windows, about one-story down, and perched on the hill, a quiet garden of manicured bushes and a large flowing fountain with a statue encrusted in a colorful tile mosaic, gushing water upwards, between the mouths of a young couple on the verge of a kiss. A roundtable full of family and friends awaited our arrival in the corner. We were the only party in the entire restaurant. Damyan had reserved the entire place. We immediately greeted everyone, while Ivan introduced each of us. The fact that appetizers and wine had already been laid out, and everyone was settled into their seats, the way only body temperature and time permits, created a somewhat awkward mood at first. It seemed all conversation had ceased as soon as we arrived. Sitting at the table, starting counterclockwise from Seb on my right, were Ivan's parents (I was pleasantly surprised to be seeing them again), Damyan's ex-wife, a trader in rare luxury watches (Ivan was given a rare gold coin watch for his NYU graduation, only a few have ever been made, the majority being gifted to incoming American presidents), a good friend of Damyan and heir to diamond fields in South Africa, an executive at Damyan's cigarette enterprise, the Head of Customs for Bulgaria, Plamen, Damyan's eighteen-year-old son Andrei, and finally myself. Damyan had a strong build, and very calm composure, not at all the sinister appearance I expected. He didn't really take notice of us at first, seeming very introverted in his thoughts. It took his son's provocation to spur conversation.

"You are from America?" Andrei asked both Seb and me.

"Yes," I replied.

"I'm a fan of Ludacris," he exclaimed in a very calm way. I think he was mainly talking to me, and probably automatically thinking I would be a fan of hip-hop. His father patted him on the shoulder.

"He is a fan of that sort of music. I have no idea why . . . " said Damyan.

"Dad," Andrei said embarrassed without raising his voice.

"He's plastered their photos all over his bedroom. Who is that one girl you have over your bed?" I could tell he was setting up a joke.

"J-Lo," Andrei said.

"Yeah that's right . . . J-Lo . . . that's the best thing coming out of that music," Damyan said, chuckling to himself.

I don't think too many people at the table understood his last comment.

"Well, Ivan has told us plenty about you guys. Traveling all over the world. Don't you guys ever tire?"

"No . . . not until we conquer Bulgaria first," said Seb. Everyone laughed at the table.

"That's right. Well, I assume Ivan is showing you guys quite a time here."

"Ivan has taken us a lot of places in such short time. We've been to Plovdiv to see the meat factory and took a drive all the way to Sunny Beach. I think my favorite place so far was Happy Restaurant." I thought Seb was pushing it with that last comment, as Happy is known for their scantily dressed waitresses, but everyone laughed just the same. We had found out Happy Restaurant was almost in every city in Bulgaria.

"I'm planning a trip," Andrei popped in.

"Yeah, he is determined to travel through Europe after high school for a year . . . a full year," Damyan said, chuckling at the audacity of that idea.

"You need to worry about getting accepted to college first, honey," Andrei's mother rung in, trying immediately to kill those hopes before they evolved any further.

"Mom. I have my whole life to graduate from college. I need some time off to get myself ready," Andrei said. I thought the idea of traveling alone a full year out of the country before even starting college to be quite a daring request at his age. The idea of foreign travel hadn't occurred to me until the middle of university. But this kid wasn't from a typical American family, and I was sure he had probably done his share of traveling already.

"We don't want you returning with children. You're too young to be ruining your life so early," she finished.

He surprisingly didn't feed into their argument, shrugged off their condemnation, and began talking about his high school basketball team and how he hoped to see an NBA game live one day. The mood definitely improved from that point on in the conversation. The main entrees came out, and we ate and drank wine indiscriminately. After the meal, Ivan, Seb, Damyan and I walked down a circular stairway out to the garden. The garden was plush green with perfectly shaped hedges bordering a sidewalk laden with burnished river stones. Damyan was very relaxed and comfortable in his skin. He didn't walk as much as glide slowly. There was an aura emanating from this guy about ten yards in circumference. Every gesture and movement was a class in non-verbal communication. It was incredible absorbing those moments of silence. His power of being reminded me of Marlon Brando in *The Godfather*. But he wasn't scary or frightening. He had a warm touch so blatantly absent from the impersonal touch of gangster movies. And to see him so embedded in his family exemplified the real reason for all his ambitions. He wasn't any different from anyone else, yet he had inherited a mystic abstract quality, something indescribable in its beginnings but obvious in its results. After ambling about the maze of hedges and towering cypress trees, he began to speak of the new business venture.

"Ivan speaks highly of you guys." A few intense seconds passed. "... and I'm hoping he is a good judge of character. The most important thing in this business or any business is trust and loyalty. That's how good business should work around here, and once you grasp this, the world is yours. You will be provided everything you need, so long as you work hard. Do I have your understanding?" He said, peering directly into both of our eyes without blinking. Seb and I both nodded yes. Then he formed an unexpected expression, one of subtle bafflement, which Ivan recognized immediately. And quickly clarified.

"They mean yes, Uncle."

"Oh. That's right." Though we didn't understand the confusion in that moment, we later found out that Bulgarians nod up and down to signal *no* and left and right for *yes*. He continued talking. "I am pleased that you guys have found the courage to travel so far from your homeland. Probably my most memorable experiences in life were traversing this great world. It is too easy becoming complacent in an environment that allows limited viewpoints. And, all societies limit viewpoints." Damyan stopped for a moment as to underline a point. We paused enthusiastically at the back of the garden, the perch overlooking the city. "Humans are like sheep in this way. We have a way of buying into our own cultural traditions many times without challenging their existence. It takes a strong mind to recognize opportunity and in turn, introduce change. Human society needs these change seekers, and it's evident you've accepted the responsibility." We sat down on a small ceramic bench, very subtle in its detail. The drabness and earthiness of its colors purposefully camouflaged it in the beauty of the surrounding shrubs. We formed a slight curve bowing out from Damyan in the center of the bench.

I rested my left elbow on my thigh not wanting to miss a gesture or word. It was amazing his ability to communicate in English. Ivan had mentioned that his uncle owned real estate in London and Monaco and South Africa, and so I had assumed he understood English. But Damyan spoke eloquently in a way uncommon to many Americans. "I must say that most of my success in business has come from isolating the real needs of human beings and not becoming distracted by restrictive cultural habits. For many people, alternatives don't exist until there is first a shift in popularity. What I mean to say is that business leaders need to be fully aware of alternatives in order to create opportunities. And you young men have already put yourself in a position of awareness. There will come a time when you have to utilize that awareness to identify alternatives for those humans sheltered by culture. I hope you will explore opportunities with our new bank venture. But whatever you do in your lifetimes, realize that you hold truths and knowledge not afforded everyone in the world. Be wise. Observe as much as possible, and don't squander your advantages. Now, I'm sorry gentlemen," he said as he boosted himself up by pushing off the bench, "but I must excuse myself. I have an important discussion with Plamen." He patted the shoulder of Ivan, saying a few words discreetly, and then glided with the same ease and aura back towards the restaurant. I could see from the windows the Head of Customs and the South African guy peering through the large windows from upstairs. They were both seemingly in deep thought. The beautiful backdrop had much to do with their mood.

"Wow. Your uncle is pretty intense."

"Yeah. I can tell he likes you guys."

Seb and I were somewhat proud being privy to this type of knowledge and foresight. We weren't rich or especially privileged. People thought one had to be rich to keep up a travel addiction. We had proven that philosophy wrong. The main obstacle to travel was materialism. The decision to buy a fancy new car, a home entertainment center, or any other reckless purchases at the onset of my career would have been my obstacle. What I wanted for my friends back home were alternatives and opportunities. I wanted them to experience more than one part of their world. I was sure these new experiences would enhance their lives.

It was satisfying witnessing Bulgaria in the transition of change. What Damyan and the entire country were experiencing in this era of modern Bulgaria was opportunity. Bulgaria and its neighbor Romania were only a couple years away from EU membership, and people were exploring the fruits of capitalism. In the spirit of opportunity, I wanted more than anything to get back to my passion. Listening to the ease with which Ivan and his uncle discussed starting a bank, the value of small countries led me to believe my idea of becoming a writer wasn't out of reach. I had more than enough material to write after three months of traveling with characters like Seb, Leo and Ivan. Plus, I had no reason to rush. As long as I continued drinking bottled water and maintaining health, as long as I continued to follow my heart and never stopped observing the globe, and as long as pencil and paper remained cheap and abundant, everything would work out for the best.

We only remained a total of three days in Sofia. Late on the third night, we dragged our bags down the steps and to the front of the building. Ivan had called a cab to take us to the train station and on to our next destination, Bucharest, Romania. Our bags were beginning to show stress, so much junk eventually had been crammed from months of random shopping and gift receiving. Furthermore, Seb and I had begun skipping the lengthy packing ceremony and now threw all our junk in haphazardly, sitting on the bag if we needed more room. We met the taxi driver down at street level and watched as he struggled to tip our bags over the ridge of the trunk. We shook Ivan's hand in a hug and thanked him for everything. As soon as we shut the doors, the driver wasted no time flooring it and speeding off into a seemingly dreary and dead darkness. Our departure had the unexpected feeling of emptiness.

Entering the station was much like stepping out at the end of the world. People of all exhaustion levels scattered the cold space the size of a small sports arena. Old wooden benches, hard and geometrically awkward, filled the heart of the drab space like ribs holding out an empty body cavity. I noticed for the first time the onset of autumn. But this place had the appearance of staying cold all year long. I couldn't imagine somewhere so gray and empty holding lively summer heat. Many benches were vacant, while others could hardly be seen through whole families of travelers. I noticed many families to be gypsies cuddled up in patchwork blankets and all colors of headscarves. There were a few backpacking foreigners waiting anxiously for the next adventure. I found a vacant bench and closely guarded our bags, while Seb went to the counter to purchase tickets.

"The next train isn't for another four hours," Seb said vacantly.

"Damn," was the only response fitting the occasion.

We pulled out extra clothing from our bags, layering garments in order to shield from the low temperatures and managed to fit on the slender slabs of wooden planks, while also leaning on our bags in the case thieves found us sleeping vulnerably. It was too late in the trip to be making tourist mistakes. A few hours passed, and I awoke as Seb was already sitting up, staring into the hull of the station. I walked over to an early morning shop, serving cheese sandwiches and eggs. None of it was appealing, but my stomach was less discriminating in hunger. We quickly ate our breakfast and headed further inside the station beyond the ticket booths and magazine stands. It hadn't occurred to me that we might be underground, until the shining of light could be seen stepping part way down a long flight of cement stairs. We managed the weight of our bags by tilting slightly forward and walking upwards. I was still tired from a lack of sleep, and at one point I almost faltered backwards by the weight. We made it to the top and to the relief of early morning light.

Light was the only thing of beauty out on the old train platforms. There were two ancient rusty trains sitting idle on our track and between the next platforms. On first sight, they appeared more valuable as scrap metal. The one waiting our platform turned alive, roaring robustly from the close acoustical distance of the other train. The roaring of the train induced sudden anxiety, and we quickly rushed to ask anyone nearby questions. There were only four other people standing next to the train. Luckily the tall man with beaten briefcase in his hand was a German on the way to Bucharest who advised us that the next train was for Bucharest. While he said this, the current train slowly began its departure. The wheels were hypnotic to watch. They rolled so slowly at first as if an old person mustering the strength to stand. The first revolution of the train's shiny metal wheels lasted for at least five seconds. Metal bars connecting the wheels began slowly rising and falling in a soothing effortless motion the way the elliptical machine glides at any local gym. The train picked up momentum and the last of the train, linked together like a cheap toy snake, followed behind until it was finally out of our sight.

At least twenty minutes had passed by when off in the distance we could see another train appearing over the horizon, already blowing its ubiquitous whistle. The train was ours. We stepped the narrow opening into our car and found a cabin to put up our stuff. I was excited about the idea of having a mobile train bed to sleep on, and though I didn't have high expectations, the bunk bed in our cabin was cramped. The sheets were the thickness and consistency of stiff cardboard and the darkness of the cabin made the starched sheets appear an indiscernible cream color. Our only light source was a tiny opaque window. It was impossible to view anything more than eclipsing shadows from the outside. Both Seb and I were still exhausted. I took the top bunk and Seb the bottom. I don't remember falling asleep or hearing the train leave. A knocking on our cabin door woke us into the same dreariness. It was a train worker asking our tickets. As soon as the cabin door opened, neither Seb nor I could fall back to sleep. Outside of our cabin in the hallway, large windows spanned the entire car. We became enthralled by the stark light and rapid movement of the surrounding terrain. Our eyes never abandoned its diverse show. Seb and I both walked like zombies into the train corridor, finally leaning on the wall facing outside. I could see out of the corners of my eyes, other passengers sharing the same view in the hallway.

There is something psychiatric about peering outside of a moving train. Here seems to be where nature and human invention collide giving way to introspective advice and listening. It was sunny outside and the countryside was fast at work. It was amazing how the train tracks seemed to blaze a c-section through middle Bulgaria, like a scalpel exposing the heart and all of Bulgaria's vital organs. Meadows of wild grass sprouted up and leaned in all directions like a hobo's hairstyle. Sycamore trees full of unstinted growth provided wide shade in the early afternoon. A couple of children, a girl and a boy, probably siblings, played among the large roots, finding seed droppings and unconsciously spreading the tree's legacy by the sheer force of pelting a stone. They both waved fervently in our direction. Wild meadows were less common than plowed fields of grain and corn. Workers ambled unenthusiastically, pulling along their mules, which were even less thrilled. They cheered up immediately as we passed by, waving and smiling with uneven mouths. Further in our trip, Seb decided to bring out the digital camera. He snapped photos of the hallway passengers, and then he stuck his head out the window taking a self-photo and getting me to do the same. Then I could see a burst of inspiration as he spotted a small caravan of gypsies ahead in the distance. The caravan had settled logistically around a valley pond. Wobbling tents in a hodgepodge of earth colors contrasted with the bright patchwork of dresses and shirts. They were too far away to notice our spying intrigue, almost too far for the camera's zoom.

    Minutes later, our train met near-darkness in a thick forest. Trees and outgrowth scraped the train's walls in a shrilling sound and a branch of pine stuck through the window nearly slapping my face. About an hour after the forest, the train passed by a small village without stopping at the station. Graffiti, obviously the work of amateurs or mischievous teenagers, sprawled across the cement walls. Old women burdened by age and weather walked along carrying bags of bread, unaware of much of the world, but still a part of its machinery, propelling its engine. The changing scenery had a dual effect on my consciousness. As if I had been a baby held and swayed in my mother's arms, the constant movement of the outside calmed my mood. The other effect was to help me reflect on all that was recent and endless. Among those universal thoughts like love and purpose and fulfillment, came intrinsically the words opportunity and hope. Seb and I, Leo and Ivan were undoubtedly fortunate to have witnessed, like alter egos, the lives of so many people across so many cultures. Still, so much of the world was unseen.

With the knowledge and awareness also came responsibility. I felt responsible to one day explain my adventures and espouse those truths I found quintessential of all human civilization. Maybe, even convert some reluctant souls to join the travel revolution and move with only one rule, that of the bottled water.